International Development

International Development

Issues and Challenges

Second Edition

Damien Kingsbury
John McKay
Janet Hunt
Mark McGillivray
Matthew Clarke

First edition 2008
Second edition 2012

Published by
PALGRAVE MACMILLAN

Palgrave Macmillan in the UK is an imprint of Macmillan Publishers Limited, registered in England, company number 785998, of Houndmills, Basingstoke, Hampshire RG21 6XS.

Palgrave Macmillan in the US is a division of St Martin's Press LLC, 175 Fifth Avenue, New York, NY 10010.

Palgrave Macmillan is the global academic imprint of the above companies and has companies and representatives throughout the world.

Palgrave® and Macmillan® are registered trademarks in the United States, the United Kingdom, Europe and other countries

ISBN 978–0–230–30322–5   hardback
ISBN 978–0–230–30323–2   paperback

This book is printed on paper suitable for recycling and made from fully managed and sustained forest sources. Logging, pulping and manufacturing processes are expected to conform to the environmental regulations of the country of origin.

A catalogue record for this book is available from the British Library.

A catalog record for this book is available from the Library of Congress.

10 9 8 7 6 5 4 3 2 1
20 19 18 17 16 15 14 13 12 11

Printed in China

Contents

List of Figures and Tables

Figures

Tables

List of Abbreviations

BRICS	Brazil, Russia, India, China, South Africa
BSS	Basic Social Services
CEDAW	Convention for the Elimination of All Forms of Discrimination Against Women
CDF	Comprehensive Development Framework
CEIF	Clean Energy Investment Framework (World Bank)
CIS	Central and Eastern Europe and Commonwealth Independent States
DAWN	Development Alternatives for Women in a New Era
FAO	Food and Agriculture Organisation
FDI	Foreign Direct Investment
FTZ	Free Trade Zones
GATT	General Agreement on Tariffs and Trade
GDP	Gross Domestic Product
GEF	Global Environment Facility
GFC	Global Financial Crisis
GNP	Gross National Product
GNI	Gross National Income
GRB	Gender-Responsive Budgeting
GSP	Generalized System of Preferences
HDI	Human Development Index
HIES	Household Income and Expenditure Surveys
HPI	Human Poverty Index
ILO	International Labour Organization
IMF	International Monetary Fund
IPCC	Intergovernmental Panel on Climate Change
LD	Less Developed
LLD	Least Developed
MDG	Millenium Development Goal
MSG	Millennium Security Goal
NGO	Non-Government Organizations
ODA	Official Development Assistance
OECD	Organisation for Economic Co-operation and Development
PPP	Purchasing Power Parity
PQLI	Physical Quality of Life Index

PRSP	Poverty Reduction Strategy Plan
SAP	Structural Adjustment Programme
SWAP	Sector-Wide Approach
UNCTAD	Conference on Trade and Development
UNDP	United Nations Development Programme
UNHCR	High Commissioner for Refugees
UNICEF	UN Children's Fund
UNREDD	UN's Collaborative Programme on Reducing Emissions from Deforestation and Forest Degradation in Developing Countries
WGI	Worldwide Governance Indicators (World Bank)
WID	Women In Development
WSF	World Social Forum
WTO	World Trade Organization

Acknowledgements

The authors and publisher would like to thank the following who have given permission for the use of copyright material:

Taylor and Francis for Table 10.1, from Grown, C., Gupta, G.R. and Kes, A. (2005) 'UN Millennium Project Task Force on Education and Gender Equality' in *Taking Action: achieving gender equality and empowering women.*

Introduction

Damien Kingsbury

The idea of 'development' of the world's poorer countries is both contentious in its meaning and in approaches to it. Yet the idea of development is central to the processes by which countries, particularly poorer countries, organize themselves. Put simply, the study of development is concerned with how 'developing countries' can improve the living standards of their citizens, notably to eliminate absolute poverty, as well as to construct a political and social environment in which such material benefit can take place. In the post-Second World War period of decolonization by which European colonial powers withdrew from their colonies in Africa, Asia and elsewhere, the aspirations that most former colonial states had for independence were often dashed upon the rocks of limited and, in some cases, reducing capacity. Existing poverty was not always alleviated and in many cases, along with corruption and inter-ethnic conflict, was exacerbated (e.g. see Hirschmann 1987; Cornwell 1999; Englebert 2000; Luis 2000).

As a result, the peoples and governments of most developed or industrialized countries acknowledged that they had and continue to have some responsibility to assist these poorer countries, to stabilize their economies, support their economic development and, hopefully, to help provide a stable and conducive material, social and political environment. At one level, this was a simple matter of self-interest – if people in poorer countries have more income, they have more purchasing power and can generate more international trade and, hence, greater wealth all around. At another level, a basic humanitarian sensibility leaves many people in wealthier countries feeling that to allow poorer people to continue to stay poor is unjust. Further, it has become increasingly clear, were there ever any doubt about it in the past, that poverty and underdevelopment have a direct correlation to a propensity for conflict, both within and between states. For much of the late twentieth century, development assistance was seen as a way to persuade poorer countries to come into one of the two major ideological camps that dominated the Cold War era – the West and the Communist bloc. The main powers

1

of each bloc unashamedly used development assistance to maintain the support of poorer countries in order to keep them in their 'sphere of influence'.

By the early twenty-first century, this bipolar ideological orientation had changed but the fear that poverty could encourage conflict, perhaps on a global scale, was given a new lease of life by the preoccupation of the United States, its allies and like-minded countries, following the events of 11 September 2001. This has led to a refocusing on at least some areas of development, intended to respond to a new perceived global 'enemy' – an anti-state, anti-materialist and in particular anti-western confederation operating under a banner of Islamist ideology.

From the viewpoint of many of its adherents, a global Islamist ideology has been seen as a foil to the perceived evils of global capitalism (or Westernism – defined as either Christian or materialist or both). And while some supporters of this form of Islam espouse a purely religious understanding of the conflict, many more are driven by desperation, poverty, inequity and dispossession. This adds up to a deep – and in many cases well grounded – sense of injustice, raising the question of whether enhanced development leading to greater global equity might dampen the zeal of at least the foot-soldiers of the movement. 'Enlightened self-interest', which was the principal ideological motivation of western donors fearful of the spread of Communism in the 1950s and 1960s, might provide a similar impetus for a renewal of development assistance today, so that increased 'development' might be seen as one thread in the 'war on terror'.

Beyond this contested element of the global order, the economic and strategic rise of China, closely followed by India, has shifted the world balance in trade and development. Not only were developed countries, notably the US, increasingly on the back foot over the rise of these two powers, the global financial crisis of 2008 onwards illustrated just how fragile the global economy could be. Development suddenly seemed no longer like a given, even for developed countries, while developing states were in many cases buffered by these larger forces over which they had little or no control.

In most discussions about development, the term itself is bandied about as though its meaning is not only commonly understood but commonly shared. This is not so. In the early post-war period, development was primarily, and often exclusively, identified with economic growth, usually measured in terms of the average income per head of population (per capita gross domestic product). However, as discussed further throughout this volume, development has a range of meanings which, while in most cases are complementary or at least overlapping, may be quite distinct in the priority they give, for example, to economic equity, to political development and democratization, to gender, or to environmental issues. This then affects their implications for action.

Even the terminology of development has changed and is continuing to change. For example, the term 'third world', which was used in the early Cold War period to describe less developed countries, was coined to contrast them to the 'first world' of the West (largely corresponding to the Organization of Economic Development (OECD) countries) and the 'second world' of the socialist bloc states. Although still used, the term 'third world' has been effectively undermined by the collapse of the second world, as well as by its overly generic and hence indistinct meaning across a wide range of varying economic and political circumstances.

The whole approach to development, assumed for years to occur through a process of industrialization, has also been questioned and is now replaced by a more nuanced approach to improving livelihoods, especially in societies whose capacity for industrialization is limited or, in effect, non-existent. The OECD world, meanwhile, which 'industrialized' or 'modernized' in the first half of the twentieth century, is now increasingly reliant upon service industries and higher technology rather than the heavy industrialized industries of that principally manufacturing-driven era. Some analysts suggest that the idea of 'modernism', which they see as corresponding to heavy industrialization, production lines and bureaucratic organization, has, for many countries, more or less passed with the advent of the increasingly diversified, globalized, high technology types of work that now characterize the leading edge of developed economies. While some countries have successfully adopted industrialization, this wider change to economic organization suggests that the path to development may differ for countries now endeavouring to lift themselves out of poverty. Some may be able to 'skip' directly to a service industry, high technology approach. Others, however, see this development as simply a high expression of modernism, and a logical conclusion of proceeding down the industrial development path.

Such considerations are, of course, a very long way from the commodity producing and subsistence economies of most of the world's states, in which wages are low, employment conditions usually bad and unregulated, and in which many facets of modern (or postmodern) life taken for granted in OECD countries exist only as a dream. Such countries also often lack technical and organizational capacity, and have limited access to resources. There has been a trickle down of technology to developing countries, but for many people clean running water is still not available, health conditions remain poor, medical support is limited or unaffordable, literacy is at marginal levels, and opportunities for personal growth are virtually non-existent.

The notion of 'third worldism' as a formula to express the common interests and joint organization of developing countries has also been challenged and largely undermined by the increasing variety of development experiences between and within these countries themselves. What really is the common feature of countries as diverse as Indonesia, Ethiopia, El Salvador and Bangladesh? Such countries are usually classified as less developed (LD) or least developed (LLD), with the latter status being used by the United Nations as a benchmark for entitlement to preferential assistance. The least developed, the poorest countries in the world, are those whose poverty is most profound, for whom special help is supposed to be available. Per capita GDP in such countries is generally less than US$2 a day and in some cases US$1 a day. What is more, for many of their inhabitants even these amounts would be regarded as a mark of wealth, as median incomes are invariably less than this. Examples of LLD countries include Laos, Cambodia, East Timor, Burma and many of the states of sub-Saharan Africa. LD countries include South Africa, Egypt, the Central American states, India and Indonesia.

Some countries previously regarded as 'third world' and generally classified as 'developing', have managed to rise above such levels, on account of beneficial location, natural resources (especially oil), colonial (or post-colonial) good fortune, or, in exceptional circumstances, the right mix of policies combined with a competent and honest government. The average income of their populations is considerably more than in the bottom two categories, yet they are still some way from the income levels of the OECD countries. Industrialization may be taking place, but it is not consistent, and their economies tend to continue to be dominated either by commodity exports or light or simple manufacturing, often combined with a high level of foreign investment and ownership. Thailand, Malaysia, Chile and Argentina all fall into such a category of 'developing' countries, as does China, Brazil and perhaps India, with each now rapidly industrializing and also moving into areas of higher technology.

Such a focus, however, privileges the economic above other aspects of life. The argument that it is difficult to consider other facets of life when one is hungry is persuasive, yet people in LD and LLD countries may still enjoy rich cultures and social structures, profound religious beliefs, as well as strong and complex social and kinship ties. And, at least as importantly, their hopes and aspirations are equal to, and often greater than, those of more economically privileged people. For example, a person consciously deprived of democracy is likely to appreciate its political advantages more than a person who can take it for granted. So too with human rights and their suppression, including those most basic desires of ordinary people everywhere, to speak freely and to be heard, to assemble and to organize around issues that affect them, and to be free of punishment, including torture, arbitrary arrest and detention, inhumane and inappropriate prison sentences and death.

Following this logic, rather than looking rather to economic indicators as a measure of development, one might consider the nature of the state: whether its agencies function adequately, whether they are corrupt or untainted, the extent to which the government is autonomous of vested interests, and whether the rule of law applies consistently and equally, and across the whole of the territory claimed by the state.

There is an assumption in such a discussion that, all other things being equal, such conditions do or should apply to all people more or less equally. Yet fully half of the world's population suffers various forms of discrimination, ranging from the 'glass ceiling' experienced by women and minorities in the developed countries, to forced abstinence from education or work in some others, and the otherwise culturally imposed roles that women are often forced to undertake, their lack of rights to redress, and their inferior status in almost all aspects of social, political and economic life. The role of women, their position in many societies, and the tension over the evolution of such positions has been one of the most troubled aspects of the development debate, and while there has been encouraging movement in some areas there has been depressingly little in others.

The issue of development, and especially material development, also implies the greater use of natural resources, often in ways that wilfully ignore the side effects, such as water pollution from industrial sources, but also in ways in which people are genuinely unaware of the consequences, such as deforestation. One might ask, leaving aside for the moment the question of resource distribution, if parents in a heavily overpopulated country where large families are favoured would understand that continuing with such a tradition, especially in an era of broadly increasing life expectancy, could directly contribute to the potential ecological collapse of their own local environment? Or, indeed, one might also ask whether a local logger engaged in deforestation is thinking about the longer term when immediate survival continues to press. And then there are those whose faith in technology and the potential 'fixes' that it might provide, offers an easy rationale for not altering their otherwise ecologically unsustainable behaviour. The world is our home, yet we seem to insist on crowding and despoiling it, with little thought for how, and if, we can continue to live in our current manner, much less what sort of 'home' we are leaving to our children, our grandchildren and subsequent generations.

Within the OECD countries, the idea of per capita GDP as the primary measure of development, as noted above, began to give way to a more widely inclusive Physical Quality of Life Index (PQLI), developed in the 1970s. The PQLI emphasized development results rather than capacity for consumption, and measured infant mortality, life expectancy and adult literacy. This was, in turn, supplanted by the Human Development Index (HDI) in 1990, which combined life expectancy (as a proxy measure for good health), per capita income and a mix of educational measures, in an effort to measure capacity to make life choices as an alternative to GDP as a way of assessing development. These measurements, in turn, are now being challenged by the additional development criteria of human dignity, religious freedom, cultural maintenance, political expression, participation and empowerment, which give meaning to the often abused term 'democratization', and other so-called civil and political 'rights'. In this, issues of 'governance' have become paramount.

In this respect, notions of 'development' continue to evolve in ways that increasingly address the range of concerns that are expressed by people in their daily lives, most notably in those countries or regions where such daily lives are often a struggle for existence, or at least an adequate existence. In particular, the expression of concerns and values that contribute to an expanding idea of 'development' are the product of an increased level of community participation in the development process. The emphasis on development has increasingly moved away from what the 'experts' say 'development' is, to what people seeking 'development' want it to be. In saying this, however, it should be understood that this process of change is only partial and not especially quick, in particular amongst the larger multilateral agencies like the World Bank or Asian Development Bank, and more traditionalist development planners.

The shift in the categorization of what constitutes development began not only to diversify 'ownership' of the meaning of development, but also to reflect the diversity of responses to the development process. Some more successful post-colonial states, for instance, have moved up the Human Development Index scale while others, for various reasons, have tended to languish or indeed slide further down the scale, and yet others have had responses that have been inconsistent, in turn reflecting a different mix of policy prescriptions and circumstances. However, it has become increasingly clear that while, for the purposes of broad study, there is some advantage to such general categorizations, as a methodological tool such a scale is only partially helpful. All countries respond to and are influenced by a range of criteria that include history, material resources, economic infrastructure, trading links, political systems, conflict and the environment. Against this, while there are similarities between some countries, no two places are exactly the same. Hence, the study of development as it applies to people in real circumstances must, if it is to be meaningful, grapple with the specific outcomes in particular contexts, and not just broad theories.

Development is, perhaps, the world's most critical problem, incorporating most of the world's pressing issues. At the same time, the subject of development has retreated to increasingly simple formulae in the minds of many of the people and governments able to address it meaningfully. Much has been achieved in the development field in improving the lives of many of the world's people, but for many others little has advanced. Based on the overall fall in official development assistance from developed countries as a proportion of their GDP, it is clear that 'fatigue' has set in, and the global contest driving much work has ended. Certainly, the gap between developed countries and many, perhaps most, developing countries continues to widen, meaning that the world is increasingly a less equal, rather than more equal, place.

In part, the problems of developing countries in 'catching up' with the developed world, or, in some cases, even maintaining their existing position, are self-inflicted. Poor and often corrupt leadership with totalitarian tendencies has all too often been experienced by developing countries over the past half century. And a refusal informally to accept as equal citizens members of non-governing ethnic groups has riven many multi-ethnic developing societies, undoing the basis for state development. However, in many cases, the problems faced by many developing countries are also a legacy of colonialism, in which disparate ethnic groups – proto-nations – were lumped together by colonial powers based on geopolitical and military reach and with little or no regard for social cohesion, existing patterns of social organization, or the need for social and capital infrastructure. Similarly, the style and method of colonial rule very often imparted to aspiring independence movements engendered little respect for, or understanding of, economic equity, legal principle, or political participation. Further, the often brutal methods of maintaining political control by many colonial powers and their often violent intransigence towards decolonization also informed and deeply influenced many post-colonial states.

Yet, it would be a mistake to see developing countries simply as a product of these historical circumstances alone. Post-(or neo-)colonial economic relationships have dominated most developing countries since, constructing them as suppliers of primary commodities to an often oversupplied world market that, as a consequence, has driven down prices and hence income available to such countries. Foreign political intervention has also been used to maintain in power governments that served elite interests, rather than the mass of the people. This process was especially notable during the period of ideological contest between the West and the Soviet bloc. Very often regimes were installed or supported not because they addressed development issues but simply because they were regarded as loyal 'clients' of one side or the other. The economic and political fallout from this policy continues to reverberate to this day.

Most notably, for over a half a century, developing countries have been encouraged to follow the industrializing lead of developed countries, borrowing heavily for (often questionable) major infrastructure projects and attempting to track along the path to economic 'takeoff' expected by early development theorists. Indeed, this fixation with an often externally imposed model of economic development has often not suited the particular conditions of developing countries and has exacerbated existing political and economic problems, or created new ones, such as deepening levels of indebtedness. There have, it is true, been some notable successes, particularly in East Asia. But a closer reading of these successes reveals a complex set of conditions that make them the exception rather than the rule. At present, only one broad model of development, based on neo-liberalism, is being promoted worldwide, but the question remains whether or not there are potentially several development models rather than the one that currently dominates.

The 'aid', too, that has been offered to developing countries to help alleviate their problems can often be seen as a means of buying off the sense of guilt of those in developed countries whose conscience is not shackled by parochial identity. Aid policies frequently target spending of aid money in the donor country on goods or services that usually have a short lifespan in the developing country and are unable to be sustained once the donor has left. In only a few cases are skills and knowledge successfully imparted to local partners in aid projects, creating a legacy of unfulfilled hopes, failed expectations and political frustration. The best, though rarest, aid projects are those that impart knowledge and skills and leave in place technology that is sustainable in local conditions. This represents the slow and incomplete transition from patronage to participation.

If most of the post-colonial era has been marked by wide-ranging policy failure on the part of many developing countries, then the developed countries also continue to bear responsibility. The policies of infrastructure development and industrialization encouraged by developed countries that required massive overseas borrowings by developing countries left a vast number of countries with crippling and often unsustainable debts. The answer to this has been further, renegotiated debt, mortgaging not just the present but the long-term future of many developing countries. And the policies that have been imposed by western governments as a condition of debt 'relief' have, in most cases, been onerous and narrowly defined, leading to cuts in basic social services such as education and health care. The tighter economic embrace of global capital, particularly since the end of the Cold War, has left most developing countries with few, if any, options about the course that is supposed to lead to development. The largely 'off the shelf' economic model that is now being handed down by organizations such as the International Monetary Fund (IMF) and the World Bank is, in reality, simply not negotiable. Yet it has been precisely this patronizing and unilateral view of the options for development that have themselves failed in the past. The 'experts' continue to believe their own propaganda and to ignore the mounting evidence. The one or two that announce that the emperor (or the empire) has no clothes are invariably cast out (see Stiglitz 2002).

Yet what has been learned about development over the past half century or so is that much of the process to date has, based on a wider set of criteria, been inadequate. Ideas in development have changed while the lives of many poor people remain much the same. It is now clear that investment in new industries to modernize the economy (1950s) has been inappropriate or inadequate; that investment in education alone (1960s) has in most cases not been sustained to reveal the benefits it could have delivered; that investment in basic needs (health, agriculture, etc.) (1970s) has not been enough or sufficiently applied; that investment in 'getting policies right' to facilitate technology transfer (1980s) has been misguided, mishandled or was simply unsustainable; and that investment in alliances that were intended to achieve sectoral reforms, especially in finance and export-led development (1990s), has not achieved the sort of gains in development that have led to a sustainable reduction in poverty on a global scale.

Remarkably, and perhaps dangerously, little attention has been paid to the physical impact that various attempts at development have had on the planet on which we all live. As noted at the Johannesburg Summit on Sustainable Development in August 2002, over the next half century the population of the world's 49 poorest countries will triple and the global population is expected to be in excess of 9 billion people. In terms of economic distribution, around half of the world's population lives on less than US$2 a day, which as noted above is understood by some planners to constitute absolute poverty, while more than 150 million children remain undernourished. Eighty per cent of the world's wealth is held by 15 per cent of its people, who also use a disproportionate share of world resources (UNPD 2001). Natural resources, including arable land, forests and sea life, are diminishing at an unsustainable rate, while more than 11,000 species risk extinction, including a quarter of all mammal species and 30 per cent of fish species (WWF 2002). Remaining forests, which produce oxygen and absorb carbon dioxide, are estimated to reduce by almost half over the next 20 years. Global warming from the production of greenhouse gases continues and constitutes perhaps the single biggest threat to the survival of the planet. Scarcity of clean water affects more than a billion people, and water loss is becoming a major problem in Africa and Asia.

Facing a less forgiving international economic and ideological order, with little scope for error, traditional 'modernist' development is being challenged by models that are more reflective, more critical and more participatory. This development challenge is reflected in efforts by some practitioners to utilize more participatory approaches to development planning, and to challenge orthodox approaches to development project design, implementation and monitoring. Greater focus on the accountability of decision makers in developing countries also reflects these more recent trends. As a result, much of the focus has shifted to giving attention to governance issues which, it has been repeatedly shown, when ignored can be manipulated by sectional interests for narrowly defined personal gain. Accountability, transparency and mandate are key themes in this more recent approach to development, with advocates for pro-poor policies, fairer international economic relations and sustainable poverty reduction challenging globalization and free-market capitalism for a greater sharing of the development agenda. This shift in focus and emphasis poses fundamental challenges to earlier conventional approaches to development, and redefines the roles that key stakeholders play in priority setting. Moral hazard and poor governance are two of the issues that are now attracting greater attention. Equally important are shifts in process that challenge development professionals to genuinely 'democratize' the development process and set out key performance indicators that do more than give lip service to the interests of the people it is intended to serve.

It is important to note that these trends were unlikely to have come forward while the Cold War continued. While developing countries remained pawns in a larger game, it was commonly regarded as too costly to the big powers to allow issues of governance, fairness or justice to play a real role in determining stakeholder influence. While there remain significant vested constraints, with the passing of the Cold War the pressures are different. Disenfranchised stakeholders are asserting their voices and poverty reduction can (and no doubt should) be a real goal of the global system.

About the book

This book is the second edition of the 2008 book *International Development: Issues and Challenges* which in turn was designed as a replacement for the 2004 text *Key Issues in Development*, to which most members of the current author team contributed and on which a number of their chapters draw substantially, although all have been thoroughly revised and updated or are entirely new or rewritten.

In common with *Key Issues in Development*, it acknowledges that development is a contested and, in some senses, unstable idea, having progressed from the early post-war years when it meant little more than increasing average income to, more than fifty years later, including a range of conditions and circumstances that impact on life in countries that continue to variously define themselves in the modern, or post-modern, world. A common understanding of a post-modern world that has evolved since the end of the Cold War is that which has transcended industrialization and largely relies on information flows and processes as the basis for its economy. Critics have argued, however, that post-modernism is in fact a variety of modernism which continues to rely on (sometimes offshore) manufacturing substrata and maintained access to primary commodities, while also using the higher level of information technology now available. That is to say, the world is increasingly locating economic sectors along state lines with different states playing different roles, i.e., high technology information providers, industrial manufacturers and basic commodity providers. The primary categories continue to exist, if in an increasingly global, rather than local, economy.

Assuming, then, that the major global economic changes involve a reorganization of states as primarily differentiated contributors to commodity, manufacturing and information components of the global economy, the questions that arise revolve around the relative weightings of these sectors and the political judgements that consent to such a reorganization. In this there is a very real tension between the structural exigencies of the 'neo-liberal' (free market-led) global economic agenda and the potential agency of politics in which allocation of resources reflects ideological (interest-based), rather than mechanistic, economic considerations. There is a suggestion in this that, following the neo-liberal paradigm, economic development is increasingly market-rather than state-led. However, this assumes that what markets achieve is development broadly defined. The neo-liberal philosophy that structurally links free markets (which are almost never actually free) and democracy (generically regarded as political development) fundamentally fails to note a long history of state intervention in markets within democratic contexts. It is also based on the assumption that markets unrestrained will deliver broadly distributed wealth, which is at best a moot point, and that competing neo-liberal economic practice is politically value-neutral which, demonstrably, it is not.

From this tension arises the question, yet again, what is the purpose of development? As discussed in this book, development continues to mean the material advancement of people, especially the world's poor. But material advancement, especially if understood as simple economic growth, is not enough by itself, and, indeed, may not even be realized without other component aspects of development which include the capacity to ensure adequate distribution of the benefits of such growth, ecological sustainability in the way the growth is achieved, and the governance to ensure that the processes to achieve such growth are agreed in a politically inclusive manner and operate under the rule of law.

Development here is, therefore, understood as a process not just of growth or, at its most benign, poverty alleviation, but also of empowerment. The universalist claims to rights, for example, as a part of an overarching (although inconsistent) globalization of standards, also includes accountability and transparency. On the other hand, the growing tendency towards localism is increasing the pressure to put decision-making into the hands of the people. In this, it has been argued by some development commentators that there is a further tension between universal prescriptions and local conditions. As discussed in the chapter on community development (Chapter 9), the application of development practice must be attuned to local conditions. Yet there are also certain normative development outcomes, including the full and disinterested application of law, and active political participation and representation of people whatever their race, sex, creed, or social status. These mutually reliant outcomes, which might be termed 'inclusive governance', both implicitly and sometimes explicitly underpin the contributions to this book. It is this underpinning, or philosophical orientation, that makes this book a somewhat more original contribution to the development debate than many others which have been far more equivocal about or disinterested in such matters.

For the purpose of the book, development means the process by which the people and states outside the industrialized world attempt to improve their conditions of life, through material and social means. Here, development implies change, affecting most, if not all, areas of life. The idea of development is a multidimensional and, by definition, interdisciplinary field in which economic, political, technological, social and cultural factors interact. Development has also been portrayed as synonymous with 'modernization', in this sense including the ideas of industrialization, economic and organizational efficiency, delineated formal political institutions and functions, the pursuit of rational decision-making and the fundamental alteration of social and cultural patterns. However, as these criteria have not proven to be universally successful, there are increasingly alternative or more inclusive paradigms for defining development.

In this respect, this book considers a wide range of what its authors believe to be the key issues in the development debate. These include definitions of levels of development, global influences on development, measurements of development, economic issues, the contribution of international aid, political and civil development (often referred to under the overused rubric of 'democratization'), the issue of gender, the idea of development as 'modernization', theories of underdevelopment, regional variation, the environment, and community development. The focus of the book is widely international and employs a geographically broad range of examples, other than where it addresses geographically specific issues (that themselves have wider implications for the field of study, such as the Asian economic crisis, sub-Saharan Africa's development failure, or the United Nations-led state-building exercise in East Timor).

Mark McGillivray's opening chapter asks the question 'What is Development?' At one level this is a basic question, but, as intimated above, it can quickly descend into a complex and contested range of responses. To this end, McGillivray updates his more detailed discussion of what constitutes development, locating at development's core the idea of poverty alleviation, and tracing its origins from the beginning of the post-Second World War era. The focus on poverty alleviation as the core of what constitutes development addresses perhaps the most basic issue in the development debate; that if people remain hungry or without adequate shelter, education or other basic services, then all else becomes redundant. This establishes the basic premise for the rest of the book.

Any study of development must trace the key debates on the political economy of development since the beginning of the post-war era. John

McKay outlines these major trends and conditions within the global system, and the dominant ideas on the nature and genesis of development. At one level, the second half of the twentieth century was an era of unparalleled growth and prosperity, if with some economic stumbles in the twenty-first centruy. But this has only occurred within certain countries or regions. A key question then, which McKay seeks to answer in Chapter 2, is why some countries have been able to prosper while others have stagnated or gone backwards. Within mainstream economic thought, there has been a strong assumption that growth in some regions will eventually 'trickle down' to the more peripheral areas, given certain conditions and policies. Thus, according to this theory, poor countries can catch up and benefit from the earlier growth experience of others and pass through a similar process of development, albeit at a later date. This is the essence of the theories of modernization that were popular in the 1950s and 1960s, and which made a return under the guise of 'neo-liberalism' from the 1980s. These ideas still inform the dominant international institutions in the development field, notably the IMF and the World Bank.

As McKay discusses, the underlying assumptions of the various permutations of free-market capitalism came under sustained attack during the 1960s, from what has become known as the 'dependency school', originating especially in Latin America. One view, put by theorists such as Baran, Frank and others, argued that developing countries could not develop in this 'trickle down' manner, because the processes of global change that gave rise to prosperity in developed countries resulted in the simultaneous impoverishment of the poorer regions. These dependency ideas themselves were also criticized, partly because of their over-reliance on global rather than local factors, but especially for their inability to account for the rapid growth that was clearly going on in parts of East Asia at the time. In turn, the economic crisis in Asia in 1997–8, the continued crisis in Africa, and the seemingly remorseless progress of globalization, partly through the expansion of the multinational corporations, has seen a revival of interest in 'neo-dependency' approaches. The chapter, then, explores the history of ideas about development, asking what has been learned from the last 50 years in terms of theory and the design of more appropriate policies.

Within development, a major consistent focus has been on development assistance, usually referred to as aid. Considering this, in Chapter 3 on aid, Janet Hunt looks critically at multilateral and bilateral aid, and the distinctions between official development assistance (ODA) and private aid programmes. The chapter assesses the contributions, styles and shifting orientations of the major multilateral aid organizations and aid donor countries, the international commitment to aid, how aid is employed in bilateral relations, and the role of non-government organizations (NGOs) in the aid agenda/s and as contributors to the effective application of aid. It also considers what aid has achieved since the beginning of the 1960s, and where it is heading in the twenty-first century. It also considers the role that development co-operation is playing towards achievement of the Millennium Development Goals {MDGs) and that future aid will play in development. Hunt sets aid within the context of other more significant factors in development, such as globalization, trade and financial policies, indebtedness (some of it aid-driven), and intrastate conflict. Her chapter also addresses public perceptions of aid and the issues of public and political support for the aid regime.

The international focus on aid has changed in the period during and after the Cold War, with aid levels declining and distribution patterns changing. Since poverty reduction is a key goal of aid (and a focus of this book), Hunt also considers the extent to which aid can contribute to poverty reduction. The question of aid and power relations raises the further question of who primarily benefits from aid, noting that aid is often far less benign than it initially appears.

Implicit in Hunt's chapter is a recognition that the material basis of development has been and to a large extent remains dominant in development thinking. To this end, McKay returns to the basis of material well-being and how that is achieved, through an assessment of how economic development policies have evolved over more than half a decade. As McKay notes, there has been a series of debates and controversies about the economic dimensions of development theory and practice, which he summarizes as ten basic points of discussion.

Initially, McKay asks and then seeks to answer how economic growth happens and what are its major drivers. While acknowledging macroeconomic policy prescriptions around exchange rates, labour costs, inflation, investment and the like, he also notes that economic formula will only work in the presence of a number of other key conditions. These include human capital, appropriate governance structures and robust political systems. He then moves on to consider whether economic growth can come easily, asks about the role of the state in the generation of growth, the appropriate roles of the state and the private sector, and the management of structural change. This then leads to the generation, absorption and use of technology, the role and rationale for foreign trade and investment and, reprising a theme of Hunt's, the role of foreign aid in growth. This chapter concludes by looking at the role of international co-operation and of international organizations and networks and, prefacing the following chapter, whether economic development is easier or more difficult in the current era of globalization.

The issue of globalization is one that looms increasingly large over many areas, not least that of development, and was therefore considered critical to include in this overall study. While in Chapter 4 Damien Kingsbury notes that development is sometimes defined in global terms, he questions the specificity of particular development issues, reflecting what some observers have called a 'global–local' dichotomy. Beyond countries, there are also wider challenges and changes to communities at all levels brought about by various aspects of globalization. As Kingsbury discusses, globalization has been broadly taken to mean economic globalization, especially of a free-market capitalist type. This implies that critiques of globalization have focused on this dominant type of globalization rather than globalization as such. Global capitalism, freed of the restraints that can be applied by states, is no longer easily restrained by a politically and often economically fragmented international community. As a result of this, Kingsbury says that in order to prosper communities must attract global capital – those that do can, indeed, prosper, while those that do not tend to wither. Kingsbury also suggests that what is said to be a reduction of state sovereignty is just another domain for elite domination, or state variation, which opens the way for exploitation.

As with development, defining globalization solely as an economic phenomenon artificially constrains its meaning. Other, non-economic, types of globalization, are equally important. These may include the spread of normative ('universalist') humanist political and social values, such as civil and political rights, political participation and representation, equality before an impartial law and so on (which is often contained within the term 'democratization'). Communication and aspects of culture are also increasingly globalized, in terms of technology, ownership and spread of media, and shared popular preferences. In these senses, development can be understood as comprising economic, political and cultural elements, all of which engage in a wider world and all of which are in some ways ultimately transformed by it. There thus remains a capacity for a normative type of globalization that implies a process intended to achieve the greatest amount of happiness among the greatest number of people.

Following from this increasing tendency towards globalization, in Chapter 8, Matthew Clarke examines the concepts, measures, trends and responses that have in large part come to define, if not the global standards, then at least the major development paradigms. As Clarke argues, at base development seeks to improve the lives of the poor.

Determining whether development has been successful in reducing poverty, however, requires poverty and responses to it to be measured. This, however, presupposes that poverty has been adequately defined. Clarke's chapter therefore begins with a review of how poverty is defined, and describes the movement from the long-held approach of it being solely a function of income to its more recent multidimensional understanding best encapsulated by the MDGs. Clarke then offers an assessment of the experience of poverty over recent decades, utilizing a large number of poverty measures and other data. He then analyses change in poverty measurements and outcomes, concluding with thoughts on how poverty might be further reduced through both local or community and national and international interventions.

Nowhere has the failure of economic development, and governance, been more pronounced than in sub-Saharan Africa, where deterioration of social and economic conditions over the past two decades has confounded development efforts. Following Asia's financial crisis of 1997–8, which raised major governance issues relating to economic development in South East Asia, the issues gained further prominence. These failures in Africa and Asia have presented major challenges to development theory and practice, and each in their different ways can be said to be at the heart of the development process. Most notably, as McKay observes in Chapter 6, rapid economic growth, collapse and a resumption of high levels of growth in Asia has posed questions for both dependency theorists and the proponents of free-market policies, while the continued crisis in Africa is an indictment of the entire development 'profession'. This chapter examines these two very different crises, and considers in particular the nature of the crises in the two regions, and the various explanations that have been put forward to account for these serious events. Working with data compiled over the past 13 years, McKay considers whether the crises in Africa and Asia were separate, unrelated events, or two symptoms of some basic problems in the global system, as well as assessing what has happened in each set of cases since then.

Within this, McKay notes the variations between countries in terms of the severity and causes of the crisis, the policies that had been adopted, or had failed to be adopted, in the period leading up to the respective crises, and the relationship between them with the onset of crisis conditions. This then leads to considering the impact of trade, investment and other liberalization policies, and the relationship between the crises and the nature of the global systems of trade, investment and finance.

Given expressions of broadly anti-western sentiment in a number of developing countries, McKay then looks at the level and nature of resentment in Asia and Africa against the West, and its economic, political and strategic implications. And continuing with a theme developed in earlier chapters, McKay also considers the relationships in various countries and regions between democracy, transparency, good governance, economic development and the crisis. He explores the extent and nature of recovery from the crisis in various countries, especially in Asia, and the policies for restructuring and reform, including the role of international and regional agencies in facilitating recovery, the extent to which these actions were effective, and what has occurred since.

In discussion of the success or otherwise of the application of economic models, issues of governance and, hence, accountability have become critical. Kingsbury notes in the following chapter some of the characteristics that have become identified with developing countries and why many of them are locked into a cycle of repression, reform and repression. As noted by Kingsbury, multi-ethnic states with low levels of institutional capacity and relative economic scarcity tend to default to patron–client relations and repression of objectors. There are debates about universal versus local values, the form and structure of the state, the principal model of political organization, about who should be included and who not and how and why, about the legitimacy of the state and the relationship between the government and the state.

Chapter 9 picks up on themes of the focus, purpose and methods of development raised by politics in developing countries to consider ideas of community development. Community development is intended to enhance the social and local decision-making process – the 'empowerment' – of people who are the target of development projects and to give them more practical political power over the goals and outcomes of the development process. Kingsbury posits that the movement towards community development reflects a fundamental reorientation of development towards a grass-roots or local-level process of democratization. Such an approach has been shown, in a number of cases, to produce real, tangible and appropriate benefits to people at the local level, as well as providing a greater sense of self worth and the capacity to make many of their own decisions. It also has the benefit of working within and preserving aspects of local culture that give meaning to community life and which assist in maintaining and enhancing the social cohesion that is necessary when successfully engaging in a process of change.

The move towards this focus on social and cultural development is derived from critiques of top-down aid projects and decision-making. Many such projects that failed to meet the needs and desires of people at the local level were often not based on local experience and were frequently unsustainable once the aid provider had left. In all, such aid benefited the aid provider, in that they were given a job and a social purpose, but had little, and sometimes negative, impact on the aid recipients. In other cases, decisions about aid projects have been taken by traditional representatives or chiefs, sometimes with the outcome that the decisions have reflected their own somewhat more limited interests to the exclusion of those of the more marginal people in their areas.

In the formative stages of this more 'grass-roots' form of development, local decision makers might require assistance and education that has been shown to be most successfully undertaken through what has been referred to as 'participatory development'. In this, the external agency works with local people in assisting them to make decisions for themselves, to reflect on their decisions and to secure such decisions against external incursions. The balancing act for the 'participatory development worker' is to assist and, where necessary, guide but to do so in a way that continues to reinforce local decision making, needs and aspirations.

Related to community development or local empowerment is the development or empowerment of women within the development context. In Chapter 10, Janet Hunt focuses on the gender aspects of development, in particular how women have largely been 'made invisible' and left out of the development process. While policies have more recently sought to include women in development, the results are mixed at best and women have always carried the largest share of the domestic material burden in societies in developing countries, beyond child-rearing and home maintenance, including domestic husbandry and agriculture, and, more recently, in paid employment. Hunt also notes that men have been more readily accommodated into the cash economy, although the benefits of their access to cash have not always contributed to the welfare of family members.

As Hunt explains, gender is understood as the socially ascribed roles of men and women in any society based on their sex. Hunt examines how gender-defined roles have been differentiated traditionally and how the development process has influenced or changed this, and how this influence or change has impacted on gender relations and the distribution of the benefits of development, often to the detriment of women.

In many traditional societies, the roles of the sexes are clearly and separately defined, in some cases with sanctions being placed on the transgression of gender roles. Gender roles in traditional societies can reflect a balance (or imbalance) of responsibilities around modes of production. However, the process of development destabilizes and reorients aspects of traditional modes of production, especially in relation to cash cropping, employed labour and the social impact of industrialization, often leaving women with heavier work burdens. Understanding the gender impacts of proposed development is a key issue.

Hunt's chapter links many of the issues raised in earlier chapters and views them through a gender lens. If development is to reduce poverty, then it must transform women's lives, since women are disproportionately represented among the world's poor. Hunt explores the relationship of gender considerations to macroeconomic trends of the past 20 years, to globalization and trade liberalization, to the environment and attempts to make development sustainable, and to the focus on community development.

While all of the preceding issues are critical to an understanding of development, it is the degradation of the earth's capacity to sustain life that presents short-term problems and critical long-term threats. That is to say, no development can take place outside the context of the physical environment, yet, until recently, this has been the most neglected area in development debate. In Chapter 11, Kingsbury therefore considers aspects of the environment that increasingly demand to be thought of as fundamental parts of the development agenda. This demand has been partly as a consequence of the rise in the profile of environmental issues in developed countries and, hence, among many bilateral and multilateral aid agencies and aid organizations, and partly in response to environmental issues that have arisen in developing countries due to increases in population and particularly as a direct result of a range of development processes. However, as Kingsbury notes, environmental issues such as global warming are not exclusive to particular countries but now constitute a threat to all. Kingsbury notes that the environmental record in development has, to date, been poor, and environmental degradation has continued at a pace that is unsustainable in absolute terms.

The environmental impact of development has manifested in a number of ways. In particular, the sheer increase in the global population – the consumption of natural resources implied in such growth and the human and industrial pollution that has been produced – is perhaps the single most important issue. As Kingsbury notes in this chapter, governments of developing countries are more inclined to go softly on such industry, as they cite their economic inability to provide alternative means of waste disposal while pointing out their contribution to employment and economic development. The same is often said about issues such as air pollution that have been shown to impact on wider aspects of the global environment, for instance the ozone layer and the increasingly critical issue of global warming. To this end, there has increasingly been discussion about 'appropriate development' and 'sustainable development', two ideas that often overlap, and these issues are discussed in this chapter.

Given the world's focus on terrorism, the issues of underdevelopment that have been argued to give it fuel, and the various development (not to mention military) resources that have been allocated to combating it, the final chapter of this book, by McKay, reviews recent thinking about the causes of terrorism and violence, and the impact that the anti-terrorism effort is having on development. Although there had been little action up until this was being written, there had been considerable rhetoric about the link between poverty and terrorism, and the need therefore to tackle poverty.

This chapter is substantially revised and rewritten in the light of recent experiences and new theoretical advances. The impact of the wars in Iraq and Afghanistan, the spill-over into Pakistan, and the expansion of terrorist activities into other parts of the Middle East such as Yemen are considered. We now think about the two-way linkages between terrorism and development in quite new ways and the intensification of the Maoist insurgency in India is also instructive here. McKay reflects on the new work on the concept of the failed (or failing) states, employing the Democratic Republic of the Congo as a relevant case study. The limits to effectiveness of international intervention in these matters have also become much clearer, and the implication of this is also evaluated.

Considering terrorism as a symptom of deeper problems, McKay sets his discussion within the growing body of theory on human security, including the wider range of conditions that are required to sustain and enhance life in a moderately predictable manner. As well as terrorism, other forms of violence are considered by McKay, including those generated by ethnic tensions

As noted at the outset, much of the world continues to focus on issues of development and, when attention is properly turned, it is widely recognized that the problems of development are global in both their reach and their potential impact. Yet at the same time the urgency felt by some about such global development issues is far from shared by all, and has resulted in this retreat from tackling the complex issues. The reduction to increasingly simplistic formulae for addressing the continuing problems of development reflects the various types of 'fatigue' that has beset many wealthier countries in relation to poorer countries. Much of this, in turn, can be attributed to the lack of ideological imperative that characterized the period from around 1950 to 1990. A new ideological imperative – that of neo-liberalism – has prevailed but it has been less generous, less sympathetic (and much less empathetic) and fairly inflexible in the choices that it has offered.

This book, then, attempts to discuss these key issues and explore some of the ways forward for development in this evolving period of global reorganization. If it provides material to work with and to consider critically, it will have gone a long way towards achieving its primary goal.

Chapter 1

What is Development?

Mark McGillivray

The term 'development' is one that has many different meanings. While many overlap, some inherently contradict each other. To many people development is either a process or outcome that is often bad in terms of its impact on people and the societies in which they live. Some others see development as both a process and an outcome, and as necessarily good. These people see development as something that should be actively sought after. And to complicate matters further, there are many others who define development in many different ways. The broad aim of this chapter attempts to identify, explain and resolve those issues by introducing and outlining various conceptualizations of development. Such an exercise is an important one: if we are to study something, it is essential to first understand what we are studying. It is especially important in a study of development, for without a definition of this term we cannot determine whether a country is achieving higher levels of development, or whether it should be considered developed, developing or underdeveloped. It is also important for development practice. Development practitioners, irrespective of whether they are involved in policy, planning or in implementing development projects, need a working definition of what it is they are seeking to achieve.

This chapter looks at various definitions of development. Such an exercise necessarily requires an examination of theoretical material about what development is or ought to be. The chapter adopts a largely chronological examination, given that many new definitions are actually responses to earlier ones. To understand the latter one first needs to understand the former. The chapter commences by introducing and critiquing various traditional or early meanings or conceptualizations of development. This is a deliberately brief discussion. More detailed treatments can be found in Leftwich (2000), Hunt (1989) and, in particular, Cowen and Shenton (1996). The chapter then examines more contemporary meanings of development, those that emerged from the late 1960s to the present. These meanings either treat development as the domination and exploitation of one group by another or as what might very loosely be described as 'good change'. The chapter favours the use of the second, largely because it forces us to reflect on what sort of change or outcomes we want to see in all countries, rich and poor, providing a framework to compare actual changes against those we would like to observe. It also allows us to consider which countries, and within countries, which people, should be prioritized in efforts to improve the human condition.

The chapter focuses predominantly on various conceptualizations that are consistent with the 'good change' approach, many that are provided by the literature on human well-being. This is followed by an empirical examination of the development record in a manner consistent with some of these conceptualizations. This involves looking at country achievements, or in some cases lack thereof, in health, education, income and related indicators. Finally, a balance sheet is provided that looks at what might be perceived as 'goods' and 'bads' and which asks us to judge whether 'development' has actually occurred. It is argued that this is essentially a subjective exercise, and a complicated one at that, which requires one to reflect on one's own personal values to judge what is important and what is not.

Traditional meanings of development

Historical progress and modernization

To many people, development means the use of natural resources to supply infrastructure, build roads and dams and provide electricity and other forms of energy, to productively utilize or exploit previously unused areas of land or to devise new forms of technology for productive use. For others, it can simply be an ordered or linked set of events or changes. It is not uncommon for someone to refer to the 'next development' in something, be it an individual's life story, a novel, a movie or a sports event or, more to the current point, a town or city, region or nation. These meanings correspond, arguably, with what most laypeople would mean by 'development'.

These layperson's definitions of development are broadly consistent, to varying degrees, with more formal definitions that were dominant in the academic and policy literatures and embraced by most development practitioners during the 1950s to late 1960s. They still appear in some literatures and are embraced by some practitioners even today, but are far less dominant. Some have their origins in literature dating back many centuries. Most if not all overlap to varying degrees and some are differentiated only by subtle differences. For our current purposes, it is sufficient to outline two that are arguably the most dominant. The definitions treat development as either historical progress or modernization. Let us briefly discuss each in turn.

Development as *historical progress* refers to the unfolding of human history, over a long period of time, in a manner that is thought to be progressive. The evolution of capitalism is often put forward as an example of historical progress. Key to this definition is what is understood as progress, and deciding whether certain historical changes are progressive is not a straightforward task. It is made all the less straightforward by many different conceptualizations of progress. The modern view of progress is based on a philosophical notion that is equated with a steady onward process, brought about by human agency, which results in a systematic transformation of the world. Human agency is in turn seen as the application of human abilities, such as intelligence and initiative.

Development, defined as historical progress, is very much linked to the Western European experience from the late eighteenth century onward. This experience saw the emergence of more materially affluent societies, the application of improved technologies that resulted among other things in better communication and transportation, greater human freedom and, in time, improvements in health and education levels.

Development as *modernization* has been described in many different ways. This very influential conceptualization of development is discussed in detail in Chapter 2 of this book, so here we provide broad details only. Modernization is a process whereby societies move through a fundamental, complete structural transition from one condition to another, from a starting point to an end point. The starting point is viewed as a traditional society that develops into an advanced, modern society. This is associated with a shift in the structure of an economy, away from a reliance on the agricultural sector. This shift sees a greater reliance over time on the industrial sector, with an increasingly large proportion of an economy's output coming from manufacturing activities. Eventually it also sees the rise of a services sector that includes the providers of health and educational services, finance, transportation and professional advice.

It should be emphasized that in its proper context modernization not only involves an economic transformation but profound social, cultural, ideological, institutional and political changes as well. In an influential paper, Huntington (1971) describes modernization as a process in which societies have more control over their natural and social environment due to the use of superior scientific and technical knowledge. Moreover, according to Huntington, the economic, social and political structures and processes actually converge over time.

Development defined as modernization or historical progress is evident in the works of two well-known writers, Walt Rostow and Karl Marx. Examining these works allows us to better understand these definitions. Rostow proposed what is known as the 'stages theory' of economic growth in his famous book published in 1960 (Rostow 1960). The growth to which Rostow refers is in the economy or economic growth, measured by year-on-year changes in the overall level of production. Rostow's theory is also discussed in the next chapter, which mainly focuses on the context in which this theory was proposed. Here our focus is on the meaning of development implicit to the Rostow theory.

Rostow's stages of economic growth

Rostow's theory is that societies pass through five stages. A society or country may be considered to be *developing* as it passes through these stages and as *developed* as it reaches the final stages. And as we shall shortly note, development is very much defined in terms of material advancement. Often this type of development is called *economic development*. The first is a *traditional society* stage. This stage is characterized by low levels of productivity and technology. The economy is dominated by the agricultural sector, with most people living and working on the land. The social structure of agricultural life is very hierarchical and there is little upward mobility: people who were born poor remained poor, and successive generations were often no better off than each other. Economic growth is very low or non-existent.

The second stage is when societies commence a process of transition. This is when the preconditions for what is termed 'take-off' into rapid and sustained growth are put in place. Accordingly, this is the *preconditions for take-off* stage. Entrepreneurial activity emerges, with a class of people willing and able to save from their incomes, thereby creating a pool of funds that can be invested. Banks and other institutions that facilitate these activities emerge, with an increase in investment in transport and communications. Modern technologies are also utilized.

The third stage is *take-off*. During this stage there are further technical advances in both industry and agriculture, the entrepreneurial class expands, new and profitable industries emerge and quickly expand and previously unexploited natural resources are increasingly used in production. This stage is characterized by two key factors that differentiate it from the previous stage. The first is that institutional resistances to steady economic growth are largely removed. These resistances might be, for example, a class of people whose interests are to retard general economic advancement, such as a landed or elite class that wants a pool of cheap labour. The second is that there are large increases in the incomes of those who not only save increasingly larger shares of this income but make these savings available to those wanting to invest in modern sectors of the economy. Savings increase by up to approximately 10 per cent of national income in the take-off stage.

Take-off is followed a long interval of sustained although fluctuating, progress as the now regularly growing economy drives to apply modern technology throughout its entire economy. This is the fourth stage, known as the *drive to maturity*. Savings and investment is in the vicinity of 10 to 20 per cent of national income and the growth of national output and income regularly exceeds that of population. The economy is now involved extensively in international trade. Commodities that were once produced at home are imported and purchased using funds obtained from exporting other commodities abroad. New industries emerge and older ones either disappear or taper off. The society adjusts its values and institutions in ways that support the growth process. Maturity is reached 40 or so years after the end of the take-off stage.

The final stage in the Rostow theory is the *age of high mass-consumption* in which the country or society is truly developed. Upon reaching this stage, societies no longer accept the ongoing application of modern technology as the fundamental objective. The consumer is king, with the economy being primarily geared towards the production of consumer durables and services on a mass basis. The leading sectors of the economy are those that supply these goods and services. Cars, television sets, washing machines, cooking equipment and leisure are the focus of productive efforts. Material prosperity is higher than ever and this modern society can unambiguously be considered as developed. Importantly, while this prosperity might not be very evenly distributed in this modern society, it would be enjoyed by all sections within it. Those who were once poor would no longer be so because economic expansion would ensure high levels of employment and a high demand for employees would ensure higher wages. This spreading of the benefits of growth to the poor is referred to as 'trickle-down', a crucial characteristic of theories such as Rostow's.

Marx's stages of historical development

Marx, in his writings first published in the second half of the nineteenth century, envisaged four stages of historical development (Marx 1970a, 1970b, 1970c, 1972). As with Rostow's stages, the implicit message from Marx's treatment of history is that a society is *developing* as it passes through each stage and achieves a higher level of *development* along the way. The level of freedom enjoyed by individuals and the ownership of private property differentiates stages. The first of Marx's stages is the *primal stage*. Individuals are overwhelmingly concerned with satisfying the most basic of human needs such as food, clothing and shelter. Higher notions such as self-expression and individual freedoms are not entertained until basic survival is ensured. All societies are thought to emerge from this primal stage.

The second stage of historical development is the *feudal stage*, in which private property exists but is held by the aristocracy. The aristocracy oppresses and alienates but at the same time is dependent upon the masses that are the subordinate serf class. This stage provides no freedom or opportunity for self-fulfilment, and increased production is achieved through the direct exploitation of the majority.

Feudalism is followed by the *capitalist stage*. The capitalist society provides private property and productivity capacity grows rapidly. An entrepreneurial, capitalist class emerges that seeks out commercial opportunity. A more modern and technically advanced economy consequently emerges that relies less on agriculture and more on industry. Marx was of the view that capitalism was best suited to achieve increases in the productive capacity of the economy. Individual freedom is, however, withheld from the proletariat (working class). This class is both exploited and impoverished, and remains alienated through its submission to wage labour. The capitalist class is enriched by the expansion of the productive capacity of the economy.

Marx's historical stages of development culminate in the fourth stage, *Communism*. The enrichment of the capitalist class and the impoverishment of the proletariat in the capitalist stage would ultimately lead to the latter overthrowing the former. The proletariat would, in particular, seize the means of production, transferring it to public or collective ownership, and encourage social relations that would benefit everyone equally. True freedom for the proletariat would then be achieved. This society would reject all previous values, realizing that class is an artificial creation and perpetuated by rulers interested only in ensuring their own self-interests and survival. That the productive capacity of the economy has been built up under the capitalist stage and the equal sharing of the benefits of this capacity means that everyone's living standards in this society are relatively high.

A critique

Traditional meanings of development, implicit or otherwise, came under great scrutiny from the late 1960s onward. Understanding this scrutiny requires us to outline the main measures of development that corresponded to these meanings. Consistent with the traditional conceptualizations of development, in particular that which equated development with modernization, was the use of the rate of growth of per capita national income, be it measured in terms of per capita Gross Domestic Product (GDP), Gross National Product (GNP) or Gross National Income (GNI), as the main indicator of whether a country was developing. Some people went so far as to even equate per capita economic growth with development, defining the latter in terms of the former.

Also consistent with the early conceptualizations was the use of the *level* of per capita national income as the main indicator of the *level* of development that a country had achieved. The World Bank, for instance, classified countries on the basis of their GNPs per capita as either low-, middle- or high-income. Countries belonging to the high-income group were widely considered as developed, while those in the low- and middle-income groups were often considered as less developed or developing countries. This does not mean that developed countries cannot also be developing, by achieving higher levels of development, just that the label 'developing' was assigned to the low- and middle-income groups. This practice continues today, but with the use of GNIs per capita for the year 2004. A low-income country is one with a GNI per capita of US$825 or less, a middle-income country is one with a GNI per capita within the range of US$826 to US$10,065, and a high-income country is one with a GNI of US$10,066 or more (World Bank 2007).

It was observed in the late 1960s and early 1970s that many economies that had followed a broadly Rostow-type modernization-led growth (or growth via modernization) strategy had achieved high rates of economic growth, with some achieving rather high incomes per capita. But this growth was not uniform, both among and within countries. Among countries, it was observed that rates of per capita economic growth in high-income countries far exceeded those of their low- and middle-income counterparts. For instance, between 1961 and 1970 the per capita national incomes in the high-income countries grew at an annual average rate of more than 4 per cent while over the same period the middle- and low-income countries grew at annual average rates of just over 3 and just under 1 per cent respectively.

These differential growth rates, combined with the fact that initial incomes in the high-income countries are by definition higher than those of the low- and middle-income countries, meant that international inequalities in per capita incomes grew over time. The rich countries were getting richer and the poor countries, while also getting richer on average, were falling further and further behind. Put differently, the poor countries were becoming relatively poorer over time. High-income country income per capita was 45 times that of the low-income countries in 1960, a ratio that many observers thought was obscenely high. By 1970, however, the former were 56 times richer in terms of per capita income than the latter and 70 times richer by 1980 (World Bank 2007).

Arguably more disconcerting were inequalities within countries. Despite the positive and often high rates of growth that were experienced by the vast majority of developing countries, there remained large sections of the populations of these countries that were largely untouched by this growth. The lives of these people were still characterized by crushing, abject poverty while tiny minorities benefited enormously. The widespread perception among observers was, therefore, that the poor benefited little if at all from the growth via modernization strategies that had been pursued in the 1960s and earlier decades. Indeed, there were many that believed that some groups within developing societies were actually worse off as a result of these strategies, if not in terms of the incomes they earned but in terms of social upheaval and dislocation, a loss of identity and cultural dislocation.

Statistics, while never adequately capturing the plight of the poor, do back up the views of the late 1960s' and early 1970s' critics of growth via modernization strategies. The experience within Latin American countries is often cited, Brazil in particular. Like many other countries in its region Brazil experienced very high rates of per capita income growth – between 6 and 11 per cent per year during the late 1960s and early 1970s. Yet large sections of the Brazilian population remained impoverished, as implied by income distribution statistics. Throughout the mid-1960s to mid-1970s, it is estimated that the poorest 10 per cent of the Brazilian population received less than 2 per cent of their nation's income. The richest 10 per cent of Brazil's population during this period is estimated to have received a little more than 40 per cent. By the early 1980s, the corresponding numbers were one and 45 per cent respectively. Income poverty data are hard to obtain for the 1970s but by 1981, after further high if not volatile annual per capita national income growth outcomes, 31 per cent of the Brazilian population, some 39 million people, lived in poverty (World Bank 2007). Brazil might well be considered an extreme example but it is broadly indicative of trends in the developing world as a whole. For instance, in 1981, after years of per capita income growth in the vast majority of countries, 67 per cent of the combined population of low- and middle-income countries lived in income poverty, some 2.5 billion people (World Bank 2007). Thus it appeared that while the developing world might have grown, the fruits of this growth were not widespread. In short, if there was any trickle-down it was clearly insufficient in its extent.

The preceding comments apply to those countries that followed what might broadly be considered a Rostow-type growth strategy. But broadly similar comments can be made about those countries that chose Marxism during the post-Second World and subsequent Cold War era, the many countries that were part of the Eastern bloc of countries, including the Soviet Union. Most if not all of these countries had achieved industrialization and had overthrown their capitalist classes. But the freedoms expected for the masses, especially civil freedoms, were not enjoyed. Nor in many cases were the expected gains in material living standards.

Contemporary meanings of development

A number of alternative meanings of development emerged from the criticisms of the modernization strategies. Some of these meanings were implicit to alternative theories of development. By this it is meant that alternative explanations of the development experiences of countries were offered, and from these theories it is possible to infer a particular definition of development. In other cases, the meanings are the result of an explicit attempt to provide an alternative definition of development. Two broad types or classes of definitions emerged: those that defined development in a rather negative manner and those that defined it in a way that is necessarily good. Let us examine each in turn.

Development as domination and exploitation

That the gap in living standards between developed and developing countries had very substantially widened throughout the 1960s and 1970s and that many hundreds of millions of people still lived in poverty in the developing world led many commentators from the late 1960s to question some of the fundamental assumptions on which modernization theories and strategies were based. These commentators tended not to question the goals of modernization but the assumption that all countries could follow a largely homogeneous development path, and that, in particular, what happened in the industrialized western world could be largely replicated in poorer developing countries. What these commentators instead saw were large volumes of foreign trade between developed and developing countries and large increases in developed country foreign development aid and foreign investment to developing countries in the apparent absence of the gains that these flows were supposed to generate. Instead, they saw countries that were marginalized and locked into a situation of underdevelopment, in which they were peripheral and subservient to and dependent on a global economy dominated by developed countries and multinationals.

A leading proponent of the preceding view was Andre Gunder Frank. Frank, like many others holding this view, drew on the experiences of the Latin American countries. As Leftwich (2000) points out, these countries had a long and intimate engagement through investment and trade with the developed world, but the processes and features of development were thought by Frank and others to be retarded and deformed, constituting what came to be known as *underdevelopment*. Frank argued that 'development and underdevelopment are the opposite sides of the same coin' (Frank 1971: 33). The school of thought to which Frank and many others belonged believed development was not about, in effect, rapid growth that led to the sorts of societies envisaged by Rostow and other proponents of modernization-led economic growth but, rather, about the domination and exploitation by the rich developed countries of their poor underdeveloped (as distinct from developing) counterparts. It was not something for poorer countries to strive for but something that should be avoided at all costs. Further details of this school of thought are provided in the next chapter.

Development as good change

In an extremely influential writing published initially in late 1969, Dudley Seers rejected the view that development was an objective or positive concept that, for example, described what was necessary for a country to achieve higher living standards for its citizens. Instead, he thought that development should be seen as a concept that requires us to identify the normative conditions for a universally acceptable aim, which for Seers was the *'realization of the potential of human personality'* (Seers 1972: 6). This conceptualization was a direct challenge to strategies that relied heavily on economic growth or that implicitly equated growth with development. He actually thought that economic growth did not solve certain social and political difficulties but could actually contribute to them.

Having defined development in terms of the realization of human potential, Seers' next task was to consider what was absolutely necessary for such realization. This led him to three related questions:

- What has been happening to income poverty?
- What is has been happening to unemployment?
- What is happening to income inequality?

Seers asserted that if all three of these phenomena had over time declined from high levels, then 'beyond doubt this has been a period of development for the country concerned' (Seers 1972: 7). He further asserted that 'if one or two of these central problems have been growing worse, especially if all three have, it would be strange to call the result "development" even if per capita income doubled' (Seers 1972: 7).

A reasonably clear case was provided for the singling out of these questions. Seers thought that human potential could not be realized without sufficient food, and that the ability to buy food is determined by income. Those living below an income poverty line cannot buy enough food to realize their human potential. Having a job – whether it be being in paid employment, being a student, working on a family farm or keeping a house – was considered to be essential for the enhancement of one's personality and for self-respect. Inequality was linked to poverty. Seers argued that poverty could be reduced much more quickly if economic growth was accompanied by reduced inequality. He also saw equity as an objective in its own right, arguing that inequity was objectionable on ethical standards.

A point often overlooked in Seers' writings is that he thought that many other factors, in addition to the reduction of poverty, unemployment and inequality, were also important for the fulfilment of human potential. He thought that this fulfilment also required adequate education levels, freedom of speech and national political and economic sovereignty (Seers 1972).

The fundamental contribution of Seers was that development should be defined as a subjective or normative concept. Development is not about what actually has or will happen – as in the writings of Rostow and Marx who saw development as historical change or those who defined development as exploitation and domination – but what ought to happen. In short, this is about differentiating between changes per se and that which we would like to see, that change which might simply be described as 'good'. This laid the groundwork for many new development conceptualizations proposed from the early 1970s through to the present. Let us now highlight some of the better known of these conceptualizations.

In the early 1970s, the International Labour Organization (ILO) focused attention on the importance of employment in developing countries for providing for basic needs (ILO 1976). The efforts of the ILO and others led to the emergence of a new meaning, which treated development as the fulfilment or satisfaction of *basic human needs*. The corresponding measure of development became the extent to which these needs were met. Basic needs are often thought to be confined to food, shelter and clothing. The ILO identified five categories of basic human needs that go well beyond these. They are:

- basic goods, including food, shelter and clothing;
- basic services, including education, health, access to water and transport;
- participation in decision-making;
- the fulfilment of basic human rights, and;
- productive employment, that which generates enough income to satisfy consumption needs.

It should come as no surprise that the ILO's flagging of a list of needs was followed by much discussion about how they can best be fulfilled. There were those who believed that basic human needs could only be fulfilled through redistributive policies that result in a more equitable distribution of income, assets and power (Green 1978). Implicit to this view was that growth-oriented strategies could not satisfy basic human needs; strategies aimed at fulfilling the latter were actually a rejection of the former. The ILO, while not rejecting redistribution policies, was of the view that high rates of economic growth were essential for a successful basic human needs development strategy.

Many more elaborate needs were subsequently articulated in the years after the ILO came up with the basic human needs approach. They included those from Streeten (1979), Streeten et al. (1981), Stewart (1985) and, some years later, Doyal and Gough (1991). These articulations tended to focus more than the ILO on needs beyond the provision of basic goods and services, such as a sense of purpose in life and work, self-determination, political freedom and security and national and cultural identity. The issue of the universality of needs, across cultures and over time, was also examined. Doyal and Gough defined universal needs as preconditions for social participation that apply to everyone in the same way. They conclude that two universal basic needs do exist – physical health and autonomy. Autonomy is viewed as the capacity to initiate an action that requires, among other things, the opportunity to engage in social action.

Discussions on development strategies and corresponding meanings of development were rich and engaging in the 1970s and early 1980s. The same cannot be said of the remainder of the 1980s. The early

1980s was a period of great economic turmoil in the developing world, largely owing to steep declines in oil prices. Many developing countries experienced serious balance of payments problems, growing public and private debt, declines in investment and high inflation. All of these problems culminated in lower economic growth rates than would have otherwise been the case. The dominant view at the time is that the best way to deal with these problems was with what might loosely be described as neo-liberal economic policies, often aimed at less government economic intervention and, above all, a primary focus on sustained economic growth. The World Bank was an active and influential proponent of similar views. Such an environment was not conducive to a more interventionist development strategy, including one aimed at satisfying basic human needs. Strategies aiming to put basic human needs satisfaction first, that were consistent with a notion of development as something other than or in addition to economic growth, were not high on the agenda of national governments and international development organizations. The 1980s can, in this sense, be seen as a lost decade in terms of the advancement of development conceptualizations.

This state of affairs changed in 1990, with the release of the UNDP *Human Development Report 1990*. In an attempt to shift development thinking and strategies away from what was thought of as an excessive preoccupation with economic growth as a goal for development policies, and back to what it saw as core values, the UNDP advanced its concept of *human development*. The UNDP defined human development as follows:

> Human development is a process of enlarging people's choices. The most critical ones are to lead a long and healthy life, to be educated and to enjoy a decent standard of living. If these essential choices are not available, many other opportunities remain inaccessible. But human development does not end there.   (UNDP 1990: 10)

The UNDP was at pains to emphasize that its concept of development was broader and more vital than mere economic growth that achieved higher average incomes. It made the powerful point that income is not an end in its own right but a means to an end. What matters, according to the UNDP, is not so much the level of income but the uses to which it is put. The UNDP invoked a powerful ally in advancing its position: Aristotle. He warned against judging societies by variables such as income and wealth that are sought not for themselves but desired as means to other objectives. Succinctly, Aristotle's view was that: 'Wealth is evidently not the good we are seeking, for it is merely useful for the sake of something else' (UNDP 1990: 9).

The UNDP not only proposed its own definition of human development but also a measure designed to show which countries had achieved the highest levels of this development and which had achieved the lowest. More generally, the measure provided a league table, a ranking, of countries in terms of the levels of human development they had each achieved. That measure is the now infamous as the Human Development Index (HDI). A detailed technical description of the HDI is not necessary for our current purposes but it combined measures of longevity, knowledge and the material standard of living into a single index. The HDI has changed since its inception in 1990 but in the original version these measures were life expectancy (the number of years a newborn child would be expected to live in a country given prevailing patterns of mortality), adult literacy (the percentage of persons aged 15 and over who can understand, read and write a short statement on everyday life) and a measure of GDP per capita adjusted for differences in the cost of living between countries (UNDP 1990). The HDI is now arguably the most widely used and reported measure of the level of development among countries. HDI scores have been published annually and are now available for more than 170 countries. The higher the score, the higher is the level of development that a country is considered to have achieved. We return to HDI scores later in this chapter.

The UNDP relied heavily on the work of Amartya Sen in articulating and designing the HDI. Sen was winner of the 1998 Nobel Prize in Economics for his contributions to the field of welfare economics. In the late 1970s, Sen began proposing what became known as the 'capability approach'. This was in the context of how inequality should be judged, with Sen arguing the case for looking at inequalities not in variables such as income but in what he referred to as basic capabilities (Sen 1980). Indeed, Sen had long been critical of the use of income as a measure of development as what was not so important was the level of income or its growth as what it was used to purchase (Sen 1985). To this extent he was in agreement with Aristotle. Accordingly, as Alkire (2002) points out, development in Sen's capability approach is not defined as an increase in income growth, or for that matter in terms of enhanced education or health alone, but as an *expansion of capability*. Capability is treated as the *freedom* to promote or achieve combinations of valuable functionings (Sen 1990). Functionings, in turn, are the 'parts of the state of person – in particular the things that he or she manages to do or be in leading a life' (Sen 1993: 31). The link between freedom and development was a theme Sen articulated further in subsequent writings. In his well-known work, *Development as Freedom* (Sen 1999a), he argued that the expansion of freedom is both a primary end and a principal means of development. More precisely, he argued that development involved the removal of the 'unfreedoms that leave people with little choice and little opportunity of exercising their reasoned agency' (Sen 1999a: xii).

So, what are these capabilities that allow one to function? Sen resists identifying a set of capabilities on the grounds it is a value judgement that needs to be made explicitly, in many cases through a process of public debate (Sen 1999a). We need to keep this point in mind later in this chapter. Yet many others have identified various lists of capabilities, or what might be interpreted as such. The UNDP has done so, in its definition of human development and choice of components of, or dimensions of development empirically captured by, the HDI. This was made clear in the *Human Development Report 1995*: *life, education, economic resources*

> The basis for selection of critical dimensions, and the indicators that make up the human development index, is identifying basic capabilities that must have to participate in and contribute to society. These include the ability to lead a long and healthy life, the ability to be knowledgeable and the ability to have access to the resources needed for a decent standard of living. (UNDP 1995: 18)

A comprehensive list of often complex capabilities is provided by Martha Nussbaum, among others. Many of these are most applicable or easy to understand at the level of an individual but can also be applied in varying degrees to countries, based on the life situations of their citizens. Nussbaum's list has been revised many times but in 2000 consisted of the following: life, bodily health, bodily integrity, senses, imagination, thought, emotions, practical reason, affiliation, other species, play and control over one's environment (Nussbaum 2000). Nussbaum describes these as 'central human functional capabilities'. It is useful to outline these capabilities in a little detail to obtain an idea of their nature. They are summarized in Table 1.1. As can clearly be seen from the table, many of the capabilities identified by Nussbaum are by no means simple in a number of respects, for example in assessing whether they have been achieved or designing policies aimed at achieving them. Clearly, the underlying or corresponding definition of development is far more complex than those outlined above. This is also evident from an examination of the equivalent lists provided by other writers, often described as dimensions of development. Alkire (2002) provides an excellent and comprehensive survey of human development dimensions and of the research that has identified them. This research, including Sen's contributions, belongs to the literature on what is now widely called *human well-being*. The capabilities that are identified in it are often called well-being dimensions, and this term will be used in the remainder of this chapter. Broadly analogous terms include the quality of life, the standard of living and, as the UNDP prefers, human development. It is now very common to equate development with these terms. Using the first, development is therefore seen as enhancing or increasing the level of achieved human well-being. This can be at the level of nations, in which matter is the overall level of well-being of its citizens, or at the level of individuals.

A key characteristic of the Sen capability approach and its extension by Nussbaum, and indeed the basic human needs approach and the writings of Seers, is that development is seen to be *multidimensional*. It is just not about improvements according to a single criterion, but multiple criteria. The extent to which this had become appreciated in the early 1990s and onwards is evident in statements emanating from the World Bank. The World Bank had long (and sometimes unfairly) been seen as a vanguard of a market-friendly, economic-growth-first approach to development strategy. It differentiated between what is referred to as 'economic development' and 'development in a broader sense' in its *World Development Report 1991* (World Bank 1991a). Economic development was seen as a 'sustainable increase in living standards that encompasses material consumption, education, health and environmental protection' (World Bank 1991: 31). Development in the broader sense was articulated by the World Bank as follows:

> Development in a broader sense is understood to include other important and related attributes as well, notably more equality of opportunity, and political and civil liberties. The overall goal of development is therefore to increase the economic, political, and civil rights of all people across gender, ethnic groups, religions, races, regions and countries.   (World Bank 1991: 31)

The pendulum had firmly swung, it seems.

The World Bank, in the above quotes, refers to the various population sub-groups (delineated by gender, ethnicity and so on), sustainability and the environment. These issues have for a number of years been highly relevant to development theory and the definition of development. Let's deal with each in turn.

Inequality of incomes among people within countries was discussed above. This type of inequality is often referred to as '*vertical inequality*' in that it refers to differences in incomes between individuals.

Table 1.1 *Nussbaum's central human functional capabilities*

Life: being able to live to the end of a human life of normal length; not dying prematurely, or before one's life is so reduced as to be not worth living.

Bodily health: being able to have good health, including reproductive health; to be adequately nourished; to have adequate shelter.

Bodily integrity: being able to move freely from place to place; having one's bodily boundaries treated as sovereign as such being able to be secure against assault, including sexual assault, child sexual abuse, and domestic violence; having opportunities for sexual satisfaction and for choice in matters of reproduction.

Senses, imagination, thought: being able to use the senses, to imagine, think, and reason – and to do these things in a 'truly human' way, a way informed and cultivated by an adequate education, including, but by no means limited to, literacy and basic mathematical and scientific training.

Emotions: being able to have attachments to things and persons outside ourselves; to love those who love and care for us, to grieve at their absence; in general, to love, to grieve, to experience longing, gratitude, and justified anger.

Practical reason: being able to form a conception of the good and to engage in critical reflection about the planning of one's own life.

Affiliation: being able to live for and towards others, to recognize and show concern for other human beings, to engage in various forms of social interaction; to be able to imagine the situation of another and to have compassion for that situation; to have the capability for both justice and friendship; having the social bases of self-respect and non-humiliation; being able to be treated as a dignified being whose worth is equal to that of others (this entails, at a minimum, protections against discrimination on the basis of race, sex, religion, caste, ethnicity, or national origin).

Other species: being able to live with concern for and in relation to animals, plants, and the world of nature.

Play: being able to laugh, to play, to enjoy recreational activities.

Control over one's environment: being able to participate effectively in political choices that govern one's life; having the right of political participation, protections of free speech and association; being able to hold property (both land and movable goods), not just formally but in terms of real opportunity; and having property rights on an equal basis with others; having the right to seek employment on an equal basis with others; having the freedom from unwarranted search and seizure.

Source: Adapted from Nussbaum (2000).

Horizontal inequality refers to the existence of inequalities between groups of individuals, typically within countries. It is based on the twin recognitions that an intrinsic part of human life is group membership and that there is a universal human need to belong, to identify with a particular group or groups (Gellner 1964; Stewart 2001). Early usage of the term looked at inequality between culturally defined groups

(Stewart 2001), but the same general notion can be applied to gender. Inequities between the sexes, members of different castes and between tribal, racial, religious or ethnic groups are considered to be different types of horizontal inequalities. As Stewart (2001) emphasizes, horizontal inequality is also multidimensional, not only relating to differences in economic outcomes (such as incomes) but social and political outcomes as well.

Concerns for horizontal inequality were heightened in the 1990s for two main reasons. The first was the increasingly apparent inequities between population sub-groups. It is not uncommon for a man to be twice as likely as a woman to be literate in developing countries (UNDP 2006). One of the best-known cases of inequities among racial groups within countries is South Africa in the Apartheid era, which ended in 1993. Some simple statistics bear this out. The average monthly wage of black workers was less than one-third of that of white workers in 1990. In 1980 the incidence of infant mortality (the number of infants dying before their first birthday) in the black community was six times that in the white community. There are of course many other examples from developing countries. These include differences between living standards or rights enjoyed of the various Hindu castes in India, between Tamils and Sinhalese in Sri Lanka, between indigenous and Indian-origin citizens in Fiji, between citizens of Albanian and non-Albanian origin in the Kosovo territory of the former Yugoslavia and between Tutsis and Hutus in Rwanda. But horizontal inequities, like vertical ones, are clearly not the exclusive domain of developing countries. They can be observed in the developed group as well. Differences in the lives experienced by blacks and whites in the United States, Catholics and Protestants in Northern Ireland and between indigenous and non-indigenous groups in Australia are examples. Indeed, the Australian example is among the more extreme in developed countries. Based on mortality rates at the time, in 2000 an indigenous Australian male could be expected to live 54 years, 24 years less than a non-indigenous Australia male. The second factor leading to a heightening of concerns for horizontal inequality related to its perceived consequences, particularly violent conflict. Such inequalities were thought to drive to varying degrees the conflicts in Northern Ireland, Sri Lanka and the former Yugoslavia, a series of coups in Fiji and the Rwandan genocide that resulted in an estimated 800,000 deaths.

Concerns over environmental degradation, the use of non-renewable resources and the like are well documented and there is little need to elaborate them for our current purposes. They are accepted and known and are widely regarded as core issues of our time, affecting all citizens, albeit to varying degrees, worldwide. The more pertinent line of enquiry is to establish how these concerns relate to how development might be defined. At a simple level one might argue that they lead us to question whether it is possible to *sustain* development levels into the future. But this is an explanation of future development levels that treats sustainability as a determinant of them. It does not embed or incorporate sustainability into a definition of development. Put differently, it does not treat sustainability as being constituent of development itself. Anand and Sen (2000) provide the grounds with which one can incorporate sustainability into a definition of development. Earlier in this chapter, a view was put that change cannot be considered as development unless it is equitable. Anand and Sen argue that sustainability should be seen as a concern of inter-generational equity, or as they put it, 'a particular reflection of universality of claims – applied to the future generations vis-à-vis us' (Anand and Sen 2000: 2030). Anand and Sen further note that:

> We cannot abuse and plunder our common stock of natural assets and resources leaving the future generations unable to enjoy the opportunities we take for granted today. We cannot use up, or contaminate, our environment as we wish, violating the rights of and the interests of the future generations.   (Anand and Sen 2000: 2030)

Sustainability can reasonably easily be seen as development, in this context.

Some comments on development as good-change definitions are warranted at this stage. It is abundantly clear that these definitions, and the interpretations or judgements that emerge from them, are far more complex than corresponding definitions implicit in modernization theories. A country according to this definition could be said to be developing if it was achieving economic or income growth per head of population. The larger or faster this growth, the more it could be said to be developing. Moreover, a country with a higher level of income per head of population than another was said to be more developed. And as we have seen, certain levels or thresholds of income per capita have been used to distinguish developed from developing countries.

For a number of reasons, such judgements cannot be as easily made if the good-change definitions are used. Let us highlight two. The first is that many of the dimensions that have been identified do not lead to precise judgements regarding changes over time, or across people or countries. Put differently, it is far from self-evident that progress in them might have been achieved or what the levels of fulfilment or achieve-ment might be. The second, and arguably more fundamental, reason relates to the multidimensionality of these definitions or the conceptual-izations on which they are based. Seers pointed to this issue when pos-ing the three questions outlined above. To illustrate, consider a situation in which a country is showing improvements in three of five key well-being dimensions, but is showing the reverse in the remaining two by the same magnitude. Is that country developing? Similarly, consider a situation in which we are asked to assess which of two countries has the highest level of development based on these five well-being dimensions. These two countries have identical achievements in the first three dimensions. But the first country has higher achievement in the fourth dimension but lower achievement, by the same magnitude, than the sec-ond country in the fifth dimension. Which country has the higher level of development? The answer to both these questions depends on the rel-ative importance one attaches to the five dimensions. Returning to the first question, if we thought the remaining two dimensions were collec-tively more important than the first three, we would conclude that the country is not developing. Alternatively, if we thought that the first three dimensions were more important than the last two, we would con-clude it was developing. For the second question, we would conclude that the second country was more developed than the first if we thought the fourth dimension was more important than the fifth and vice versa.

The issue of how to weight or assign relative degrees of importance to well-being or quality of life outcomes is a huge issue in the assessment of development levels and trends. In an ideal world, we would have the scientific information to be able to weight these outcomes. But we do not. We do not, for example, have the results of a worldwide survey in which people were asked to rank what outcomes are most important to them. Nor is there consensus on what determines well-being outcomes. This was an issue that the UNDP grappled with in the construction of the HDI. It is widely accepted that the weights attached to the compo-nent variables of the HDI should vary. Yet in the absence of information on how to assign values to these weights, the UNDP opted for the sim-plest alternative, which was to give each an equal weighting. This means, for instance, that an improvement in health is just as important as an improvement in education or income of the same magnitude in assessing development changes based on the HDI. At this point it is instructive to recall Sen's view on identifying a set of capabilities, which was that this rests on a value judgement that needs to be explicitly made. The same point can be made about valuing development out-comes. In the absence of the required scientific information, one must ultimately make an explicit value judgement in assigning different values or weights to given outcomes on the basis of personal preferences, subjective or otherwise.

Applying development definitions

It is now appropriate to apply some of the development conceptualizations outlined in this chapter by looking at country classifications and development achievements. Specifically, we look at development achievements in terms of the modernization-led growth and good-change definitions. The former leads us to focus on income levels (as they reflect historical growth rates) and the latter leads us to look at achievements in such areas as health and education. This in many respects is an unavoidably empirical exercise. As such it is necessary to again invoke the caveat stated above, that statistics while useful do not adequately capture the plight of the poor. This does not mean that we ignore statistics, just that we recognize their limitations. We start by looking at how countries are classified.

Country classifications

For much of the second half of the twentieth century countries were classified as either first-world, second-world and third-world. The first-world countries were those that had industrialized and achieved high per capita incomes and belonged to the OECD. The second-world countries were those that were part of the Soviet bloc and the third-world were in essence, all other countries. The first-world countries were considered developed, so too typically were the second-world countries. The third-world countries were considered developing or less developed. While these classifications were influenced by political criteria, it was for much of the second half of the twentieth century that the first-world countries were richer in terms of per capita income than second-world countries, and the third-world countries were poorer still. So, to this extent, the division between developed and developing countries was consistent with the growth via modernization definition of development.

The usage of the terms 'first-world', 'second-world' and 'third-world' came under increasing question in the late 1980s and 1990s. This was for two main reasons. The first is that many of the third-world countries were as rich as those in the first-world group and richer than all in the second-world group. Indeed, there was so much diversity in the third-world group that people began to question the usefulness and usage of the term. The second was the collapse of the Soviet Union. Many of the countries that emerged from the Soviet Union as independent states were extremely poor and by income standards alone could clearly be labelled as developing. These classifications are still largely used today in official circles despite these changes. While the first-, second- and third-world terms are not used, those that would have been labelled third-world are officially classified by the United Nations and other official international organizations as 'Developing Countries': 150 countries or territories were classified as developing in 2010. Most of the former Soviet bloc countries are now classified as Central and Eastern Europe and Commonwealth of Independent States (CIS) countries (UNDP 2010b). Full lists of the countries belonging to these and all classifications mentioned in the remainder of this chapter can be found on the *Human Development Report 2010* (UNDP 2010).

A number of changes in country classifications have occurred over time. The Czech Republic, Hungary, Poland and Slovakia are all former Soviet bloc countries that are now part of the OECD and as such are generally considered as developed countries. The Republic of Korea (South Korea, as it is more widely known), Mexico and Turkey have in the last decade moved from the developing to the OECD group. Many anomalies remain, however, and for this reason the developing countries group remains highly diverse. Many countries in the developing group should clearly be treated as developed. Singapore and Hong Kong have very high well-being or living-standards levels by international standards (Hong Kong is in the top twenty countries in the world in terms of income per capita) and yet are still in the developing countries group. The reasons for this are largely political, as certain benefits in terms of access to concessional international finance and trade opportunities, for instance, accrue to countries in the developing group. In partial recognition of the diversity of the developing country group, the United Nations has for many years assembled a 'least developed country' group, based purely on developmental criteria, including income per capita. Countries in this group are those considered by the UN to have the lowest levels of development, as its name implies. In 2010 this group consisted of 23 countries or territories (UNDP 2010).

Two additional methods of classifying countries and the corresponding country groups are widely used. The first is to classify countries according to per capita income levels. This is how the World Bank arrives at its above-mentioned income group classifications. As mentioned, it has been common to treat low- and middle-income countries as developing or less developed and high-income as developed countries.

The income thresholds used change over time, getting larger each year. In 2008, 41 countries were classified as high income, 93 as middle income and 59 as low income. Singapore and Hong Kong are in the high-income group and yet are still included in the UN developing countries group. All of the Central and Eastern European and CIS countries are either in the low- or middle-income group (and not the developing countries group). The second country groups are based on the HDI, with countries being divided into low, medium and high and very high human development categories. As such, these groupings are consistent with a multidimensional development conceptualization that is broadly consistent with the Sen capability approach, albeit taking into account a rather narrow selection of capabilities. In 2010, 38 countries are classified as very high, 45 as high, 75 as medium and 24 as low human development. Note in particular the dominance of the low human development group by sub-Saharan African countries. All but one of these countries (Afghanistan) are sub-Saharan African (UNDP 2010).

Development profiles

Let us now take a closer look at development levels by looking at the development profiles of individual countries and not just the group to which they belong. Which countries have the levels of development and which have the lowest? It would be particularly insightful to base this exercise on a comprehensive range of well-being dimensions (or capabilities) but limitations in the availability required to do this restricts us to only relatively basic dimensions. Table 1.2 helps in this regard. It identifies the 20 most developed and 20 least developed countries based on both the HDI and income per capita. Income per capita is measured using Purchasing Power Parity (PPP) GNI per capita. Such a measure is adjusted to take into account differences in price levels between countries, and as such gives a better idea of the purchasing power of incomes across countries and hence in material living standards. For instance, if one country had a PPP GNI per capita that is twice that of another, a person earning that income in the first country could buy approximately twice the number of equivalent goods and services than someone earning half that income in the second country.

All of those in the top 20 HDI group are high-income countries. The vast majority of countries in both top 20 groups are European. Both bottom 20 groups are dominated by sub-Saharan African countries. All 20 bottom HDI countries with the exception of Afghanistan are from that region. The only bottom 20 income per capita countries not from sub-Saharan Africa are Nepal and Haiti. Note also that there is a lot of

Table 1.2   *Top and bottom 20 countries, 2008*

Human Development Index (HDI)			Income per capita		
Top 20					
Rank	*Country*	*HDI*	*Rank*	*Country*	*GNI per capita ($PPP)*
1	Norway	0.938	1	Liechtenstein	81,011
2	Australia	0.937	2	Qatar	79,426
3	New Zealand	0.907	3	Norway	58,810
4	United States	0.902	4	United Arab Emirates	58,006
5	Ireland	0.895	5	Kuwait	55,719
6	Liechtenstein	0.891	6	Luxembourg	51,109
7	Netherlands	0.890	7	Brunei Darussalam	49,915
8	Canada	0.888	8	Singapore	48,893
9	Sweden	0.885	9	United States	47,094
10	Germany	0.885	10	Hong Kong	45,090
11	Japan	0.884	11	Netherlands	40,658
12	Korea, Republic	0.877	12	Switzerland	39,849
13	Switzerland	0.874	13	Australia	38,692
14	France	0.872	14	Canada	38,668
15	Israel	0.872	15	Andorra	38,056
16	Finland	0.871	16	Austria	37,056
17	Iceland	0.869	17	Sweden	36,936
18	Belgium	0.867	18	Denmark	36,404
19	Denmark	0.866	19	Germany	35,308
20	Spain	0.863	20	United Kingdom	35,087

→

overlap between the groups: most in the top 20 HDI group are in the top 20 income per capita group and the same applies to the bottom 20 groups. Recalling that the HDI includes measures of health and education, this reflects the statistical reality that, in general, countries with higher levels of these variables also have higher incomes.

The development record

Let us conclude our empirical exercise by looking at the development record over recent decades. Has the level of development, worldwide, increased, decreased or remained the same over recent decades? We again base this exercise on rather basic well-being dimensions, relating to health, education, income and sustainability. The answer to the preceding question is not at all straightforward. 'It depends' is probably the

Table 1.2   *(continued)*

Human Development Index (HDI)			Income per capita		
Bottom 20					
Rank	Country	HDI	Rank	Country	GNI per capita ($PPP)
150	Zambia	0.395	150	Nepal	1,201
151	Gambia	0.390	151	Rwanda	1,190
152	Rwanda	0.385	152	Comoros	1,176
153	Malawi	0.385	153	Mali	1,171
154	Sudan	0.379	154	Chad	1,067
155	Afghanistan	0.349	155	Ethiopia	992
156	Guinea	0.340	156	Guinea	953
157	Ethiopia	0.328	157	Madagascar	953
158	Sierra Leone	0.317	158	Haiti	949
159	Central African Rep	0.315	159	Malawi	911
160	Mali	0.309	160	Mozambique	854
161	Burkina Faso	0.305	161	Togo	844
162	Liberia	0.300	162	Sierra Leone	809
163	Chad	0.295	163	Central African Rep	758
164	Guinea-Bissau	0.289	164	Niger	675
165	Mozambique	0.284	165	Guinea-Bissau	538
166	Burundi	0.282	166	Burundi	402
167	Niger	0.261	167	Liberia	320
168	Congo, Dem Rep	0.239	168	Congo, Dem Rep	291
169	Zimbabwe	0.140	169	Zimbabwe	176

Source: Data from UNDP (2010).

way to respond. The development balance sheet, shown in Table 1.3, helps illustrate this point. It distinguishes between what might be called good change, progress or development from less pleasing changes. The former are labelled alternatively as deprivation, disparity or, consistent with the development as domination and exploitation paradigm, underdevelopment. If we look at the development record over the last 45 to 50 years, we cannot help but be impressed by the substantial progress that has been made in many areas. The left hand side of the balance sheet in Table 1.3 makes this abundantly clear. People are now living much longer, many less children are dying before reaching their fifth birthday, far more people are literate, incomes have increased tremendously and consciousness of environmental and sustainability issues has increased substantially in recent years. To these extents, the development record is impressive, levels of development are higher than ever

Table 1.3 *A development balance sheet*

Progress, Good Change, Development	Deprivation, Disparity, Underdevelopment
Health	
• The life expectancy of a person born in a developing country in 1960 was 47 years. By 2008 this number had risen to 67 years. Worldwide, average life expectancy increased from 53 to 69 years over the same period.	• A person born in a high-income OECD country in 2008 is expected to live 13, 23 or 38 years longer than one born in the same year in a developing, least developed or sub-Saharan African country, respectively.
	• In many OECD countries life expectancy had exceeded 80 years of age in 2008. Life expectancy in 2008 was 44 years in Afghanistan and Zimbabwe and 45 years in Lesotho and Zambia.
• The number of children in the world dying before their fifth birthday fell by 80 deaths per 1000 children between 1960 and 2009. In developing countries it fell from 233 to 66 deaths over the same period.	• In 2009 8.1 million children still died before their fifth birthday.
	• A child born in a developing country in 2009 is 12 times more likely to die before reaching its fifth birthday than one born in a high-income OECD country.
Education	
• The percentage of developing country adults who were literate rose from 64 in 1970 to 80 in 2008. In the least developed countries it more than doubled, from 26 to 68 per cent, over the same period.	• More than 770 million adults were illiterate in the world in 2009.
	• In many developing countries more than half of all adult females and in 10 sub-Saharan African countries, more than seven out of every 10 females were illiterate in 2007.
	• It is not uncommon in developing countries for a male to be twice as likely as a female to receive a secondary school education.
Income and wealth	
• Developing country per capita income (GDP per capita adjusted for purchasing power) increased more than sixfold between 1960 to 2009, from $758 to $4968. World per capita income increased over the same period from $1,737 to $9,514.	• More than one billion people – one fifth of the world's population – live in conditions of extreme income poverty, surviving on less than $1.25 per day. In at least 12 developing countries more than half the population lives in extreme income poverty.

→

Table 1.3 *(continued)*

Progress, Good Change, Development	*Deprivation, Disparity, Underdevelopment*
	• Income per capita (GDP per capita adjusted for purchasing power) in sub-Saharan Africa fell from $1,760 in 1980 to $1,537 in 2000. In high-income OECD countries it increased from $19,669 to $30,553 over the same period.
	• Income per capita (measured using GNI per capita adjusted for purchasing power) among OECD high-income countries in 2009 was seven, 17 and 26 times that in developing, sub-Saharan African and least developed countries, respectively. Liechtenstein's purchasing power parity GNI per capita in 2009 was 460 times that of Zimbabwe.
	• In the early 2000s the richest 20 per cent of the world's population held 75 per cent of world income, while the poorest 20 per cent held 1.5 per cent.
	• In the early 2000s 2 per cent of the world's adult population held more than 50 per cent of world personal assets.
Environment and sustainability	
• Environmental consciousness has increased worldwide in recent decades and most countries have ratified the major international environmental treaties, including the Kyoto Protocol.	• World carbon dioxide emissions rose from 4.0 metric tons per person in 1983 to 4.6 metric tons per person in 2007. In OECD high-income countries they rose from 11.2 to 12.2 metric tons per person over the same period.
	• The world's largest carbon dioxide emitting country over the decade from 1998 – which contributed more than one-fifth of total world carbon dioxide emissions during these years – still refuses to ratify the Kyoto Protocol.

Sources: Data from various issues of the UNDP *Human Development* Report and the World Bank *World Development Indicators* and from Davies et al. (2006).

before (at least in recorded history) and the world is a better place as a consequence.

But it must be emphasized that this picture is an average or aggregate one. It does not necessarily apply to all people in all countries of the world and ignores a number of disparities. It is, in short, a partial story as the right-hand side of the balance sheet reveals. Despite improvements in child mortality and literacy, 8.1 million children died in 2009 before reaching their fifth birthday and more than 770 million adults are illiterate. Life expectancies have plunged in recent years in sub-Saharan Africa in recent years, owing to the HIV/AIDS pandemic. A person born in Zimbabwe in 2008 can only be expected to live for 37 years based on current mortality rates in that country. Just over 1.4 billion people still live in extreme absolute income poverty, despite the very large increases in average incomes. Incomes per capita actually fell in sub-Saharan Africa between 1980 and 2000. Disparities have also grown, quite substantially in some cases. A person born in a high-income OECD country in 2004 given prevailing mortality patterns in that year might be expected to live 33 years longer than one born in those countries classified by the UN as least developed. The richest 20 per cent of the world's population in the early 2000s held 75 per cent of world income while the poorest 20 per cent held 1.5 per cent. Two per cent of the world's adult population holds 50 per cent of the world's personal assets. Finally, the increase in environmental awareness notwithstanding, carbon dioxide emissions are still on the rise worldwide and some countries have not ratified key international environmental agreements.

The main conclusion emerging from Table 1.3 is that despite the progress that has been made, the world remains a place of widespread deprivation. Much more still needs to be done, and the world could be a much better place. The differences in health achievement have already been noted, especially the gaps in life expectancy between developing and developed countries. The ability to live a long and healthy life is core human development dimension. More generally, good health has important instrumental values with respect to other dimensions. Illness can prevent a child from going to school and an adult from going to work. For these reasons some additional comment on differences in health achievement is worthy of comment. Figure 1.1 shows average levels of life expectancy of the 10 per cent of countries with the highest life expectancies alongside those of the 10 per cent of countries with the lowest life expectancies for the years 1962 to 2002. It shows that while life expectancy in the first group has continued to growth, it has fallen in the second group since the late 1980s.

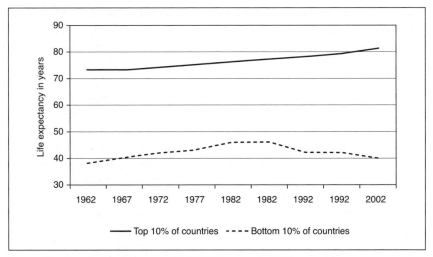

Source: Constructed using data reported in McGillivray et al. (2009).

Figure 1.1 *Health status, 1962 to 2002*

So, let us ask the above question again. Has the level of development, worldwide, increased, decreased or remained the same over recent decades? If one looks at the general picture and ignores disparities, then on balance the answer to this question based on the evidence just presented is probably 'yes'. It might differ, of course, if one looked at information based on a large range of well-being or related dimensions. But if our conceptualization of development includes a concern for equity, the answer is not so clear. Recall what Seers wrote about development, that if one or two of unemployment, poverty and inequality has grown worse, it would be strange to call the result development. Inequality seems to have grown worse. Has there then been development? To emphasize a point made above, the answer will depend on how highly we value equality. If it has an especially high value, then we might conclude that the level of development in the world has declined, and not risen as many would assert.

Conclusion

This chapter outlined various meanings or conceptualizations of development. It commenced by looking at traditional conceptualizations. This included the definition implicit in the modernization approach to development, which saw development largely as economic growth. The chapter then examined more contemporary meanings of development, those that emerged from the late 1960s to the present. These meanings are those that either relate to the domination and exploitation of one group by another or to what might very loosely be described as 'good-change'. Most attention was devoted to the latter, This was on the grounds that these definitions are particularly useful because they force us to focus on and consider what sort of change or outcomes we want to see in all countries, rich and poor, providing a framework to compare actual changes against those we would like to observe. The fundamental premise of the chapter is that defining development, and deciding what is development and what is not, or whether development has actually occurred is a necessarily subjective exercise. It is also a rather complicated exercise, requiring one to reflect on one's own personal values to judge what is most important and what is not as important.

Given this, let us conclude with some more questions, in addition to those asked in the preceding section of this chapter. What is your definition of development? Is it based on multiple dimensions or on a single dimension? Put differently, what criteria does a country need to satisfy to be considered to have achieved higher levels of development? It might be useful to write down your own definition (ideally limiting it to a sentence) and revisit it from time to time as you work your way through this book, and especially when you have completed reading it.

Chapter 2

Reassessing Development Theory

John McKay

In this chapter we explore the key ideas put forward, especially in the last half century or so, on development and underdevelopment, and place these concepts within the context of the major trends, conditions and prevailing ideologies within the emerging global system. The dominant ideas on the nature and genesis of the very process of development have themselves gone through a series of transformations during this period, but strong counter-arguments have also emerged constantly. Thus the history of ideas on development can be characterized as a series of revolutions and counter-revolutions, and in many cases the key ideas from a particular period have re-emerged in a new guise at a later date. We also argue that most fundamental changes take place in response to crises of various kinds that challenge accepted paradigms, and the global financial crisis (GFC) – discussed in detail in Chapter 6 – has since 2007 shaken the foundations of the global economy and has had a major impact on our thinking about competing theories of development.

Notwithstanding periodic episodes of crisis, the last 50 years have been characterized by unprecedented growth and prosperity, but only within certain countries and regions. A basic question, then, must be why some countries have been able to achieve spectacular progress while others have stagnated or even gone backwards. Within mainstream economic thought there has been a strong assumption throughout this period that growth in successful regions will eventually trickle-down to the more peripheral areas, given appropriate policies. Thus, poor countries can catch up and benefit from the earlier growth experiences of others, and pass through a similar process of development, albeit at a later date. This is the essence of the theories of modernization that were popular in the 1950s and 1960s, and which, in a modified form, made a return to the mainstream of policy-making in the 1980s. However, these prescriptions have come under sustained attack ever since the 1960s from a number of different directions. The first criticisms came from what became known as the 'dependency school', originating especially in Latin America: the underdeveloped world could not develop in this trickle-down manner, because the very processes of global change that gave rise to prosperity in the North resulted in the simultaneous impoverishment of the countries of the South.

These ideas were also criticized, partly because of their overreliance on global rather than national factors, but more particularly for their alleged inability to account for the very rapid growth that was going on in parts of east Asia at the time. If growth at an unprecedented rate was possible in South Korea, Taiwan and the other 'Tiger' economies, there could be nothing wrong with the global system as such, it was argued. The problem must rest with the internal policies of the poor countries: to be successful they needed to do more to emulate the East Asian 'miracle' economies. The onset of the Asian financial crisis in 1997 gave support to this view. However, the onset of the GFC a decade later has once again challenged this dominant view: the ability of the Asian nations to rebuild their economies so quickly after their own crisis, and now they have emerged relatively unscathed from the GFC it has again forced us to think anew about the Asian development model and the rapidly growing global influence of a number of Asian countries.

Mainstream ideas of modernization have also been criticized from a quite different direction. Several authors have questioned the often unspoken assumption that the aim of development is to deliver to every global citizen a lifestyle similar to that now prevailing in the rich countries. They have dismissed the idea that development must always be the same as 'modernization', which is in fact nothing less than 'westernization'. This perspective has also been taken up by the growing environmental movement that has argued that it would be physically impossible for everyone in the countries now poor to live the sort of lifestyle now prevailing in North America or Western Europe. The costs in terms of resource depletion, pollution and general environmental degradation would simply be too great.

Still other commentators have suggested that in the development debate there has been far too much reliance on economic factors alone, and that, in fact, processes of political and social change are equally relevant. Indeed, many would argue that for effective development to take place it is usually essential to consider a range of social and political factors.

In spite of these criticisms, for a number of years after the end of the Cold War the mainstream paradigm was very strongly entrenched. However, beginning with the turmoil in Asia, the continued crisis in Africa, and now most importantly the impact of the GFC, we are now seeing the emergence of interest in 'neo-dependency' approaches, and in the older Marxist concepts of imperialism.

This chapter will explore these major currents of thought and will evaluate some of the major theories that have been advanced. However, the main focus will be on what we have learned from the last 50 years of development theory and how this might be reflected in the design of more effective policy approaches.

The global context for development ideas and policies

Ideas in development theory and practice cannot be divorced from the broader assumptions, aspirations and beliefs of any age. These more general modes of thought set the scene for more specific discussions of what development is, or should be, and the most appropriate policies and methods that can be harnessed in the search for this elusive prom-ised land of happiness and prosperity. It could be argued that debate about development, its nature and how to achieve it, is *the* central issue in the whole of western social science. The early towering figures in the field, writers such as John Stuart Mill and Karl Marx, were essentially theorizing about development. The Enlightenment was fundamentally concerned with progress towards an ideal society, and how the har-nessing of rational thoughts, policies and actions might allow the real-ization of this goal. But similar ideas of progress can be found in other non-western modes of thought. In Japan, for example, a distinctive approach to the philosophy of economics was developed with a focus on 'administering the nation and relieving the suffering of the people' (Morris-Suzuki 1989), a notion that is close to the concerns of develop-ment. In traditional China, Confucius (who died around 479 BC) was convinced that he lived in an age of acute crisis – perhaps similar in some ways to our own times. He was, he believed, witnessing the col-lapse of civilization (Leys 1997), and his entire project was concerned with the ways in which a better society might be built and governed. Interestingly, the Chinese government is now reviving Confucian ideas as a way of stabilising a society undergoing breathtakingly rapid change (Bell 2008).

The genesis of modern development thought in the West is usually dated to the end of the Second World War. The European colonial empires had expressed some concern earlier for the improvement of their subject peoples, but it was really only after 1945 that development was seen as a worldwide priority. New technologies and logistical sys-tems developed during the war were seen as being modified to fight a new battle against global poverty. The initiation of the Marshall Plan for the reconstruction of Europe, a similar plan for Japan, and the establishment of the major Bretton Woods institutions, notably the World Bank and the IMF, signalled a new determination to avoid the economic and social problems of the 1930s that heralded a global conflict. However, there have been numerous changes of fashion in development thought since 1945, reflecting the ebb and flow of a series of wider debates.

The first of these concerns the position and role of the nation state as the fundamental unit of analysis and policy-making. The system of international relations that emerged in the post-war world centred on the United Nations and related institutions enshrined the special position of the sovereign state as the recognized authority over the space defined by its national boundaries, as the legal body able to pass laws and initiate policy, and as the only legitimate user of armed force to ensure its stability and will. Thus the field of development studies generally uses the nation as its primary unit of analysis, and most statistics are collected on this basis. However, the growth of broader economic and political units such as the European Union as well as the ratification of significant international treaties has challenged some of the traditional powers of the state. At the same time a large number of regions within individual countries have been campaigning for, and in some case achieving, much greater autonomy. Thus the powers of national governments are being whittled away from above and below, a process which some have called the 'hollowing out of the state'. However, in the aftermath of the GFC some commentators are questioning whether such processes will continue. Responses to the crisis have dominantly involved actions by national governments to shield their economies, shore up key corporations such as banks, stimulate employment and so on. A related question concerns the extent to which the government of a nation can act as the most important catalyst for change and the key controller and co-ordinator of all kinds of development programmes. In the 1950s and 1960s, there was a general assumption that governments must play these key roles and be the organizers of a wide range of services; however after the 1970s there was a long period in which the private sector was seen as much more important. The conviction that markets can deliver the benefits of development more effectively than governments is a central tenet in the neo-liberal paradigm that has held sway for so long, and which has resulted in what Toye (1987) has called the 'counterrevolution' in development thought. There were always important differences between opinions in various countries here. Support for the minimalist state came most enthusiastically from the

United States, the United Kingdom and Australia, while much of Western Europe retained its traditional range of government responsibilities. The transformation of Asia into an economically powerful region also suggested new creative possibilities for government activities, with governments central to progress in Korea, Taiwan and Singapore, and more recently in China. Some writers have even suggested that the Asian model of development brought together the most useful aspects of the capitalist and socialist systems into a new 'third way' that was the most efficient way yet devised of generating growth (Johnson 1987; Wade 1990). For some time after the Asian financial crisis of 1997 many commentators dismissed the continued value of this Asian development model, but the continued growth of Asia, the realisation that many aspects of this model have still survived including in China, plus the impact of the GFC have now reopened discussion of this whole area.

Notions of power are central to development thought – some would even argue that power is the pivotal concept in the whole corpus. During the Cold War, both the United States and the Soviet Union saw aid and development programmes as a major weapon in the battle to gain support for their ideologies and systems. Genuine independence of policy was not favoured by either side, hence the rise of the non-aligned movement. However, some leaders were able to play off one side against the other, gaining benefits from both. The end of the Cold War saw an end to both these constraints and opportunities. Whole regions of the globe, especially in Africa, suddenly became peripheral to the global system and were simply ignored by western politicians, businessmen and investors. This situation has changed again after the terrorist attacks on the United States on 11 September 2001. In the 'war on terror' we have returned to the Cold War slogan that 'either you are with us or against us'.

In the period since the end of the Cold War it has become common to regard liberal democracy as the only viable economic and political system in the modern world. Francis Fukuyama (1992) called this the 'end of history', in the sense that the long period of conflict between rival ideological systems was over, raising again the question of whether there is only one way of achieving development and creating a modern nation. However, this assumption has come under sustained attack. The whole debate about 'Asian values' at a time when growth rates in that region were clearly superior to those prevailing in the West was one form of questioning. The environmentalists' view that not all nations can possibly have the lifestyle prevailing in the West has already been mentioned, but other authors are now raising some rather different but

just as difficult questions. Hernando de Soto (2000) has asked why capitalism has triumphed in the West but has been so spectacularly unsuc-
cessful in a number of other regions. Oswaldo de Rivero (2001) has
raised the prospect that not all economies can ever aspire to sustained
growth and development: many are simply non-viable. Thus the old
assumption that development can be achieved by all if the 'correct' policies are implemented is being increasingly questioned.

These debates raise further questions about democracy, freedom and
the involvement of local communities in the process of development.
Nobel prizewinner Amartya Sen (1999a) has proposed that we should
regard development as freedom from tyranny, poor economic prospects,
social deprivation, inefficient public facilities and so on. Freedom and
democracy are of course noble aims, but open to a wide range of alternative interpretations. Not surprisingly, a number of Asian commentators, confident in the economic success of their region, have proposed
that Asia can develop its own form of democracy and its own definition
of human rights. These concepts would not be the same as the western
ideals but would be just as valid (Mahbubani 1998; de Bary 1998;
Bauer and Bell 1999; Bell 2000). Finally, the question of democracy and
freedom raises the question of how far we see development as being a
process initiated and implemented by outside forces and actors, or as an
essentially an internal transformation fuelled by local initiative and self
help. The emphasis in the field on the role of outside 'experts', the incul-
cation of new and foreign values and methods, and the central role of
aid all have conspired to downgrade the role of local mobilization. This
is especially true in an era of globalization, when many commentators
predict that cultural and economic convergence on some kind of international best practice is bound to take place. In the present era, the
whole question of the relationships between globalization and development theory is opening up as a new battleground in the conflict of ideas
and ideologies (see, for example, Jomo and Nagaraj 2001; Petras and
Veltmeyer 2001; Schuurman 2001).

Theories of modernization

None of the complexities, counter-arguments or self-doubts introduced
in the previous section was allowed to cloud the simple but powerful
message espoused by the proponents of modernization theory. During
the 1960s and part of the 1970s, within all of the social sciences there
appeared studies in aspects of modernization, each couched in the particular language and concepts of the particular discipline, but all carry-

Modernization Theory) [handwritten]

ing the same beguiling promise: all nations however poor were able, with the implementation of 'correct' policies, to achieve a modern standard of living by following exactly the same growth path as that pioneered by the western nations.

Examples of such studies can be found in sociology, geography and political science, but it was in economics that the seminal work was published, with the appearance of Rostow's *The Stages of Economic Growth* (1960). But this is more than just a study in economics, which is part of the reason for its influence over the years. Rostow, as he has made clear in some of his later reminiscences (Rostow 1984), has always had a strong interest in economic history and has also written in detail on the importance of politics in the development process (Rostow 1971). Yet, somewhat paradoxically, his many critics have derided his attempts to produce a universal theory of development, one largely divorced from the historical and institutional realities of particular societies, and have been particularly scathing about his political positions.

Rostow proposed that the path to development and modernity involved the movement by any nation through a series of stages:

- the traditional society
- the pre-take-off society
- take-off
- the road to maturity
- the mass consumption society

Rostow's 5 stages [handwritten]

The framework is full of hope – every nation has the capacity to pass through these stages and achieve mass consumption. The image of take-off is particularly evocative, full of power and hope, as the nation is able to launch itself into a bright new future. The book was also written as a deliberate counter to the numerous Marxist theories that were appearing at this time. The subtitle of the book – 'a non-communist manifesto' – written at a time when communist expansion was feared in all parts of the underdeveloped world, emphasized that successful development could be achieved without revolution. The most important mechanism in the whole process, the fuel needed to achieve take-off, was investment derived principally from domestic savings. If the savings rate could be moved from the normal 5 per cent of GDP to 10 per cent or more for a sustained period, then take-off could proceed. A major role of the political system, especially in the early stages, was to create the organizational mechanisms and the political will to achieve these sustained increases in savings and productive investment. Rostow was at pains to point out that there was nothing automatic or inevitable about these processes. Unless economic policies and political systems were managed effectively, then a nation's move from one stage to another could stall.

While roundly criticized, this theory has been widely quoted and used by both theorists and policy-makers. In a number of more recent interviews and books, Rostow has claimed that history has entirely vindicated his theory. The fall of the Soviet Union has demonstrated the unviability of the communist alternative, while the success of East Asia has underlined the importance of high rates of savings and investment (Rostow 1990).

Rostow's theories and their symbolism matched the mood of their time. There was much discussion in policy circles of the need to escape the 'vicious cycle of poverty'. There were several versions of this concept, but in general terms it described the ways in which the processes of poverty and underdevelopment were self-reinforcing. Low or non-existent rates of growth meant that savings and investment rates were low. Insufficient was invested in productive facilities of various kinds, ensuring that low levels of growth persisted. Funds were not available for better schools, universities or hospitals, ensuring that the nation could not find a way out of its poverty through investment in its human resources. Lack of investment in roads, ports and other infrastructure kept the economy working at low levels of efficiency. A way out of this persistent cycle of poverty was needed, and the modernization theorists provided a hope that this might be possible.

The Harrod–Domar growth model, which also became popular at this time, provided some economic sophistication to the emerging propositions (Hettne 1995). Growth could be self-sustaining, leading to a 'virtuous cycle of growth'. Increases in output and income would be accompanied by a higher marginal propensity to save, leading to more investment and a new round of expansion and income growth. This model, based on Keynesian theory, also proposed that initial impetus for growth could come from foreign aid, providing the first round of investment in the absence of domestic savings.

The emphasis on modernization within economics was mirrored by a range of other (and some would say complementary) studies in other social sciences. In politics, for example, there was much research on political modernization and the generation of more effective political institutions, inevitably made in the image of the West. In geography, a number of studies concentrated on 'spatial modernization', involving the spread of infrastructure and other symbols of modern life, and the gradual expansion of the *core* into the more backward *periphery*. In psychology, too, there was an attempt to explore the ways in which more 'modern' personality traits could be engendered and fostered.

Perhaps most influential was the work going on at this time in sociology, and most important here was the work of Talcott Parsons (1937: 1951). He attempted to develop a grand theory of 'social action', seeing human activity as voluntary and intentional but set within a symbolic realm and a natural environment. He identified four major functional subsystems – the economy, the polity, the social community and the fiduciary system – and argued that as societies modernize these systems they become more elaborate and the roles of individuals are increasingly differentiated. It is not surprising then that Parsons has been called 'the theorist of modernity' (Robertson and Turner 1991).

There were, however, some genuine attempts to make modernization theory more sophisticated through what has become known as *dialectical modernization theory* (Martinussen 1997). This attempted to unravel the complex relationships between the 'traditional' and 'modern' sectors. Gusfield (1976), for example, argued that traditional institutions could be revitalized through contact with modernizing influences in other parts of society. This represented a significant advance over the numerous studies of the 'dual economy' that saw a much clearer distinction between the modern and more traditional parts of the society.

Some assumptions in the rather optimistic modernization framework were questioned by Gunnar Myrdal (1957) and Albert Hirschman (1958), both of whom demonstrated that both 'virtuous' and 'vicious' cycles could operate simultaneously to produce growth in some areas and stagnation in others. Earlier economic theory had been used to suggest that inequalities would not last long because labour would migrate from low-wage areas to regions where rewards were higher. Similarly, capital would move to regions where the returns were higher, usually in areas that were currently backward but had high investment potential. Thus, growth would take place in the more backward areas, removing the initial inequalities. Both Myrdal and Hirschman attacked this kind of equilibrium analysis. Myrdal suggested that two kinds of forces would be at work. *Spread* effects would serve to distribute growth from richer to poorer regions or countries, while *backwash* effects tended to intensify existing inequalities. The relative strength of these two forces would depend on a range of circumstances and policy frameworks: thus processes of *circular and cumulative causation,* could often lead to ever-deepening levels of inequality.

Many of Hirschman's idea were quite similar, but he developed a particular analysis of the role of government in the management of these processes. He argued that development is by necessity an unbalanced process, and it would also be unrealistic to expect government planners to invest in various sectors of the economy in a finely balanced way. In particular, he considered the balance between investment in *directly productive activities*, such as factories or plantations, and the infrastructure needed to support these facilities, which he termed *social overhead capital.* Growth may occur by concentrating on the development of infrastructure, thereby reducing production costs and encouraging further investment in production, or the reverse may be preferred. If production is privileged, inefficiencies in infrastructure will appear, forcing catch-up investment. Either strategy might work, and the choice of the more appropriate would depend on local circumstances. The work of Hirschman and Myrdal grew out of the tradition of modernization studies, and used some of the same theoretical assumptions, but their attention to the persistence of inequalities provides a direct link to some of the more radical critiques that began to appear in the 1960s.

The challenge of dependency theory

During the 1960s it became clear that inequalities were not being narrowed as conventional economic theory had predicted: rather, the world was becoming increasingly divided between the powerful *core* regions and the impoverished *periphery*. In Myrdal's terms, the *spread* effects were being overwhelmed by the much more powerful forces of *backwash*. One of the regions where this reality was most pronounced was in Latin America, and it was from here that an influential set of new theories began to emerge – what became known as the *dependencia* or dependency school.

Much of the initial impetus for this mode of thought came from the work of the United Nations Economic Commission for Latin America, and in particular from the work of Raul Prebisch. The central argument – now known as the 'Prebisch thesis' – was that the basic assumptions of neo-classical economics did not exist in the real world. The economic landscape did not primarily consist of small producers and buyers, each operating in a perfect marketplace with none able to exert power over these market processes. Rather, global commerce took place between the rich and powerful developed economies and the much weaker peripheral countries. Not surprisingly, the rules of the trading system were systematically manipulated in favour of the powerful western-based corporations to the benefit of the already rich countries (DiMarco 1972). In particular, Prebisch rejected the orthodox Ricardian arguments in favour of each nation specializing in the output of goods for which it had a particular comparative advantage, and trading these goods through the international system. He argued that none of the 'late industrializers', such as the United States, Germany and Japan, had been able to use such a strategy for their development. Rather, they had gone through the early stages of industrialization behind protective tariff walls until they felt competitive enough to confront the global market on equal terms. Specialization would not encourage industrial development of the kind needed in Latin America; instead the region would be condemned to a peripheral position as a supplier of primary products. (raw goods ... ?)

These arguments were taken a stage further, and given much greater exposure, in the English-speaking world by Andre Gunder Frank, who in 1967 produced his classic *Capitalism and Underdevelopment in Latin America*. He argued that development and underdevelopment are in fact simply two sides of the same coin. The rich countries achieved growth by systematically exploiting their colonies and the rest of the underdeveloped world and this process had been going on for several centuries, at least since the Spanish penetration of the New World. By the twentieth century, no part of the globe was too remote to remain untouched by the impacts of the international economic system of imperialism and domination. Thus it was nonsense to regard, as Rostow had done, the underdeveloped world as in some kind of pristine initial state. The poor countries had in fact been underdeveloped in the process of incorporation into the global system, and the structural changes that had been imposed upon them made future development of a real and autonomous kind much less likely. Once the goods in which they specialized were no longer needed by the world market, or if a cheaper source was found, they would be simply discarded without the possibility of returning to their old internally oriented system of production. The poorest regions of Latin America were not those that had been ignored by the world market: rather they were those that had in the past had a very close relationship but had outlived their usefulness. Latin America as a whole, he suggested, had progressed most during the two world wars when the countries at the core of international capitalism had been otherwise engaged and the periphery was left to develop in its own way.

Many similar ideas were developed at roughly the same time by Celso Furtado (1964), who argued that capitalism had expanded throughout the globe, particularly after the industrial revolution in Europe: no region was left untouched, and in all cases new hybrid structures were left behind, with profound implications for future development prospects. The penetrated economies were generally characterized by the existence and interaction of three distinct sectors:

- a 'remnant' economy consisting mainly of subsistence farmers, but with a small amount of cash crop production;
- a domestic sector producing goods and services for local consumption;
- the internationally oriented sector producing goods for the world market.

This classification was used as the basis for a later analysis of the Brazilian situation (Furtado 1965), written at the time of political and economic crisis. Here he dealt with the class implications of the structures of underdevelopment. Many earlier theorists had dismissed the role of the elites in Latin America as simple collaborators with international capitalism in the exploitation of their lands, but here Furtado presents a much more nuanced analysis, pointing out that there is a real diversity of class interests in Brazil. Most lacking was an elite committed to the generation of autonomous industrialization, and institutional arrangements would need to be flexible enough to allow such a group to assume power – a crucial advance in development thought that we will take up again with reference to the successful industrialization of east Asia. Furtado himself then returned to a general analysis of Latin America (Furtado 1969), which represents one of the fullest statements of the dependency thesis. The export of primary products, he urges, cannot advance development at all, but more importantly the structures of the economy and the society strongly inhibit any movement towards a more productive and sustainable future. He called for a complete reform of institutional arrangements, the exercise of political power and relationships with the outside world – and with the United States and the multinational corporation in particular. New technologies needed to be developed and harnessed internally, and in the early stages at least, the state sector would have to play a leading role as a catalyst for development. The countries of Latin America could achieve many of these difficult tasks more easily by developing productive arrangements for regional co-operation. While these basic assumptions and propositions were generally accepted by many later theorists, a number of writers developed particular components of the analysis in more detail. Three of them, all of which have particular relevance for current debates, are considered briefly here: Arghiri Emmanuel, Samir Amin and Immanuel Wallerstein.

Emmanuel (1972) produced what at the time was a very influential analysis of the ways in which international trade reinforces income inequalities at a global level. Goods exported from high-wage countries have a consistently higher price on the world market compared with exports from underdeveloped countries that have much lower wages, not because these first-world exports are inherently more valuable but because rich countries have the political power to manipulate the markets and set prices favourable to their own products. This argument, although widely criticized in several quarters, is still repeated by some authors in the current debate about globalization and the supposed benefits of large-scale expansion of world trade.

Amin's particular contribution, on the other hand, was to elaborate Furtado's analysis of the internal structures of underdeveloped countries (see, for example, Amin 1976, 1977). He looked at the development of both the export-oriented and domestic sectors, and at the linkage (or lack of it) between the two. Areas involved in export activities, usually of primary products, would have higher wages than found in the rest of the economy, but the multiplier effects of these investments would be far less than in developed economies. Most of the supplies of specialized machinery would come from core countries, as would even some of the food and more luxury items consumed by the labour force. This lack of productive linkage meant that the two parts of the economy were quite isolated from each other. The export sector would in fact have its closest relationships with the areas to which its output was exported, again in the core countries. Amin termed this separation between sectors *disarticulation,* a characteristic feature of almost all underdeveloped countries. The maintenance of the export sector required the compliance of members of the local elite who would be bought off through higher wages, corrupt payments or the supply of luxury goods. The obvious gaps between rich and poor would inevitably cause deep resentments that could lead to political instability and, to ensure the maintenance of order, large sums would have to be spent on the import of military hardware and on rewards to the military forces to ensure their loyalty. This would exacerbate a balance of payment situation already made dire by the progressive decline in the relative value of the primary products being exported. The shortfall in hard currency could only be met by opening up yet further mines, plantations or other export activities but this would lead to yet another spiral of deepening disarticulation and internal inequality.

Wallerstein's contribution has been voluminous and has partly involved some very detailed historical analysis of the emergence and development of the global economy, founding a whole school of analysis that has become known as *world systems theory* (see, for example, Wallerstein 1974, 1979, 1984, 2011; Hopkins and Wallerstein 1982). But he is also important for his introduction of an entirely new category into the debate about the structure of the core and the periphery. He pointed to the need for a category of countries that acted as go-betweens or mediators between the rich and the poor nations, and could help to diffuse any tensions that might arise from global inequalities by providing examples of what could be achieved within the system. This group, which included countries like Australia, Canada, Spain and South Korea, he termed the *semi-periphery*, and their role was to demonstrate that revolution or even drastic reform was not at all necessary.

As we have seen, in much of dependency theory there was the assumption that external forces were all-powerful and simply swept away any lingering remnants of the old structures. As a number of critics pointed out, this is clearly too extreme, and even in the newer versions of modernization theory important interactions between the modern and traditional sectors were postulated. A number of the later dependency writers attempted to remedy this shortcoming, notably Fernando Cardoso (Cardoso and Faletto 1979; Cardoso 1982). In these writings, they point to the complex configuration in various Latin American countries of competing or co-operating groups and classes, each influenced by external forces and each attempting to use these external elements to their own advantage, although no class or group is strong enough to control this environment.

Dependency theory has also been criticized from a variety of other perspectives. A number of Marxist scholars have taken issue with the methods and assumptions used, suggesting that they are a misrepresentation of the true Marxist position. Several writers have argued that the dependency theorists have missed the true essence of capitalism and instead have portrayed it as a simple zero-sum game. Bill Warren (1980), for example, has argued that while it may have a number of abhorrent features, capitalism is necessary to strip away the original feudal situation found in most underdeveloped regions, and this can only be accomplished by outside imperialist forces that are essential for its establishment, which is in turn a prerequisite for the transition to socialism. From the other side of the ideological spectrum, several critics have pointed to gains that have been made in the development of a number of countries, especially in Asia. These have been contrasted with the performance of those countries that have attempted a more self-reliant approach, and it is to this 'miracle' of growth in Asia that we now turn.

The Asian miracle: challenges for modernization and dependency approaches

It has been claimed, with justification, that the spectacular growth that has taken place in east Asia since the 1960s represents the most profound and rapid economic, social and political transformation that has ever taken place. Former US Treasury Secretary Larry Summers has calculated that during the Industrial Revolution in Britain, within an average human life span, standards of living rose by perhaps 50 per cent, a noticeable improvement. But in contemporary Asia a person may well have experienced an increase of some 100 fold, or 10,000 per cent (Mahbubani 2008). It is little surprise, then, that the Asian experience should have attracted so much attention and presented such a challenge to all existing theories of development (see, for example, Berger and Borer 1997; Rowen 1998; Leipziger 2000). The recent history of the region has generated an enormous literature and spawned a number of comparative studies seeking to explain why Asia has been so much more successful than either Latin America or Africa (Gereffi and Wyman 1990). However, there is still no agreement about the Asian experience and what its implications are: each side in the debate has attempted to enlist the Asian success story to support its own entrenched position.

The modern-day descendants of the modernization theorists have stressed the importance of adherence to neo-classical postulates in countries such as South Korea, Taiwan and China. The key to success, they argue, was the avoidance of any protectionist tendencies. Rather, the entire emphasis was on exports as the engine of growth. Competitiveness in export markets required close attention to labour and other production costs, and to the careful management of macroeconomic policy and exchange rate settings. Continued competitiveness also demanded an ongoing programme of reform, resulting in progressive privatization of government enterprises, trade liberalization, structural adjustment, reforms in corporate governance and the fundamental democratization of the political system.

The responses of the adherents of dependency theory have also been predictable. In the early stages of the developments in South Korea, for example, a number of critics questioned how 'real' this development was, arguing that this was a classic example of dependent development, relying on politically motivated support from the United States and essentially exploiting low-cost labour resources. Unflattering comparisons were made with North Korea's emphasis on self-reliance. Yet as the evidence of continued progress mounted, and as the North Korean competition faltered, the emphasis switched to the lauding of the South Korean model of autonomous development. It was emphasized that the early stages of industrialization took place behind high tariff walls, and the government played a very important role as initiator and co-ordinator of new initiatives (Amsden 1989; Wade 1990). The nature and role of the South Korean state has received particular attention. Peter Evans (1995), for example, has argued that east Asia has been far more successful than Latin America because the state has been both *autonomous* and *embedded*. Unlike its counterparts in Latin America, the state in Asia has not been hostage to particular vested, class interests, but has been autonomous and able to act independently in the interests of the whole nation. Yet the state has been closely integrated into society, positioned to receive messages from all parts of the community and able to interact on all of these levels, and in particular with the business community, to ensure that plans and targets were effectively met.

Yet, the Asian experience has also presented some different challenges to development theory by highlighting some factors that are outside all of the major existing theories. One set of writers has highlighted the role of culture in development, and pointed to the wide variety of experience in different parts of the world, thus questioning the generality of any development theories. Much has been made of the common Confucian heritage in Korea, Taiwan and China. This philosophy emphasizes the ethical responsibilities of both rulers and the ruled and was useful in instilling a high level of work ethic and response to authority in these countries. Confucianism also places great reliance on education and self-cultivation in the development of society, and as a result the level of investment in education has been extremely high. Comparisons have been made between what has been called the 'Confucian rate of growth' and the lesser performers, labelled, for example, the 'Hindu' and the 'Buddhist' levels of performance, although the recent growth performance of India has resulted in some reformulation of these generalizations. More broadly, the Asian experience has drawn attention to the capacity of the state to initiate and control growth (Weiss and Hobson 1995), and to the importance of skills and initiative.

Some commentators have also pointed out that both Korea and Taiwan had a special strategic position during the Cold War, being American allies on the frontline against communism. This allowed them to gain special advantages from the United States, including access to military and development aid, and preferential access to American markets for their products, especially in the early stages of growth. The western world generally turned a blind eye to the blatant copying of products and technology, something that would not be tolerated now.

Rather than supporting one of the existing models of development, a number of researchers have suggested that the Asian model of growth is in fact a case unto itself. Asian companies have been energetic and entrepreneurial, have concentrated on improving their productivity levels and have been able to develop new product lines and penetrate new markets as older lines become less profitable. Yet, the prevailing ethos of the societies has been generally much more egalitarian than in countries such as the United States. There has been great attention to the avoidance of the grosser forms of income inequality, giving a much greater sense of social cohesion and stability. At the same time, some of the strengths of more centrally planned economies were utilized, especially in the early stages of development. The state was both active and efficient, avoiding the lethargy and waste that characterized the Soviet system. Importantly, the population felt that it was involved in a great and vital national enterprise, and was willing to work enormously hard and make sacrifices in the interest of future generations.

But this successful experience and the later onset of the Asian crisis leads us to two further questions, both of which are concerned with the question of the applicability of this model to other parts of the underdeveloped world. First, several commentators, as well as policy-makers from around the world, have urged various governments to adopt the Korean or Taiwanese models of development but it is far from clear whether such a transfer can work. As we have seen, many aspects of the Asian transformation can be interpreted as being very culturally and historically specific. Cultural values in regions such as Africa are far different from those in Korea, and countries could not now expect to derive the economic advantages that Korea and Taiwan were able to derive during the Cold War. Even if it were possible to transfer development models in this way, do nations that adopt such a high-growth path to development risk the sort of damaging crisis that befell Asia in 1997? Is it possible to adopt these methods in the early stages of growth and then undertake a careful and appropriately sequenced series of reforms that can avoid later instability? This latter question is of great relevance to China at the moment. Many features of the Korean model, including the creation of some large conglomerates based on the example of the Korean *chaebol,* have been adopted but there are fears about how the economy will be adapted and reformed in the longer term.

The neo-liberal ascendancy

Since the 1980s, development thought and policy has been dominated by what has become known as neo-liberal thought, or what Toye (1991) has called the New Political Economy. In part, this has resulted from a particular reading of the important Asian experience described above, as well as the decline of the dependency movement as a result of criticisms both from within and outside the 'progressive' strands of development thought. The movement also gained much momentum from the fall of the Soviet Union, and the consequent discrediting of socialist alternatives to capitalism, which gave rise to a more self-confident West willing to reassert many of the elements of the old modernization model (Colclough and Manor 1991).

Certainly, there are many elements that demonstrate a simple return to modernization, notably the often unstated belief that there is one path to development which all nations can follow in a series of stages. The goals of development are also portrayed as unproblematic, involving a simple movement toward the modernity that is portrayed as so successful in the West. All good comes from external sources, with outside norms and methods being essential to the breaking down of traditional barriers to growth. Many of the core mechanisms for growth are also similar to those cited in the earlier period. Savings rates are still a central element, supported by foreign investment. But, importantly, the role of government is simply dismissed. Elites and politicians in particular are uniformly portrayed as rent-seeking villains, willing only to look after their own narrow interests rather than the good of the entire society (Toye 1991). Thus, while markets may not be perfect, they are portrayed as infinitely preferable to governments controlled by a 'kleptocracy'. Indeed, market failures are seen as more often resulting from an excess of government interference in the economy rather than from a dearth of regulation. Government services, even including health and education, must be pared back in the interests of balancing the budget and creating an environment conducive to foreign investment. Similarly, foreign exchange rates must be managed (i.e., devalued) to encourage export competitiveness.

Many of these policy measures have been promulgated by international institutions, notably the IMF, to deal with the periodic crises that have plagued much of the underdeveloped world. But it is also true that much of the neo-liberal doctrine is embedded in the large body of literature supporting the move towards globalization, and it is this set of beliefs that was so fundamentally challenged by the onset of the GFC.

Globalization, the global financial crisis and development theory

In the early years of the new millennium, the central talking point, both among policy-makers and the general public, was globalization. There even seemed to be a general agreement that this new wave of change was inevitable and that all nations must either seek ways of accommodating the new reality or risk irrelevance as the rest of the world marches into this glittering future. Yet there was surprisingly little consensus on exactly what the term meant. At one level, it can simply involve the expansion of economic activities such as trade and investment across national boundaries. But it is frequently used to highlight closer economic integration, greater policy reform and openness and greater interdependence between countries. More controversially, the term has sometimes been used to describe (or predict) tendencies of convergence by all countries towards similar political systems, lifestyles and even tastes in entertainment or fast foods. There were certainly dissenting voices even at the height of enthusiasm for this new order, but the onset of the GFC in 2007 has added a whole new dimension to the debate – underlining old warnings and raising completely new ones. An added impact of this crisis has been to hasten the shift that was already taking place from the old centres of economic and political power in Europe and North America to the 'developing economies', and particularly those in Asia, nations with rather different priorities and strategies. In the process the whole notion of development is being redefined as well the theoretical and policy frameworks utilised in achieving progress.

Given the looseness of the concept of globalization, it is not surprising that a number of voices have long been raised to criticize several of the claims that have been made in its name. John Gray (1998) has challenged one of these basic tenets, that this is a new era involving a profound set of changes to many aspects of global economy and society. Rather, Gray suggests, there have been several similar periods before in world history – in the mid-nineteenth century and again in the years leading up to the First World War in particular – when there were high levels of international trade and investment. In these earlier cases, the experiment with laissez-faire economics proved to be short-lived, principally because of the extreme levels of income inequality that were generated in the process. This polarization led to political instability that quickly forced new systems to be adopted. In both earlier examples, the life of the experiment was no more than 10–15 years. Thus, Gray argued, globalization is merely the return to a failed experiment, and this current incarnation is bound to disappear quickly in the same way, and for basically the same reasons.

Not surprisingly, the remnants of the old dependency school have also criticized globalization as yet another manifestation of the western desire to dominate and exploit underdeveloped countries. The existing world order is being remade to serve the greed and class interests of a small elite, and the capitalist state is being restructured to serve this new kind of imperialism (Petras and Veltmeyer 2001). Many groups have felt marginalized and even exploited by this powerful set of global forces, and we have recently witnessed a number of mass demonstrations against globalization and what are regarded as some of its key institutions, the World Trade Organization, the IMF and the World Economic Forum, for example.

The supporters of globalization argue that the best chance for growth in the poorer countries remains with the liberalization of world trade and the reform of internal policies. Currently, there is lively debate raging about the empirical evidence on whether the gap between rich and poor countries is in fact growing or declining as a result of these policies. One group led by members of the United Nations Development Programme argues that the gulf is getting wider, while others suggest the opposite. Dollar and Kraay (2002) have argued that inequality has in fact decreased since 1975, mainly because of rapid growth in China and India, and 'globalizing' countries have done much better than others. However, several other commentators have questioned these figures and the assumptions behind them.

Moving beyond these arguments, a number of elements of a new agenda for development have been proposed by some writers who are responding to what they see as innovative elements in the global debate. The whole modernization approach has been seriously questioned by those seeking to go beyond what they regard as an outmoded modernist paradigm. Any attempt to impose a unidirectional or single path to development has received some harsh criticism from those researchers using a postmodern approach that stresses a whole new agenda concerned with knowledge, identity, meaning and the like (Schuurman 2001; Parfitt 2002). Some have gone so far as to suggest that the whole development project is now moribund or at has at least reached a serious impasse, and we have entered an era of 'post-development' (Sachs 1992b; Rahnema and Bawtree 1997).

In part, this introduces a whole new set of concerns into the debate but many of the older issues are also rejected or turned on their head. The assumption that the underdeveloped world can be treated as a homogeneous and undifferentiated whole is completely dismissed. The development path of a society, and indeed its choices about the goals of development itself, are historically conditioned and are heavily influenced by the pattern of institutions that has emerged over the years. We should not regard any set of institutions, not even the market, as indispensable or the best choice – everything depends upon the context and the historical legacy. Similarly, the overarching belief in progress that characterized the modernist approach has been replaced for some by a greater sense of pessimism or a desire to avoid the most dangerous risks. The state, regarded for so long by many as the guardian or even the catalyst of development, is now seen by this group as part of the problem. Rather, they argue, our real hope is with civil society and its struggle for emancipation. This of course raises some serious issues about the old methods of development assistance and the role of aid and the 'expert'. The process of development is here conceived as a form of discourse, one shaped by disparities of power. Escobar (1995) has argued that development is not a set of aims or knowledge, that is gradually uncovered and acted upon, but an imposed set of constructs and values. The western concern has been to win markets, gain access to raw materials and avoid being swamped by massive increases in the populations of impoverished countries. The West, with its blind faith in technology and the effectiveness of planning, has treated the third world as a child in great need of guidance. Accordingly, this school argues that all earlier categories of development thinking have fallen into the trap of paternalism, or what is often called now 'trusteeship' (Cowen and Shenton 1996; Parfitt 2002). The aim of development must be to escape from this 'impasse' and reflect the real needs and goals of the people involved, although it is far from clear how this is to be achieved (Sharp and Briggs 2006; Sylvester 2006; Simon 2006.)

Another important element in the current debate concerns the role of different kinds of political and economic regimes in encouraging or inhibiting growth. Not surprisingly, the neo-liberal mainstream argues that western-style democracy is essential to progress, although some interesting counter-arguments are now appearing (see, for example, Clague 1997; Rodrik 2011). Not surprisingly, given our earlier discussion, much of the counter-argument is coming from Asian countries that see themselves as being successful but not necessarily following conventional or western models. In an interesting study, Sylvia Chan (2002) argues that the common label of 'liberal democracy' contains two different elements that may in fact be contradictory – many of the strongest supporters of economic liberalization are opposed to many democratic ideals. Similarly, we need to recognize three key elements of 'liberty' – *economic*, *civil* and *political* liberty – and three key conditions that need to be achieved to promote growth – *security*, *stability*, and *openness and information*. After surveying the Asian growth experience, she concludes that such liberties and outcomes have in fact been achieved under national systems that are not democratic in the western sense but are more congruent with local histories and institutions.

While this argument was still raging the global economy entered a new and extremely unstable phase culminating in the GFC and its numerous aftershocks that are continuing right down to the time of writing. For some the entire edifice of neo-liberal thought has been shown to be worthless or even reckless and dangerous, and had brought the entire global financial and economic system to the brink of disaster. However there have been concerted attempts by many with a strong vested interest in retaining the pre-GFC system – with the finance houses of Wall Street and the city of London very much to the fore – to drag public opinion and policy makers back to 'business as usual'. Yet in spite these efforts it does seem that the old modes of neo-liberalism have been seriously wounded, although it is not yet clear whether the damage will prove fatal. At the very least, as Robert Wade (2009) has put it, even if there are strong pressures from powerful elites to return us to the familiar ways of thought and action, it is now more possible to consider some alternative paradigms and policy agendas. The basic problem is that although neo-liberal approaches have been roundly attacked, no well articulated alternatives have so far emerged (Rodrik 2006), but in some ways what we are now seeing is a healthy reappraisal of the entire architecture of development theory, with some key elements of the old received wisdom now being re-thought. This process is far from complete, but the elements of a new approach may well emerge from the following central questions that are briefly introduced here and discussed in more detail in the chapters on the economics of development and on the impact of the global financial crisis and of economic instability more generally.

First, and perhaps most basically, the inherent superiority of market mechanisms for the allocation of resources and in the design of a whole range of policy instruments in all areas of development – something that as we have seen has been an article of faith for some time – is now under serious question. It is not just that markets were patently incapable of dealing with the crisis of 2007 – and for many critics they were seen as being part of the problem – but some key theoretical constructs backing up long-held assumptions about the role and efficiency of markets have been shown to be shaky to say the least.

Related to this point, the neo-liberal slogan that governments were part of the problem rather than the solution has also been challenged. With the widespread and catastrophic failure of markets, governments were the only line of defence against complete system failure, and were forced to pump billions of dollars into their economies. This has generated widespread taxpayer anger, and there have been many calls for much stronger regulation regimes. Just how far this political process goes depends upon how much longer the crisis continues – at the time of writing continued fears about sovereign debt in Europe and the United

States suggest that the instability still has a long way to go, with unpredictable consequences. But it is clear that debate about the appropriate role of the state in the whole process of development has returned to centre stage (Tanzi 2011).

One clear dimension of the developments leading directly to the global crisis was the 'unhitching' of the financial sector from the 'real' economy. In a provocative new book Satyajit Das (2011) has noted that once upon a time economies were about making useful things but now we construct immense and artificial financial structures that give immense riches to a few but put at the risk the vast majority of the population. Virtually all aspects of the economy – and indeed the society more generally – have been 'financialised' and brought within the realm of the market. Goods and services that were once thought of as unambiguous public goods – for example water supplies – have been privatised in many countries. Similarly, many food staples now traded on world markets have attracted the interest of speculators, and speculation on wheat, rice and other basic items has been seen by many as being a major contributor to the rapid increases in food prices in the last few years.

Overall, it could be argued, the world is now much more unstable than it has been for some time, and this is creating a lack of security across many dimensions for many millions of people, but especially the most vulnerable. As part of the debate about the causes and consequences of the GFC it has been argued that the processes of financial sector growth and the increasing reach of the market have exacerbated degrees of inequality at all levels, and this inequality has been a major contributor to the rise of instability and the generation of crisis (Vandemoortele 2009). The creation of a small number of very rich individuals and a mass of poor people has reduced aggregate levels of demand and simultaneously created dangerous levels of social and political instability.

At a more general level, the GFC has forced everyone to think about the politics involved in financial and economic policy issues: the need to take what some regard as the old-fashioned field of political economy seriously may be one of the most important consequences of the crisis in terms of development theory and policy. In thinking about the new global political economy surely one key impact of these recent events has been the hastening of the transfer of global power from the West, and in particular the US, to the rising powers of Asia, and notably China. This will have all kinds of implications, many of them quite profound. It has always been clear that dominant theoretical and policy paradigms can only be established and maintained with strong pressure from a major global power. The US exerted the power necessary to establish and defend the neo-liberal orthodoxy, but with the decline of Washington and the rise of Beijing things will be different. China is of course actively promoting its interests and the strengths of its development model with a deliberate campaign to enhance its 'soft power' through a well-financed 'charm offensive' (Kurlantzick 2007).

A key consequence of this renewed attraction of Asian approaches to development policy and planning is that the role of the state – and indeed the very nature of the state – has returned as a central issue of our age. The fact that China's economy is still under very direct control of the state, that a significant proportion of the economy is still state-owned, that the nature of China's links with the global economy are tightly constrained and that the country was able to weather the GFC so well, has not gone unnoticed in the rest of the developing world (Subramanian 2011). The need to strengthen state capacity and regulatory reach has emerged as one of the key lessons of the GFC: the state should now not be seen as a key problem but as an indispensible part of any viable solution. Markets unaided cannot be relied on to deliver the benefits of development since market failures are endemic, even in developed countries. This lesson is certainly being heeded in a wide range of countries where various kinds of 'state capitalism' have been established. Aware of the economic power of capitalist systems but unwilling to trust the operations of uncontrolled markets, several countries are using carefully regulated markets to create wealth but are ensuring that the funds are used as the government sees most appropriate (Bremmer 2010).

This re-evaluation of the role of the state also raises questions about the future of democracy. Halper (2010) fears that with the rise of China authoritarian forms of government will again become more attractive, but Dani Rodrik (2011) presents a rather different kind of argument about the future of democracy. He suggests that after the GFC we now realise that the simultaneous pursuit of democracy, self-determination and economic globalization is not feasible. If nations need the ability to defend their own economies and citizens at times of financial crisis, and if the frequency and impacts of such crises are to be lessened, then it is the nature of globalization that must be re-defined: we must return to the idea that international economic rules need to be subservient to domestic policy, not the other way round. A less ambitious globalization would be better for the vast majority.

At a rather different scale of analysis, the fundamental shifts in global power that are in process have given rise to a series of important studies on why, some two centuries or so ago, the West rose to a position of unchallenged world dominance, what factors were crucial, and how this leadership position of the North Atlantic powers is being challenged by developing Asia. Kenneth Pomeranz (2000) has shown that at the time of Britain's industrial revolution some areas of China were equally well positioned to take off but were left behind by a rapidly expanding Europe. The explanation for this 'great divergence', he argues, was that parts of Britain had easy access to high quality coal deposits essential for early industrialisation, but even more important were the major advantages, including raw materials of various kinds, provided by the acquisition of extensive new colonies. Taking a much longer historical perspective, Ian Morris (2010) similarly concludes that the biggest advantage that the West had was one of geography, and in particular easier access to the vast resources of the New World. Geography will continue to be an unequal force in the future, but he speculates that the uneven consequences of climatic change will be a major factor in future development, and Asia's proximity to an arc of instability stretching through much of Africa through the Middle East and India and into South East Asia will cause many problems. Niall Ferguson (2011) has also weighed into this debate arguing that there were six major factors that allowed the West to gain global dominance – intense competition within Europe itself; the scientific revolution in the seventeenth century; the rule of law and representative government; the development of modern medicine; the emergence of the consumer society; and the work ethic. All of this allowed sustained capital accumulation, but by now the East has absorbed all of this technology and its associated lessons, while the West has sunk into a massive crisis of debt that could destroy the whole edifice quite quickly, a process highlighted and intensified by the GFC. Thus, development theory now has to grapple again with these large scale and long-term issues, questions that were familiar in the writings of the Marxist historians, but which for some time were submerged by the more immediate analyses of the neo-liberals.

But this kind of analysis also raises some new questions that will challenge our established theories. For the first time for several centuries developing Asia is replacing the North Atlantic region as the main driving force of the global economy, and the G8 and the other cosy clubs of the rich nations are challenged by new groupings such as the BRICS (Brazil, Russia, India, China, South Africa). Will the old imperial relationship between the rich and powerful be re-established, albeit in a revised form, or are, for example, China's relationships with Africa and Latin America very different from British or French colonialism? Michel and Beuret (2009) report that many Africans believe that China is not just interested in economic exploitation – offering generous assistance with infrastructural, health and educational development – but the evidence of this is still rather sparse.

Perhaps the most fundamental question of all for development theory relates to the whole nature of the debate – if indeed the developing economies are now poised to become the main driving force of global growth while the West is entering a prolonged period of austerity and low growth. Nancy Birdsall (2011) has even asked whether the GFC might mark the end of 'development' as an idea to be replaced by a more global agenda for co-operation. This is all far from clear, but there is no doubt that we live in extremely interesting times for our discipline, as the tsunami that was the GFC necessitates a fundamental reassessment of development's theoretical underpinnings.

Chapter 3

Aid and Development

Janet Hunt

As development thinking has changed, so have fashions in aid. This chapter considers the various ideas and approaches that have shaped international development assistance for over half a century, looks at the various motives for co-operation and assesses the current state and role of development co-operation in light of globalization. It also considers the role that development co-operation is playing towards achievement of the Millennium Development Goals and that future aid will play in development.

The purpose of aid

Underlying development assistance is the idea of an implicit 'international social contract'. That is, there is a broad understanding amongst developed countries that in order for the world to become a moderately equitable place, or at least to alleviate some of the worst suffering, there needs to be some form of international assistance. For some developed countries, this follows a perceived sense of responsibility following the process of decolonization. For others, it is intended to assist less developed states to reduce the probability of their further decline and potential for instability. Many donors provide aid not only for humanitarian reasons, but to enhance their own economic, political and strategic interests, through encouraging their exports, or shaping the economic policies or political persuasion of recipient countries and 'stabilizing' other states. The alternative term 'development co-operation' perhaps captures some of these mutual benefits that have often been influential in the nature and direction of aid.

Historical background

It is generally believed that the idea that wealthier countries could assist poorer ones to develop originated at the end of the Second World War.

However, its origins are really earlier than that, since between 1929 and 1941 the League of Nations provided China with 30 technical experts in areas such as health, education, transport and rural co-operatives (Rist 1997: 65). Following the war, assistance started on a much larger scale with the formation of the United Nations and its specialized agencies, and the establishment in 1944 of the International Bank for Reconstruction and Development (IBRD) and the International Monetary Fund (IMF). The initial role of the IBRD, better known as the World Bank, was to raise capital for the reconstruction of Europe and Japan, while the IMF was to promote international monetary stability. The first loans to developing countries were to Latin American countries in 1948 and 1949 (Hellinger, Hellinger and O'Regan 1988: 14; Ryrie 1995: 4–5).

US bilateral assistance began in 1948, with the Marshall Plan to assist with Western European reconstruction in the face of advancing communism in Eastern Europe; soon foreign economic aid was integrated with military aid to meet Cold War objectives (Zimmerman 1993: 8).

The idea that there could be a concerted international effort to address poverty and underdevelopment is attributed to President Truman, whose inauguration speech announced continuing support for the UN, the Marshall Plan, and the establishment of NATO. His fourth point was aid: 'We must embark on a bold new program for making the benefits of our scientific advances and industrial progress available for the improvement and growth of underdeveloped areas' (Rist 1997: 71). The late 1940s and the 1950s was a period of optimism, in which people believed that it was indeed possible to eradicate hunger and misery resulting from underdevelopment, perhaps within a decade (Hoffman 1997).

The underlying theory was that growth in developing countries would create development, and that it would be achieved through large investments of capital, coupled with technical expertise. The emphasis was on modernization and industrialization, using surplus labour from rural areas to achieve import substitution (Tarp 2000: 19–23). Keynesian economic theory was the order of the day, with its emphasis on government investment adding further intellectual support for the value of providing foreign aid.

European aid programmes developed strongly in the 1960s as European countries recovered from war and were in a position to join the effort to assist the developing world. In particular, as decolonization of Asia and Africa proceeded, former colonial powers, such as France and Britain, launched major development assistance programmes to their former colonies.

Although the Organisation for Economic Co-operation and Development (OECD, i.e., 'developed') countries account for by far the largest proportion of aid, it is important to recognize that non-OECD countries, particularly the Eastern bloc during the Cold War, were involved too. USSR was initially active supporting Eastern European reconstruction, but later turned its attention to other Cold War 'fronts', notably in Asia and parts of Africa. For much of the Cold War period, the USSR and its Warsaw Pact allies accounted for almost 10 per cent of aid (Manning 2006: 372) and China assisted African countries such as Tanzania and Somalia from the 1960s onwards (Nayyar 1977; Manning 2006; Klare and Anderson 1996). Following the end of the Cold War and as a result of economic 'opening' in the former communist world, Russia and some other Eastern bloc countries themselves became recipients of OECD aid.

In the lead-up to and during the oil boom of the early 1970s, Arab countries also provided assistance to developing countries. Indeed, in 1978, aid from OPEC countries reached a peak of 30 per cent of global aid (Manning 2006: 373), though it subsequently declined. Today these countries remain active again, along with other so-called 'emerging donors', countries such as Turkey, Mexico, Korea and Brazil, along with China, India and Russia that actually continue long-standing roles (Manning 2006; Kharas 2009; Kragelund 2008: World Bank 2010a).[1]

Perhaps what is new about these emerging non-DAC donors is the scale and assertiveness of their efforts and the competition they are bringing into the aid system (Woods 2008). Some 30 or more such countries now provide aid (Paulo and Reisen 2010) and some are already equalling or surpassing the smaller DAC donors in the amounts of aid they provide. Their aid is often tied to procurement of goods and services in the donor country and complemented by trade and investment (Paulo and Reisen 2010; ODI 2010; Chun, Munyi and Lee 2010). Indeed aid from Arab countries, especially Saudi Arabia, Kuwait and the United Arab Emirates, averaged 1.5 per cent of GNI in the period 1973–2008, more than double the UN target and five times the average of DAC countries (World Bank 2010a).

Interestingly, the idea of providing aid through non-government organizations preceded these government initiatives. The origins of non-government aid can be traced to between the First and Second World Wars, often in response to the victims of war and conflict, although it should be recognized that the Red Cross had already been established as early as 1863 (Stubbings 1992: 5), while 'proto-aid' charitable organizations, notably Christian missions, existed prior to that. As Smillie notes (1995: 37–9), Save the Children was founded in 1919 to help the child victims of the First World War. Foster Parents Plan (now Plan International), which began in 1937, was a response to the Spanish Civil War, again to help the child victims. Oxfam began in 1942, during the Second World War, to provide famine relief to victims of the Greek civil war; CARE started by sending food parcels from the USA to Europe in 1946 and World Vision began slightly later in response to the victims of the Korean War. These are among the major international non-governmental organizations (NGOs) today.

The role of the private sector in development co-operation, through major philanthropic foundations such as the Open Society Institute and the Bill and Melinda Gates Foundation, has flourished during the 1990s. And the latest development in giving has been the emergence of significant online philanthropy, through websites such as GlobalGiving and Kiva that link individual donors to projects in developing countries (Desai and Kharas 2010: 1113). It remains to be seen how this particular trend will affect the direction and effectiveness of privately gifted aid.

How much aid, to whom?

In the early years of aid, it was felt that 6 per cent economic growth was needed in developing countries to address the poverty and misery people were experiencing. To achieve the necessary capital investment to gain this level of growth, it was suggested, would require 0.7 per cent of the GNP of the developed nations (Jolly 1999: 36–7). This is the origin of the target for aid set in 1970, but still current today, more honoured in the breach than in its realization. Only five of the 22 member countries of the OECD Development Assistance Committee – Denmark, Netherlands, Sweden, Norway and Luxembourg – meet the 0.7 per cent target (OECD 2010b: 99).

After initial growth during the 1970s, between the early 1980s and the late 1990s, aid levels fell steadily from around 0.36 per cent GNP to an average of 0.22 per cent GNP (German and Randel 2002: 149) despite rapidly growing per capita wealth in OECD countries in that period (Padilla and Tomlinson 2006: 4).

Following UN members states' commitment to the Millennium Development Goals in Year 2000, and in particular, the G8 'Gleneagles Agreement' of 2005 to increase total aid by $50 billion by 2010 (Tomlinson 2010: 157), total ODA experienced an unprecedented increase, growing by 30 per cent in real terms between 2004 and 2009 (UNDP 2010: 32). Today the average level of aid provided by DAC donors has risen to 0.31 of GNI. It peaked at 0.32 per cent GNI in 2005 but has declined unevenly since then to its 2009 level of $110.4 billion (Tomlinson 2010: 155). The Gleneagles Agreement target was missed by some $20 billion (Tomlinson 2010). Historically, the pattern of aid growth has always been uneven (Tarp 2000: 85; German and Randel 2002: 145; Padilla and Tomlinson 2006: 3).

While US aid was significant in the early decades, by 1980 the European countries were providing more than twice as much as the US (Ryrie 1995: 10). In dollar terms the US, the UK, Germany and France now contribute the largest amounts of bilateral aid, and the European Union members of the DAC provide a total of 58 per cent of all DAC aid (OECD 2010b: 97); the contribution of the USA as a percentage of its GNI is small, 0.19 per cent of GNI in 2008 (OECD 2010c: 172). However, over the decades, Official Development Assistance (ODA) has grown in volume from some US$8 billion a year in the first half of the 1950s (in 1987 value) until the total value of OECD aid peaked at US$122 billion in 2008 (Tomlinson 2010).

In efforts to bring greater focus onto the quality and direction of aid, not simply the volume, over the years, two significant indicators have been used. One relates to the proportion of aid going to least developed (LLD) countries and less developed (LD) countries, the other to the proportion of aid being spent on Basic Social Services (BSS), such as health services, education, potable water and sanitation (Jolly 1999). The emphasis on the LLD countries reflected concern in the UN and among NGOs at the distortions of aid that led to relatively high proportions flowing to middle-income developing countries. The measure of Basic Social Services was proposed by UNICEF and UNDP at the World Summit on Social Development in 1995 as part of a proposed compact in which 20 per cent of development assistance and 20 per cent of developing country government expenditure should be devoted to basic services in areas such as health, family planning, education, nutrition, water and sanitation. Expenditure on sectors such as basic health and basic education in 1995 and 1996 were a mere 1.8 per cent and 1.2 per cent of total ODA respectively for the 12 donors who managed to report against these measures, but the idea never really took off (Randel and German 1997: 249).

Most recently, attention has switched to the extent to which aid is being directed towards achieving the MDGs, a set of eight goals with clear targets and measurable indicators, agreed at the UN Millennium Summit in September 2000, which to some extent address the above concerns in a new guise. In this case, more serious measurement and reporting regimes have been instituted (United Nations 2006), and the significant financing gap to achieve the goals by 2015 was calculated, although not filled (Padilla and Tomlinson 2006: 3). A further measure of aid quality introduced by NGOs in 2010 in their annual critique of official aid, 'The Reality of Aid', is the calculation of 'real aid'. 'Real aid' discounts three areas of expenditure DAC donors are allowed to count as part of their ODA: debt cancellation; the costs of supporting developing country refugees for their first year as residents of donor countries; and the estimated costs of educational infrastructure for developing country students studying in donor countries. NGOs argue that these cannot be viewed as legitimate aid expenditures (Tomlinson 2010: 152–6).

The geographical distribution of aid has changed significantly over the decades. These shifts reflect the changing dynamics of development, as Asian countries like India and China make gains in poverty reduction while high levels of poverty persist in Africa. In 1961, almost a quarter of all aid went to the Middle East and North Africa, 20 per cent to South Asia and less than 10 per cent to sub-Saharan Africa (Ryrie 1995: 12). By 2008, 41 per cent of ODA went to Africa, 12 per cent to the Americas, 40 per cent to Asia and 8 per cent to other regions (Tomlinson 2010: 173).[2] Since the mid-2000s, Iraq has topped the recipients list, with Nigeria and Afghanistan also major recipients (OECD 2010a). In fact, since the inception of the 'War on Terror' three countries – Iraq, Afghanistan and Pakistan – received 17 per cent of all new aid committed from 2000–08 (Tomlinson 2010: 160).

Shifts have also occurred in the sectoral distribution of aid. In the early period there was a very strong emphasis on economic infrastructure development, but the largest allocation is now to social infrastructure (40 per cent). In 2005 aid expenditure on debt relief, a dubious use of aid, peaked at 28 per cent but has now reduced to 10 per cent of ODA. Since 2000 an increased amount of aid, averaging 8.3 per cent annually, is spent on emergency humanitarian assistance. Whilst some increases reflect major emergencies such as the 2004 Asian tsunami and the Kashmir earthquake in 2005, a sharp increase in 2008 reflected increases to Afghanistan and US food aid to Ethiopia (GHA 2010). Despite their high public profile, support to NGOs is less than 5 per cent of official development assistance (OECD DAC 2006 and 2007).

Usually around 70 per cent of aid is provided through bilateral channels, that is, directly from one country to another. The remainder, apart from the small amount through NGOs, is provided through multilateral organizations, which include the various specialized UN agencies such as the World Food Programme, the World Health Organization, UNICEF, UN High Commission for Refugees and United Nations

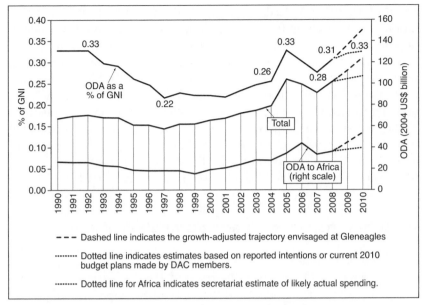

Source: OECD *Development Co-operation Report Summary 2010*, p. 2.

Figure 3.1   *DAC members' net ODA 1990–2008 and DAC Secretariat simulations of net ODA to 2009 and 2010*

Development Programme. The international financial institutions, especially the concessional arms of the World Bank and the various regional development banks (e.g., Asian Development Bank, Inter-American Development Bank), are also included. Some new multilateral funds, such as the Global Fund to fight AIDS, tuberculosis and malaria, have earned growing support. However, the share of ODA through multilateral channels, which has generally hovered around 30 per cent of ODA, is eroding slightly. The share of ODA to United Nations agencies in particular has dropped in the last decade (OECD 2010d).

Aid from emerging donors is not included in the DAC calculations of ODA, and issues arise about the definitions and transparency of such aid from some of the emerging donors. What is clear is that they tend to emphasize the productive sectors of the economy rather than social sectors in their assistance (Kragelund 2008).

However, beyond ODA and non-DAC aid from 'emerging donors', aid from all private sources (such as NGOs, religious groups and private philanthropy) at US$60 billion per year is growing fast and now getting close to the level of bilateral aid (at $73 billion per year) and is attracting more scholarly attention (Kharas 2009; Hudson Institute 2010; Davis and Dadush 2010). Indeed, research is highlighting the overall fragmentation of aid, resulting from the new range of donors and the proliferation of institutions within donor countries that now provide aid.

Also attracting more attention is the development value of remittances sent by developing country workers overseas back to their home countries. These have grown rapidly since 2002. At $338 billion in 2008, these far exceed ODA, and have been relatively steady even through the global recession. The largest recipients are India, China and Mexico, but in a number of countries remittances, though smaller, now account for more than 25 per cent of GDP. These include Tajikistan, Tonga, Moldova, Kyrgyszstan and Lesotho (Hudson Institute 2010: 58–71).

What has shaped levels and distribution of aid?

There can be no doubt that colonial histories, foreign policy and trade objectives have had a major influence on both the levels and distribution of aid. In particular, the Cold War and other geopolitical objectives have shaped aid levels and distribution, thereby reducing aid's effectiveness in poverty reduction (World Bank 2002c: 5; Human Rights Watch 2002).

This has been particularly the case for the US and a number of larger aid donors (by volume) such as France. Tarp (2000) shows that aid from smaller countries, such as Sweden, has been better shaped by the needs of recipient countries than that of other, larger donors.

The dramatic skewing of US aid in favour of Israel and Egypt for foreign policy purposes illustrates the geopolitical use of aid (Zimmerman 1993). As Ryrie says:

> In 1991, one country, Egypt, received no less than 32 per cent of American aid and Israel, a relatively rich country, 8 per cent. These figures exclude military aid. Nicaragua and Honduras between them received another 4 per cent, while the whole of sub-Saharan Africa got 3.6 and India, 0.8 per cent.   (Ryrie 1995: 13)

Such a distribution was clearly not needs-based. If aid has not been wholly effective in relation to its publicly promoted humanitarian objectives, it may have been far more successful in achieving its other, less trumpeted, yet often more calculated goals.

Some of the better known abuses of aid include Japan's allocations to leverage votes from small states to support its pro-whaling stance in the International Whaling Commission, and the way numerous donors promote trade through a host of mixed credit schemes (see for example Bain 1996).

Another commercial aspect of aid has been the fact that over decades much of it has been 'tied' to developed country providers. Such involvement of private sector companies based in donor countries has been roundly criticized as costly to developing countries. Tying may require firms who manage projects to be registered in the donor country, procure commodities, such as food aid, from donor sources, and place donor country expatriates in developing countries as technical advisers (Simons et al. 1997: 187; Randel and German 2002: 14-15; Padilla and Tomlinson 2006: 14, OECD DAC 2007a). Technical assistance (supply of developed country 'experts') is also a large component of total aid. In 2002, still 38 per cent of total bilateral ODA was technical co-operation (Randel, German and Ewing 2004: 21) with the World Bank suggesting that 100,000 foreign technical experts were employed in Africa alone in 1999 – an incredible number.

The linkage of tertiary education places to universities in donor countries is a further aspect of aid tying, which has also distorted educational aid strongly in favour of tertiary education rather than basic or primary education. For example, examining Australia's educational assistance in the first half of the 1990s, around 70–75 per cent went to tertiary level while only 6–10 per cent went to primary and secondary combined, despite the fact that research has consistently shown high social rates of return for spending on primary education (Simons 1997: 130–33).

Overall, some progress has been made since 2000 in untying aid, with recent figures suggesting only 17 per cent of 2007 aid was tied (Clay, Geddes and Natali 2009). However, the large US food aid contribution remains tied, and technical assistance (which is excluded from this figure) remains at 2002 levels as a proportion of total aid. In 2008 at the Accra High Level Forum, donors pledged to plan the further untying of their aid, but even when aid is untied it seems donor-based companies still gain a high percentage of aid contracts (Tomlinson 2010: 176).

The post-Cold War decline in aid since 1992 has been accompanied by a rise in private sector investment in selected developing countries, notably China and Latin America. This was the period when debt rescheduling and structural adjustment lending began in earnest; donors recognized that debt service repayments, sometimes greater than the aid countries received, were crippling certain low-income highly indebted developing countries, so policy change was needed.

Aid has also been shaped by new agendas, and since the 1990s, influenced by the view that it is only effective where 'good policies' are in place. 'Good policies' really mean policies consistent with the so-called

'Washington Consensus', or the particular brand of neo-liberalism being promoted by Anglophone countries in the donor community. At the same time, a commitment to the 1996 DAC goals, and the subsequent MDGs agreed in 2000, to halve the proportion of people living in poverty and their associated social goals has influenced donor governments to re-assess where aid was going, what effect it was having and whether the goals could be reached. The focus turned to assisting those countries where poverty is significant but where 'good governance' policies were in place (Dollar and Levine 2006). Yet initially donors varied considerably in the extent to which their aid was really focusing on achieving the MDGs (Baulch 2004) and Tomlinson noted that, despite aid growth, there was initially not a real shift to the MDG sectors of education, health, food security and poverty reduction; rather foreign policy and debt reduction drove the direction of new aid spending. However, since 2008, the focus on MDGs has improved, with 42 per cent of new aid going to support their attainment (Tomlinson 2010).

However, it is fair to say that from 2001 foreign policy objectives have reasserted themselves in aid agendas – signalled in December 2001, when the USA pledged Pakistan over US$1 billion in debt forgiveness, investment, trade and refugee relief (Jefferys 2002: 3). This was clearly associated with the US Government's 'war on terror' policy (Human Rights Watch 2002) and its need to maintain a close alliance with Pakistan because of its engagement in neighbouring Afghanistan. OECD countries have since seen development co-operation as a useful tool in their fight against terrorism: 'OECD aid to Afghanistan increased tenfold between 1999 and 2003' and 'in the case of the UK, Iraq became the top recipient of bilateral aid in 2003/4 ... usurping India' (Howell 2006: 125). Indeed, between them, these two countries received 37 per cent of the total new aid funds from 2002–06, most of the rest going to debt relief, technical co-operation and other emergencies (Padilla and Tomlinson 2006: 14). Iraq, Afghanistan and Pakistan remain major aid recipients in 2008, indicating the continuing impact of the 'war on terror' on aid disbursements (OECD 2010a). And while the OECD DAC's agreement to allow debt write-off to count as ODA may have contributed slightly to reducing indebtedness it failed to contribute new aid money to developing countries. In addition, donors such as the USA, Australia and Denmark have incorporated anti-terrorist activities through a range of programmes criticized as dealing with threats to the rich through programmes intended for the poor (Padilla and Tomlinson 2006: 11; Spillane 2004: 167; Hameiri 2008). Thus just as an 'aid effectiveness' agenda was gaining ground, the geopolitics of the 'war on terror' began to undermine it again. However, the effectiveness agenda has recently returned, in part no doubt sparked by the debate about the extent to which the MDGs are being met and in part due to the higher profile of increased aid budgets, particularly at a time of global financial recession.

What has aid been like?

Though the goals of aid have remained much the same, the ways donors aim to achieve them have altered considerably over the years. Moseley and Eeckhout found that: 'The project aid component of aid budgets has declined severely from the early 1970s (sometimes to the point of collapse) and other aid instruments have expanded to fill the vacuum, notably technical co-operation, policy-conditioned programme aid, support for the private sector and for NGOs and emergency assistance' (Moseley and Eeckhout 2000: 131).

In the early 1970s the 'Basic Needs' approach extended the 'development project' into new areas, such as agricultural development, health and education. The processes of development immediately became more complex and less predictable than the earlier physical infrastructure projects. In particular a trend towards large 'integrated rural development projects' greatly increased the complexity of development tasks. The weaknesses and problems that such projects faced led to greater focus on government policy environments as a key factor in successful development.

Following the oil price shocks and the US dropping of the gold standard, and the consequent economic upheavals, at the end of the 1970s, Keynesian economic policies gave way to neo-classicism. In line with this, the World Bank's promotion of Basic Needs Approaches ended, and attention turned to macroeconomic policies. The economic recession at the beginning of the 1980s, and the associated debt defaults first triggered by Mexico, led to a major rethink in development circles. An aid mechanism was needed now which could quickly help stabilize the economies of deeply indebted poor countries, where private sector investment had dried up. Thus began lending and balance of payments support that was predicated on IMF-directed 'structural adjustment' programmes, requiring recipient countries to liberalize and deregulate their economies. By the mid-1990s, the World Bank had also moved towards emphasizing structural adjustment packages, which became 'about a third of World Bank lending and just under 20 per cent of the bilateral aid budgets of the OECD countries' (Moseley and Eeckhout 2000: 136–7); many countries are still experiencing those processes in

2010. As Moseley and Eeckhout note, there were at least three major problems with this type of assistance: weak implementation, ineffectiveness in stimulating economies, and negative side effects.

Though countries undergoing structural adjustment found that their export trade improved, investment deteriorated, poverty increased as services reduced and the impacts on growth were unconvincing (Moseley and Eeckhout 2000: 136–9). Many developing countries became more vulnerable to negative influences on the trading environment, such as hyper-competitive pricing for imports against a local manufacturing market, and in a bid to compete primarily on the basis of low wage rates, developing countries tended to bargain each other downwards, which had a negative impact on levels and distribution of income (Morrissey 2000).

Thus the next phase was to shift to other mechanisms, notably through the private sector and, on a much smaller scale, through NGOs. For example, there were significant increases in World Bank funds to the International Finance Corporation which supports private sector development in the developing world (Ryrie 1995: 121–61). The OECD emphasizes that, in general, 'countries which have used market opportunities and developed dynamic private sectors have fared better than those that have not' (OECD 1989: 78–9). It urges donor governments to assist developing countries to meet the preconditions for developing a vibrant private sector (OECD 1989). The abolition of monopolies, strengthening competition, an appropriate regulatory environment, efficient banking, transport and communication facilities are among these requirements which aid began to address.

A more recent mechanism for aid goes beyond 'projects' to the development of sector-wide approaches, or SWAPs. These are specific programmes within a sector with specific objectives which fall somewhere between the project level and the macroeconomic support of structural adjustment lending. SWAPs are favoured in poor, highly aid-dependent countries and have been most frequently used in health and education sectors. These SWAPs enable donor funds to be integrated into sectoral budgets to expand programmes in agreed ways and, in theory, facilitate donor co-ordination to support developing country government planning and priorities. However, in reality, the weakness of donor co-ordination, and the extent of donor intervention and oversight, means that such strategies are far from the ideal in giving recipient governments a greater chance to drive development (Randel and German 2002: 17: Cassity 2010).

Many donor countries are changing the mechanisms through which aid is provided to try to make it more effective, although the problem of 'donor proliferation' remains significant, (Acharya, de Lima and Moore 2004; Frot and Santiso 2010; AusAID 2010a). Fengler and Kharas observe that 'growth in aid agencies has proceeded as fast as growth in aid dollars.'(2010: 6). They have documented 233 multilateral aid agencies and 56 donor governments with official aid agencies, some with several agencies that are involved in development programmes. Add to this a vast array of private funding agencies and the complexity of the aid system becomes apparent.

The emphasis on greater donor co-ordination and support for developing country planning has flowed from earlier initiatives by the World Bank to promote the Comprehensive Development Frameworks (CDFs) and Poverty Reduction Strategy Plans (PRSPs) at national level. These frameworks embraced a wide range of development partners beyond national governments, while the PRSPs were intended to be participatory exercises to assist governments to focus on policies and programmes to reduce poverty. Their success appears to have been limited, due in part at least to a failure to appreciate the political power dynamics operating in recipient countries (Booth 2011). It is within this context that greater support for SWAPs and budget support has been emerging. Old policy 'conditionality', which is generally considered to have failed, has been replaced by new efforts to generate greater aid effectiveness through a raft of reforms.

Central to these reforms is the *Paris Declaration on Aid Effectiveness* (2005), developed through the OECD Development Assistance Committee. The aim of this Declaration is to reform aid management to reduce transaction costs for developing countries in aid administration, as aid flows increase. Its key principles are: developing country ownership of development policies, strategies and co-ordination; alignment of donor aid flows with national development strategies, with a single related framework of conditions or success indicators; greater harmonization of donor approaches to aid management; a focus on results; and mutual accountability for development performance. As well as the SWAP and PRSP mechanisms discussed above, budget support and basket funding (the latter involves donors jointly funding a programme or sector, or a budget) are increasingly being used to give effect to the Declaration. The *Accra Agenda for Action* adopted in 2008 extends the attempt to improve aid, through commitments relating to predictability of aid, use of country rather donor systems as a first option for aid delivery, changing conditionality away from donor prescriptions to recipient country development objectives, and further untying of aid (OECD DCD-DAC n.d).

However, despite all the effort to implement these principles for a more effective aid system, aid 'fragmentation', a new term in the aid lexicon, remains a major problem, with a number of obvious costs. Fengler and Kharas' research revealed that Cambodia receives over 400 donor missions each year 'and government officials report spending 50 per cent of their time meeting and reporting to donors.' (2010: 15). Some developing countries may have more than 2000 official development projects per year (Frot and Santiso 2010). And while the number of aid projects has dramatically increased, their average size has significantly reduced in the last 10–15 years (Fengler and Kharas 2010; Frot and Santiso 2010). Volatility of aid levels is a further problem particularly in countries in which political and security considerations play a large part in donor aid flows (Fengler and Kharas 2010: 17–19) or when 'the number of donors to a country is small, and when the aid budget is heavily concentrated within the forms of aid which are "reactive" to the recipient country's predicament, such as food aid, emergency aid, and program budget support aid' (Bulíř, Gelb and Mosley 2008: 2046). Strategies which reduce aid fragmentation and volatility, while retaining some flexibility, are seen as important for effective aid, along with approaches which align better with developing country budgets and priorities (Moon and Mills 2010).

While these aid effectiveness initiatives have been underway, the number and scale of natural disasters and complex humanitarian emergencies drove a considerable expansion of emergency relief funding during the 1990s and the 2000s. OECD aid for emergencies, around US$1 billion in 1990, had reached some US$10 billion by 2005, or 10 per cent of all aid (German and Randel 2002: 151; OECD DAC 2006, Table 18). With continuing emergencies in Sudan, Afghanistan, Ethiopia, Palestine and Somalia, humanitarian aid continued to rise to almost $12 billion in 2008, nearly 12 per cent of total ODA (excluding debt relief); it is likely to have dropped back to around 10 per cent of ODA by 2009 (GHI 2010: 5). However, as Jefferys (2002: 2) shows, emergency humanitarian aid is rarely dispersed according to need; rather it depends on the geopolitical interests of donors and, often as a result, the media profile of particular humanitarian situations. For example, major floods in Pakistan were much slower to attract funds than the Haiti earthquake for a number of possible reasons, including the less dramatic media that floods generate compared to earthquakes and a lack of confidence in the Pakistan government (Burki 2010). In another case, the enormous response to the 2004 Asian tsunami which led to US$7,100 being available for every person affected contrasts starkly with the US$3 per head available for those affected by the Bangladesh floods of the same year (Tsunami Evaluation Coalition 2006).

Many of the recipient countries of humanitarian assistance are conflict-affected states, and the ability of local and international humanitarian players to provide aid 'in a neutral, impartial and independent way' (DARA 2010: 9) and maintain humanitarian space in such locations has become more difficult. In particular, in places such as Afghanistan and Iraq, military forces have also been involved in aid activities, blurring the distinction between neutral humanitarian aid workers and combatants. Even in other types of emergency, such as Haiti's earthquake, military forces have been involved in the response to a far greater degree than in the past (GHI 2010: 9). The increasing politicization and 'securitization' (i.e. the use of aid to assure donor security) of aid risks distorting aid agendas and priorities and challenging the ability of humanitarian workers to meet the needs of affected populations (Collinson, Elhawary and Muggah 2010; DARA 2010; GHI 2010; Hamieri 2008; Jacoby and James 2010; Lischer 2007; Save the Children 2010).

Other major changes in aid in more recent decades have reflected greater attention to social and environmental rather than just economic aspects of development. The struggle to gain recognition that aid could contribute to gender inequality when it should be enhancing gender equity has been a long, hard one (see Chapter 10) and, whilst all donors now have gender policies, the translation of policy to practice is more difficult. Official donors have also adopted NGO language about participation, empowerment and community development, but rarely has the full import of these approaches been implemented. Genuinely inclusive and participatory aid requires major shifts in processes, attitudes and behaviours to really transform power relationships at organizational and interpersonal levels (Groves and Hinton 2004). These are hard to achieve, even for their original proponents, though Hickey and Mohan find that where participation is based firmly on citizenship rights, there appears to be some success (Hickey and Mohan 2005). Yet efforts to bring a rights-based approach to development co-operation, have struggled to gain legitimacy and enjoy practical application. In addition, changing global circumstances have brought a range of other aid agendas to attention, among them preventing the devastating spread of HIV AIDS, combating the trafficking of people, and promoting drug control through support to farmers to convert from growing opium to other crops.

Another area in which it has been difficult to make progress is the environmental sustainability of aid efforts, despite the attention brought to these issues by the Rio Earth Summit in 1992 and advocacy by environmental NGOs. The impact of climate change, particularly on agricultural and food production, and the likelihood of more frequent extreme weather events in developing countries, is, however, renewing attention to the link between environmental factors and development. In particular, debate is around how climate change mitigation and adaptation measures should be financed (Ayers and Huq 2009; Macintosh 2010; Porter et al. 2008; Tomlinson 2010). To date, the Global Environment Facility (GEF), established in 1991, is the financial mechanism for four United Nations environmental conventions (Porter et al. 2008). Since 2002 it has included a number of special funds which 'finance projects relating to climate change adaptation, technology transfer and capacity building in the various sectors, including energy, transport, industry, agriculture, forestry and waste management, as well as in economic diversification' (Porter et al. 2008: 13). The World Bank has also been a major financier in the area of climate change, particularly through its Clean Energy Investment Framework (CEIF) (Porter et al. 2008: 14). It also established a 'prototype carbon fund' in 1999 that has stimulated the development of 10 similar funds worth over $2 billion (Porter et al. 2008: 14). However, the Bank has been roundly criticized as its funding for renewable energy and energy-efficiency projects ($109 million in 2005) pales to insignificance in the face of its continuing funding for power generation projects through fossil fuel development and large dams (over $2.5 billion in 2005) (Porter et al. 2008: 17).

A further initiative is the UN's Collaborative Programme on Reducing Emissions from Deforestation and Forest Degradation in Developing Countries (UNREDD), launched in 2008. It is intended as a carbon-offset scheme whereby carbon emitters (whether corporations or governments) purchase carbon credits generated through the maintenance of carbon-storing forests in developing countries. Thus it provides financial incentives to developing countries 'to retain carbon stored in forests through reduced logging, fire, farmland expansion and infrastructure development. The UN estimates that financial flows for greenhouse gas emission reductions from REDD (now referred to as REDD+) could reach up to US$30 billion a year' (Considine 2010:1).[3] However, many risks have been highlighted that could jeopardise the extent to which such a scheme (or similar others) would significantly reduce deforestation or degradation and associated carbon emissions (Macintosh 2010). In addition to these major initiatives, and complicating the picture, many aid donors have developed or are developing their own climate change responses and funding mechanisms (Porter et al. 2008). Furthermore, there is concern that Climate Change expenditure, meant to be additional to donor's ODA commitments, does not divert ODA away from other important development priorities facing poor people who are not responsible for greenhouse gas emissions (Tomlinson 2010: 172–5).

How effective has aid been?

Clearly the stated purposes of aid are related to economic growth, the reduction of poverty and the alleviation of suffering. Aid is thus, correctly, assessed against such criteria. Over the years there have been some successes but they are not as great as many think they should have been. One reason for this is that aid has in fact been badly distorted by other agendas, whether diplomatic, strategic, or related to the economic self-interest of donor countries.

Because of the above-mentioned distortions, the efficacy of aid has been ambiguous. However, while recognizing the ambiguity of aspects of aid and its efficacy, Cassen notes that aid has helped make possible a number of significant achievements, from raising food production to building infrastructure (1994: 224). According to Cassen et al.: '[T]he majority of aid is successful in terms of its own objects. Over a wide range of countries and sectors, aid has made positive and valuable contributions' (1994: 225). More reprehensible failures from the donor side, according to Cassen, include using aid for commercial or political ends without regard for its supposed development objects, or from failing to learn from past mistakes in its application. However, Cassen does not discuss the 'reprehensibility' of aid misuse by recipient countries, for example, through corruption, redirection of aid and so on.

One approach to assessing the effectiveness of aid is to examine evaluations of aid programmes. The World Bank published a review of evaluations of development assistance in 1995 that drew five conclusions about the conditions that were necessary to make aid effective. These were:

- ownership by the government and participation of affected people – linked to the government's own commitment to poverty reduction;
- strong administrative and institutional capacity – an environment of 'good governance';
- sound policies and good public sector management – meaning governments facilitating open markets and investing in infrastructure and people;
- close co-ordination by donors – to simplify aid management for recipient governments;
- improvements in donors' own business practices – to focus less on inputs and more on effects of development at the country level. (World Bank 1995)

The emphasis on sound policies reinforced a continuing focus on con-ditionalities associated with World Bank and IMF loans provided as part of debt relief programmes. Such conditionalities have attracted considerable criticism and, despite indications that they are frequently too numerous and poorly implemented, they persist. A study of loans to 20 developing countries between 2002 and early 2006 indicated that, on average, 67 conditions were placed on World Bank loans to these countries. Notably, many of these related to controversial privatizations of essential services, such as energy or water supply; trade liberalization measures; and various measures unrelated to poverty reduction priori-ties (Kovach and Lansman 2006).

Much of the debate about the effectiveness of aid has been at a macro level, and has focused on the extent to which aid has contributed to growth in developing countries. The Burnside and Dollar (1997) study has been particularly influential in donor circles. It concluded that 'aid has a positive impact on growth in a good policy environment' (Hansen and Tarp 2000: 116). This fed into the World Bank's own study authored by Dollar, *Assessing Aid,* in 1998. Such work shaped a great deal of aid thinking since the late 1990s, in that a strong emphasis was placed on countries having sound policies in place. At a time when donors were reducing the number of countries to which they provided aid, to gain more focus and effectiveness in their aid programmes, con-sideration of developing country policy environments appears to have played a significant part in their selections (Battaile 2002: 2–3).

Hansen and Tarp (2000), who reviewed these studies of aid effective-ness, suggest that Dollar's and Burnside's conclusions are at best ques-tionable. They revisit the same data but conclude instead that aid has a positive impact on growth even where policies are poor. When other studies are also considered (e.g. Hadjimichael 1996), the conclusion they draw is that aid has a significant impact on growth, 'as long as the aid to GDP ratio is not excessively high' (Hansen and Tarp 2000: 118; Tarp 2000: 45). As they point out, in any case, the countries whose pol-icy environments are most conducive to good aid results may be those who need aid least. On the other hand, there is also the view that coun-tries that most need aid can quickly become aid dependent and fail to develop their own economic foundations, or that inappropriate aid sim-ply establishes a higher level of external debt (see Kanbur 2000: 410–16).

In a major review of aid effectiveness studies over 50 years with find-ings relating to the relationship between aid and growth, McGillivray et al. (2006) indicate these studies reveal that, in the absence of aid, growth would be lower but they find no consistency in the results about the policy contexts in which aid works. However, there appears to be some evidence that there can be decreasing returns to higher levels of aid within countries, that relatively stable levels of aid, rather than volatility, increase effectiveness; that aid has greater impact on growth in countries outside the tropical zones, and that aid is only effective when the country is politically stable and its benefits are greater if a country is more democratic. Burnside and Dollar have also refined their argument to emphasize that institutions, rather than policies, are what matter for aid effectiveness. McGillivray et al. also note that the evidence suggests 'that aid clearly worked at the micro level' (2006: 1045) in contrast to the debate about its macro outcomes.

Overall, a reassessment of these neo-liberal policies, associated with reducing the scope of the state and enhancing the scope of the market, is now developing. This came about largely because empirical evidence demonstrated that during the period of neo-liberalism overall economic growth had been slower than in earlier decades, the gap between the rich and poor countries widened and Africa in particular, which had been the subject of many of the 'Washington Consensus' prescriptions, performed poorly. East Asian countries, on the other hand, did well but their success, initially used to bolster arguments in favour of export-led growth, was reinterpreted to recognize the interventionist policies and appropriate mix of state and market mechanisms that had led to their achievements (Onis and Senses 2005). Most particularly, the success of countries such as Vietnam and China, whose active industrial development policies clearly differed from neo-liberal prescriptions, have demonstrated that states can play some critically important roles in development.

The emerging 'Post-Washington Consensus' articulated by Onis and Senses (2005), and supported by economists such as Joseph Stiglitz (2002), suggests that actions by states can improve the functioning of the market, for example by good regulation of the financial system, but at the same time the market can improve the functioning of states. The key point is that it is competition between public and private services, rather than privatization itself, which may drive efficiencies. Other important roles for the state include investment in education and infrastructure, support for dissemination of new technologies, and pro-poor interventions (Onis and Senses 2006: 274–5). Thus recent thinking about development focuses on the performance of both the state and market simultaneously, 'institution-building and democratic governance' and 'the importance of additional policies to deal with key social problems such as pervasive unemployment, poverty and inequality' (Onis and Senses 2006: 277). Indeed, Booth's research tracking development of Asian and African countries over 50 years shows that while institutions matter, policies are important as well. The more successful Asian countries had all 'adopted policies that combined (i) macro-economic balance, (ii) rural-biased public investment and (iii) economic freedom for smallholders', whereas none of the African countries had done so (Booth 2011: s8). In particular Booth highlights the importance of agricultural policies, a point emphasised as far back as the late 1970s.

One of the most recent consequences of the intense debate about the effectiveness of aid and accountability of donors is the call for greater transparency about where aid goes and what it does. The first Aid Transparency Assessment was published in 2010, finding a wide variation in donor transparency and a lack of comparable data (Publish What You Fund 2010). Another response, particularly among civil society organisations, has been the development of charters and standards, initially for humanitarian response, but now covering development work as well (HAP International 2008: The Sphere Project 2004: INGO Accountability Charter 2006). However, as Eyben (2008) points out, it is important to reflect on the *processes* of mutual accountability, address the power imbalances and engage in relational dialogue that respects diversity of views and allows for adaptive learning if aid is to become more effective.

Criticisms of aid

Yet, even as new calls for an emphasis on poverty reduction and recognition of the failings of the Washington Consensus gain some traction, criticisms remain about the power inequalities implicit in the aid system, and indeed in the wider global political and economic arrangements which keep poor countries poor.

For example, NGOs argued that as a result of the 'Post-Washington Consensus', the 'governance' agenda was being distorted to allow the powerful international financial institutions further opportunities to impose their policy agendas on developing countries, creating unrealistic and non-democratic demands on them for major public sector reform (Randel et al. 2004). NGOs argued for a greater focus on democratic accountability mechanisms and a human-rights based approach to development which would enable poor people to act as citizens, rather than be the objects of externally imposed policy prescriptions.

Non-government organizations had earlier made concerted criticisms of a number of major aid projects, specifically those supported by the World Bank and/or the Asian Development Bank, such as Kedung

Ombo, Narmada and Arun (Nepal). These campaigns led in turn to a range of demands for changes in World Bank *policies* in areas such as information disclosure, resettlement, an Inspection panel to monitor Bank compliance with its own policies, indigenous peoples' policy and various improvements in environmental and social policies (Fox and Brown 1998; Rumansara 1998; Siwakoti 2002).

Of course aid has always had its critics, both from the left and the right of the political spectrum. Some focus on aid as a concept, which distracts from other more significant reforms needed or which fails overall to deliver its claimed benefits, others on the failings of specific projects or types of aid. Quite early on, the Basic Human Needs approach to aid was criticized for being an attempt to thwart developing country efforts to push for a new International Economic Order (Galtung 1997). Others asserted that development assistance was simply a new form of post-colonial control and imperialism: 'Whatever the form of aid, or even trade, we see no realistic way in which rich nations can transfer resources to the poor without pursuing their own profits and expanding their own power' (Weissman 1975: 13). Over a quarter of a century later, the non-government organizations which together write and publish *The Reality of Aid* asserted that the conditionalities increasingly associated with aid enable the donors to exert power over developing countries. The trends of the 1980s and 1990s, as they say, brought about a new global order 'dramatically at odds with the New International Economic Order' (Randel and German 2002: 6).

As they pointed out, despite the rhetoric of the Development Assistance Committee about a new emphasis on partnership and ownership of development programmes and projects, the donor country imposition of countless conditionalities served to push the Washington Consensus policies onto aid-receiving countries, particularly through economic adjustment programmes. The contrasts between the policies that developing country governments were forced to pursue and those enjoyed by developed countries is the ultimate hypocrisy which NGOs decried: 'southern governments are forced to privatise and liberalise, while OECD restrictive practices, tariff and non-tariff barriers cost developing countries US$160 billion a year' (Randel and German 2002: 5). Hancock (1989) also criticizes official development assistance as a concept, though his grounds are different and, unlike NGOs, he has no faith that it can be reformed. He argues that the bureaucratic institutions that manage aid are secretive, bloated and self-serving. He is particularly critical of a host of failed and unsustainable projects that have often left governments indebted while donor-country private corporations responsible for the project implementation walk away with handsome profits. Furthermore, relative to other economic flows, he says, aid is insignificant, and indeed, writing at the end of the decade, he notes that the so-called 'donor' countries have in fact been net recipients of funds from the developing countries since the early 1980s. At the same time, Hancock says there is enough aid to do harm:

> it is often profoundly dangerous to the poor and inimical to their interests; it has financed the creation of monstrous projects that, at vast expense, have devastated the environment and ruined lives; it has supported and legitimised brutal tyrannies; it has facilitated the emergence of fantastical and Byzantine bureaucracies staffed by legions of self-serving hypocrites; it has sapped the initiative, creativity and enterprise of ordinary people and substituted the superficial and irrelevant glitz of imported advice.   (Hancock 1989: 189)

Easterly has reinforced arguments made earlier by Bauer (1993) that aid is not the solution to raising living standards in developing countries. He argues that the $2.3 trillion spent on foreign aid since its inception have failed to impact on growth and the world's poor and the reasons are frequently to do with poor governance and politics, which aid cannot resolve (Easterly 2006). McGillivray et al.'s research (2006) suggests that the first claim cannot be sustained, but the second may hold where politics leads to instability. However Easterley has renewed his critique arguing that despite claims that aid donors are supporting development of democracies, in fact since 1972, on his calculations, around a third of all aid has consistently gone to dictatorships. Whilst the end of the Cold War was expected to change this practice, Easterly argues that the 'war on terror' now helps explain its persistence, particularly in relation to Central Asia and Ethiopia (Easterly 2010). Moyo (2009) reiterates many of the themes of earlier critiques of aid but goes further to assert that because of these, aid to Africa should cease within five years and African governments should instead raise development funds themselves, for example from international capital markets, a rather bleak prospect following the global financial crisis.

Aid in an era of globalization

One major purpose of official development assistance had been to supply capital to the developing world but by 1977 private capital flows to developing countries had already exceeded official development assistance by a ratio of two to one (Williams 1997: 43). As globalization proceeded, the question emerging was, 'What specific role would development assistance play in a world in which private financial flows were increasing so rapidly'? Between 1990 and 1996, private international finance to developing countries increased dramatically from US$44.4 billion to US$256 billion – more than six times the aid flows. However, the bulk of the investment was directed to around a dozen countries in east Asia and Latin America, notably China. Very little is flowing to the Least Developed Countries, nor are the social sectors the targets of this investment. Private investment also has its dangers. In 1997, the financial collapse in East Asia which reverberated through Thailand, South Korea and Indonesia in particular, illustrated the dangers of rapid withdrawal of speculative capital and the collapse of a country's currency; and after the 2008 GFC private capital sources significantly reduced (Chibba 2011).

As noted, some three trillion dollars is being traded daily on global foreign exchange markets (Seguino 2010: 190). At the start of the 2000s, one week of currency exchange was worth more than a whole year's worth of trade in goods and services globally and more than 40 per cent of these transactions involved round trips of less than three days (Oxfam 2002: 36). This rapid movement of speculative capital leads to great volatility and instability in financial markets and has the capacity to suddenly plunge millions of people into poverty. So, while flows of private finance have contributed to the development of a limited number of nations, the problem with the global capital flows from a human development perspective is their size and volatility and their capacity to undo development gains virtually overnight.

Of course the impact of risky financial activity, particularly as a result of the failure of regulation to keep pace with the high risk new financial instruments being utilized in the financial powerhouses of the world, led to the global financial crisis in 2008. This crisis had considerable impacts for the developing world, coming as it did hot on the heels of a food crisis and energy crisis. The World Bank estimated that these crises had already pushed some 64 million people back into extreme poverty and the depth of poverty people were experiencing was also worsening (World Bank 2010: viii; United Nations 2010: 7). Already over a billion people were food insecure according to the Food and Agriculture Organization (FAO) as a result of falling agricultural production, population increases and higher food prices; these combined with higher energy prices, were creating stresses for poor people in developing countries even before the financial crisis took effect. The impacts of the GFC on developing countries are varied and as yet, their full impact has not been fully assessed, but reduced trade and limited access to capital for investment will contribute to slower growth; those dependent on trade with severely affected developed countries, such as Mexico which has a high level of trade with the USA, are especially hurt.

Of course much of the theory of globalization has rested on the promotion of trade as a driver of economic growth. According to Oxfam, 'the potential of even a one per cent increase in world export share for each developing region could reduce world poverty by 12 per cent' (Oxfam 2002: 7). Yet, as they go on to show, trade theory is not being borne out in practice for much of the developing world, as poor people, far from benefiting from global trade expansion, are losing out. And trade restrictive practices by the developed world are frustrating developing countries' aspirations. Oxfam estimates that the total cost to developing countries of all export restrictive practices is over US$100 billion annually.

Thus trade liberalization has proceeded in a highly asymmetric manner. Many developing countries have been forced to liberalize by conditionalities attached to structural adjustment loans but developed countries have resisted any equivalent policy shifts, blocking equitable access to their markets for developing country produce. When average per capita income in low-income countries is just over $400 per year, and US farmers receive average subsidies of $21,000 per annum, something seems seriously awry (Oxfam 2002: 112–13). Unless trade liberalization proceeds in a more equitable manner, current trends which are seeing a widening of the gap between developing and developed countries in their share of world income are likely to persist and even worsen (Oxfam 2002: 66–70). Wade (2008), for example, argues that key trade-related agreements on investments (TRIMS), services (GATS) and intellectual property rights (TRIPS) negotiated since the 1990s make illegal many of the industrial development policies used by the successful east Asian countries, which favoured national firms, and entrench current global wealth hierarchies. The Doha Round of the World Trade Organization negotiations that started in 2001, intended as a 'development round' to assist developing countries, has as yet failed to reach any agreement which could address these problems.

One consequence of globalization has been the use of aid to boost the private sector, support the financial sector and support trade liberalization policy generally. Kragh et al. review the various aid instruments that donors have used to stimulate the private sector (Kragh et al. 2000: 319–30), noting that while this type of support remains only a small part of official development assistance, it could contribute to poverty reduction as well as overall growth. Morrissey (2000: 375–91) notes that aid can be used both for short-term compensatory assistance as countries liberalize trade, or to support the development and necessary infrastructure for regional trade agreements. Kovsted (2000) recognizes that, following a series of international financial crises since the 1980s that impacted negatively on developing countries, aid is also now being used to help strengthen the financial sectors of developing countries, reducing the risks of 'systemic failure'. Such assistance can also aim to safeguard the economy 'against excessive volatility and contagion from both domestic and international financial markets' (Kovsted 2000: 333), for example through improved financial information and analysis and better regulation. Interestingly, one of the more popular forms of support has been to micro-finance institutions that appear to meet donor interests in both stimulating markets and assisting the poor simultaneously.

Both trade and the growth of private sector investment in developing countries may have the potential to supersede official development assistance but the geographically limited benefits and the negative trends associated with both these phenomena lead one to conclude that official development assistance will still be required by many of the poorer countries for some time, even as more rapidly-growing countries such as China, India, Brazil, South Africa and others start to assert themselves as significant in the global economy. In particular, China is on track to become the largest economy in the world within a decade, although that does not imply that poverty, especially in its more remote areas, will have been eliminated.

It is arguable that widening inequality and the stresses and strains of globalization have also contributed to the number of intrastate conflicts in the 1990s. Dealing with the consequences, Addison says is 'now *the* most important set of issues facing the donor countries and their development, foreign policy, and military institutions' (Addison 2000: 392). Certainly this issue has come to the fore since the turn of the century, in the context of a very changed aid environment since late 2001 – the global 'war on terror'. And notwithstanding the broader impact of the combined food, energy and financial crises of the late 2000s, the use of aid in conflict or post conflict environments remains very much to the fore.

Conflict and state-building

The role of aid in 'fragile,' 'failing' or 'failed' states, or in conflict and post-conflict environments, has become a significant area for practice and study. This had begun in the 1990s but took on new urgency and new meaning after 2001 when the emerging view rendered the South 'as a source of international crime, terrorism, and conflict that contributed to global instability' (Howell 2006: 123). Fear that failed states would be havens for terrorists galvanized donor countries to engage seriously with these issues, and provided a perceived legitimacy for more aggressive intervention (Duffield 2005: Hameiri 2008). As the Administrator of USAID said in 2006: 'Unlike the Cold War, we are now menaced more by "fragile states than conquering states" ... opening up the developing world to economic opportunity and expanding the ranks of democratic states are now vital to our own national security' (Natsios 2006). Such thinking lies behind interventions in Afghanistan and Iraq that remain contentious. Of course, the use of aid in conflict settings is not new but the scale and frequency of aid operations in association with UN-led peacekeeping is what has changed, and it is likely that this trend will persist in the future.

Many aid organizations have worked hard to ensure that the victims of conflict are assisted in ways that avoid fuelling violence through a deeper appreciation of the dynamics of conflict (Anderson 1999). Apart from the obvious role of aid in assisting refugees and displaced people affected by conflict, aid is being used in the transition to peace and democracy, for example in supporting peace talks and monitoring peace agreements, the establishment or re-establishment of the state institutions, macroeconomic assistance, the conduct of elections, supporting justice systems (including international criminal tribunals for the former Yugoslavia and Rwanda), landmine awareness and clearance and the restoration of livelihoods in the longer term. The complexities of providing aid in these contexts should not be underestimated, particularly where political instability persists and power shifts constantly at many levels. Indeed, the dependence of newly emerging states, such as Afghanistan, on foreign security forces and donors may itself contribute to the legitimacy problems such nascent states face (Suhrke 2006).

These issues have generated considerable research and debate about strategies donors can use in situations where states are 'fragile', 'failing' or 'collapsed', terms which often obscure more than they reveal about the causes and possible solutions, and the complex processes of state formation and capacity development involved (Nelson 2006; Millikin and Krause 2002; Rosser 2006; Fritz and Menocal 2006). Different donors take a range of different approaches to such problematic contexts, for example, some take a 'peace, human security and basic needs' approach; others an 'economic development and good governance' approach; and others a 'global security' approach. Some combine two or even all of these (Fritz and Cammack 2006). A clearer picture is developing about the relationship between nation-building (the development of citizenship identity among a population), state-building (establishing the formal institutional structures of a state) and peace-building (building mechanisms and processes for resolving violent conflicts, engaging in reconciliation and establishing lasting peace). Lessons from research on aid for peace-building emphasize recognition that understanding that politics matters, while not allowing aid to be politically driven. Research also stresses the need to maintain good development principles, build state capacity (including extending the reach of government to the rural areas), engage for the long term and invest considerable resources. The need to deal with the causes of conflict and conflict players is also evident (Fritz and Cammack 2006).

However, not all writers believe this rational approach will succeed. Duffield (2002) draws attention to the huge growth in the 'shadow economies' – the informal sector and the illegal cross-border networks and flows of cheap goods, entire parallel systems to the formal economy, officially unregulated but controlled by powerful players. This shadow economic network sustains warring parties in conflict zones, enabling them to conduct modern warfare. These networks and flows have also sustained people, provided them with essential goods, food, medicines and consumer items unobtainable or unaffordable through other channels. Liberal globalization, he argues, has created the spaces within which these shadow systems have flourished. Such systems, he argues, 'resist liberal norms and values' (Duffield 2002: 1059). Duffield sees the aid system, with its own public–private networks of practice, as a new approach to imposing a 'will to govern' over these 'borderlands' as part of a wider security system; for him, the rediscovery of 'development' as the solution to these borderland 'crises' fails to recognize the reality that an alternative modernity is being practised within them, one that challenges liberal systems. Failure to understand this, he believes, may lead to further disillusionment with the outcomes of such redoubled aid efforts.

Of course the contribution of aid to peace-building, however successful or otherwise it might be, is but one use of aid as a 'public good'. A global 'public good' may be considered any issue that has trans-boundary benefits, or addresses trans-boundary problems. Among the most obvious are global environmental challenges such as climate change, deforestation, trans-boundary pollution, the spread of disease, especially HIV AIDS, drug trade and people trafficking, and reducing population growth (Kaul 1999). This motivation for aid involves its use for these purposes, which may in some cases, distract from the poverty-reduction focus.

Already a significant proportion of development assistance is being spent on these types of activity. Interestingly, as Hopkins (2000: 436) points out, many of these global public goods initiatives provide some global regulation in the face of market failure and thus present an alternative to the neo-liberal paradigm. They also, however, reflect the use of aid for purposes of self-interest to developed countries. The most recent developments in aid, which link it tightly to western security objectives, illustrate this clearly. Other examples include the sums being spent on slowing or halting the flow of people to developed countries and combating the trade in illicit drugs. Interestingly, the broadened agenda for development assistance may be one of the factors that have led to political support for some of the increases in aid announced since 2002. There are difficult tensions between maintaining the focus of aid on poverty reduction and building political constituencies in the developed countries for increased aid budgets. The 'global public goods' use of aid may build support but it clearly creates the risk of pursuing multiple objectives that cannot all be met and which may even conflict at times.

The Millennium Development Goals and poverty reduction

While security concerns may have driven increases in aid, and indeed may shape to a large degree where that aid goes, there is a competing framework that provides an important official agenda for aid. This is the set of Millennium Development Goals agreed to in 2000.

In the 1990s, a series of United Nations World Conferences on aspects of social development set a series of goals for governments to achieve. These fed into an important meeting of the OECD Development Assistance Committee in 1996, which also placed great emphasis on effective partnerships and 'locally owned' development strategies. Donors agreed to a series of poverty reduction and social development goals to be reached by the year 2015. However, despite the apparent desirability of the goals, there was criticism that they had been adopted unilaterally by donors through the OECD mechanism. The adoption by the United Nations at its Millennium Summit in 2000 of the eight similar, but somewhat developed, Millennium Development Goals, dealt with this criticism and forged a wide global commitment to them. Significantly the MDGs, unlike their predecessors, include commitments by developed countries in areas such as aid, trade and debt relief, and they are backed up by a series of concrete indicators for each goal. The most recent UN report on progress indicates that despite setbacks resulting from multiple crises in the late 2000s, 'The overall poverty rate is still expected to fall to 15 per cent by 2015, which translates to around 920 million people living under the international poverty line – half the number in 1990' hence meeting the global MDG poverty reduction target (United Nations 2010: 4). However, the report recognizes that progress is uneven, both in terms of where it is occurring, and in terms of the eight different goals. Progress for example is extremely slow on Goal 5, improving maternal health, and progress on gender equity (Goal 3) generally seems sluggish, although progress on the primary education goal (Goal 2) is better (yet it still won't be reached, particularly in sub-Saharan Africa). And while proportions change, the absolute numbers of people in poverty in 2010 remain high (1.4 billion) and the number of malnourished has actually risen (United Nations 2010). Kabeer (2006) highlights the real challenge of meeting the MDG targets in relation to what she terms 'durable inequalities'; these result from various group identities or categorizations such as caste, ethnicity, indigeneity, or other 'devalued identities' or spatial disadvantages.

Importantly, the development targets have caused donors to focus more closely on the quality and effectiveness of aid, and particularly its impact on poverty reduction, rather than on more general measures of growth and development (Simons et al. 1997; DFID 1997, 2000 and 2010; Ministerial Review Team 2001). For example, DFID's White Papers placed significant emphasis on eradicating poverty, although as Slater and Bell (2002) note, they did not challenge the virtues of neo-liberal globalization or acknowledge that there may be contradictions between the poverty eradication goals and the widening inequality which current forms of globalization are creating. However, DFID's most recent review indicates that the UK will work for a better regulated world economy (DFID 2010: 7).

The debate about poverty has been further stimulated by the publication of Jeffrey Sachs' book *The End of Poverty* (2005). Sachs, an economist formerly associated with orthodox structural adjustment policies, argues that ending poverty is possible with the right investments in a range of capitals that the extreme poor usually lack (human, business, infrastructural, natural, public institutional and knowledge capital). Sachs has been criticized for simply repackaging modernization, uncritically urging the deeper integration of peripheral countries into the highly unequal global marketplace, downplaying the historically important role of states in development and failing to address ecological and other critiques (Sneyd 2006). His work certainly ignores the development critiques of other 'post-development' writers such as Escobar or Shiva (Pieterse 1998).

However, attention to 'pro-poor growth' within a modernization paradigm has certainly increased in the early twenty-first century. Pro-poor growth is the type of economic growth attained within a policy context which favours the poor, rather than one in which growth increases relative inequality (World Bank PovertyNet 2006). However, globally, growth has stalled following the GFC, and this will affect the achievement of the MDG poverty reduction goal particularly in some regions, at least in the short term. The big improvements have been in China and (to a lesser extent) India with their huge populations. Sub-Saharan Africa, western Asia and parts of Eastern Europe and Central Asia are unlikely to achieve the poverty reduction target (World Bank 2006c: Roberts and Cave 2010; United Nations 2010). Unfortunately, despite approximately one-third of the current one billion people living in poverty being indigenous peoples, the donor community has paid little attention to the specific factors which contribute to their poverty and how to address those in the context of the MDGs (but see United Nations Department of Economic and Social Affairs 2006).

In the early 2000s, the UN Millennium Project estimated that the amount required to fill the financing gap for every low-income country to reach the MDG goals would be 'US$73 billion in 2006 rising to US$135 billion in 2015' (UN Millennium Project 2006). This led to a growing interest in 'innovative sources of finance' to supplement the contributions of ODA. Whilst debt reduction through the World Bank's Debt Relief for Heavily Indebted Poor Countries programme was seen as one way in which additional funds could be released for social investment, a number of other ideas were proposed, some of which could have dual benefits. These include global environmental taxes; a small tax on air travel; the financial transaction tax (also known as the Robin Hood tax) – a very small tax on all foreign exchange transactions; creation by the IMF of Special Drawing Rights, with contributions by donor countries; an International Finance Facility with funds from capital markets; increased private contributions through NGOs and private foundations; a global lottery or global prize bond; and facilitating increased remittances from emigrants to developing countries (Atkinson 2006; HM Treasury 2004 and 2006).

Whilst some of these proposals appear not to have progressed in the last five years, others are already happening or are still squarely on the table. Most movement has been in the area of financing for health aid with a range of innovative measures being explored (Sandor, Scott and Benn 2009) Already, an air ticket levy scheme started in 2006 has been adopted by 13 countries, and is contributing to programmes relating to AIDS, tuberculosis and malaria (Sandor, Scott and Benn 2009:1). It is also clear that remittances and philanthropic contributions are growing fast. Remittances increased globally from \$289 billion in 2007 to \$338 billion in 2008, despite the GFC; although the growth of remittances to the Latin American and Caribbean region in that period was very small, obviously affected by the weak economic situation of the USA (Hudson Institute 2010: 60). Whilst there has been some debate about their development value, Gupta et al. (2009) found that in Africa remittances do contribute directly to poverty reduction and financial development. Philanthropic and private giving is also rising to close to the level of bilateral contributions as has already been mentioned (Hudson Institute 2010; Kharas 2009). The financial transactions tax is still being considered, fuelled in part by the fact that it was excesses of the financial sector which caused the GFC, and there is an argument that, having been bailed out, they should now contribute back. Campaigners have suggested a tax rate of 0.05 per cent on currency transactions, which in 2011 could raise \$650 billion dollars per year (www.robinhoodtax.ca/howitworks). The IMF has indicated that such a mechanism is technically feasible and the idea is gaining momentum (Howlett 2010).

Some point out that more funds are lost to developing countries through capital flight than they receive in ODA, so measures to prevent such losses would be extremely valuable (Boyce 2002). For example, capital flight from Indonesia in 1997 was said to amount to \$70 billion, at that time approximately equivalent to the country's total foreign debt, which underpinned the radical devaluation of its currency. Malaysia, on the other hand, imposed restrictions on the flow of capital and by 2002 had effectively recovered from the 1997 economic crash.

The future of aid for development

Whatever the future sources of aid financing, it is clear that aid has come full circle and is returning to its political origins. The paradigm of development, as first envisaged in the 1950s, has changed. Today the key concept is not 'development' but 'globalization'. For those who hold the reins of power, this means economic globalization according to an (only slightly softened) neo-liberal agenda.

Thus for the foreseeable future, aid will continue to be used to advance both the western security agenda of tackling 'terrorism' and neo-liberal economic and political agendas. Aid will support strategic interventions and the building of 'fragile states'; it will also help countries develop their markets and promote democracy. However, the difficulties of trying to graft foreign political institutions and processes onto certain countries where the underlying values and principles are not agreed, and the very idea of 'nation' is contested, seem to be overwhelming.

Aid will also be used strategically to secure access to or control of scarce natural resources as pressures on soil, land, water and marine life and forestry resources increase over the next decades. It is likely that the future will see a significant increase in conflict over the control and management of such natural resources. The role of emerging donors such as China is particularly relevant in this regard. Moore and Unsworth note that, 'The Chinese make it very clear that they want access to oil, other commodities, and markets for manufactured products' (Moore and Unsworth 2006: 711), while studiously avoiding any conditionalities or concerns about governance common to western donors. Chinese companies, banks and educational institutions are serious about doing business in Africa and likely to have increasing influence (Moore and Unsworth 2006; Kragelund 2008). This of course is no different from Japan's similar interest in assisting countries that can supply its raw materials. Although some legitimate concern may exist about the potential of emerging donors like China to undermine some of the well-developed DAC system principles, in many ways emerging donors are no different from DAC donors in linking their own foreign policy and trade interests to their aid programmes; western concerns about China's role in Africa seem somewhat overstated (Kragelund 2008; Tan-Mullins, Mohan and Power 2010) but the significance is that China is a non-OECD player that, along with India and a number of other developing countries, such as Brazil, is gaining considerable international clout. This will change power balances in the aid system.

Donors will of course vary in their emphases, as will the strategies applied to different aid-receiving countries, according to geo-strategic and political factors, their engagement with or marginalization from global trade and their adherence to neo-liberal economic frameworks. But the above trends will particularly shape the programmes of the largest donors.

The NGO community and the alternative globalization movement in civil society will no doubt keep the pressure on to see the Millennium Development Goals met as fully as possible in the remaining years to 2015 and for the effort to be renewed and enhanced in subsequent years. The continuing emphasis will be on transparency and effectiveness of aid and accountability for outcomes to the poor; this is also likely to lead to a more vigorous debate about the other conditions necessary, beyond aid, if these targets are to be fully achieved, even after 2015. Pressure will continue to mount from the developing world and among global activists and NGOs, particularly for faster and more meaningful action on trade, particularly market access for agricultural goods to Europe and the USA, without the large concessions in other areas (such as services) that the developed world is demanding of the low-income countries. The push for the financial transactions tax will also continue. One irony, however, is that as donors seek to promote democratic governance, the western security agenda is being widely used to curtail civil liberties, constrain dissent and restrict democracy, a trend likely to reduce accountabilities to the poorest in the developing world (www.whiteband.org). And new aid modalities, such as budget support, may redirect aid away from civil society groups that are essential to promote wider participation in development and increase pressure for good governance.

But aid, debt and trade cannot be viewed in isolation from other signals the world sends to the warlords and dictators of the poorest, conflict-ridden states. The secretive nature of huge deals that international resource companies strike with government elites around oil, minerals and other resources encourages corruption and enables governments to avoid accountability to their people. The demand from the West for narcotics fuels an illegal trade that also promotes corruption and violence, the consequences of which are all too evident in countries such as Afghanistan and Burma. The proliferation of arms, many of which are manufactured in the developed world, fuels deadly conflicts in the South that impede development (Moore and Unsworth 2006). These wider interconnections between the rich and poor worlds need to be exposed and resolved. For example, the trade in 'conflict diamonds' and the role of trade in other minerals (such as cassiterite) and cocoa, in fuelling conflict have been highlighted in recent years (Grant and Taylor 2004; Global Witness 2007; Schure 2010). Aid alone will never solve these sources of poverty, corruption and violence; only concerted and comprehensive approaches that challenge powerful forces in the developed as well as the developing world can ultimately address them.

Notes

1. Korea became a member of the Development Assistance Committee of the OECD on 1 January 2010.
2. Figures total more than 100 per cent due to rounding.
3. REDD+ would also include forest conservation, sustainable forest management and increasing forest carbon stocks.

Chapter 4

Globalization and Development

Damien Kingsbury

There is much to separate and distinguish developing countries and each needs to be understood in its own context. However, there is also much that developing countries share in common, in terms of their internal structures and conditions and their relations with and links to the rest of the world. In a significant part, where developing countries do experience internal conditions in common, this is a consequence of their external relations and the increasing standardization or homegenization of those relations. In particular, how development has been defined, the methods of achieving development and the conditionalities that have been applied to developing countries have all reflected an increasingly standardized global agenda. Even the material and cultural aspirations of many in developing countries have increasingly come to reflect a more global set of influences, as have the means by which culture is dispersed. While particularities remain local, the shared and imposed circumstances of development reflect an increasing tendency towards the global.

One of the commonalities between developing countries is that a significant proportion of their populations live in poverty, with many living in absolute poverty. Most developing countries are also overwhelmingly net exporters of a small number of, usually unprocessed, primary goods and simple manufactures, and net importers of complex manufactured goods, especially technical and electronic goods, and services. Where developing countries do export manufactured goods, they are often textiles, clothing and footwear, or of simple construction, older technology, or only partially processed manufactures.

Where people in such countries have a job, or some means of income, there is a good chance they will have or have access to a small, portable transistor radio, which plays music based on a popular three minute format (although often with quite distinct regional variations), as well as broadcasting some news and other current information. For many, this is their primary source of information about the world beyond their immediate environment. If these people live in or visit a big city, they might pass by an American-style fast-food outlet, where the price of a meal is as much as most people would be lucky to earn in a day, or, in some cases, in a week. However, the customers of this fast-food outlet, who might arrive by a fairly new – Korean, Chinese, Indian or Brazilan – car, may be wearing brand-name sports shoes and jeans, and drinking an American-brand soft drink with their fashionable treat. Perhaps for work or for entertainment, such people might also use the Internet, and be immediately exposed to the vast range of ideas, perceptions, values and interests that circulate around the globe more or less without restriction.

The government of this country would probably hold elections and thus claim to reflect the common aspirational political standard of 'democracy', although irregularities could be widespread and patron-client relations remain an important source of political power, in large part due to the relatively recent adoption of a representative voting system. The government would also most likely be a recipient of an IMF structural adjustment package as a consequence of earlier, poorly invested or squandered loans for infrastructure projects. However, to qualify for this further loan, the government will have had to significantly cut its public service, including funding for schools and teachers, and public clinics and hospitals and their staff.

Such a government is also likely to have reduced tariffs on imported goods, but for many years found that prices for its export commodities had fallen by around half, in real terms, until the early 2000s, which placed further pressure on government revenues. Since then, commodity prices have increased, if unstably so, but from 2006 basic food prices leapt, while moderating slightly in 2008, and increased again in 2010–11. This means that in many cases, poor people who had to rely on purchasing food were pushed to the brink of starvation. Competing against subsidized commodities, especially food and other agricultural products, in developed country markets has disadvantaged exports. If the gap in income between rich and poor in this country was not getting any greater (and it would have already been significant), there is a fair chance that it was not reducing much either. In many cases, however, the income gap was indeed growing (e.g. see Shari 2001) in particular within African and Latin American states, although the absolute divergence in global wealth peaked around 1970 and was broadly, if conditionally, reducing thereafter (Cole and Neumayer 2003). These are just some of the possible, and probable, circumstances for a person in a developing country in the era of globalization.

The issue of development, almost by definition, encompasses states across the globe and has, as a consequence, been defined in global terms. From the formulation of development models to the provision of aid, loans and other funds to multilateral, bilateral and NGO aid projects, the response to issues raised by the development question has been one defined in global terms. This has been, in some cases, quite appropriate, and in others not. Similarly, the impositions and advantages of global economic integration and linkages, including through banks and other financial institutions, foreign multinational corporations and foreign direct investment, and other aspects of global integration, such as communication and culture, have impacted on almost all developing countries in one form or another. This has left many developing countries facing what has become a 'cookie-cutter' or 'off-the-shelf' format for future development. One size, or policy programme, is suggested to fit all, especially by the international agencies that are so often the arbiters of 'correct' policies.

While many of the issues facing developing countries are similar, the particular circumstances for each country vary, often even within a single country. Similarly, with a process of global integration occurring at a state level, local communities have increasingly looked to themselves, their context, their past and their cultural markers as a means of defining or preserving local identity in the face of a potentially homogenizing and sometimes alienating world. So too have some governments asserted a local particularism or cultural relativism, positing the culturally specific as exempt from global norms. However, in the field of politics, this has most often been by way of denying local political aspirations or asserting a claimed particularism in opposition to claimed universals (such as civil and political rights). Unfortunately, the use, and abuse, of power has a universal quality that transcends local particularity in equal proportion to more positive universals (see Avonius and Kingsbury 2008).

In terms of local context, the pressures that arise, for example, in a tropical country with high rainfall and relatively high soil fertility will be quite different from those of a semi-arid or arid country; mountainous territory will have different requirements to flat ground; industrialization raises different issues to agriculture; a literate work force will have different capabilities and expectations to an illiterate one; and so on. Beyond countries, there are in some cases also issues that correspond to groups of countries within a particular region, for example in trade policy (e.g., ASEAN). And there are, of course, wider challenges and changes to communities at all levels brought about by various aspects of the process of global integration.

The meaning of globalization

Of the thousands of texts that have been written on 'globalization' in recent years, most have their own definition, not all of which agree.

However, the broadly prevailing (but also most generalized) view of globalization is that it is a proposed or actual situation where there is a process or series of linked processes that lead towards greater interaction or integration between states and within states. The primary context for both the process and the outcome is economic, being manifested as an increasingly integrated or interdependent global market (see WTO 2007). Stiglitz (2006) posits globalization as the closer integration of the countries and peoples of the world which, in turn, has derived from the reduction in costs of transportation and communication and the breaking down of barriers to the flow of goods, services and capital across borders.

Kearney's survey of globalization (2001) opted for economic criteria accounting for 90 per cent of the globalization phenomenon, allocating the difference to political, cultural and environmental criteria. Such an integrated market is understood to operate on the principle of laissez-faire or neo-liberal capitalism, in which barriers between states, such as tariffs, should no longer exist and in which local economic unities (such as local regions or states) compete on the basis of comparative advantage. Comparative advantage might be, for instance, a specialization in a particular form of production, or it could be what a country does best or, in some cases, at all. For many developing countries, their 'comparative advantage' is low wage rates, which is simply selling down the cost of labour as the lowest common economic denominator. In principle, economic globalization could also be met through the standardization of central economic planning (the theoretical model employed under 'communism'), although this was not achieved in practice. That is because the contemporary global economic condition in which there is a tendency towards integration was made possible, in practical terms, by the collapse of such centrally planned economies ('international communism'), and the claimed failure of state interventionist or Keynesian economic policies in otherwise capitalist societies (despite the success of state interventionist capitalist societies such as Singapore).

However, many proponents and critics of economic globalization also argue that the world remains a long way from an idealized free-trade model. Some even suggest that pro-free traders are less interested in free trade, as such, but rather the untrammelled pursuit of profit that can be achieved by free trade where that suits, or by government intervention or protection where that alternatively suits. The global financial crisis (GFC) from 2007 was illustrative of this tendency, with banks and other trading organizations pressing for greater deregulation under which financial regime they were individually rewarded for engaging in increasingly risky lending practices. When the financial bubble burst, a number of major financial institutions collapsed, leading to a major credit squeeze and a consequent fall in credit to marginal industries as well as the drying up of consumer confidence. In order to reduce the worst effects of the GFC, governments engaged in costly bail outs of large if marginal industries, including banks and major manufacturers (e.g. see IMF 2009).

Critics of globalization argue that the notion of free trade based on comparative advantage works primarily to the benefit of industrialized countries that can take advantage of cheap labour and goods produced in developing countries. Where free trade does not deliver such advantages to developed countries, some developed countries employ protectionist policies to support globally non-viable but domestically politically important industries (legislated United States farm subsidies of US$270 billion between 2002 and 2012 being a prime case in point). That is to say, what has been happening has been less economic globalization, which implies a degree of equal access, than it has been an internationalization of capitalism, which does not imply such an equality of access (Beck 2000: 199–200). Even the IMF has recognized that economic globalization has not been an unmitigated success, stating that: 'a large part of the world's population – especially in sub-Saharan Africa – has been left behind by economic progress. As a result, the disparities between the world's richest and poorest countries are now wider than ever, with increasing incidences of poverty within countries' (IMF 2002: 1, see also UNDP 2011).

While the economic definition of globalization is probably the most important, because it impacts directly on how people live, other interpretations of globalization include a more generalized interdependence, the collapse of time/space, communications, culture, political institutions, global institutions, and levels of global intervention. Many also identify the collapse of effective distance, at least for some, via improvements in transportation and communication, as critical aspects of globalization (see, for example Giddens 1991, 1995; Lubbers 1996; Lubbers and Koorevaar 1998, 1999; Tehranian 1999; Herman and McChesney 2000; Robins 2000; Thompson 2000; Sparks 2007; McPhail 2010). Tehranian, in particular, notes that communication is the defining quality of the post-industrial age and that it is as a consequence of enhanced communications that globalization has been able to both occur and to occur in particular ways. Conversely, it has also been the globalization of communication that has allowed for a global response to globalization – a social globalization aimed at limiting the free reign of unfettered economic globalization (Held and McGrew 2007: ch. 11; Florini 2000: 1923). Gurtov (1994: 6–11) suggests that interdependence generally is the defining characteristic of globalization and sees that occurring in both positive and negative ways, citing previously local types of issues arising across international boundaries, including responses to investment and ownership, voluntarist aid programmes, legal disputation, terrorism, and so on. Globalism, therefore, can, in many respects, also imply a cross-pollination of influences or a tendency towards a common point. This can apply to economics but equally to politics and socio-cultural matters.

One controversial and much discussed, but poorly documented, aspect of globalization has been its impact on cultures and the capacity for the preservation of tradition and custom. The symbols of globalization, such as television and generic clothing (image and self-image) and the elite culture of consumerism, have become commonplace if not universal, while the impact of material aspiration has entered almost every corner of the globe. For many, the 'protection' of cultures is critical and, in cases where there is an unthinking onslaught, the gradual acclimatization to external influences is often preferable to complete social dislocation. However, the preservation of culture assumes that culture is or can be static and that preserving the particular in the face of the encroaching universal is a fraught process not guaranteed to succeed. There is in this, though, an assumption that what amounts to culture is inviolable or somehow fixed, despite changes within cultures beyond the impact of globalization. There are numerous examples of traditional patterns of behaviour being not only at odds with increasingly globalized norms of behaviour but with members of their own community. Cultures that have customs that oppress women are far from universally freely endorsed by those women, while cultures that imply economic or political repression or subjugation may have a long history but are not always universally subscribed to. And then there is the notion that even in an increasingly homogenized world, there is or can be a uniformity of culture or of cultural responses and that material conditions, environment and history will all continue to contribute to shaping a range of world views.

In all of this, there is the equation submitted by Amartya Sen that the purpose of development should define its application, and (in a slightly less utilitarian but more complex way) he defines development as being a process intended to achieve the greatest amount of happiness among the greatest number of people. This happiness, he says, comes from freedom to do and achieve things, and freedom from negatives, such as hunger, illiteracy and oppression. Sen's version of development, too, represents a type of globalization but a positive type with which most anti-globalization critics would feel fairly comfortable.

The IMF goes so far as to say that globalization is not about economics so much as it is a 'political choice in favour of international economic integration, which for the most part goes hand in hand with the consolidation of democracy' (IMF 2002: 1). The assumption here is that countries exercise 'choice' in liberalizing their economies and that as they do so they will also liberalize their political institutions. The structural logic implied here is that economic liberalization will lead to economic growth which will, in turn, lead to the development of an educated middle class which will, in turn, press for greater democratization. While there have been some instances of economic 'choice' and of political liberalization that agree with this proposition, there have also been many more examples of states that have liberalized their economies through coercion, often while maintaining authoritarian political structures. Capitalism has been shown to be a prerequisite for democracy but democracy has not been a prerequisite for capitalism.

One way in which development and globalization fit neatly together has been in the development paradigm that 'development' equals economic growth, which in turn, implies industrialization. The standard development model implied a standardized development outcome. This has been shown to be far from the case, consequently raising questions about the evenness and depth of the globalization process, and the influence of local conditions. In these senses, development can be understood as comprising economic, political and cultural elements, all of which engage in a wider world and all of which are in some ways ultimately transformed by it.

Related to the idea of the globalization of ideas, but with less of a structural linkage than that between economic and political development, is what Beck calls a 'cosmopolitan democracy', or the establishment of 'cosmopolitan rights for all' (Beck 2000: 93). Beck notes that rights, as such, are best protected for those who enjoy them when they are enjoyed by all. However, as Beck also notes, assuming a 'realist' international relations theory position (in which states achieve beneficial outcomes primarily through the capacity to impose their will), the paradox in such 'cosmopolitanism' is that rights are only guaranteed by states in what is still largely an anarchic world order and that guaranteeing rights beyond states implies global governance which, to date, exists at best very impartially and often ineffectively. There is, however, a view of what constitutes 'universal' human rights that is normatively applicable, regardless of circumstances. The UN Declaration of Human Rights is one such vehicle for the expression of such values, as are the International Criminal Court, the International Court of Justice and the 'Responsibility to Protect' paradigm, while global organizations such as

Amnesty International and a number of transnational NGOs also pro-mote universalist agendas. As Pettman notes, human rights are a general moral claim to matters of fundamental interest (Pettman 1979: 76) and, as such, apply to the condition of being human, rather than to being the citizen of a particular state. Similarly, the idea of 'democracy' has become increasingly universalized, if only in rhetoric (see Chapter 7). However, while normative terms are prone to being over-used and reduced in meaning, their acceptance as representing a set of ideas around which codes of behaviour are supposed to cohere in turn, at least to some extent, represents a global agreement. So too is there global acceptance, it could be argued, of the idea that within each polity there is, or should be, a type of social contract to ensure that states and their elites function more or less in the interests of all citizens and in which citizens agree to work more or less co-operatively to the larger benefit (and, where states and elites fail to function as such, they are recognized as being dysfunctional or malignant). The problem, of course, is that the normative quality and practical application of such 'agreement' is largely defined by each country's elites, often to their own benefit, and the capacity of the global community to formally enforce such norms, through a conventional monopoly of violence, does not functionally exist. Where the 'global community' does enforce sets of 'norms', they are more often interpreted and enforced by a small num-ber of key states (e.g. NATO in Kosovo and Libya), and in some cases appear to reflect at least some of the fundamental interests of those states (e.g. the US-led war in Iraq) rather than a larger global norm. Such states can and do argue that the interests they represent are global and sometimes they are endorsed, or not blocked, by the UN Security Council. However, the character of such representation of global inter-est necessarily implies a particular perspective and that perspective may not be, for a variety of altruistic as well as self-serving reasons, univer-sally shared.

In response to what is perceived as unilateralism, another phenome-non that can be and sometimes is global in its reach and aspirations is 'terrorism' (that is, acts of attempted political persuasion by the use of terror) which has been highlighted in the period since 11 September 2001. It is overstating the situation to suggest that terrorism literally reaches into homes across the globe and in significant part the impact of terrorism, as it has manifested in North America, South East Asia and Africa, has come from the global reach of the news media. However, in the post-Cold War era, via the news media, terrorism has reached into homes across the globe in a symbolic sense and its targets have been manifestations of developed global identity (embassies of the primary global power, the World Trade Centre, foreigners' night clubs, foreigners' hotels and so on). Because of the somewhat diffuse and seemingly unconnected nature of its targets, the geographic breadth of its reach and its global aspirations, terrorism in the early twenty-first century has increasingly become portrayed as the primary trans-global threat (USDS 2002, 2006).

Key globalization organizations

Globalization is represented by two broad tendencies, one of which is increasingly pervasive, sometimes recognized by its symbols, but which is otherwise not easy to pin down. Of this tendency, the global reach of American-styled popular music and English-language films, associated western styles of clothing and the generic use of English (particularly its popular terminology) stand out, although shifting across to a more specifically identified arena are global brand names, such as Coca-Cola, McDonald's and Nike (or Pepsi, KFC and Adidas). Such branding, however, starts to imply not just familiar signification but also global corporate reach of such readily identifiable names that include Exxon-Mobil, Microsoft and Toyota (or Royal Dutch/Shell, IBM and General Motors). Less readily, to most people, are 'faceless' organizations such as Citigroup, Itochu and Axa, or mining companies such as Rio Tinto or AngloAmerican. These are typical of the world's largest transnational corporations. But it is global 'public' institutions that perhaps most fully carry the standard of globalization. Such institutions in some ways fulfil the types of functions found under the governments of sovereign states, yet there is no global government for them to answer to. In this way, these organizations are sometimes perceived as being a law unto themselves, running a global agenda but on behalf of unstated interests.

These are organizations that represent what could be called 'global interest', or which are explicitly in favour of globalization. These organizations have come to be publicly identified with globalization, and to some extent with the juggernaut quality that globalization represents to many people. Most influential among these organizations are the World Trade Organization (WTO), the International Monetary Fund (IMF), the World Bank (WB) and the United Nations (UN). The first three are targeted at various aspects of economic development within the context of a global economy. The UN and its numerous agencies tend to focus more on global security through the political, humanitarian and social aspects of global development.

The WTO is the world's main international organization to promote order and co-operation in world trade and, as such, is the world's dominant pro-globalization multilateral organization (see Supachai 2002). The WTO was created out of the 125- member state Uruguay Round of the General Agreement on Tariffs and Trade (GATT) negotiations in 1995. The primary difference between the WTO and the GATT is that the WTO is a permanent organization with judicial power to rule on international trade disputes, whereas the GATT was based on a series of meetings, or 'rounds', without permanent status and with no judicial power. The WTO also covers services while the GATT included only trade. However, like the GATT, the focus of the WTO includes tariffs and non-tariff barriers to trade, natural resource products, textiles and clothing, agricultural and tropical produce, other articles covered under the GATT system, anti-dumping regulations, subsidies, intellectual property, dispute settlement and services. According to the WTO, its purpose is to achieve by consensus 'legal ground rules for international commerce' that are then ratified by member state legislatures to increase the flow of trade (WTO 2002a). The WTO has a rule-making and dispute settlement function that is, in effect, legally binding on member states and which has been strengthening since the WTO's inception (see WTO 2011, Gagne 2000).

Of particular relevance within the context of development, the WTO represents a large proportion of developing countries, with three-quarters of its membership self-defined as developing countries, less developed countries (LDC) or least developed countries (LLDC) (the abbreviation 'LLDC' is also used to refer to land-locked developing countries). In principle, special provisions for developing, less-developed and least-developed countries are put into all WTO agreements, including 'longer time periods to implement agreements and commitments, measures to increase their trading opportunities and support to help them build the infrastructure for WTO work, handle disputes, and implement technical standards' (WTO 2002a: 6). According to UNCTAD, the 49 least developed countries are identified by the UN as such in terms of low GDP per capita, weak human assets and a high degree of economic vulnerability (UNCTAD 2002b, 2010). At the time of writing, the key definition for 'least-developed country' was based on a daily per capita income level (even though this said nothing about median per capita GDP which is a more accurate assessment of how most people in a given country actually live). The level for determining LLDC status was at the time of writing US$900 per annum, which potentially included a very much larger number of developing countries than the former measure of US$2 per day. Further, this calculation did not base itself on purchasing parity power (PPP) (the relative capacity for a denominated unit of currency to purchase a set good in a particular environment). The definition for what constituted LLDC was also determined by restrictions on trade capacity or opportunity, and other related criteria. But even if a WTO member announces that it is a developing country, this does not automatically mean that it will benefit from the unilateral developing country preference schemes, such as the Generalized System of Preferences (GSP): 'in practice, it is the preference giving country which decides the list of developing countries that will benefit from the preferences' (WTO 2002b). More importantly, since the formation of the WTO, none of the countries that were members of GATT that have negotiated accession have been allowed to use the transitional periods set out in the WTO Agreement. It is also worth noting that under GATT, tariffs were primarily reduced between developed countries that also benefited from a subsequent increase in trade. In this, many developing countries were left further outside the global trading environment (Martin and Schuman 1997: 108–14). As a minor concession under the WTO, however, developing countries were eligible to benefit from technical assistance provided by the WTO Secretariat and WTO Members (WTO 2005).

Perhaps less identified as a globalizing institution than the WTO, the IMF has been at least as pervasive in reshaping the global macroeconomic climate, and, in particular, in bringing to heel many states that have otherwise been reluctant to accept the full and far-reaching effects of access to globalization via economic deregulation. The main impact of such deregulation has been in the flow of global finance which leapt from $17.5 trillion in 1979 to over $3,000 trillion by the end of the 20th century (Held et al. 1999: 208–09; see other references in this collection) and which dominates all other forms of global capitalism, including stock markets and the like. The IMF was established in 1946 as a part of the Bretton Woods Agreement of post-war reconstruction to promote international co-operation on finance, encourage stability in exchange rates and orderly systems for exchanging money between countries, and to provide temporary assistance for countries suffering balance of payments problems. Especially since the late 1970s, the IMF has played an active role in lending money to redress balance of payments problems caused by previous bad loans. In doing so, through what it calls 'structural adjustment programmes' (SAPs), the IMF has commonly imposed free-market 'reforms' on countries that have requested loans. SAPs commonly consist of raising interest rates to reduce domestic consumption and to attract foreign capital, reducing tariffs and non-tariff barriers to trade, reducing commercial taxation rates, establishing 'free- trade' (non-taxable) zones for foreign investment, and cutting government spending, most commonly in administration, education and health. Like the WTO, the IMF believes that world prosperity is enhanced by greater exchange between nations and these policies are intended to facilitate the integration of developing economies into the global market.

Also established under the Bretton Woods Agreement is the IMF's sibling organization, the World Bank (WB) which is, in effect, a global development bank or a multilateral bank that provides long-term (and lower interest) loans primarily for major infrastructure projects, such as water and sanitation, natural resource management, energy supply and so on. Increasingly, in practice, the WB also helps to restructure broad economies, through what it calls 'adjustment projects', which support governments undertaking policy reforms, such as improved public sector management. Because of its policy of providing 'soft loans' primarily for development projects, the WB does not attract the criticism that is sometimes directed at the harder-focused IMF. However, being derived from the Bretton Woods Agreement of 1944 for post-war reconstruction and to stabilize global currencies, the ideological orientation of the WB and the IMF is closer than even their sometimes overlapping functions, and the WB also uses its economic leverage, notably through the 'Integrated Framework' for 'trade capacity building', to encourage borrowing countries to adopt free trade or pro-economic globalization policies.

While the WTO, IMF and WB are 'inclusive' economic global organizations, not all 'global' institutions are as nominally inviting. The Organisation for Economic Co-operation and Development (OECD) is composed of 34 members that are exclusively developed or industrialized countries, including in North America, Western Europe (including Czech Republic, Hungary and Poland) and Japan, South Korea, Australia and New Zealand. While it claims to support a broad and socially equitable agenda, including governance, development and sustainability (such terms having widely interpretable meaning), the OECD's main function is to provide economic arguments for globalization, such as data demonstrating the positive contribution made by multinational corporations to economic development. In that it includes countries from around the world, but does not include non-industrialized states in its membership, the OECD's perspective tends to be driven by the rather narrowly defined economic interests of global capitalism that, as noted, have been claimed to lead to structural global imbalances.

While the WTO, IMF, WB and OECD are orientated towards achieving global economic outcomes, the other major global institution is the United Nations. The purpose of the UN is to promote and maintain international peace and security through friendly relations and dispute resolution, and to support human rights (1948 Universal Declaration of Human Rights, United Nations). In large part, this role came out of a global desire to promote peace and international harmony following the catastrophe of the Second World War. The globalizing aspect of the UN derives from its requirement that its 192 member countries (as of 2011) commit to being good global citizens, abide by UN agreements and conventions and support its various agencies. UN agencies include the Security Council, the Economic and Social Council, the Trusteeship Council, the International Court of Justice, and offices including the High Commissioner for Refugees (UNHCR), Conference on Trade and Development (UNCTAD), the UN Children's Fund (UNICEF) and the UN Development Programme (UNDP). The UN is also linked to the IMF, WB, World Health Organization and similar intergovernmental organizations through co-operative agreements. The UN recognizes that broader global responsibility requires international institutions, and also supports the case for reform of international institutions, including its own Security Council, to make them more representative. Related to the above, the UN has sponsored a Global Compact to establish and promote a shared set of core values regarding labour standards, human rights and the environment. In this sense, the UN is as close to a global government as exists, although the fact that its agreements and conventions largely rely on the co-operation of member countries means that it has very little scope for enforcing its decisions and they are, consequently, frequently observed in the breech.

New or old?

The public idea of globalization has gained currency since the 1980s and in particular from the 1990s, following the end of the Cold War and the subsequent opening up of global markets. However, the term itself was first coined in the 1960s, following the rise of transnational corporations. A number of theorists even argue that it began with the first circumnavigation of the globe in 1519–22 (despite that set of linked voyages being a rather tenuous venture), or that the 'world system' (i.e. globalization) goes back some 5,000 years (see Frank and Gills 1992, 1993). Global exploration proceeded quickly and by the end of the nineteenth century global trade and investment, as a proportion of global capital, was at a record high. At the same time, those few parts of the world not already colonized were becoming so. This event, or series of events, not only integrated virtually all parts of the world into common administrative groupings, it also reorganized much of the economic activity in the colonies towards providing unprocessed or semi-processed goods for European and North American markets. In this respect, the colonies were linked to what were to become the developed countries in ways that implied their structural economic subservience and which set many of the opportunities or lack thereof that came to define the newly independent states in the post-colonial era.

The First World War brought global economic expansion to a halt and, although it continued again in the 1920s, it was severely buffeted by the Great Depression of the 1930s. However, during this time there were also increasing global standards applied to measurements of weights, distance, time and space. The post-Second World War period saw the emancipation of virtually all of the world's colonies and marked an era of both greater global interaction and greater global competition, not least between two great rival ideologies: capitalism and economic central planning (generally, although inaccurately, described as 'communism' or 'Marxism'). The 'long boom' from the early 1950s until the mid-1970s, saw consumer-driven global capitalism develop at a functionally unprecedented rate. This paralleled the struggle of most post-colonial states to become economically functional within the increasingly globalized system (as discussed in other chapters).

Other aspects of globalization from this time included major improvements in global communications, especially through telephone and satellite technology and an increasing level of international air travel that speeded up communications and enhanced both international business and the global spread of ideas. The aforementioned collapse of economic central planning (signified most clearly by the tearing down of the Berlin Wall and the end of the Soviet Union), the advent of computerization and the related introduction of the internet shifted global communication, and hence global business, to another plane, seemingly to 'shrink' the world, at least for the lucky billion or so who live in developed countries or who comprise the elite in developing countries. Notably, the flows of trade and finance that have ensued are now at unprecedented levels (see further discussion of this in Chapter 6), and this alone is argued to be a, perhaps the, defining characteristic of globalization. And along with unprecedented production, trade and integration, so too have the by-products of such development become global (see Chapter 11). For most, however, globalization has not meant greater access to global resources but being buffeted by material circumstances that are often the consequence of decisions taken by otherwise unconnected people on the other side of the globe. And for many who do have access to that most pervasive medium of global communication – television – the global messages are overwhelmingly trite and often culturally and spiritually corrosive.

While there is no doubt that globalization exists as an idea, there are varying perspectives on what globalization actually means and to the extent of its pervasiveness. These views could be broadly categorized according to hyperglobalists, sceptics and transformationalists.

Hyperglobalists

Hyperglobalists are broadly that group that could be called the 'boosters' of globalization; those whose theoretical arguments give legitimacy to others who act often in their own interests. The hyperglobalists, exemplified by Kenichi Ohmae, regard the world as dominated by transnational corporations that in an unregulated environment are the source of efficiency, unstoppable progress and are vehicles for the creation and dispersal of wealth on a global scale (at least to those countries that embrace such globalization). Within this, the capacity for states to erect barriers to global trade has reduced their legitimacy in such a global environment (Ohmae 1991, 1995, 1996, 2005). This view of globalization posits it as the ultimate expression of modernism (which one development paradigm held as synonymous with development) and as the logical endpoint for human development.

The hyperglobalist position argues that globalization is a fact and that it is and should be unstoppable. The primary statistic to support the hyperglobalist case that the world is indeed economically integrating, and at a vastly increased rate, is the turnover of foreign exchange, which increased by 10 times between 1979 and 1997 relative to global GDP (Guillen 2001: 6). By 2011, foreign exchange turnover had reached just under US$4 trillion a day, or 20 per cent more than in early 2007 (IBT 2001). Hyperglobalists argue that economic globalization is to everyone's benefit, often in the near to middle term. Proponents of this position cite evidence to support the assertion that inequalities in global income and poverty are decreasing, claiming that this is a consequence of states complying with the largely free market requirements of economic globalization. The World Bank, for example, argues that where poorer countries have lowered their tariff barriers they have increased employment through shifting industry towards export-orientated markets, which generally earn more than industries that compete for local markets. The World Bank cites the example of China's engagement with global trade, and its growth in income from $1,460 per capita in 1980 to $4,120 in 1999 and $11,000 in 2011 (calculated for purchasing parity power). Or to look at it another way, in 1980 American citizens earned 12.5 times as much as Chinese but by 1999 the difference was only 7.4 times (though this still represents a strong advantage). The World Bank also claims that income disparity is decreasing in Asia and Latin America (although this was before various financial crises beset some Asian and Latin American states – see Prasad et al. 2003 for an alternative view from the IMF). In such circumstances, lower incomes tend to reflect lower education and productivity standards, although as capital accumulates there is a capital shift towards more capital- and knowledge-intensive industry that generates high income. Where poverty has increased, this has reflected a failure to integrate into the global economy (World Bank 2002a, 2002b).

Indeed, in many countries, notably in East Asia but also in some cases in Latin America, per capita GDP has increased relative to the United States (WB-GNI 2002) However, in many cases this is a consequence of a complex array of factors, including history, proximity or access to natural resources and markets, industrial predisposition, and prior industrialization or infrastructure development. Further, such statistical information is not based on the exchange rate between currencies, i.e. it is not denominated in single-currency (such as US dollar) terms. Rather, such analysis is based on the parity purchasing power (PPP) of particular currencies within their own countries and there are numerous arguments to suggest that, while PPP gives a better indication of real income value, it does not provide an overall, especially macroeconomic, picture (nor does it distinguish between lower-cost local products and higher-cost, often higher technology, imports).

While the hyperglobalization group argues that globalization does not make the world more economically unequal (see Lindert and Williamson 2002), there is no absolute agreement on this point. Duncan suggests that globalization may indeed increase economic inequality in some countries, notably through the economic 'shocks' this can induce. But he suggests that this can still be overcome through 'risk management' and other internal structural adjustments. And he still says that poverty is rising in countries that do not open themselves to globalization (Duncan 2000). Similarly, the UNDP generally favours the advantages of globalization, but note that it also has 'negative, disruptive, marginalizing aspects' (UNHDR 1999: 1).

Sceptics

The sceptics' position on globalization is generally that if it does exist, it has been overstated, that it is not especially new and the effects on world trade are primarily amongst the developed economies of North

America, Western Europe and Japan. This, sceptics say, represents an increase in economic internationalization but not in economic globalization; that domestic investment remains greater than foreign investment, that the volume of trade is small relative to the size of trading economies, that most companies locate most of their staff in their home countries and that large areas of the world are little touched by such internationalization or globalization (Hirst and Thompson 1996; Wade 1996: 66–84). Such sceptics also note that, far from becoming an anachronism in a 'borderless' world, the state is stronger that in any previous period (a view that found renewed impetus from the unilateral 'realism' of the US post-11 September 2001). Not only is the state stronger or more unilateral, at least in some cases, sceptics claim, but there has also been a significant rise in the number of independent states over the primary period of contemporary globalization, from 159 UN members in 1990 to 192 by 2006 (UN 2006), with numerous more attempting to assert independent state status.

However, while the state is still understood as the primary manifestation of collective political will, the increase in the number of states in significant part reflects the failure of pre-existing states, and the consequent assertion of a more local political identity. Moreover, most of the states that have come into being in that period were beholden to multilateral organizations for their political or economic survival and were in that sense more a product of globalization than a reaction to it. Finally, the increase in the quantity of states did not imply a qualitative assertion and, while there were more states, the capacity of states to exercise independent authority in the realm of macroeconomic policy had diminished significantly over this period. There were, however, exceptions to these macroeconomic 'rules'.

The Prime Minister of Malaysia, Mahathir Mohamad, was one of the more successful critics of globalization, rejecting IMF intervention and policies in Malaysia following the 1997 South East Asian economic crisis and instituting monetary and financial controls which saw Malaysia recover from the crisis more quickly and thoroughly than its neighbours. After that, Mahathir continued to accept capitalism and foreign investment while lambasting the laissez-faire aspects of globalization, arguing that the 'one size fits all' policies pursued by the WTO, IMF and WB 'tend to favor the agenda of richer countries that dominate them' and 'hinder the ability of the individual country to choose the set of policies that suits its own development needs'. In particular, Mahathir espoused the 'selective' acceptance of globalization, in particular the timing, manner and extent to which a country participates in globalization. He also argued for the selective protection of strategic industries 'for the good of the country'. To that end, a country must retain a decisive and independent political leadership (Mahathir 2002). Various Latin American states, in particular Venezuala and Bolivia, have also opposed what they argue is unilateral intervention by such agencies, with varying degrees of success.

Positioned at the further end of the sceptics scale are those oppositionist groups that not only doubt the claims for globalization but which regard it as being actively negative. The broad view represented by such groups claims that rather than globalization leading to a reduction in income inequality, it actually increases such inequality, through the failure of the global 'trickle-down' effect (in which the spending of the rich contributes to the wealth of the poor) adequately to 'trickle down'. In particular, they often cite the UNDP 1999 Human Development Report, which notes that over the decade to 1999 the number of people earning $1 or less a day had remained static at 1.2 billion, while the number of people earning less than $2 a day had increased from just over 2.5 billion to 2.8 billion. Of the world's 42 poorest countries, only one had shown a meaningful increase in per capita GDP between 1980 and 2010 (UNDP 2010a), while the UNDP's rdeveloped 'multidimensional measure of poverty' showed that 1.75 billion people lived in poverty, of whom 1.44 billion lived in less than US$1.25 a day (UNDP 2010b). The 1999 report also noted that the gap in global income between the world's richest 20 per cent and the world's poorest 20 per cent has increased from 30:1 in 1960 to 82:1 by 1995 and had got progressively worse from that time (UNNS 2008). While there were net global improvements in some areas, such as the reduction of infant mortality, this could not be attributed to globalization as such. A range of other indicators did, however, show that the world's poorest countries largely remained exceptionally poor, and in many cases were slipping by comparison with developed countries (UNHDR 1999: ch. 1; HDR 2006).

Further, the poorest 20 per cent of the world's population enjoyed just 1 per cent of global GDP, global export markets, foreign direct investment (FDI) and the world's telephone lines. The world's richest 20 per cent, by comparison, enjoyed 86 per cent of global GDP, 82 per cent of the world's export markets, 68 per cent of FDI and 74 per cent of the world's telephone lines. According to Oxfam:

> The world's 48 poorest countries have seen their share of world trade decline by more than 40 per cent since 1980 to a mere 0.4 per cent ... The agriculture and textiles sectors, in which poor countries are most competitive, remain subject to a prohibitive array of high

and escalating tariffs, quotas, and seasonal restrictions. (Oxfam 2002; see also Kamal-Chaoui 2000)

Another way of looking at it was that the world's richest 1 per cent earned as much as the world's poorest 57 per cent (Elliott and Denny 2002).

Like Oxfam, organizations such as The South Centre and the Group of 77 (developing country groups) are critical of the IMF and the WB for failing to live up to their rhetoric on poverty alleviation and, through structural adjustment policies, in many cases exacerbating poverty. Such organizations also call for developing country debt to be cancelled, particularly where such debt is low in absolute terms but also unsustainable. They were also critical of the WTO for promoting policies that encourage trade at the expense of developing countries (South Centre 2008).

Depending on the method of analysis, most of the critiques of capitalist globalization could be understood as variations on a left-liberal political agenda. That is, such critiques tend to posit equity of distribution before capital accumulation and the supremacy of the social and political over the economic. In particular, there is a wholesale rejection of the idea that markets should function without accountability beyond 'market forces', reinforced as a result of the GFC. As a consequence, this coalescing of groups around such core ideas has resulted in a competing form of globalization in which networks of groups, organizations and even countries combine to pressure or protest against economic globalization's otherwise seemingly unstoppable march. A key network in the anti-economic globalization debate is the World Social Forum (WSF), the explicit leftist orientation which looks towards rebuilding leftist politics through a loose alignment of like-minded organizations within a globalized context. While the WSF is a global organization, it was founded in Brazil and its orientation has remained with the world's poorer countries. In this, it 'stand[s] in opposition to a process of globalization commanded by the large multinational corporations and by the governments and international institutions at the service of those corporations' interests, with the complicity of national governments' (WSF 2002: pt 4). Various (mostly quite small) left-wing political parties around the world have constructed generally similar Marxian critiques of economic globalization, seeing it as essentially the global spread of capitalism in which the global poor are exploited by the global rich, while a number of organizations have arisen specifically in response to economic globalization, notably around specific meetings of the WTO (e.g. Genoa 1998; Seattle 1999).

Following from, and in some aspects related to, the sceptics' position, within the critique of globalization there is also a significant environmental debate which is critical of globalization's pursuit of profit at the expense of the natural environment and the exploitation of developing countries' often lax environmental regulations. This follows on from globalization's lack of commitment to or exploitation of the local, in which neither foreigners nor elites are directly subject to the consequences of local environmental degradation. Organizations such as Friends of the Earth, Greenpeace, the World Wildlife Fund and others are all critical of the environmental record of global capitalism, notably over global warming, deforestation and the depletion of other non-renewable natural resources and the production and inappropriate disposal of harmful by-products.

Friends of the Earth, for instance, have constructed a 'WTO environmental scorecard' that identifies WTO decisions that have had a direct negative environmental outcome. These include 'dirty' petroleum products in Venezuela, overturning European preferences for Caribbean (low pesticide) bananas, overturning a European ban on hormone-treated beef and against a US ban on shrimp fishing that harmed turtles and other sealife (FOE 2002) and arguing against genetically modified foods (FOE 2005). Greenpeace similarly notes that trade liberalization has been undertaken without an environmental impact assessment, that it has not introduced environmental precautionary measures and has side-stepped responsibility on international environmental law such as the Kyoto Protocol on Climate Change (Greenpeace 2001). Many such organizations argue that there needs to be trade sanctions to enforce environmental goals. Interestingly, these organizations are themselves global, although representing very much an alternative vision to the conventional global free-trade developmentalist model.

Transformationalists

Within the globalization debate, there is a group that has been identified as 'transformationalists' which in some areas intersects with the sceptics' position and which sees globalization as part of a historical process of multiple transformations. These transformations vary from place to place and time to time in terms of extent and intensity of change and the speed and impact of such change (Held et al. 1999). In some senses, the transformationalist understanding of globalization corresponds to the debate between modernism and post-modernism, the former equating with hyperglobalization and the latter with a transformationalist understanding. In particular, the plural quality of the transformationalists' understanding, emphasizing difference, inconsistency and diffuse centres of power, contrasting with the actual or claimed singularity of hyper-globalization. Giddens has argued, for instance, that the process of globalization has been uneven and, while it co-ordinates, it also aids the process of inter-state fragmentation, with states proceeding less in a uniform direction than displaying opposed or competing tendencies (Giddens 1990: 64, 175), a process magnified by the GFC (Sassen 2011). In a not unrelated manner, many observers note that globalization is less 'global' than it is regional, being reflected not only in increased trade and investment between OECD countries but also through the development of trading blocs or groups, such as the North American Free Trade Agreement, the European Union, the Association of South East Asian Nations, the Southern Common Market (Latin America), West African Economic and Monetary Union, the Asia-Pacific Economic Co-operation forum, and others.

Others, meanwhile, have argued that the process of globalization has produced a complex series of inconsistently related outcomes that serve to create uniformity in some spheres at some times but competing tendencies in others. The distribution of income within developing countries could be a case in point, with many developing countries manifesting an increasing gap in income distribution. Kohl and O'Rourke noted that in east Asia, income inequality fell while economic growth was led by export demand that was, in turn, supported by higher education levels. However, where export growth exceeded educational capacity, income inequality grew. They also note that while factors other than globalization appeared to be more important in determining income inequality, the 'shocks' introduced by globalization could and often did exacerbate such inequality (Kohl and O'Rourke 2000: 44–6). And even in a relatively successful economy, such as Malaysia, income inequality shifted only slightly over the 20 years from 1970 to 1989 (Yusoff et al. 2000), while in Argentina globalization was recognized as being a significant contributor to income inequality (Bebczuk and Gasparini 2000). However, in other cases, the impact of globalization has been at best ambiguous, on balance has been matched by a global gap in income (HDR 2006) and in some cases has been clearly positive (e.g. Singapore, Taiwan, Hong Kong).

In this, the political value-judgements applied to the policy implications of globalization, especially economic globalization, are paramount, at least in those states able or willing to assert a degree of autonomy from the globalization paradigm (Rodrik 2011). Perhaps in this the distinction needs to be made between developed and developing countries, and the economic capacity for diversification between developed countries (types of complex manufactures and information-based systems) and between developed and developing countries, and the relative homogenization of economic capacity (simple primary exports and labour intensive production) on the part of many developing countries. Within this, it should be noted, a small number of countries have made the leap from developing to developed status, in particular the 'four tigers' of East Asia. But the conducive circumstances of these countries have been identified as specific and their feat has not been widely replicated.

In all of this, the alleged modification of state sovereignty is in one sense just another domain for elite domination. It is less that state sovereignty is being reduced but that there is a variation in the role and function of the state, in particular variation that has implications for dividing elite and common interest along international lines which can in turn manifest as corruption, oppression and so on. The 'state', as an idea, is only sacrosanct for those who have, or who believe they have, a vested interest in its maintenance. To this end, the state, as an institution, has had variously to accommodate differing sources of pressure; from international institutions in the realms of economics and politics on one hand and demands from 'localisms' (community groups, separatists, etc.) on the other, which have tended to weaken the institutional independence of many states and to some observers have led to a 'hollowing out' of 'globalized' states. The biggest impact on the functioning of the state has, therefore, been in how states rearrange themselves in light of such external influences. The hyperglobalists' singularity implies a Fukuyama-ist 'end of history' which instead of achieving hegemony has remained challenged and it is probable that the 'democratic fatalism' – the inevitable advent of democracy as the political expression of liberal capitalism – implied in this totalizing idea is mistaken. But in the global contest of ideas and information, the normative and historical claim to such a singularity is perhaps the greatest intellectual challenge to the idea of the state.

'Realism'

In some areas of debate and as noted above, globalization is taken to mean economic globalization, especially of a laissez-faire capitalist type. There are two points worth noting here. The first is that there is little new about global trade or what might be called global 'economic imperialism'. The second is that there is implied to be something wrong with economic globalization as such, whereas this more probably refers to global laissez-faire capitalism. Critics of economic globalization would, on the face of it, be happier with a more equitable global distribution of wealth that would, by definition, also constitute 'globalization'.

Global capitalism, of the free-market type, has developed a life of its own, though in ways that could not be easily constrained by what remains a politically and often economically fragmented international community. In simple terms, if global capital is unhappy with one site of investment it can, relatively simply, pick up and move to another. The logic of this process is that, in order to prosper, communities must attract global capital and those that do (and do so within proper investment guidelines) tend to prosper, while those that don't sink. Yet in order to appear attractive to global capital, communities often have to undercut their competitors which in turn calls forth their competitors, also cutting in what amounts to a downward cycle, if not spiral, of poverty. The wage structures of Indonesia and the Philippines well illustrate this cause-and-effect model, with both competing against each other for foreign investment on the 'comparative advantage' basis of low wages.

There is, however, some debate about whether the term 'realism', in its international relations sense, accurately describes globalization. Assuming 'realism' to mean the capacity of states to protect their own interests or impose such interests on others, a critical assessment of globalization would argue that it does reflect the 'realist' policies of the world's economically developed states, not least of which is the US. However, another analysis could argue that the interdependence implied in globalization is at odds with the independence implied in realism, that realism tends more towards protectionist economic policies, and that alliances are displaced by collective security (Gurtov 1994: ch. 2). However, a critical analysis of both realism and globalization would suggest that they are variations on the same theme, that they both enhance the capacity of selected states, that WTO/IMF/WB prescriptions do function as a type of protectionism and that collective security is only limited to those states that are part of the globalization alliance or which are strategically important to the globalization agenda.

This then posits a type of 'neo-realism' in international relations, in which dominant states define domestic policy in spite of globalizing tendencies, in which the give and take of international relations is increasingly negotiated (although with the obvious capacity for pressure) and in which states themselves are seen to be acting less on behalf of the direct interests of their citizens as much as on behalf of ideological assumptions about what is best for the state, which include what might be termed its other 'stakeholders', such as the corporate sector and, in some cases, government institutions. That is, the role of the state is becoming redefined or reorganized rather than disappearing (Held and Young 2011).

Conclusion

There is a case to suggest that globalization slowed in the last years of the twentieth century and again early in the twenty-first century, not least in response to the Asian economic crisis of 1997 and the GFC of 2007. But this was a temporary slowdown and did not mean that the process of globalization was in decline, at least not for the foreseeable future. That is, the various elements of globalization do appear to be progressing more or less inexorably. For those who abhor globalization and see little or nothing positive in it, this may well be cause for dismay. For those who champion or look forward to it, it is cause for some satisfaction. But for most, it simply is, in much the same way that the formation of nations in the nineteenth and twentieth centuries was, in part a constructed process and in part an imposed consolidation of political and economic territorial imperatives. There were then many who felt (and may still feel) uncomfortable about such territorial incorporation but on the whole the idea of ordering of the global community into states was a necessary precondition for political survival.

In one sense, the linkages and interdependencies that have come to characterize intrastate relations are coming to be replicated on a global scale. In the way that the train, mail and telegraph increased regional integration, so too global shipping, airlines, telecommunications and the Internet are increasing global integration. The oil for the machinery of national integration was industrialization, most successfully brought about through capitalism and the trade it implies. The oil for the machinery of global integration similarly remains capitalism and the trade it implies and expanded communications and the cultural integration that implies.

The difference between national integration and global integration, however, is that national integration and the terms upon which it was founded largely followed a long integration of regional peoples, whereas global integration has been relatively sudden, at least in its post-communist phase, and unaccountable in its application. Further, the construction of states has implied both rights and obligations on the part of both the state and its citizens, and within that a type of social contract. The notion of global rights and obligations exists in public rhetoric but is a very long way from being supported in the objective conditions of the lives of a very large proportion of the world's population, especially in terms of distribution of global income. In economic terms, states increasingly have global obligations that are functionally paid for by their citizens. However, in so far as 'rights' exist, they exist in practice at the state level, with global intervention occurring only where a case can be made that such intervention is in the clear global interest (or in the interest of a global power with the capacity to persuade others). Similarly, in so far as there is potential for a 'social contract', there is little doubt that if the world was one political community much of it would decry its conditions and question its position in such an agreement.

This, then, reflects the reality of globalization, which is that, regardless of the rhetoric of its usefulness, its capacity to produce growth or other forms of development, it is essentially a unilateral arrangement that reflects particular ideological views (see Cox 1996: 23). This unilateral arrangement, or the ideology it represents, does not necessarily reflect the views of the people of developed countries (although it may if they understood what sorts of compromises they might have to make in a more equitable, sustainable world) but of the major corporations and the governments that are symbiotically linked to them. In this sense, capitalism is more able to proceed in a laissez-faire manner globally than it is within states. Equally, the moderating factor on state-based capitalism, which is government that in theory represents the will of its citizens, does not exist in the 'anarchic' international environment. It is from this point that globalization and development can proceed in one of two general directions.

The first direction is that, corresponding to economic relations and the agreements that allow them to exist, global institutions will come to form the machinery of a functional global government, operating as an effective federation joined in common interest. As global capitalism develops, it may be that it will need to ensure that developing countries do in fact grow richer (if in a more sustainable manner) in order to continue to provide the markets that capitalism cannot survive without. This will then require that the obvious imbalance in global wealth in part be addressed through sheer economic necessity. The other direction that globalization can proceed in is, after having fantasized about genuine laissez-faire economics which have historically never existed, capitalism's free-market theorists will achieve their goal of unregulated (or 'self-regulating') economic activity with no role for 'government'. Unfettered capitalism's internal logic will, according to this theory, ensure the greatest potential for global growth and the most pragmatic distribution of economic good. An alternative view is that such unfettered capitalism will simply see the accumulation of wealth in some places, but not in others. The problem with this scenario, however, is that, even assuming that such theory can translate in practice before short-term greed produces environmental unsustainability, the social and economic cost that is already being borne by much of the world's population will increase and will, almost inevitably, result in some form of political response.

It has been argued, for example, that global Islam's critique of the West is in large part fuelled by such structural inequality, expressed as repression (see, for example, Chirzin 2002) and that this has in turn created the grounds for radical and terroristic responses. In this it has employed the communications tools of globalization, although these have been used to profoundly reject globalization's laissez-faire policies. Less religiously motivated, it was a similar (though perhaps not as profound) economic imbalance that prompted the rise of theoretical and then practical state-based 'communism' in the late nineteenth and early twentieth centuries, initially expressed as terror and then as revolution. As noted by Plekhanov in the Russian context over 100 years ago, the underprivileged 'suffer not only from the development of capitalism, but also from the scarcity of that development' (in Kochan 1963: 204). It was the failure to address the shortcomings of both capitalism and the distribution of capitalism's benefits that led directly to the Russian Revolution of 1917, in which three decades of high-level foreign investment was appropriated by the Bolsheviks (Kochan 1963: 174, 199–200). It would take little imagination to conceive of a similar global response to global capitalism's capacity for rapaciousness. However, in this there may be a glimmer of hope. Recognizing the radical option as a response to an unrestrained global capitalism, it may be that, as occurred in states a century or so earlier, there will be a compromise in which the demands for equity are tempered by moderation and reform and in which the desire for unrestrained profit is similarly tempered. As an illustration of this possibility, however, the GFC only led to some relatively mild controls on the financial sector and not to the substantial overhauling many had called for. It may be that there will be further crises before such a balance is struck. But without a balance between developed and developing countries, and between global capitalism and global responsibility and equity, the future looks more rather than less bleak.

Chapter 5

The Economics of Development

John McKay

While most of us accept that development is about much more than economics and growth, there is no doubt that academic and policy debates have been dominated by economic considerations. Work in this area has a long and conspicuous history and has attracted some of the best minds in the history of analytical thought, and not only in the western world. In the period since the Second World War, there has been a whole series of debates and controversies about the economic dimensions of development theory and practice but these can be summarized in ten basic questions that will be used to structure discussion in the rest of this chapter.

First, how does growth happen and what are its major drivers? Trying to understand the origins of growth is perhaps the most basic question of all, and one which absorbs the constant attention of the poorer countries. For some, it is simply a matter of following the right policy recipe – managing exchange rates, labour costs, inflation, investment and the like. But, others suggest, this economic formula will only work in the presence of a number of other key conditions. Human capital must be available in adequate amounts and with the required skills. Appropriate governance structures must be in place to regulate the actions of individuals and companies, and to avoid problems of corruption or exploitation. Political systems must be robust enough to avoid disputes over access to resources or to the various benefits of development boiling over into destructive conflicts. This in turn raises the issue of whether it is possible simply to put in place one kind of economic system, such as liberal democracy, and then expect all other positive outcomes to flow automatically, or whether the various societal domains are much more discrete.

Second, is growth an easy process or does it require much effort and sacrifice? It has been suggested that with the removal of some of the 'unnatural' constraints on development, for example old corrupt elites or inward-looking governments, growth will occur spontaneously and naturally without the need for any further inputs. But other theorists and practitioners contend that in fact growth is difficult and only achieved at a great price. There are many false starts and wrong turns, and all the required conditions and inputs must be available at just the right time and place. Growth to them is a conditional and contextual process that must proceed in the correct set of sequences.

Third, in the generation of growth what are the roles of the market and of the state? If growth is seen as easy and natural, this usually rests on the assumption that market forces can be effective almost single-handedly. Some basic regulation may be necessary but government involvement should be kept to a minimum. The extreme opposite of this view is represented by the now largely discredited centrally planned economies of the Soviet era, but many more moderate commentators have suggested that what is needed in the stimulation and management of growth is a creative and mutually supportive partnership between the state and the market, and this was the basis of the Asian economic miracle. This debate has been given added impetus after the onset of the global financial crisis (GFC), and one key argument presented here is that the state is once again recognized as being central to all parts of the growth process and of the broader development agenda (Tanzi, 2011).

Fourth, what are the appropriate roles of the state and the private sector? Similarly, it has been contended that while the private sector can contribute a great deal to the generation of growth, governments are needed to guarantee the availability of certain key elements such as political stability, education and effective infrastructure. Governments can also provide financial incentives and facilitate co-operation between private and public institutions such as research centres.

Fifth, how can processes of structural change be managed, and how can costs be ameliorated? Development does not involve a single period of transformation but is a never-ending process of continual change and renewal. Structural change of this kind is always messy or even chaotic and, while society as a whole may benefit in the long run, some groups may have to bear great costs and hardship. This raises issues of how such intensely political processes are to be managed effectively, and how the costs as well as the benefits are to be apportioned.

Sixth, how can technology be generated, absorbed and used? Most theorists now recognize that growth processes, especially since the industrial revolution, have been partly driven by technological progress, and in the modern world the competitive position of all nations depends on their ability to generate or at least gain access to appropriate technologies. Even in advanced economies, this often requires creative alliances between universities, private companies and government research institutes but for less developed countries the tasks involved are even more fraught. This is particularly so in the early stages of development, when educated personnel are usually scarce, and in the difficult transition from simple, labour-intensive activities to more demanding higher-value industries. Countries such as China are now investing massively in upgrades of their technological base and this is creating problems for smaller nations with more limited financial resources.

Seventh, what is the role and rationale for foreign trade and investment? Much economic theory has been developed to support the notion that free trade is of benefit to all nations at every stage of development and will result in optimal efficiency in the use of scarce resources. However, in practice most countries have used various kinds of tariffs, quotas or other restrictions to benefit their own producers and such issues still make it difficult to move further with international agreements under the World Trade Organization. At various times, theories have been put forward in favour of certain kinds of restraints on access to particular markets until local industries have had time to establish themselves. Similarly, some commentators have argued that foreign investment should be limited until local companies have been able to acquire sufficient resources and experience to be able to compete.

Eighth, what is the role of foreign aid? One of the enduring problems of development is to explain how countries can make the initial move to a higher level of growth, after which the process may become self-sustaining. Many writers have suggested that foreign aid can provide such an impetus, and allow the construction of essential infrastructure, educational facilities and the like. Indeed, much of the practice of non-government development agencies as well as large official programmes of assistance is based on such a proposition. However, some critics have suggested that aid, if not carefully targeted, can crowd out national enterprises and stifle local initiative.

Ninth, what is the role of international co-operation and of international organizations and networks? Many of the same questions about aid apply equally to the activities of international organizations such as the World Bank and the various regional development banks. There has also been fierce controversy about the role of the IMF in supplying policy advice to national governments, especially in times of economic crisis.

Tenth, is economic development easier or more difficult in the current era of globalization? There is no doubt that the international economic and political environment facing developing countries now is very different from that prevailing when, for example, the original 'Tigers' of Asia began their spectacular transformation. However, there is little agreement about whether in fact it is now easier or more difficult to begin the development transition. Some argue that it is more difficult now that the rules of world trade have made illegal many of the strategies used by the developed as well as the Asian countries to achieve their rise. By contrast, others suggest that, given the massive availability of foreign direct investment, development is now easier to achieve if the right policies are followed. The debate around globalization has also renewed interest in the old question of the relationships between development and income inequalities.

In this short chapter, it is impossible to go into details in an area that is so broad and to do full justice to all of the debates that have raged over the centuries; however, the aim is to at least introduce some to most influential schools of thought on these key questions. The discussion is based around the first basic question concerning the drivers of growth but contrasting views on the other issues are also introduced. However, in the later part of the chapter there is a consideration of one of the key development issues of our age: the complex interrelationships at the international, national and more local scales between economic growth and inequality. Is inequality an inescapable result of processes of growth, especially in the earlier stages of the process? Has globalization resulted in an intensification of tendencies towards larger gaps between the rich and the poor? If large numbers of poor people can be lifted out of poverty, does it matter if at the same time the gaps between rich and poor are becoming larger? Is there evidence that growth rates can be maximized if in fact policies to minimize inequalities are pursued at the same time, which is a common interpretation of recent experiences in east Asia? Given the momentous shockwaves flowing from the global financial crisis (GFC) do our ideas and policy prescriptions need to be re-evaluated? These are policy issues that many analysts have also suggested are central to issues of political and social stability, and to the whole question of motivation and mass mobilization.

The main drivers of growth: competing schools of thought

The classical and neoclassical school

As was noted in Chapter 2, this set of theories has been clearly dominant both in the academic literature and in the policy formulations of the key international institutions, and has been so since at least the eighteenth century – however it already has been argued that some fundamental challenges have been thrown up by the GFC which began in 2007. The Europe that the major classical theorists knew was only just emerging from a past in which rapid economic growth had not been the norm, and one in which there was a delicate balance between population and resources. In such an environment the logical assumption was that population growth would depend upon the availability of those commodities necessary to support life, and food in particular, and that in any period of growth there was a constant race between the growth of population and the increased availability, largely through technological progress, of the those things needed to support life. Malthus of course made this constant battle between population and resource availability central to his arguments, believing that the geometric increases in population were bound in time to dwarf any gains that might be made through technological development.

For these classical thinkers – such as Adam Smith and John Stuart Mill – the output that could be achieved from any economy was dependent upon the supply of labour, the total stock of capital, the size of available land and other natural resources and the level of technology that could be applied to the productive process. However, a significant increase in the supply of land, which was by far the most important resource at the time, was seen as out of the question. This was also an age of relative capital scarcity, which was crucial since they believed that the rate of technological progress was dependent upon the availability of new capital sources. The creation of new investment capital was directly dependent on the rate of profit, which was in turn related to the supply of labour and the level of technology available in the production process. As wage levels and household incomes increased, more food and better housing could be obtained, and this generally meant that more infant children survived to adulthood and were able to enter the growing labour force.

As will be obvious, there is a good deal of circularity in the argument: the total system grows through what we now know as a pattern of circular and cumulative causation – each success leads to a further round of expansion. But by the same logic any failure or contraction is successively spread and magnified throughout the system. While the supply of all factors of production was limited and finite, the one element that was perhaps most open to change was the supply of capital for investment, and this was dependent in large part on the rate of saving that could be achieved. But all of these early theorists had a view that at some time in the future a mature and essentially stationary economy was inevitable, albeit at a relatively high level of prosperity: none of these theorists was able to foretell the impact of the riches that became available for the New World and later from the numerous colonies that were acquired by the dominant powers.

Another common observation on the classical school is that since these writers lived in economies that were still predominantly agrarian, their arguments were built around single-sector entities that had the supply of land at their centre. However, as has been pointed out by some later reviewers (for example, Benjamin Higgins 1958), Malthus was something of an exception in this regard. He noted that as development proceeds there is an accompanying process of structural change, resulting in a diminished share of total output coming from the agricultural sector. Thus he foreshadowed much later analysis that would assume a dual or multi-sector economy in which the structure and dynamics of each sector were rather different. He also argued that increasing returns to scale were a particular characteristic of the emerging industrial sector, and this has important implications for the usual classical assumptions about the inevitability of stagnation in mature economies.

It is likely that all classical theorists were well aware of the role of the entrepreneur in stimulating investment and technological progress, but this ingredient was not really introduced as a major element. However, this was taken up as a key explanation for progress by Joseph Schumpeter (1934), who saw growth not as a process of the steady accumulation of resources, labour and investment but as essentially unstable and episodic. He was of course the product of the twentieth century and not surprisingly saw the world in rather different terms from his classical forebears. Crucially, he argued that this technological upgrading was the direct result of the activities of creative entrepreneurs. Successful economies are those that are able to encourage and reward such creative contributors, and this will necessitate the emergence of a national income distribution that provides incentives for this creative class.

After the Second World War, as problems of post-conflict reconstruction and the development of the former colonies came to the fore, there emerged renewed interest in theories of growth. This can now been seen as the birth of modern growth theory which has been dominated by neoclassical thought, firmly grounded in the assumptions and methods of the classical thinkers but attempting to reflect the new realities of the world which these theories sought to explain. This group of theorists agreed on a wide range of issues but controversies existed about a number of key questions. One debate concerned that assumption of constant returns to scale that was inherited from the classical school. Many neoclassical theorists have been happy to retain this assumption, while others maintained that in the modern economy, as the size of production units increases there are often extra efficiencies in output. Secondly, some writers have argued that the growth of a number of key factors of production is exogenously determined, while others have suggested that most of these processes are endogenous to the system. Some economists, following Schumpeter, believed that technological development is the result of outside forces – particularly investment in education and the ability of the social and political system to generate creative entrepreneurs – while others have stressed that technological process is largely a process internal to the economy mostly driven by 'learning by doing'. The general tendency in modern growth theory is to rely more and more on endogenous models, based largely on the ideologically driven assumption that the neoclassical economy is a self-contained and self-sufficient system that need not rely on outside stimulus. A third issue relates to the role and origins of human capital growth that has been central to the debates about the east Asian growth model.

It is generally recognized that the neoclassical school was heralded by Robert Solow (1956) through the formalization of his growth model that assumed that in a competitive capitalist economy there are constant returns to scale and diminishing returns to all factors of production. Both labour and technology are exogenously determined and grow at a constant rate. Crucially, with these assumptions the economy converges to an equilibrium. Much later theorizing derives from this model, although some of the assumptions, and hence the convergence on equilibrium, have been questioned.

But in this period there also emerged a range of theorists that began to add a much greater level of sophistication to the debate. Several key criticisms of the established growth theory had begun to emerge, some of which have already been noted. Many researchers had high expectations, or perhaps unrealistic hopes, of just what ought to be explained by these economic theories and felt compromised by the fact that in a number of areas key factors were determined externally to the models. Second, the expected convergence of incomes between countries did not seem to be happening. Third, it was clear that many of the limits on the expansion of crucial factors of production that had been assumed by the classical theorists could no longer be justified. Importantly, the growth of the labour supply was accelerating rapidly as new medical services became available. Fourth, the rapid technological advances that had been generated by both world wars and had then revolutionized factory production in particular meant that technological change needed a much more central place in any explanation of growth. Finally, empirical evidence was also supplying ample evidence to challenge the assumptions of constant returns to scale.

In the 1940s and 1950s, three particularly interesting theorists attempted to deal with these criticisms. Rosenstein-Rodan (1943) looked at the question of increasing returns to scale, arguing that these resulted from technical progress within the factory system and that increased labour productivity was derived from new methods of industrial training and from the creation of social overhead capital. He was a champion of what has become known as the theory of the 'big push', arguing that a minimum quantum of investment was necessary to kick-start growth, something that could not be achieved by small increments of finance. Also important was Nurkse's (1952) work on why income disparities between countries persisted, and in particular why capital did not flow at this time from rich, high-wage countries to poorer nations. His argument was that in poor countries beset by vicious cycles of low levels of productivity and small markets, investment levels were depressed. Equally influential has been Arthur Lewis's (1954) seminal work on the influence of surplus labour on patterns of economic development. He portrayed underdeveloped economies as essentially dual in nature, consisting of a small modern industrial sector and a large subsistence sector with extensive disguised unemployment. The existence of this pool of surplus labour should facilitate the expansion of the modern sector, which could draw in large amounts of cheap labour without causing wage increases. These were all important contributions, and Ros (2005), for example, has argued that these ideas were far more relevant to the real world situation that was emerging than much of the later theorizing.

What in fact happened, to cut a long and complex story very short, was that the field became dominated by two issues. The first was the concentration on the supply of investment capital as the element that could perhaps be stimulated more easily and which could then initiate a virtuous cycle of growth through increased productivity, output, wages growth and profitability and hence a new round of enhanced investment, something already discussed in Chapter 2. Secondly, there has been special concentration on the role of technological change and the resultant increases in productivity, and on the creation of new human capital. Paul Romer (1986) argued that investments in research and development are central to the creation of increasing returns and technological progress can free the economy from any tendency to converge on an equilibrium.

So far I have concentrated on theories that attempted to account for growth within single countries but in fact international trade and investment have become increasingly important in the global economy and hence have also attracted a great deal of attention. Adam Smith is recognized as the creator of the concept of absolute advantage, according to which nations should concentrate on the production of goods in which they hold some kind of cost advantage. But it was Ricardo who extended this argument to include the case for specialization in national exports that had such an advantage, and who argued that partner nations in trade would all benefit from this kind of exchange. This has been the basis of much work within mainstream economics, which has attempted to provide ever more technically sophisticated support for this basic proposition. However, a number of strong criticisms, or at least qualifications, of this unreserved support for the benefits of international trade, and in particular increasingly free trade, have emerged (see, for example, Dutt 2005; U. Patnaik 2005).

Marxist and neo-Marxist theories

The relationship between the theories of Marx and his followers to theories of development and underdevelopment is of a rather different order to the propositions of the more orthodox neoclassical persuasion. Mainstream economic theory, and the policies derived from it, has always been seen by its adherents as being equally applicable to all nations regardless of their different histories or institutional systems – what has now become known as a 'one size fits all' approach. By contrast Marx first put forward a complex set of theories to explain the dynamics of capitalist economies, and then postulated a set of relationships between those nations that had made the transition to capitalism and the rest of the world.

Marx's theories, set out particularly in the first volume of *Das Kapital* and with Friedrich Engels in *The Communist Manifesto*, are simultaneously explanations of developments in the spheres of economics, politics and social life, but it is the particular economic basis of the capitalist system that underpins everything. While all societies must enable the life of their citizens to continue through the production of food and other material needs, capitalism is unique in that all production is geared to the market exchange of commodities. The 'true' value of these commodities consists of the amount of human labour that has been devoted to their production but the capitalist is able to sell his products at a higher price, the exchange value. Wages must be paid by the owner to the workers to at least allow them to stay alive and reproduce the next generation of labour but wages are not set at a level equal to the exchange value of the goods produced. The difference is the surplus value, the basis of profits for the capitalist class. The capitalist system is inherently competitive and over time individual companies are faced with the problem of declining profits. This is partly overcome by the even greater exploitation of workers through the imposition of longer working hours or lower wages, and the existence of a 'reserve army' of the unemployed ensures that this has to be accepted by workers. There is also strong pressure to introduce new technologies. At the social and political levels of analysis, Marx subscribed to a basic notion of historical materialism; people make and remake their lives through their productive activities, and it is the economic basis of society that produces a particular cultural superstructure. Crucially, workers within the capitalist system are alienated from the products of their labour, since the labour process is increasingly controlled by others, and consists of repetitive and specialized tasks within a complex division of labour. Thus there is none of the satisfaction of producing the complete and finished articles that was available to the earlier craft workers. Workers are also degraded through ever increasing levels of exploitation and hence are more alienated from each other as well as from the capitalist class (Hobsbawm 1998; Stedman Jones 2002; Wheen 2006).

Marx has been called the first real development economist in that he studies both development *under* capitalism and the development *of* capitalism (U. Patnaik 2005). As has often been noted, Marx was very concerned with the historical origins of capitalism, and the particular (or perhaps unique) juxtaposition of forces that allowed it to emerge in Europe, processes that involved momentous struggles. The gradual expansion of commodity production resulted in the weakening of merchant capital, but rather more was needed to really allow capitalism to flourish, and the question of other key factors in this issue of transition has fuelled much debate. A related question that Marx addressed concerned the lack of a similar capitalist revolution in countries such as India and China that had been rather richer than Europe until quite recently but were now rapidly falling behind. His response to this issue was to put forward the concept of the 'Asiatic mode of production'. Village subsistence economies were both unlikely and unable to move towards a capitalist mode of production, and the class of nobles that extracted surplus from village production used this wealth for conspicuous consumption rather than for the initiation of more productive economic systems. Marx's key contribution, though, was to put together the historical issues of the transition to capitalism in Europe with the question of why the rest of the world was falling behind into a single overarching process of capitalist dynamics. Basic here was the concept of *primary accumulation*, which provided the means for the transition to capitalism and heralded in the system of labour essential for the new economy. Also crucial was the inevitable movement towards the *centralization of capital*. Processes of primary accumulation were facilitated by the extraction of surplus from the rest of the world and this process became ever more efficient and exploitative through the centralization of capital into ever larger companies – insights that many claim make Marx still the most convincing analyst of contemporary globalisation.

These ideas have been built on by a range of theorists and political activists that have become known as the neo-Marxists. Perhaps most influential, and this includes policy making in some countries down to the present, has been the emergence of the Latin American school of dependency theorists, a movement that has already been introduced in Chapter 2. But it is important to look at the economic underpinnings of this kind of theorizing and assess its historical accuracy and usefulness in policy terms.

Within these broad neo-Marxist schools approaches, it is important to distinguish between *structuralist* and *dependency* approaches. Influenced by Keynesianism as well as by Marx, the structuralists saw the dual North–South division as crucial both at the international and national levels (Saad-Filho 2005). Markets are often very poor at dealing with the priorities for change in such a situation and there is a strong case for government intervention. Structuralists argue that free trade and the international division of labour work systematically in favour of the rich countries and against the developing world, because of the long-term deterioration in the terms of trade for the products coming from the developing world. The only way out of this structural imbalance is for developing countries to undertake their own independent programmes of industrialization. But there are severe problems associated with local industrial growth: the private sector is often weak and savings rates often low and hence strong government intervention is again essential.

As we have already seen, the dependency theorists went much further in their critique of economic orthodoxy, arguing that the West had become rich initially through the exploitation of the periphery, thereby facilitating the process of primary accumulation, and that this transfer of surplus value from the poor to the rich continued in the current phase of the centralization of capital. Thus the dependency theorists were pessimistic about the strategies proposed by the structuralists, including the creation of national manufacturing capacity. Nothing short of a fundamental recasting of international economic and political relations within a socialist model would have any real impact on the lives of the world's poor.

The Asian model of development

The Asian model revolves around much more than a set of economic concepts and policies. It has grown from the very political and social foundations of some very distinctive societies, but in terms of the economics of the Asian model, it is the role of the state that has given rise to most controversy. The theory of the developmental state has drawn on a number of important strands of economic thought that highlight the key roles that governments can play (Chang 1999). Rosenstein-Rodan's theory of the 'big push' was one such key foundation as was Alexander Gerschenkron's (1962) work on late industrialization in which he affirmed that, as global production increases and hence the minimum scale of efficient output is raised, so the size of investments must also increase markedly, and only through state involvement can nations seek to join the club of industrialized powers. In Japan, more recently in South Korea, Taiwan and Singapore, and later still in China, the role of the government has certainly been central. Governments had clear and detailed strategic plans for the development of their economies and indeed their wider societies. Key industries were identified, protected and supported until they were strong enough to be competitive in world markets. Extremely large investments were made in physical infrastructure, such as ports, roads and telecommunications systems, and in social infrastructure, especially education. In most cases, competition within key sectors was carefully managed and emerging 'national champions' were often given a monopoly position. Trade union activity and hence wage increases were carefully controlled in the name of maintaining export competitiveness, for it was the emphasis on exports of manufactured products that was also a very distinctive component of the Asian model. At the same time, the lack of market discipline within most individual industrial sectors was replaced by strong government supervision (Amsden 1989, 2001: Woo Jung-en 1991).

Two relatively recent developments have now brought the Asian model into a rather different perspective. The onset of the Asian financial crisis in 1997 was seen by some as completely discrediting this form of development theory and policy; however, more recent developments in the region, and some new interpretations, have forced us to rethink many of these hasty judgements. Second, the rise of China and its continued dramatic growth have also redirected our attention to theoretical and practical approaches coming out of Asia that are both plausible and effective, both within their own terms and as models for other developing countries.

The seemingly inexorable rise of China is particularly significant but can it be considered as part of the tradition of the Asian development model? Many commentators from the orthodox economic school have argued that China's success has been grounded on its abandonment of its old Communist agenda in favour of a capitalist system, but this would appear to be a gross oversimplification. Liew (2005) has argued that history, geography and institutional structure are all important in the choice of paths to development, and in particular the role of the Chinese Communist Party – albeit undergoing constant reform in the post-Mao period – has been central. The party has been able to reinvent itself and hold its monopoly position over power, and the market has been used as a tool of state power rather than as a replacement for it. Similarly, Baek (2005) has argued that the China has adopted many features of the earlier East Asian developmental model, maintaining strong control over the financial system, supporting to a large number of state-owned enterprises and fostering a range of national heavy industries.

The example of China has renewed interest in the old question of 'flexible rigidities' in East Asia (Chang 2007b). Orthodox economic theory makes a strong push for complete flexibility in markets, in allowing entry and exit of firms in any sector, and in the role of the financial system. But as Dore (1986) has pointed out, countries in East Asia have attempted to set out a strong vision for the future, have developed industrial policy frameworks for key sectors and, at least in the earlier phases, have controlled the banks and the provision of credit very carefully. This has inevitably meant some degree of 'rigidity'. However, at the level of the individual firm, and especially for smaller enterprises, there has been a greater emphasis on flexibility, allowing entrepreneurs to take advantage of new opportunities.

The challenge of the global financial crisis

The onset of the GFC has challenged many aspects of the conventional wisdom on the initiation of growth processes and, importantly, on the ways in which sustained progress can be maintained in the face of potential instability. The crisis and its implications are discussed in detail in Chapter 6, but here we consider some of the most important implications of this turbulent period, which at the time of writing is still reverberating through the global system. Of the myriad impacts, perhaps four are most important and likely to be long-lasting in their influence: the need to rethink some of our key theoretical assumptions on economic growth processes; the return of the state as a central actor in the initiation and maintenance of global and national growth; an acceleration in the rise of Asian nations, and China in particular, as key players in the global economic, political and strategic systems; and, the stagnation of the West and the concomitant rise in the relative importance of some of the developing economies.

As has already been noted in Chapter 2, a key impact of the GFC has been to call into question the supposed 'magic' of the market. Markets, which in the theories of many neo-liberal writers had been assumed to be infallible, self-correcting and self-regulating guides to current and future values as well as future risks, were shown to be in fact unstable and unreliable, prone to both mass panic and hysteria. Critiques of markets and their operations have, since the GFC, come from a variety of directions. Historical analysis has shown that over a long period, beginning with a number of crisis periods in the nineteenth century, markets have failed at crucial times, plunging national economies and the global system into serious recessions (Krugman 2008; Cassidy 2010; Ahamed 2009; Fox 2009; Shiller 2009). High level mathematical analysis, using fractal techniques, has also shown that markets are much more random and unpredictable than most commentators had believed (Mandelbrot and Hudson 2004). Much attention has also focused on risk and debt, the ways in which these can build up to dangerous levels and threaten the whole global economy (Reinhart and Rogoff 2009; Das 2011; Roubini and Mihm 2010).

As part of this new theoretical challenge to orthodox positions the question of the state has once again become of extreme interest, from a variety of perspectives. In the developed world the massive intervention by governments to prop up their financial systems and protect jobs – not always successfully – raised fundamental questions about relations between the state and the market. How long should such intervention continue, and to what extent should taxpayers be protected from future crises of this kind by improved regulation of the economy? Also basic is the question of in whose interests is the state intervening – a question that could equally be posed in the developing world. Duménil & Lévy (2011), for example, argue that we should not be surprised that the state would intervene on behalf of the ruling elites, and we should not expect any long-term change to come from such intervention, but other writers have taken a quite different view. In the developing world the role of the state that had been so downplayed in recent years especially by the key international organizations is now being reconsidered.

As we have seen, state intervention was a key element in the Asian Development Model, and the enormous attention given to the rise of Asia since the onset of the GFC has included a renewed interest in the Asian model including the potential for interventionist state action in a number of new areas. China now has a much greater influence in Africa, Latin America and a number of other developing regions and this is obviously giving much greater emphasis to Chinese approaches to development.

At the same time, the stagnation that is currently afflicting the economies of the United States and much of Europe is reducing the attractiveness of these models for developing countries and reducing the amount of investment available from the developed world. A number of developing economies, notably the so-called BRICS (Brazil, Russia, India, China and South Africa), are becoming much more important both economically and as models. The decline in the power of the United States suggests that the unipolar moment that occurred immediately after the end of the Cold War is being replaced by a multi-polar system, and as we have seen in Chapter 2 some commentators are speculating that this may mean the end of the whole 'development agenda'. It is to these kinds of policy debates that we now turn.

Policies to stimulate growth

Many of the theories considered in the first part of this chapter, and in particular the orthodox theories, did not emerge in response to the problems of the poorer countries. Rather, they related explicitly to the explanation of growth in the already developed economies. It was assumed rather that these emerging economies would simply follow the same development paths as the now rich countries had done earlier. Thus, for much of the period after the Second World War, the new Bretton Woods institutions, and notably the World Bank, followed what might be called 'common sense' modernization strategies that attempted to reproduce the western experience of growth. The particular emphasis was on the provision of infrastructure – roads, railways, ports, airports, dams and the like – that would facilitate development. All of this changed, however, in two opposing kinds of strategies. In a few nations, socialist or neo-Marxist solutions were attempted but the triumph of the neo-liberal agenda in the West encouraged the more widespread application of similar policy prescriptions. Thus the developing countries joined the mainstream. At the same time, the reaction in some quarters to the globalization experience and the related re-emergence of theories of imperialism and exploitation has also put some poorer countries at the forefront of a new kind of struggle. The example of rapid growth in Asia is also being seen by some as providing a justification for a new kind of policy direction. Thus, development theory and its policy recommendations have moved from being regarded as a marginal and exotic backwater to the very centre of intellectual ferment, and the impact of the GFC has significantly intensified this trend.

Orthodox policies and the Washington Consensus

In 1994, John Williamson wrote a landmark paper in which he set out what seemed to be the generally agreed policy framework within the Washington development institutions. His particular focus was on Latin America but his formula was rapidly applied to the rest of the developing world. The Consensus, which distilled the economic orthodoxy of the day, was based around the three pillars of macroeconomic discipline, microeconomic liberalization and globalization and involved ten policy reforms, or 'Ten Commandments':

1. *Fiscal discipline with small budget deficits.* Macroeconomic stability is essential for continued growth, with low inflation a key component, but this can be undermined by large budget deficits.
2. *Avoidance of investment in sectors that offer low returns but that are politically sensitive or controlled by key pressure groups.* Government expenditure in particular needs to be carefully planned and controlled.
3. *Broaden the tax base and cut marginal tax rates.* Tax systems need to provide adequate incentives as well as sufficient revenue.
4. *Financial liberalization is essential.* The supply of credit, the setting of interest rates and similar financial decisions are more appropriately determined by the markets than by the government.
5. *A unified exchange rate should be set at a level that induces export growth.* Exports are central to inducing wider growth processes and non-traditional exports in particular need to be encouraged.
6. *Trade restrictions should all be rapidly replaced by tariffs and these should be progressively reduced.* Quantitative restrictions on trade give windfall profits to privileged importers, while tariffs, which instead channel this revenue to the government, can be gradually whittled away.
7. *Barriers to foreign direct investment should be removed.* FDI is more stable than either portfolio capital or bank loans and should be encouraged.
8. *State-owned enterprises should be privatized.* This would raise the efficiency and the profitability of these industries.
9. *Regulations that impede the entry of new firms or that restrict competition should be removed.* This allows the economy to become more competitive, and protects consumers.

10. *Individual property rights should be protected by the legal system.* Such rights should also be extended to the informal sector. (Adapted from Williamson 1994: 26–8)

In his later writings, Williamson has examined many of the criticisms that have been made of this kind of policy framework (Williamson and Mahar 1998; Kuczynski and Williamson 2003; Williamson 2004). He maintains that the agenda has generally stood the test of time quite well and the major recommendations remain valid. However, from the outset he acknowledges that the name is guaranteed to evoke in many quarters strong emotions of resentment against United States arrogance, interventionism and even imperialism. He also argues that some policies that have generally become associated with the Washington Consensus were not part of his original formulation. He draws a clear distinction between his proposed set of reforms, which are firmly within the *neoclassical* tradition, and the newer *neo-liberal* doctrines that were fostered by the Reagan administration in the United States and by Margaret Thatcher in Britain. He stresses that his original formulation did not advocate minimalist government, the slashing of government services, supply-side economics, monetarism, nor the rejection of income redistribution as an assault on property rights and a serious disincentive to both companies and employees. He also stresses, in the light of the 1997 Asian crisis, that the premature deregulation of the capital account can have disastrous results unless a sufficiently strong and regulated financial and banking system has been developed, hence the sequencing of reforms needs serious attention (Stiglitz 2002).

Over the years since Williamson's original formulation, and partly in response to a number of criticisms, there has emerged an 'Augmented Washington Consensus', which concerns itself particularly with issues of governance (Beeson and Islam 2005). Targets include central bank independence and inflation targeting, public sector reform, the creation of more flexible labour markets, adherence to WTO standards and other benchmarks for the business and financial sectors, strengthening financial systems and governance, pursuit of democratic reforms, and the enunciation of poverty reduction strategies.

But a much more fundamental critique of the Washington Consensus has been undertaken by Stiglitz (2006). He has argued that the whole process has been a failure and that a 'Post-Washington Consensus Consensus' has begun to emerge. Most basic of all, he suggests, is the failure of theoretical and policy analysis to understand the economic structures of developing countries, and to recognize that there are fundamental differences between individual nations: one size does not fit all. Markets alone cannot produce outcomes that are either efficient or just, especially in an environment of rapidly changing technology. All societies seeking growth need to spread the risk associated with innovation and investment and must take care of the concurrent improvement of educational systems, physical infrastructure and the like. International institutions have created unfair rules in global relations and have foisted deeply flawed policy prescriptions on developing countries, he insists. Only national governments can play the indispensable regulating, co-ordinating and distributive roles, and these national policymakers need to be closely involved in negotiations at the international level: more successful development strategies cannot be arrived at within Washington alone.

Challenges to economic orthodoxy: Marxist policies revived

In spite of the some of the more triumphalist predictions made at the time of the downfall of the Soviet Union, Marxist modes of analysis have undergone something of a revival in recent years. The continuing difficulties that the United States is facing in Iraq have led several commentators to suggest that its power is now on the wane and that the 'unipolar moment', that period of unchallenged power that the US enjoyed after the end of the Cold War, is over (Wallerstein 2006). Problems with the US budget and balance of payments situations, the resultant blow-out in international borrowings by Washington and the inherent instability in the global system that this creates may hint at the unravelling of US hegemony (Arrighi 2005). However, other Marxists have argued that such an analysis underestimates the control that the US now has over the global financial system, and this is central to understanding the dynamics of continued US imperialism.

Panitch and Gindin (2005) suggest that under the guise of globalization what we have seen is the imposition of a new capitalist, imperialist empire based on four principles. First, the former fragmentation into national units has been replaced by a seamless, global capitalism. Second, the US has assumed responsibility for the creation and management of this system. Third, the US has actively structured and limited the options of elites based in other states. Finally, international financial institutions have been essential for the mediation and structuring of this new global system. This has elicited some resistance, especially in the developing world, since this integration blocks the emergence of any real kind of coherent national development.

This kind of analysis has also been undertaken by David Harvey (2003) who has similarly argued that a new kind of imperialism is emerging, and has been taken a stage further with his analysis of the GFC (Harvey 2010). The driver of these changes has been the crisis of over-accumulation that has plagued capitalism since the 1970s. In response, new markets and production capacity have emerged around the world but this also involves the creation of intense international competition. This is inherently unstable and involves frequent upheavals and crises, as in Asia in 1997. Threatened in the realm of production by new competitors in Asia, even though much of this has derived from the investments by US-based multinationals, the US has moved to assert its dominance through the financial system, backed by its unchallenged military superiority. But it is far from certain that this financial control can last for ever. The massive savings and investments coming out of Asia, many of them now allowing east Asian countries to control key assets in the US, may in fact herald a change in the balance of power.

In terms of policies, the re-emergence of radical political and economic initiatives in Latin America is based largely on resentment at what is seen as a new kind of US imperialism. However, the policies themselves appear to have changed little from the economic nationalism promulgated by the dependency school in the 1960s. There has not yet been a real attempt by Marxist scholars to spell out the real policy options that are available based on their detailed analyses – but this problem of moving from theory to workable practice has always been one of the weaknesses of this school of thought. The most promising direction at the moment seems to involve something of a convergence between Marxist and East Asian approaches exemplified through the rapid emergence of China, which at least in theory remains a communist state.

Challenges to economic orthodoxy: the Beijing Consensus

The term 'Beijing Consensus' has been around since at least the mid-1980s, but it was popularized in a paper by Joshua Cooper Ramo (2004) and since then has taken on a variety of economic and political connotations. In his formulation, Ramo argued that the rise of China is having enormous ramifications both inside the country and in the wider world. China is achieving nothing less than the reshaping and reordering of the international system through the introduction of 'a new physics of development and power' (p. 2). This promises to other nations the development of not only new and effective development policies but also ways to achieve true independence and freedom of action within a new international order and is therefore a replacement of the highly prescriptive Washington Consensus. It is based around three key 'theorems', he suggests:

- Rather than assuming that developing nations must start with simple and often outdated technologies and then graduate to more leading-edge approaches, it urges the immediate adoption of the most modern innovations 'to create change that moves faster than the problems that change creates' (p. 12).
- In periods of rapid change, it is impossible to control everything from the top. Sustainability and equality are central to new policy directions, so that income growth and quality of life are maintained, and social disruption and instability are minimized.
- Self-determination must be maintained through the creation of the leverage necessary to resist any hegemonic powers that might seek to dominate the nation.

In terms of economic policy, we have seen that China has already adopted many of the tenets of the Asian development model as it emerged in countries like Japan, Korea and Taiwan, and all three of those nations have a significant stake in the current Chinese economy, tending to maintain and reinforce many of these methods and approaches. Such economic models are now being transferred into Africa and Latin America as China quickly expands its influence there. While China's search for reliable supplies of resources is certainly seen for what it is, a number of writers have seen evidence that Africa is being transformed in a very positive way that contrasts with earlier periods of western involvement. The terms of trade for commodity producers have improved markedly, ameliorating many of the long identified problems of the 'resources curse' (Gonzalez-Vicente 2011) while investment in infrastructure and in social services has also been vastly increased (Friedman 2009).

But it is in the political and security domains that the particular attraction of the Beijing Consensus rests. Beijing now offers a rallying point for all those who oppose what they see as a US-oriented project of imperialism, as well as the exploitation that goes hand in hand with the policy prescriptions of international organizations such as the IMF and the WTO. Certainly a number of commentators in the West have expressed some alarm about the growing popularity of the Beijing Consensus in many developing countries. Chief among these is Stefan Halper (2010: x) who fears that:

China's governing model is more appealing to the developing world and some of the middle-sized powers than America's market-democratic model. Given a choice between market democracy and its freedoms and market authoritarianism and its high growth, stability, improved living standards, and limits on expression – a majority in the developing world and in many middle-sized, non-Western powers prefer the authoritarian model.

As such, this approach encourages the use of state power to achieve key national goals and this includes the continued use of methods that the rich countries were able to adopt during the earlier phases of their rise but which they now seek to deny to poorer nations now seeking a development transition of their own. In what is now a very influential book in much of the developing world, Ha-Joon Chang (2002) argues that it is a tragic mistake for richer countries to attempt to deny developing countries the right to adopt policies and institutions that are most appropriate to their needs and their current stages of growth, and more recently Chang (2007b, 2010) has made a broader attack on the ways in which the rich nations control the development and globalization agendas. Robert Wade, in looking at the legacy of his own important book on the role of the state in Taiwan's development (Wade 1990) makes similar points. While governments in rich countries are allowed much flexibility in setting policies aimed at upgrading those industries most crucial for their stage of growth, WTO regulations severely restrict such intervention in industries that are important for nations in transition to industrialization. This seems designed to ensure that already wealthy countries will not be challenged while underdeveloped countries will remain trapped in poverty. It is to this kind of perceived unfairness in the current global system that the Beijing Consensus has a particular political resonance (Wade 2004).

We must be careful of course to try to separate the impact of the intellectual arguments that have surrounded the success of east Asia as a whole from the narrower appeal of China's foreign policy agenda. China is now heavily involved in trying to further its own economic prospects through the signing of large resource deals with a range of countries around the world but at the same time it has launched what has been called a 'charm offensive' to further its general influence in the world. In Africa, for example, a recent World Bank Report has argued that economic growth in east Asia generally, and in China in particular, offers the continent its own 'Silk Road' (Broadman 2007).

Two kinds of criticism have emerged of these initiatives from Beijing. The orthodox economic response has of course been to question the wisdom of adhering to the east Asian-style industrial policies. For example, Noland and Pack (2003) argue that growth in Asia was the result of good macroeconomic management and the contribution of industrial policies was minor or even negative. Hence the case for other countries following such policies is weak and, under current rules governing world trade, may be illegal. Other critics have pointed to Chinese support for African regimes with somewhat questionable human rights records, suggesting that principles of non-interference in the internal affairs of others may not be justified in such circumstances.

There is also the question about the role, if any, of industrial policy and government initiatives as countries attempt to move up the value-added chain into more technologically advanced forms of production. Emphasis on technology is one of the key elements of the Beijing Consensus, and certainly Chinese planners express concern that China must take care not to be trapped in the role of a low-cost, low-technology producer. The difficulties that both Korea and Taiwan have experienced – and indeed are still suffering – as they attempt to consolidate such a transition to high technology status serves as an important object lesson in the immediate region.

A great deal has been written about the next stage of east Asia's growth, especially in the light of the Asian crisis of 1997 (for example, Gill and Kharas 2007; Gill, Huang and Kharas 2007). While much of this work has echoed the assumptions of the dominant economic orthodoxy, there are an increasing number of voices coming out of Asia itself suggesting a return to some of the ideas of the developmental state, albeit in a significantly modified form (for example, Park 2003; Chang 2007b). Such writers argue that a significant state role is still needed to accomplish some of the key tasks that will be necessary for a successful transition to a new kind of economy: co-ordination and planning for complex new situations, development of innovative vision, building of new institutions of various kinds and the management of the conflicts that are bound to accompany such profound societal changes (Chang 1999). Globalization does not reduce the need for state action, rather there needs to be redefinition of the key tasks that must now be undertaken to control and mould these forces to meet national needs through the management of currency appreciation, investment flows and industrial restructuring (Weiss 2003).

Conclusion: growth in a globalizing world

By way of conclusion, it is essential to consider the prospects for growth in the current environment and ask whether it is now easier or more difficult for nations to be successful in making a transition to a more prosperous future. Central here is the question of whether the processes of globalization are relatively stable or not – and the impact of the GFC has raised serious doubts here – as well as the issues of whether income inequalities have risen or fallen in recent years, and how the various mechanisms of globalization are linked to particular outcomes.

Growth and inequality

There is now a very large literature on the question of the relationships between globalization and income inequalities at various scales of analysis; however, in this very acrimonious debate there is still little agreement. Supporters of globalization such as Dollar and Kraay (2002) and Bhagwati (2004) have asserted that global inequalities have in fact decreased markedly, while writers such as Stiglitz (2006) and Galbraith and Berner (2001) come to the opposite conclusion. In part, these differences reflect problems of data but there is also a question of the appropriate scale and focus of analysis. It has been argued that China and India are so large that their recent success provides bias at the global level, while for much of Africa and Latin America, for example, the picture is much less encouraging. In addition, Garrett (2004) has suggested that while in aggregate terms the poorer countries, again India and China in particular, may have done well from globalization, and there has also been rapid growth in most rich countries, there is a real problem for middle-income countries.

There is also a question of what measures of inequality are appropriate for such an analysis. Most writers have focused on absolute measures of poverty and on the number of people living below some key threshold level of poverty. Bhagwati (2004) has stressed that in China poverty declined from 28 per cent of the population in 1978 to 9 per cent in 1998. However, others have underlined the importance of measures of relative poverty. While many people now have higher incomes, they feel left behind because of the more rapid progress of others, and of the elites in particular. Some time ago, Denis Goulet (1971) introduced the concept of the 'shock of underdevelopment'. The poor may have always been with us but in an age of mass communications they are now made painfully aware of their poverty on a daily basis, and in particular they measure their own disadvantage relative to the rich people they now see on television and in films.

Also important here is the question of changes in income inequalities between countries as against within individual nations. Both are important, but in political terms resentment against fellow citizens seen as being unfairly advantaged may be more potent, and may even threaten the stability of globalization itself. One important element in the east Asian model, particularly in the early years, was its strong element of egalitarianism. This goes back to a rather different tradition of economic thought in east Asia. The Confucian heritage stressed the societal goals of universal order and harmony and gave particular emphasis to the obligations of rulers towards the welfare of their subjects. In Japan, a dominant school of economic thought emerged which stressed the need for 'administering the nation and relieving the suffering of the people' (Morris-Suzuki 1989). It is also significant that in China today a great deal of emphasis is being placed on the need to rectify, in the name of both equity and political stability, the great imbalances that now exist between the prosperous coastal regions and the much more backward inland areas (Shirk 2007).

In a major survey of this evidence, Kaplinsky (2005) puts forward what is perhaps the most persuasive conclusion. The experience of globalization has been extremely mixed, with some winners and many losers. Companies seeking new opportunities in developing countries are very discerning about the particular advantages of each location, hence some are chosen but many are not. Poverty then is not a simple lagged effect, with all nations being able to eventually share in global prosperity. Indeed the emergence of even a small number of large-scale producers like China would result in massive saturation of world markets. Also, some locations that have advantages at some time may also be abandoned later in favour of new opportunities. Thus, development is a highly complex and situational process, and this has important policy implications.

Implications of globalization for growth theories and policies

The rather inconclusive picture that emerges from the literature on the relationships between globalization and income inequalities makes it difficult to give a precise answer to the question of whether growth is now easier to attain for latecomers. On the one hand, the success of a number of Asian countries, China and India in particular, is seen by many as a shining example of just what is now possible. The process of 'industrial learning' that, as we have seen, has been central to Asian growth, and the flood of foreign direct investment in the region, has certainly had a major impact but outside Asia the picture may not be quite so rosy. Worse still, the growth of China may be making it even more difficult for other countries to compete for both markets and foreign investment.

There is also the issue of countries that have achieved some development being able to make the major transition to higher value-added kinds of production. This brings them much more into competition with the already developed countries and has been the subject of much debate in the context of the rules governing world trade. This is particularly significant in the case of China, which if it could successfully make such a transition could serve as a major market for a whole new generation of low-cost producers of simple industrial goods.

If Kaplinsky (2005) is right, some nations may be able to use their special locational advantages to attract international or local capital but what is clear at the moment is that most countries in the developing world now see themselves as trapped by a global system that is stacked against them and is generating increasing levels of inequality. This is a very dangerous situation that is threatening the very future of globalization itself. Similarly, Niall Ferguson (2005) has argued that the current situation – characterized by imperial over-reach, rivalries between major powers, unstable alliances, rogue regimes and increased terrorism – is ominously like the situation before the First World War when globalization also crumbled, with disastrous results. As we will explore in Chapter 6 the GFC has brought such issues into sharp relief, and raised the additional question of the ways in which inequalities at various geographical scales contributes to the high levels in system instability that we are now experiencing.

Chapter 6

Continuing Crises: The Developing World and the Global Financial Crisis

John McKay

The traumatic impact of the global financial crisis (GFC), and its continuing aftershocks right down to the present, have intensified our interest in systemic breakdowns of this kind and heightened debate about their causes, impacts and the most appropriate ways to deal with them. Crises of this dimension, or those as serious as the Asian crisis of 1997–8, are very traumatic events in their own right, resulting in losses of income and assets that affect very wide sections of the community, and with ramifications such as job losses that can often be seen for decades afterwards. But the GFC seems to have been of such a scale and impact that our thinking has been revolutionised. Earlier crises – at least in the period since the Great Depression of the late 1920s and 1930s – have been relatively localized and hence could be blamed on purely local conditions or follies. But the GFC began in the United States, quickly spread to Europe and then implicated much of the rest of the world to a varying extent, and thus raised some awkward questions about the global financial and economic architecture, and some even urged that the very survival of the capitalist system should be debated.

For many analysts, crises have always been of great interest because of what they can tell us about economic and political systems in various countries and regions, and at the wider global level, but even more fundamentally, crises are usually the periods in which national or international systems undergo profound changes or are transformed by outside pressures. During periods of relative prosperity, or at least stability, the pressures for change are much less urgent and as a result there is a tendency for existing ways of operating to continue. It is only when some form of crisis creates a national or international emergency that change is forced on often reluctant governments and wider communities.

However, there may also be a danger inherent in regarding crises as unusual or even aberrant phenomena. A number of writers have pointed out that periodic crises seem to be an integral part of the international capitalist system, or perhaps of all political and economic systems yet devised. Stiglitz (2002) has argued that we should not really be surprised that Asia suffered a crisis in 1997–8: rather we should ask why, contrary to previous experience in all other regions including Europe and North America, the region had been so remarkably stable and dynamic since the 1960s. This raises some interesting and fundamental questions about how the global system and a range of international organizations are structured.

Global and regional crises in historical context: learning the lessons

The renewed interest in the longer-term historical evidence of crises at the global level and in various countries and regions is not just about learning the lessons of previous crises to avoid or at least minimise the impact of new ones, important as this is. Far from being isolated such events can be seen as causally related: each crisis sheds yet more light on the structure and dynamics of the global system, illustrating how the various parts of the whole interact with each other, and how the resolution of each new event helps set the scene for the next convulsion. Paul Krugman (2008) has called this kind of study *depression economics*, a field that many misguided economists thought had been long consigned to the footnotes of economic history. Seen from this perspective, the Asian Financial Crisis of 1997–8 was not just an event confined to one region as the result of local errors but essentially one of the harbingers of the GFC.

Most attention has focused on the Great Depression of the 1930s and the contrasts or commonalities with the experiences of the 1980s, 1990s and now of course the GFC. But there has also been a return to the historical analysis of several periods of upheaval during the nineteenth century, and some important reinterpretations of earlier evidence (see, for example, Fishlow 1985; Ghosh 2001; Kindleberger and Aliber 2005). It is no accident that most interest has been generated by those crises that have threatened to have serious impacts on the West: if a crisis is no longer just out there in Africa or wherever, even if troubling images appear nightly on the world's television screens, it is much less disturbing than one that threatens to strike at the rich nations.

But this intense level of enquiry, resulting now in a very large literature, has failed to yield any consensus on the predominant causes of these crises. The conventional view, enshrined in the Washington Consensus and its later manifestations, stresses that crises are essentially caused by internal policy weaknesses and an inability to strengthen market-based systems throughout the economy. But this dominant paradigm has received a great deal of criticism from a number of directions. Several commentators have criticized the exclusive concentration on the internal causes of crisis, arguing that external factors are often just as important, and in many instances paramount. The structure of the international financial system itself, the activities of hedge funds and other new financial instruments, the policies of the international agencies such as the IMF, the policies of stronger western countries (especially the United States) and the activities of multinational corporations have all been cited here. But more fundamentally, a number of writers have argued that crisis is the direct and inevitable result of the ways in which various regions have been incorporated into the global capitalist system. The precise details vary from region to region, and many forces are specific to particular historical periods but, as we shall see in relation to Africa, Asia and Latin America, crises have been explained by some researchers as the result of long-term structural factors rather than specific and internal policy failings (see, for example, Frank 1980; Arrighi 2002).

These fundamental differences of opinion on the causes of economic crisis inevitably lead to sharp conflicts over the most appropriate policy responses to the onset of a crisis. The policy prescriptions that flow from the Washington Consensus are, of course, restricted to internal policy reforms. By contrast, those writers who have emphasized the external or global causes of crisis have paid more attention to the restructuring of international financial institutions and of the basic architecture of the global economy. The IMF has been criticized for being too concerned with the need to pay back loans owed to international lenders, often with dire consequences for the welfare of local residents. As we shall see, the IMF has also been criticized for its failure to learn the lessons of the Great Depression of the 1930s. It is now accepted that the policies put in place initially to deal with the Great Depression were entirely inappropriate and in fact made matters even worse. Yet it was just such contractionary policies that were imposed on Asian countries in 1997 – and now on Greece – when what was needed was a strong stimulus to encourage growth, and industrial expansion in particular (Stiglitz 2002). What such critics argue is that the international financial system has become progressively more unstable, and given recent events this viewpoint deserves some attention.

How has the risk of crisis increased in recent years?

Even well before the onset of the GFC, a number of analysts were suggesting that the risk of crisis was significantly greater than it had been some decades ago. Attention has been focused particularly on the changing volume and nature of international financial flows, the progressive removal of state regulations controlling such flows, and the ways in which the introduction of these new financial systems has been supported by alliances between some governments in the developed world and the emerging financial industry (Crouch 2011).

There is no doubt that the volume of international financial flows has increased dramatically since the 1970s. In earlier periods, the amount of money flowing between two countries was made up of two components: first, payments for goods traded, and second, investments and loans from one country to another. Both of these flows continue to be important, and both have grown dramatically in recent years; however, these items have been overwhelmed by new components, especially speculative capital. Daily turnover in the world's currency markets just prior to the GFC was around $1.2 trillion, with much of this activity speculative in nature, but the fastest growing part of the financial sector in recent years has been derivatives, financial instruments often of a complex nature derived from a more basic financial instrument, and this was estimated to be worth $600 billion per day in 2008. These amounts dwarf the value of world trade, global investment flows and indeed the size of even the largest foreign exchange reserves. Even so, investment flows of various kinds are increasing very rapidly. Total cross-border capital flows – made up of equity and debt security purchases, international lending and deposits and foreign direct investment – stood in 2007 at $6.4 trillion per year, and was growing much more rapidly than global GDP (IMF 2007). In part, this reflected the growth of assets under management by pension funds, hedge funds and the like: total funds in this area are now around $53 trillion. But it is now accepted that perhaps 95 per cent of the capital moving across borders is speculative in nature, and financial authorities even in the largest and richest countries are very limited in their power to act in the national interest against such speculators.

A fierce critique of this new world of speculation has been developed by Susan Strange (1986, 1998). She has coined the term *casino capitalism* to describe this new phase in the global economy, but she has more recently argued that it is now better to talk about *mad money*. This frenetic movement of capital has a clear logic, she argues, but it is simply the logic of short-term profit, with no thought of the consequences for nations or communities. Even more recently Satyajit Das (2011) has coined the term *extreme money* to describe the ever more frenetic pace of change in the financial world.

Several factors have given rise to this new situation. One of the most important of these has been the rapid growth in the amount of money available on world financial markets. This growth in liquidity began in the early 1970 when rapid rises in the world price of oil flooded the markets with *petrodollars* seeking profitable investments. This source of money was quickly supplemented in August 1971 when President Nixon, in an attempt to solve the problems that the United States government was having in financing the Vietnam War, unilaterally abrogated the Bretton Woods system, refusing to allow the continued exchange of US dollars for US gold reserves. Still more money became available on financial markets in the 1970s and 1980s as the result of rapid industrial development in East Asia and increases in oil revenues received by producers especially in the Middle East. So much money became available for investment that only a small fraction of it could be absorbed into traditional channels. Thus the second factor in the development of this new economy has been the rapid emergence of new financial instruments and products and, equally importantly, the reform of existing government regulations to allow them to flourish. Banks were progressively freed from many of the limitations that had previously restricted their activities and even more important was the emergence of a new range of non-bank financial institutions. Foreign exchange rates were progressively deregulated, allowing markets rather than governments to set these rates. But for these new financial products to work more effectively and speedily, new technologies were needed for the instantaneous transfer of funds across the globe, and these were soon available thanks to advances in computer and satellite systems. However one vital piece was still missing: a push strong enough to overcome the reluctance of some governments to give up the national controls that still existed in many economies, and which were seen by many officials (correctly as it turned out) as necessary for continued stability in the financial sector. This final impetus was provided by the emerging alliance between the United States government and the dominant players on Wall Street. The US government used extremely tough measures to ensure that even the most reluctant governments were persuaded to deregulate their systems, and in particular remove any restrictions on inflows of capital (Varoufakis 2011).

In speculation, as in the casino, bets are being made, this time on the future value of currencies, commodities, or shares, and some punters will win and others will lose. Given the instability that often results in hardship for ordinary citizens in the countries affected, would it not be more desirable to remove much of this uncertainty in markets by returning, for example, to more regulated exchange rates? The answer is that it is the very uncertainty inherent in the new system that allows some people to make very large amounts of profit from speculation.

There have also been important developments in the more traditional sectors, now frequently called the *real economy* – a telling comment on the nature of much financial activity! In spite of continuing protectionism in the European Union and the United States, restrictions on world trade through tariffs and other means have been progressively reduced through a series of agreements negotiated within the General Agreement on Tariffs and Trade (GATT), which soon after the conclusion of the Uruguay Round in 1993 became known as the World Trade Organization (WTO). This is one factor in the rapid growth of world trade, which since 1945 has expanded some twelvefold, compared with a fivefold increase in global output. But this increase in trade also reflects a growing internationalization of production through expanded foreign investment, especially by large, multinational corporations, a process that began on a large scale in the 1970s. At this time, profit levels for the large corporations of the developed world were being hit by a combination of three factors. First, the shocks to the international finance system provided by the Vietnam War and the dramatic increases in the world price of oil in 1972–3 and 1979 pushed up cost structures for many companies and resulted in strong inflationary pressures in many countries. Second, the 1970s were also a period of rapid wage increases in much of the developed world, with serious consequences for inflation and production costs. Third, the global recession triggered by the oil price increases resulted in a significant and extended drop in demand for many industrial products. The result was a crisis in profitability for established companies, resulting in strenuous attempts to cut costs. The strategy favoured by many corporations was to move production offshore to cheaper locations, saving particularly on labour costs. But for this to be successful, several new features had to be in place. Global production networks, in which components made in several locations are brought together for final assembly and export to world markets, can only work effectively if cheap and efficient transport is available. This was provided by a complex of innovations that has become known as the 'containerization revolution'. A global network of production also requires an efficient and reliable means for monitoring, controlling and co-ordinating production and quality levels. This became available through rapid advances in computer and satellite technology. Perhaps most important of all, the institutional basis had to be available in the new host countries to ensure that investment could be made on favourable terms. An increasing number of national governments, especially in Asia, were willing to provide such a favourable environment for foreign investment as part of their emerging strategies of export-oriented industrialization. This movement towards international production has continued to the present, resulting in a rapid growth in the levels of direct foreign investment (FDI).

A number of writers have argued that the recent rapid increases in FDI flows have heralded a new period in the nature of global financial flows. Eichengreen and Fishlow (1998) have contrasted this new era with earlier episodes on the basis of the dominant form or origin of financial flows, recognizing three distinct periods and modes of investment:

1. *The era of bond finance.* This was a long period of distinctive international financial flows originating in the nineteenth century and consisting of loans guaranteed by government, municipal or private organizations. Strong bond markets emerged in London, Paris, Berlin and Amsterdam to service the emerging capital markets particularly in the United States, Canada, Australia, Latin America and Russia. This early period was somewhat volatile, with frequent defaults. Much of this investment was in infrastructure projects. In the early part of the twentieth century the United States emerged as an exporter of capital rather than an importer and by the 1920s a number of financial intermediaries emerged, notably investment trusts. The nature of the projects being financed and the countries of destination also changed, widening to include some much more risky markets. The system received a fatal blow in the global Depression of the 1930s, with most countries defaulting on their debts.
2. *The era of bank finance.* The late 1960s and early 1970s saw a period of rapid increase in liquidity, resulting from increases in oil prices, and the emergence of new financial instruments, supported by a new consensus on the need for financial reform and liberalization. At the same time new financial markets emerged, notably the eurodollar market, and these actively pursued possible new investment destination in the developing world. Large investment flows took place initially to Latin America, but then to East Asia and Africa. When the burden of this debt became too much and when it became clear that a substantial proportion of the money had been invested in unproductive projects – what Susan George (1988) has called castles in the sand – the result was the crisis of third-world debt.

3. *The era of equity finance.* This period has been characterized by an emphasis on investment in shares in companies around the world, and Eichengreen and Fishlow date this phase from the end of the 1980s. By then, there had been significant changes in the financial regulatory systems of many countries, but equally important was the emergence of pension funds and insurance companies as major investors. By 1990, lending to Latin America was greater than at the peak of the bank lending period, and flows to Asia were also very large.

More recently, and particularly in the period following Asia's strong recovery from its own period of crisis and the dramatic rise of China, Asian investors in particular have purchased very large quantities of US government bonds, financing the very large budget and balance of payments deficits. Continued high levels of savings in Asia have allowed the build-up of massive debts in the US and these global imbalances have been seen as one of the major causes of the GFC (Eichengreen 2007).

Seeking to understand the causes of crises: the return of Marx, Keynes and Minsky

One of the results of the GFC, as has been underlined in earlier chapters, is that the conventional wisdom about growth and development has been seriously challenged, really for the first time in several decades. One area in which the old certainties have clearly been demolished is in the theoretical approaches to understanding the origins and propagation of crises, and the appropriate policy responses. Here we consider the new relevance of several theorists who had been largely ignored for many years and evaluate the strengths of their approaches to the current situations. In particular we look briefly at the theoretical positions of Karl Marx, John Maynard Keynes and Hyman Minsky, all of whom have returned to prominence since the onset of the GFC, as well as some more recent theoretical contributions.

Marx (1818–83) first became interested in the phenomenon of crisis at the time of what became known as 'the great crisis of 1857–8' triggered by the failure of the Ohio Life Insurance Company, and incorporated some of his ideas in his *Grundrisse*, laying the foundations of a more general theory of crises within capitalism. Basically, Marx concluded that recurrent crises were the result of problems in the sphere of production: capitalism's unrelenting drive for accumulation resulted in regular periods of overproduction and hence a falling rate of profit. This could only be resolved by the liquidation of some of this surplus production capacity, and the jobs associated with it, until a new level of output was reached that could be sold. Thus crises were the necessary and regular mechanisms of adjustment, albeit resulting in a great deal of pain to both capital and labour.

The GFC has revived interest in the Marxist concept of overproduction, and particularly important here has been the work of Robert Brenner. He has shown that the average rate of profit of corporations in developed countries has suffered a steady decline since the early 1970s (Brenner 2006). Intense competition between advanced nations, advances in manufacturing technologies and the emergence of a range of new industrial nations – particularly in East Asia – dramatically increased total output and put downward pressure on prices and hence levels of profit. A number of other Marxist scholars have questioned aspects of the theoretical basis of Brenner's work (for example Smith 2010), but there has been widespread support for the general thrust of the argument. More recently Brenner and others have re-evaluated the theory of overproduction in the light of the onset of the GFC, taking the crisis as a vindication of their approach.

But other Marxists have seen the growth of the financial services industry in a somewhat different light. Peter Gowan (1999) argued that the twin developments of neo-liberalism within the United States and globalization at the international level were used by vested interests, supported by the US government, to create what he called the 'Dollar-Wall Street Regime – a potent economic tool to advance US national interests. Political and even military pressures have been used to maintain or impose local regimes willing to go along with this emerging institutional structure. These arrangements are presented as logical or even inevitable concomitants of economic and technological change but are in reality politically motivated and extremely destabilizing, with serious results for the poorer economies that are incorporated into the global financial structures, but also producing damaging cycles of boom and bust in the advanced capitalist economies. Building on these kinds of observations Duménil and Lévy (2011) have argued that the GFC was not the result of overcapacity but of the inherent instability of the global financial system. Neo-liberalism, they argue, was introduced by the ruling elites after the 1970s to recapture the income share that had been lost during the earlier period of redistributive and progressive policies introduced after the Second World War. The results were dramatic. In the period leading up to the Second World War the top 1 per cent of US households received some 13 per cent of the total income of all households, but this declined to 9 per cent by the 1970s. The introduction of the range of policies that became known as neo-liberalism reversed this decline, and by 2007 the pre-war share of total income had been restored, but this frantic dash to acquire high levels of income through financial services expansion created instability, culminating in the major crash in 2007–08.

One more general feature of the debate that has emerged after the GFC has been the resurgence of Marxist inspired theoretical analysis, and the best of this work has involved a carefully considered review of the whole opus of Marxist research on the causes of crisis. Particularly useful here is the thoughtful review by Panitch and Gindin (2010) of the strands of critical analysis that have developed in this area since the original contribution by Marx himself in the 1850s. They make three key points:

- Crises are historically specific, therefore any analysis must be based on a thorough understanding of the conditions of accumulation and the general economic environment – profits, wages, the structure of trade, availability of credit, the dynamics of class structures and the dynamics of class – state relations.
- This form of contingency analysis must also be extended to explanations of the duration of particular periods of crises and the ways in which these are resolved.
- It is also crucial to understand how the resolution of one crisis leads to the emergence of new systems and relationships, and how these set the scene for the next crisis.

The authors illustrate such a mode of analysis by presenting their summary of how the GFC happened, building on an earlier but more detailed statement (Panitch et al. 2008). The nature of capitalism had been progressively transformed throughout the period since Marx was writing, and this had profound implications for the types of crises that have emerged: competitive capitalism had given way to monopoly capitalism, and this in turn had been replaced by 'financialized' capitalism. High levels of leverage and risk taking were encouraged, leading to ever greater dangers of instability, which in turn spawned new kinds of hedging and risk spreading. The state, far from retreating as was proposed by neo-liberal theorists, became even more important as the final guarantor of the system, but while this was essential for the confidence of the financial markets it also invited 'moral hazard' and encouraged the emergence of speculative bubbles. Mortgage finance, especially in the US, became a key element of financial expansion, encouraged by government subsidies of various kinds designed to integrate the working class still further into the system and provide a political buffer – through constant expectations of increasing house prices – against any feelings of resentment at the stagnant or declining levels of real incomes resulting from the neo-liberal policies adopted by successive administrations. Household debt, encouraged by these expectations of expanding equity in real estate, also fuelled consumer demand and hence the manufacturing sector. It was this house of cards that came crashing down in 2007–08.

Just as the work of Marx has been revived and some extent re-interpreted in the light of more recent developments, so there has been renewed interest in the theories of John Maynard Keynes (1883–1946), whose ideas were originally formulated in response to the Great Depression of the 1920s and 1930s. In his *General Theory of Employment, Interest and Money* published in 1936 Keynes contradicted all of tenets of the classical economic thought that were dominant at the time. Contrary to the prevailing assumption that markets and investors had perfect access to information and were thus able to evaluate any future risk, Keynes argued that uncertainty and responses to unknowable risk were at the heart of the economic behaviour of both investors and consumers. Future expectations were generally based not on rational calculation or on Adam Smith's 'invisible hand' but on conventions, stories, rumours and a strong element of crowd behaviour as people seek social ratification for their decisions, be they optimistic or pessimistic. Thus herd behaviour in the market always amplifies both booms and busts. Crucially, Keynes argued, when aggregate demand collapses at the onset of a downturn the response of businesses is not to reduce prices – as the economic theory of the time postulated – but to slash output and hence employment. But this in turn leads to a further reduction in demand, resulting in a spiral down into deeper crisis. The only effective policy response here is for governments to stimulate demand through making money available to investors as cheaply as possible and by undertaking capital works of various kinds, generating budget deficits for a time if necessary.

Robert Skidelsky, who through his monumental three-volume biography as well as many other writings has done more than anyone to argue for the continued relevance of Keynes, has interpreted the GFC in the light of what Keynes believed or would have argued in the light of the current environment (Skidelsky 2009). The importance of uncertainty has certainly been highlighted. At the onset of the GFC most mainstream economists believed that most economic actors possessed enough knowledge and information to make rational decisions based on accurate prediction of the risks involved. This so-called 'efficient market theory' has in Skidelsky's opinion been blown completely out of the water by recent events, and yet a surprising number of economists still seem to hold to this irrational faith. While the onset of the GFC resulted in massive Keynesian-style government spending, Keynes himself argued that the role of government should not be confined to providing stimulus to demand at times of crisis but in enacting policies designed to maintain full employment at all times, and to minimize the chances of recurrent crises. Above all Keynes was passionate about big moral issues such as the aims and limits of economic growth, and in the aftermath of the GFC, many of the more thoughtful economic analysts now urge a return to the macroeconomics of Keynes (for example, Taylor 2010) and a greater emphasis on the big issues that are central to this book, notably development and income inequalities.

A more recent contribution to the theory of crises has been made by Hyman Minsky (1919–96), a researcher who was generally ignored during his lifetime but who is now central to the discussion of how to manage the post-GFC world. Minsky claimed that his major inspiration was the work of Keynes, but in fact many of his key concepts differ markedly from that earlier model. Minsky, writing much later than Keynes, placed the financial system at the centre of his concepts of economic dynamics and crisis. Keynes believed that the financial system could amplify movements towards crisis, but for Minsky finance was the major cause of instability. Modern capitalist economies, he argued, have an inbuilt tendency to create speculative booms – what he calls a dynamic of *upward instability* resulting in *system fragility*. During periods of relative stability and prosperity, there is a tendency for entrepreneurs to feel confident enough to take on higher and higher levels of risk. Systems of *hedging*, under which debt servicing costs are more than covered by expected revenue flows, may be replaced by *speculative financing* systems, which rely on windfall profits for the refinancing of debt, and these in turn may be transformed into some kind of *Ponzi* scheme in which there must be constant borrowing in order to service existing debt costs. If enough businesses increase their risks in this way the result is an extremely high level of *system instability*. At this stage even a relatively trivial random shock will be enough to trigger a crisis – no major exogenous event is necessary. This is what has become known as a *Minsky moment*, and a number of writers have interpreted the onset of the GFC in just this way.

But even though Minsky was writing much closer to our own time than the two earlier theorists there are strong suspicions that the structure of the financial system has been transformed sufficiently to confound a number of Minsky's observations on both the causes of crisis and the policy tools needed to deal with such instability. Dymski (2010), while acknowledging that GFC has shown the main contours of Minsky's analysis to be profoundly correct suggests that the stubborn refusal of the US economy to respond to government stimulus measures is the result of recent changes in the financial sector that Minsky could not foresee, especially the changing roles of banks and other financial institutions (see also Das 2006).

The work of these three thinkers – Marx, Keynes and Minsky – could all be classified as theories that are fundamentally critical of existing systems, hence it is hardly surprising that supporters of the status quo have preferred proposals that favour some degree of modest reform, or even what Robert Wade (2008) has called 'incremental muddling through'. At one extreme, some commentators have argued that while instability may be inherent in modern capitalism the returns in terms of high growth rates during periods of prosperity are so much greater than under any other system that the costs from relatively infrequent bouts of crisis can be absorbed relatively easily and should simply be endured. At the other end of the spectrum there have been suggestions for quite serious reform, particularly in the regulation of the increasingly dominant financial system (Chirot 2011). This follows the logic of Keynes and assumes a key role for government in the ongoing prevention of future depressions. Much of this work has also involved the systematic study of various bouts of recession or crisis, particularly since the Great Depression of the 1930s, drawing common and ongoing lessons and highlighting the ways in which the risks of instability have increased over the years.

Other explanations for the GFC, and ideas to prevent a recurrence

As was noted at some length in Chapters 2 and 5, the recent history of development thought has been dominated by faith in the market as the most effective allocation mechanism for resources of all kinds in every conceivable situation, but this blind faith in the superiority of market mechanisms has been perhaps the most obvious casualty of the GFC. Even if many economists and policy makers still cling to this article of faith the old certainty has gone, and other quite different possibilities are at least being considered. A whole series of new studies have emerged on why market mechanisms are prone to fail, and much attention has been given to the psychology of markets that is at the heart of many of these problems.

Market mechanisms are of course based in part on the assumption of rational individuals armed with clear ideas on their desires and preferences, as well as perfect information about both the present and the future, but in practice few if any of these prerequisites exist. After reviewing the experience of a whole range of bubbles and crashes – starting with the Dutch Tulip Bulb Bubble of 1636 – Kindleberger and Aliber (2005) come down very firmly in favour of the Minsky model, pointing to the key question of the availability of credit. When optimism is high and a bubble is building, credit is more easily available and hence the level of mania is exacerbated, while when a crisis hits, credit is cut off even for viable borrowers and the crash intensifies. This view has been strongly supported by Reinhart and Rogoff (2009) with massive amounts of data from a whole range of crises over some eight centuries. Not only are highly indebted companies and national economies extremely vulnerable, but policy makers and entrepreneurs refuse to believe the lessons of the past, arguing that this time things are different and all the old problems have been solved! As John Cassidy (2010) and Justin Fox (2009) have both stressed, most mainstream economists have chosen to ignore the growing body of research on the psychology of economic behaviour, preferring instead to believe that the economy was a self-correcting mechanism that would quickly shrug off the impact of any speculative bubble. This was certainly the view of Alan Greenspan, the former Chairman of the US Federal Reserve, but in a speech in 1996 he did warn about the possible emergence of 'irrational exuberance' in markets – and after the GFC this phrase has become his most famous utterance (Shiller 2009). However few if any monetary authorities have yet to repudiate the theory of the self-regulating market, or put in place any coherent policies to counteract these tendencies.

The GFC also ignited widespread criticism of the behaviour of the banks and other financial institutions, and in particular, the excessively high salaries and bonuses paid to staff even during times when the industry was suffering gigantic losses and was relying on government bail-out packages to stay afloat. But again, while various politicians have railed against these excessive remunerations there seems to be little appetite to take any firm measures. In this blame game it is clear that the financial institutions have simply been taking advantage of a lack of government regulation. This is not just a matter of unreasonable executive salaries, but of government complicity in the development of a culture of risk taking, excessive borrowing and highly leveraged investment (Crouch 2011). Paul Mason (2009) argues that the repeal by the Clinton Administration of the Glass-Steagall Act of 1933 – which had ensured the separation of investment banks from deposit taking banking institutions – confirmed what had been happening in the financial industry for a number of years, culminating in the birth of modern investment banking. One result was that over the last 20 years, and for the first time, the size of the financial market has greatly eclipsed that of the real economy. Investment banks became all-powerful heralding the 'off balance sheet decade', in which innovative ways to hide the debt being accrued by clients were invented, and also the development of the 'shadow banking system' designed to circumvent the regulations under the 2004 Basel II agreement for companies to maintain adequate capital cushions.

In part this dilution of regulatory oversight reflected an alliance between government and the finance industry in the US in particular, or at least a dangerous belief that what was good for Wall Street was in the interest of the nation (Mattick 2011). The role of central bankers in the disastrous handling of the Great Depression ought to have been a warning, as Ahamed (2009) has argued, but history has not been part of the education of most students of this field in recent years. Criticisms of regulatory systems and policy frameworks at the national level have been matched by questions at the international level, targeting in particular the key global organizations such as the IMF and the World Bank. The role of the IMF, an institution that many commentators believed was being marginalized before the GFC, has now come to the fore, but questions are being asked about the role of a 'lender of last resort' both in terms of how the GFC could have been managed better and in the avoidance of future crises.

The GFC has also highlighted a widespread failure to understand the broader context in which economic processes have been taking place and the serious consequences that can ensue. Particularly important in the field of international development are the implications of inequality at various geographical scales, and the consequent emergence of serious global imbalances. A number of Asian countries have accumulated very large foreign exchange reserves, and a prime example here is China, which by the first half of 2011 held reserves of $US3045 billion. Some of this – along with similar reserves from other countries in east Asia and the Middle East – has been invested in US securities of various kinds, essentially funding much of the large borrowings of the US government as well as its corporations and private citizens. Asia's frugality has supported western debt-driven excess. For the late developers the best strategy – as Rajan (2010) has noted – was clear: export to grow, use cheap labour resources to start the process, and gradually move up the technology ladder as capital stocks and human resources improve. Yet it is these imbalances in the global economy – caused by high levels of debt and huge trade and budget deficits in the West and equally large foreign exchange reserves, savings and trade surpluses in some key developing economies – that are seen by many as the fundamental cause of the GFC (see, for example, Eichengreen 2007; Roubini and Mihm 2010). This theme is explored in more detail in the following section, which examines the role of Asia in the GFC and the implications of the crisis for the future of this dynamic region.

Asia and the global financial crisis

We have already seen in Chapter 2 that the dramatic rates of growth achieved in a number of east Asian countries from the 1960s onwards posed a major challenge to analysts of the processes of development, and the catastrophic crisis that hit the region in 1997 also gave rise to widely varying theories about the causes and implications of these events. Some commentators argued that the causes of the Asian crisis were basically *internal* and resulted from the growing contradictions and inefficiencies that had emerged within the economic and political systems of these countries. Their policy response called for fundamental reforms of corporate governance, economic policy-making, the political systems and the relationships between the government and the private sector. By contrast, other researchers suggested that, while there were certainly some internal shortcomings, the basic causes of the crisis were essentially *external,* relating particularly to the problems in the structure of the international financial system. Their policy responses centred on the need for a new architecture of regulations governing these global flows of funds. The GFC has now given much support to this latter view, suggesting that the Asian crisis was simply part of a series of warning tremors before the full force of the shock waves hit in 2007. But one clear result is that after the GFC Asia's role in the global economy – already growing rapidly before 2007 – has been greatly enhanced, and this is in large part the result of the ways in which Asia responded to its own earlier crisis.

The onset of the Asian crisis is usually dated to July 1997 when in response to intense pressure from international markets the currencies of Thailand and Indonesia were floated in quick succession, leading to massive devaluations that were interpreted by international investors as a warning signal about the economic vulnerability of the whole region. Before the end of the year, the contagion of crisis had also spread to South Korea and there were fears that the country would default on the payment of its international loans. The South Korean government was forced to call on the International Monetary Fund for assistance and the largest ever emergency loan of $US 58.3 billion was put in place. Similar, but smaller, loans were also obtained by Thailand and Indonesia. A number of other countries in the region were also affected by the crisis, notably Malaysia, but the governments did not find it necessary to seek IMF assistance. The impact on the most affected countries was catastrophic. The Indonesian economy declined by at least 14 per cent in 1998 and by some estimates inflation was running at 60 per cent. Both Thailand and Korea experienced declines of around 6 per cent, closely followed by Malaysia at 5.1 per cent. Unemployment became a serious problem throughout the region, resulting in marked increases in poverty levels.

Given the magnitude and importance of these events, it is hardly surprising that the Asian crisis has generated an enormous literature from a wide variety of disciplinary, theoretical and ideological perspectives (see, for example, Jomo 1998; Jackson 1999; Pempel 1999; Agenor et al. 1999; Haggard 2000; Woo et al. 2000; Stiglitz and Yusuf 2001; Chang 2007a). However, there is a wide divergence of opinion on the basic causes of the catastrophe, its policy implications and the appropriateness of the conventional management measures invoked by the IMF.

As was noted above, one major school of thought has paid particular attention to the internal causes of the crisis, stressing failures of macroeconomic policy and corporate governance. Much of this literature was unashamedly triumphalist, proclaiming that the Asian model, which had for many years been touted by some as more effective than the orthodox neo-classical paradigm, did not work after all. The aspects of policy failure that have been stressed by different authors and with relation to specific countries include: prudential regulation, and in particular the monitoring of the banking sector; corporate governance, and especially the assessment and management of risk; the management of exchange rates; the encouragement of too close relations between government and the private sector, leading to cronyism and corruption; an inadequate emphasis on technological upgrading and other means of increasing productivity; and an inappropriate willingness to bail out companies that are in trouble, rather than allowing inefficient firms to fail and thus encourage others to lift their performance levels.

These attempts to place responsibility for the Asian crisis squarely on the policy failures of the governments involved have been countered by a number of authors who have instead pointed to failures in the international system. Most influential among these is Joseph Stiglitz, a former chief economist at the World Bank and chair of President Clinton's Council of Economic Advisors. He has given detailed evidence on US economic policies in Korea, arguing that these were central to the onset of the crisis (Stiglitz 2002). As early as 1993, there were discussions within the US government about ways of opening up the lucrative Korean market to a variety of US companies. In particular, Wall Street was keen to see the liberalization of the Korean capital market to allow greater foreign penetration. A number of critics urged caution, arguing that this action was premature and needed to wait until the necessary legal and regulatory frameworks had been developed in Korea, otherwise there was danger of serious instability. However, local US interests prevailed and Korea was pressured to undertake rapid deregulation. The result was a very rapid inflow of capital for a time but when the panic of 1997 set in there was an equally dramatic reversal. The fragile financial system could not cope and this premature liberalization of the capital account is regarded by Stiglitz as the single most important cause of the crisis.

Whatever the truth of these allegations, they were certainly believed by large segments of the population in many Asian countries. Widespread anti-American and anti-IMF feeling resulted in a concerted attempt by Asian governments to build stronger financial defences around the region, to work more closely together and to develop a strong regional financial body to reduce any possible future dependence on the IMF. This is the logic of a number of initiatives, such as the agreement in Chiang Mai (2010) to establish a regional monetary agreement, moves to strengthen Asian co-operation through the ASEAN Plus Three system, and discussions about the establishment of an Asian Monetary Fund (Frost 2008). Asian countries have also been very much to the fore in discussions about reform of the architecture of the international financial system, to provide greater protection to nations from the impact of speculation and unchecked money flows of the kind that destabilized Asia in 1997 (Eichengreen 1999). Above all, many Asian nations sought to insulate their economies by amassing massive foreign exchange reserves, acquired through aggressive export promotion efforts, and as we have already seen this resulted in the emergence of serious global imbalances that many have seen as a major contributor to the onset of the GFC.

Several commentators have argued that what has in fact emerged in much of east Asia is a bitter ideological and policy struggle between the neo-liberal school and a more nationalistic group that stresses the need to return to some of the core values of the Asian model, albeit with some modification. In a volume edited by MacIntyre, Pempel and Ravenhill (2008) to mark the 10th anniversary of the crisis, four major arguments are advanced about change in Asia since 1997:

- The desire to protect the region from any recurrence of the disaster of a decade earlier had forced significant changes to the political economy of the region, in particular, new initiatives on regional co-operation, banking regulation and social safety nets. But there had been an overall lack of uniformity in response to the crisis – rather each country adopted its own approach.
- The long-standing Asian focus on achieving equity along with growth was generally reaffirmed, however in some countries income disparities continued to widen.
- The crisis gave weight to critics of the old government-led model of development, and encouraged greater market liberalization.
- The response at the regional level was also very strong, resulting in important measures for financial co-operation and the creation of safeguards – such as currency swaps and the creation of a regional bond market – to insulate the region from future crises. As a result Asia is now a much more coherent and institutionalised region.

But some critics have taken issue with some key elements of this assessment, particularly in relation to national reforms and the role of the state. There have been reforms, but also some reversals of earlier policy initiatives, and the existing domestic policy and economic regimes are, in the views of many, substantially intact (Robison and Hewison 2005; Beeson and Islam, 2005, Hundt 2005). Even in the countries most directly affected by the crisis there has not been the wholesale movement to neo-liberal approaches that many had predicted. The actions of the IMF and a number of western governments in the immediate aftermath of the GFC continue to be seen by many in Asia as an attempt to impose neo-liberal prescriptions on an unwilling region that had its own ways of stimulating growth (Klein 2007). Wade (2004) has argued that in many cases Asian countries have deliberately tried to give the impression of going along with IMF prescriptions but in fact they have returned to many of the policies that had been dismantled during the 1990s. There has been a return to the practices of the developmental state but often – with WTO rules and norms in mind – 'below the radar'. There was a widespread feeling in much of Asia that the 1997 crisis was the result not of internal shortcomings but of a premature liberalization of the financial system, largely in response to intense pressure from western governments. This explanation has been given added weight by the GFC, and many Asian commentators are urging their governments – and those of the developing world more generally – to eschew such early liberalization and avoid the impacts of financial shocks originating in the West (Stiglitz 2010; Wade 2009). In many cases political elites have simply used the new situation to their continued advantage, while the state has also used new opportunities to re-invent and re-legitimise itself, as is arguably as influential in the economy as it ever was.

Of crucial importance in this debate is the question of China and the precise model it has used to generate its spectacular growth. Many commentators from the orthodox economic school have argued that China's success has been grounded on its abandonment of its old communist agenda in favour of a capitalist system, but this would appear to be a gross oversimplification. Wang Hui (2009), for example, has argued that China's history of revolution and its more recent phases of development are all part of single discourse of modernity, and calls for an entirely new model. By contrast, Huang (2008) argues that from the 1980s onwards the state-controlled sector based in the urban areas has become dominant, stifling progress in the more entrepreneurial rural areas. However, there seems to be strong support for the notion that China is basically following the lead of Asia's earlier developers such as Korea. Liew (2005) has argued that history, geography and institutional structure are all important in the choice of paths to development, and the Chinese Communist Party has been able to reinvent itself and hold its monopoly position over power: and the market has been used as a tool of state power rather than as a replacement for it (see also McGregor 2010). Similarly, Baek (2005) has argued that the state has continued to maintain strong control over the financial system, gives strong support to a large number of state-owned enterprises, has fostered a range of national heavy industries, and has based its growth on the fostering of both export competitiveness and of domestic savings – all familiar features of earlier growth strategies in east Asia.

In one key respect, though, the Asian model – particularly in the form that emerged after the Asian Crisis – is being modified. In response to the evidence that global imbalances were a contributing factor in the GFC there has been much pressure on China to put more emphasis on its domestic economy rather than a single-minded search for higher export levels (Pei 2011; Rajan 2010). Political pressures have also emerged within China for such a move, with many commentators warning of the dangers of continued income inequalities between regions and also calling for more attention to improving standards of living and thus increasing internal consumption. The Chinese leadership has signalled its willingness to enhance the domestic economy and local demand, with some particular attention to the problems of many rural areas, and this should also increase the imports of foreign goods – a trend that will increase as the Chinese economy matures.

In Chapter 5 we have discussed the so-called Beijing Consensus and how this model is now being exported to much of the developing world. Indeed, the greatly enhanced role of both China and India in the global economy is one of the lasting impacts of the GFC, although the trends were clearly apparent in the preceding years, and as is explored in the next two sections of this chapter this is having a profound impact on processes of development in both Africa and Latin America.

Africa and the global financial crisis

In spite of some recent successes in some countries, sub-Saharan Africa is still clearly the most impoverished region of the world, and many statistics could be cited to illustrate different facets of this unfortunate condition. In 2009 annual per capita income was $1,681, only half that of the poorest parts of south Asia and less than one-seventh that of Latin America. Average life expectancy is only 50 years, again the lowest in the world, and the region also has the highest rate of infant mortality. Two million children die annually before their first birthdays: infant mortality rates have risen to 107 per 1,000 compared with 69 in south Asia. Some 70 per cent of the world's HIV AIDS cases are in Africa. Around 40 per cent of the population lacks access to safe water and 33 per cent have no access to health services (Mills 2010).

This is certainly a crisis but, unlike for example the Asian financial crisis, this is not a short event with a quick onset and a relatively rapid recovery. This has been a long, slow deterioration, especially since the 1970s: in more than half the continent the average person is poorer than in 1970 (Moss 2007). The causes are complex and multifaceted, embedded in pre-colonial, colonial and post-colonial history and in the cultural history of Africa's diverse population. Space only allows us here to consider just some of the most important factors involved, and examine the ways in which the continent was affected by the GFC.

Arrighi (2002) and others have argued that one of the most important causes of the African tragedy is the form in which Africa has been incorporated into the global economic and political system. By the time of European colonization in the late nineteenth century, Africa had already been devastated by several centuries of Arab and European slave trading from the region and this was exacerbated by decades of further exploitation. Many of the African states that achieved independence in the 1960s had very arbitrary boundaries, cutting through many ethnic groups, and many had difficult geographies because of their size, shape, harsh terrain, poor climates or uneven population distributions (Herbst 2000). The fragmented nature of many African societies and political systems, with many tribal antagonisms, worked against the consolidation of state power. Few if any states were able to mobilize the resources needed to compete in the new, globalizing economy that emerged from the late 1970s onwards and many faced civil wars, insurrections or armed conflicts over access to scarce resources. Recently, Africa has suffered from a large number of internal conflicts, certainly more than any other region, and by 2001 the number of internally displaced people had reached 13.5 million (Mills 2002). In many states, the major priority of the ruling elites has been the consolidation of their own power and wealth rather than programmes to enhance the wealth of the total society.

A lack of adequate human resources has been a particular problem for the continent. To make matters worse, Africa has suffered from a serious flight of skilled people in recent years. It is estimated that 60,000 doctors, engineers and university staff left Africa between 1985 and 1990 and this exodus has continued at a rate of 20,000 per year since then (Mills 2002, 2010). Add to this the impact of a range of debilitating diseases and the extent of Africa's skills problem becomes very clear.

A further basic problem facing Africa has been its clear marginalization in the global system that has emerged since the late 1970s, and especially since the end of the Cold War. During the Cold War, a number of debilitating wars by proxy were fought in Africa by the superpowers but few if any economic benefits were received. Since the early 1990s, Africa has been largely seen as irrelevant in global economic, strategic and political terms. The continent now accounts for less than 1 per cent of annual global financial flows (UNCTAD 2002b). China alone now attracts more than 10 times as much FDI per year as the whole of Africa. International investors see Africa as poor, politically unstable, lacking in human resources and with inadequate infrastructure. There are also few domestic sources of investment, given the low level of average incomes, and as a proportion of wealth or exports African countries remain among the most heavily indebted in the world. Savings rates in Africa are the lowest in the world, less than half of those found in Asia, and some 40 per cent of all the domestic wealth that does exist is held outside the continent.

Partly as the result of the failure to create productive export industries capable of generating significant export earnings, Africa has been unable to make any headway in paying off the debt that has been accumulated over previous decades, but particularly since the 1970s. In 1999, Africa's debt was estimated to be some $201 billion. In many African countries, external debt became larger than total GDP and in some cases debt servicing requirements in terms of interest repayments alone far exceed total export revenues (Gibb et al. 2002). A debate continues over the question of how the international community should respond to the continuing burden of debt in poor countries, many of them in Africa. One influential group has lobbied for the forgiveness of debt under the banner of the loose alliance called Jubilee 2000. In 1996, the World Bank created its Highly Indebted Poor Countries (HIPC) Debt Initiative to allow poor countries to break free from these past debts. By 1999, $3.4 billion had been set aside for debt relief, but Jubilee 2000 has consistently argued that much more needs to be done. In 2005, the largest donors agreed to give further debt relief, with up to 100 per cent reduction in some countries, although some campaigners have urged wider coverage for the programme (Moss 2007). Critics of debt relief, on the other hand, have argued that there is no point in cancelling debts until there is tangible evidence of real reform in Africa, otherwise yet more external assistance will be wasted (Easterly 2001). These problems are exacerbated, Moss (2007) contends, by a largely ineffectual aid industry that is confused and fragmented: the aid agencies are becoming part of the problem rather than offering a solution.

Poor economic performance and poor quality leadership and governance are widespread problems, but as Clapham, Herbst and Mills (2006) point out, the record has been particularly bad in Africa's large nations, such as Nigeria and the Democratic Republic of the Congo. In east Asia, some large nations, Japan and more recently China, have provided real leadership for their regions but in Africa it is really only the smaller states such as Botswana and Mauritius that have had any real success, and this has had limited spill-over effects.

Given this multitude of problems, what are the prospects for reform and reconstruction? There have been many grand plans for African reconstruction in the past, including a series of studies by the World Bank (1981a; 1984a; 1986), the Lagos Plan of Action produced by the Organization of African Unity (1981), and the United Nations *Plan of Action for African Economic Recovery and Development, 1986–1990* (United Nations 1985). The actual impact of these ambitious programmes has been very disappointing.

But many commentators in Africa suggest that globalization, if handled well, can provide a new way out for the continent. In particular, the rise of India and China and the increased prices being offered for the minerals and other resources with which Africa is well endowed may offer a way forward. Asia offers both large markets and growing industries that can absorb not just traditional exports like cotton but also food and consumer goods. Tourism from Asia can also be a key earner of foreign exchange. Thus, while Africa may have been marginalized by the West, Asia can be the new Silk Road (Broadman 2007). Critics have questioned whether China's exploitation of Africa's resources will be any more benign than was the earlier colonial rape of Africa, pointing out that almost all Chinese investment has been in resources, and oil in particular, often in countries like Sudan that have questionable development credentials. However, others have suggested that if handled carefully China and India can help the continent to higher levels of growth: it is for Africa to make decisions and plan for its own future (Winters and Yusuf 2007). An optimistic view has been presented by Friedman (2009) and Gonzalez-Vicente (2011) who argue that China is already in the process of transforming parts of Africa, not just by increasing demands for resources but by exporting entrepreneurial methods and more general Asian dynamism, and incorporating Africa into Asian industrialization. China's method of operation, it is argued, is fundamentally different from earlier western investors and the results can be much more positive and less exploitative. But China's 'hands off' approach to local political regimes means that there are dangers in some situations of enhancing the power of regimes that are certainly anti-development: there is a need for local communities to be more active in making sure that they are involved in determining their own futures.

This theme of Africa needing to take hold of its own destiny is now a common refrain among commentators from all parts of the continent. Governance and leadership problems and issues of ethnic and religious conflict have dogged the region and can only be solved by the African nations themselves. This has become even more urgent since an implicit bargain has been struck between Africa and the major economic powers: Africa will reform itself in return for significantly increased assistance of various kinds. It was self-help and African internal reform that was central to the launch of the New Partnership for African Development (NEPAD). This is a joint initiative of the African leaders themselves, but it has been endorsed by a meeting of the World Economic Forum in Durban in June 2002 and by a meeting of the G-8 in Canada later in the same month. In July, also in South Africa, the African Union was launched, replacing the old Organization of African Unity, and this was partly meant to symbolize a new and united beginning to co-operation in the region in support of

Chapter 7

Politics, Governance and Development

Damien Kingsbury

To the casual observer, politics in developing countries commonly appears to be beset by, if not mired in, problems of limited political representation, poor governance and corruption, with only occasional and often poor engagement with notions of democracy and with a propensity to various degrees of failure of state institutions. To a considerable extent, this perception is based on a history of failure of developing countries to consistently conform to a modernist western model of political processes, the value of which has been the subject of lively debate. More specifically, however, developing countries have each faced a range of economic, social and institutional challenges, some of which have been successfully overcome and many of which have not and which can undermine political stability. Within this framework and recognizing that individual countries face specific historic problems, there are elements of consistency between the issues they have faced and which allows a general analysis of development politics which can be applied when understanding specific case studies.

This chapter sets out the main features of politics in developing countries, attempting to show how the relationships between these elements forms a complex interweaving of factors that preclude providing simple answers to their multi-faceted problems. The chapter begins with identifying how the origins of developing countries through colonialism and post-colonial experiences shaped their experiences, the successes and failures of post-colonial political identity, the politicization of militaries, tensions between economics and politics, regime change and issues in democratization and authoritarian government. It then continues to address issues of governance, the relationship between the state and society, regime change and what has often been put as the normative imperative of democratization.

This chapter is based on the idea that 'development', which proposes processes by which people can improve their lives, is in large part shaped by the political and social freedoms and accountabilities. The idea of development has traditionally been focused on economic development, or improvement in the material welfare of people. Some commentators, notably politicians in developing countries, have even argued that economic or material development should take precedence over political development, and that political development should be put on hold to ensure that fragile or conflicted political environments do not hinder efficiencies of organization necessary to lift poor countries out of poverty. In some cases, this position has also been allied with the view that political development, especially if that means democracy and civil and political rights, are a foreign imposition, do not necessarily accord with pre-existing political values, and may constitute a form of imperialism.

Related to the view that economic development should take precedence over political development – that people will be unconcerned about politics if they do not have enough to eat – is the view that higher levels of material development are necessary to sustain higher levels of political development. That is, if people lack food security or they are illiterate, they will not only be less concerned about politics but less able to meaningfully participate in a given political process. A countervailing view is that if people have the opportunity to freely express themselves, and to hold their politicians accountable, they are more likely to be able to ensure there is adequate distribution of food and other available material goods, including education (see Sen 1999a). This then raises the fundamental question of whether it is economics that drives politics, or politics that drives economics, or what has been referred to as the debate about the competition between structure and agency. These issues will be discussed within the context of contemporary theory on wider interpretations of governance and evolving political practice.

The origins of developing countries

Of the world's developing countries, most came into existence in the period following the Second World War, in which struggles for liberation that had begun to find their voice in the 1920s and '30s became more compelling in the post-war era. Even those states that were not formally colonies were often defined by aspects of the colonial experience, not least in terms of their borders and the status of their external relations. The major exception to the post-war experience of decolonization was in Latin America, which had largely shed the imposition of colonialism in the early nineteenth century. But even its subsequent experiences tended to reflect the broadly shared experiences of later post-colonial states.

There have been two defining qualities of developing countries that derive from their post-colonial status. The first is that the successor states have almost all been based upon prior colonial boundaries, usually reflecting colonial convenience rather than prior ethno-linguistic unity. The second is that most developing states came to independence through a military struggle, with military forces and ideology subsequently coming to play a major role in the orientation of the state.

Having achieved independence, many developing countries have frequently failed to sustain the sense of unity of purpose that liberation helped engender, and have also not sustained their commitment to either a generalized sense of freedom or a representative, accountable and participatory political process. The aspirations often associated with independence – that independence will address the problems that beset the colonized territory – have commonly exceeded the capacity of the newly formed state to deliver. Indeed, such aspirations were often confronted by reduced state capacity as a result of war and the loss of colonial expertise, organization and capital. Expectations of improvement in the lives of the people concerned not only went beyond that which the colonial power was able to provide, but were further out of touch with the reduced post-colonial environment (Chandler 2010: 170).

The gap between post-colonial expectation and the (lack of) capacity to fulfil it invariably produced disappointment (Jefferess 2008: 163), often alienation and, in some cases, anger. In multi-ethnic post-colonial societies and in particular within the context of post-independence material scarcity, there has been a tendency for political leaders to reward their political supporters at the expense of other groups (Grawert 2009: 138). This form of patron–client relations was often based along specific ethno-linguistic lines, although exceptions arose where patron–client groups form around other areas of geographic or, more commonly, economic interest. That is, where the bonds of a united struggle against colonialism may form an initial sense of unity, this unity was not always maintained in post-colonial era.

In an open or plural political environment, such as post-colonial democracy, this lack of unity can manifest as political opposition and dissent. In cases where governments have little initial capacity, they may struggle to maintain organizational control and consequently had a tendency to close political space and thus revert to forms of authoritarianism, often employing repressive colonial-era legislation (see Collier 2009: 173–6, 186 on the relationship between state capacity and post-colonial democracies). In cases where such governments have derived from a military or revolutionary background that reflected a high degree of non-consultative hierarchical organization, such organization is reflected in the political style and orientation of the new government.

Political identity

Independence movements in colonial territories were frequently accompanied by a rise in the assertion of a nationalist identity, usually cohering around their opposition to the colonial authority. But because most colonies were constructed according to geographic convenience rather than along ethnic lines, they usually included distinct tribal or ethnic groups, many of which traditionally had ambivalent or even hostile relations. Moreover, it was a common practice of colonial powers to employ one ethnic group in a position of advantage over others, as a mechanism for recruiting ethnic groups in support of the colonial enterprise (e.g. see Horowitz 1985: 527), for example the German favouring of minority Tutsis in Rwanda, the British favouring of minority Tamils in Ceylon (Sri Lanka), French favouring of ethnic minority Vietnamese in Cambodia and Laos and Dutch favouring of minority Dutch East Indies (Indonesia) eastern islanders over majority western islanders in military capacities. In some cases, post-colonial states succeeded in developing a sense of coherent national identity, for example in some Latin American and Arab states. In others, however, attempts to compel loyalty to the new national project failed, especially where some ethnic groups felt discriminated against on the grounds of their ethnic identity and where the 'civic guarantee' of equal inclusion failed to apply, including many sub-Saharan African (most countries at one time or another), south Asian (Sri Lanka, parts of India) and South East Asian states (Myanmar, Laos, Indonesia, Philippines). This was particularly so where a specific ethnic group with a grievance within a reasonably geographically coherent area did not acknowledge the legitimacy of an administration from a separate location or over the claimed area, or where that sense of legitimacy was never adequately established or was lost, illustrated by separatist movements that affect or have affected many developing countries.

Post-colonial states in particular have tended to exhibit vertical or regionally based ethnic group tendencies, where they are constructed from multiple pre-existing ethnicities and where the civic function of the state, in which all citizens are treated as equal, is weak. Given that most post-colonial countries are 'ethnically diverse' (Collier 1998) and often have weak civic institutions, there is a tendency for such states to coa-

Desch (1999) has argued that civilian authority over militaries works best where a state faces high external threats and low internal threats. Civilian control of the military works worst, according to Desch, where a state faces high internal threats, such as separatism or revolutionary movements, and low external threats. In those conditions, the military is more likely to see itself as a political actor or as the protector of the state, often justified by the role played by militaries (or their precursor guerrilla organizations) in independence movements. In conditions of high internal and external threats or low internal and external threats, Desch suggests that civilian control over the military sits in between the two extremes. In developed countries, however, the tendency has been for low internal and external threats to equate to greater civilian control over the military (see Lasswell 1941, see also Dains 2004). Militaries in developing countries also appear to have interpreted as an internal 'threat' a perceived or actual lack of competence by civilian leaders.

Huntington (1957) argued that the most effective method of asserting civilian control over the military is to professionalize them, but this was based on the US model and assumed a capacity to do so. This capacity to profesionalize the military is often not present in developing countries and in particular where the state is unable to meet the full costs of the military and hence militaries engage in private businesses outside civilian control (e.g. Indonesia, China, Vietnam, Burma, Laos, among others), meaning they are less accountable to civilian governments.

Notably, too, when military organizations do influence or exercise political authority, they are by definition hierarchical, closed and relatively authoritarian (see Huntington 1957). This is especially the case where the military derives its ethos from revolutionary idealism, in which its role in the securing of independence is usually only the first step on the road to a wider social transformation.

Where society is otherwise initially disorganized or where alternative legitimate sources of power have not yet become established, or where the post-independence development project either heads towards failure or actually fails (e.g. Afghanistan, Somalia, Sudan), military control is regarded by power-holders as necessary to maintain state organization or, in some cases, cohesion. This then has the capacity to devolve into a situation where the newly independent authority may lose legitimacy through its exclusive, non-participatory and non-representative system of organization, or where it compels often geographically and ethnically specific reluctant citizens to remain within the state. Again, a significant element of this tendency towards political closure in the face of state incapacity set against growing frustration and disappointment came to characterize many new developing country governments, when tensions between increasing political closure on one hand and growing frustration on the other spilled over into violence. Governments moved to assert their authority, as was again demonstrated in many Arab states in 2011, but a breakdown of state institutions in a number of instances led instead to near state collapse, in some cases resulting in the even stronger assertion of the status quo, in others a generalized chaos and disfunction but, very often, eventually in regime change (e.g. Egypt, Tunisia, Libya).

Democracy, democratization and regime change

In the period since the end of the Cold War, there has been an upsurge in the number of states around the world that define themselves as 'democracies'. This is in part due to the electoral processes employed in a number of former Soviet states and the turn towards electoral processes in formerly authoritarian client states that have since lost the patronage of one or other of the two former superpowers. However, not all regime change has been democratic, democratic change is not inevitable and it is possible for democracies to revert to other, less or non-democratic forms of political organization. Further, what is claimed to be 'democratic' may not be that, or it may be a procedural democracy, employing a relatively free electoral contest, but failing to provide a range of more substantive democratic qualities such as the separation of powers between government institutions, equitable and consistent rule of law, civil and political rights such as freedom of speech and assembly, or the opportunity to fully participate in the political process (see Schumpeter 1976; Dahl 1986; Burton et al. 1992: 1; Grugel 2002: 6).

In debates above democracy and democratization, Fukuyama (among others) argues that there is only one final form of democracy – liberal democracy associated with free market economics (Fukuyama 1992). This implies either a grand, singular vision, or a circumscribed or minimalist understanding of the meaning of the term 'democracy'. Assuming the grand, singular (and usually unreflective) vision, there is no effective room for debate or alternative, as this model casts itself as an absolute, which is in turn reflected in dogma. Such 'democratic absolutism' has frequently run contrary to the political experience or preferences in developing countries, even where they accept a substantive democratic model, for example, with a higher degree of economic intervention. As a result, there has been considerable debate over the value and appropriateness of a 'one size fits all' democracy, not least in developing country contexts.

There have also been a number of objections to democracy, which have frequently been adopted by non-democratic governments to rationalize their political structure and orientation. Pre-democratic governments such as monarchies have generally been opposed to democracy on the grounds that it stands in opposition to hereditary right to rule, which in turn has become acculturated into the societies they govern. Authoritarian governments also argue that democracy promotes social division, short-term interests over long-term planning (e.g. see Kaplan 2005; Hoppe 2001). In some cases, they also argue that democracy can imply a tyranny of the majority. Communist governments have also argued that democracy is a subterfuge for capitalist control of society and that the only political choices are those between parties or individuals representing versions of exploitative capitalism.

There has been a long-expressed view that notions of democracy are culturally specific and are not transferrable to non-western societies (e.g. see Zakaria 1994). 'With few exceptions, democracy has not brought good government to new developing countries...What Asians value may not necessarily be what Americans or Europeans value', Lee said by way of defending what were claimed to be 'Confucian values' (Han et al. 1998). Similarly, Halper has argued that democracy is a dead idea and that China's authoritarian model will come to dominate the twenty-first century (Halper 2010). Both Lee's argument and that of China also argue in favour of economic efficiency over political participation.

Related to the view that economic development should take precedence over political development – that people will be unconcerned about politics if they do not have enough to eat – is the view that higher levels of material development are necessary to sustain higher levels of political development. Consistent with these views, particularly up to the 1990s, was the argument that suggested that developing countries could not 'afford' liberal government and that only strong government could deliver desired development outcomes. This argument was particularly strong in east Asia and was justified by citing the examples of the 'Asian Tiger' economies of South Korea, Taiwan, Hong Kong and Singapore, none of which enjoyed liberal government during the period of their economic development (though each of which enjoyed specific opportunities that assisted their economic development). Each of these east Asian states was described as a 'developmental state', referring to relatively high levels of state autonomy from vested interests as well as relatively high levels of intervention in economic planning, regulation and performance. While this model, originally based on the Japanese experience with its Ministry of International Trade and Industry (MITI) under the Liberal Democratic Party rule between 1955 and 2009 (with an 11-month interregnum in 1993–4), has tended to function in states with limited political plurality, political closure is not a prerequisite for relatively high levels of such intervention. To illustrate, there was a relatively high level of government intervention in the Swedish economy until the 1990s.

The argument put by more authoritarian governments in favour of political closure was, following the 'developmental' model, that if people lack food security or they are illiterate, they will not only be less concerned about politics but less able to meaningfully participate in a given political process, or what has been termed by some as 'rice before rights' or the 'full bellies thesis' (see Howard 1983). A countervailing view is that if people have the opportunity to freely express themselves, and to hold their politicians accountable, they are more likely to be able to ensure there is adequate distribution of food and other available material goods, including education (see Sen 1999a).

In cases where democracy is established, there can also be a democratic tension around the acceptance of a plurality of views, some of which might be antithetical to further such openness (e.g. majority imposition, or voting to end voting) and which may set up points of conflict within a society still struggling to come to grips with low levels of institutional and organizational capacity. Many developing countries struggle to overcome these tensions and can and sometimes slip into chaos, often ended when the military or another authoritarian party imposes its own undemocratic will. This then raises the issue of regime change, which in developing country contexts may be towards or, more likely, away from open, plural political models.

The issue of regime change is critical in the process of political development and is often at the point at which options for democratic openings occur (e.g. the 'Revolutions of 1989' in which a number of Soviet Bloc states adopted democratic practices). However, at the point of regime change, there may be a fatalistic belief that political change necessarily produces positive, democratic outcomes. By regime change, what is meant is a fundamental shift of political values, and is more commonly not via an orderly handing over of government within an established and agreed political framework (with the exceptions to this general trend being among some former Soviet bloc). The literature on regime change suggests that it usually follows a period of rising political tension and that its common feature is political instability in the period leading up to, surrounding and following it. As a consequence, regime change can be accompanied by political violence, especially between groups representing the status quo and aspirants for change.

Superfluous use of words! *unfucking necessary.*

The causes of regime change are various, but change that is internally driven tends to reflect a failure of the existing system to either fulfil the basic requirements of a key social sector or sectors, such as rural or urban workers, the middle class, business owners, traditional oligarchs, or the military. This failure to fulfil such sectoral interests may reflect a basic ideological position that predisposes the government to ignore or oppose particular interests. It may also reflect a government's incapacity to function in favour of its preferred interest sector, such as where the government becomes excessively corrupt, factionalized or otherwise unable to exercise authority, or where its key institutions cease to meaningfully function. In this respect, regime change is most commonly a consequence of horizontal, interest-based political change (class-based revolutions). A government either tends to represent one horizontal group by replacing another, or a horizontal group or coalition of groups replace their own, failed government. Regime change is rarely vertical because vertical divisions that are so strong as to successfully challenge a government tend to want to establish a separate state. Absolutely successful vertical challenges are rare (the USSR, Yugoslavia, Bangladesh, Eritrea and East Timor being notable exceptions), while partial successes such as greater regional autonomy are more likely (for example, Spanish regional autonomy, Finland's Åland Islands, Indonesia's Aceh, and so on). Vertical regime change may also occur in tribal societies, such as Afghanistan or Rwanda, where the government tended to reflect the assertion of specific tribal interests within the state.

oh really.

The period of regime change is the point at which there is greatest political flux and hence both opportunity and threat. Where there is opportunity, it is often understood in terms of the resolution of a negative (usually associated with the end of a chaotic or dysfunctional government or dictatorship). Sometimes, however, this change may be away from plural government towards a more closed or authoritarian political model. Even where new forms of government may have the external characteristics of democracy (such as in the Philippines in 1986, or Indonesia in 1998), there may be partially or completely hidden components that fundamentally compromise the capacity of the general population to meaningfully participate in political affairs or to be genuinely represented (see O'Donnell 1996 for discussion on this broader topic). That is, where regime change is towards democracy, it is often procedural rather than substantive.

Beyond this, regime change is not by definition towards a normatively more desirable or participatory outcome. Although the tendency towards the end of the twentieth and early twenty-first centuries has been for regime change to move away from authoritarian models, it can also impose non-democratic or authoritarian rule. More recent examples of this negative form of regime change, between 1999 and 2006, include Pakistan, the Central African Republic, São Tomé and Príncipe, Guinea-Bissau, Haiti, Mauritania, Nepal and Thailand, along with attempted coups in numerous other countries.

As discussed, regime change can be from or to any other particular regime type. O'Donnell and Schmitter (1986) identify eight basic political model types, each characterizing degrees of democracy and liberalism, although interestingly, in contrast to other interpretations of economic liberalism which usually imply laissez-faire capitalism and equate liberalism more or less to economic equality. Assuming, however, that liberalism implies the greatest economic freedom for the greatest number (a variation on the utilitarian theme) rather than the greatest economic freedom for whoever is able to exercise it if at the expense of others, O'Donnell and Schmitter's interpretation can be accepted as liberalism, though of a more political than purely economic type.

At the most authoritarian end of their scale, O'Donnell and Schmitter identify autocracy, or 'dictadura', as constituting low democratic capacity and low levels of liberalization, moving to or from a plebiscitary autocracy usually via a coup or revolution. Moving towards a medium level of liberalization while retaining low levels of democratization is characterized as liberalized autocracy, or 'dictablanda', which might characterize a number of authoritarian but not dictatorial regimes (such as Singapore). Instituting limited political democracy with medium liberalization, or 'democradura', opens the next political category, characterizing less authoritarian but still restrictive regimes, such as in Malaysia and perhaps the democratizing states of sub-Saharan Africa. States moving towards popular democracy, representing high democratization with low liberalization might be characterized by India or Sri Lanka before the effective limitation of the latter's political space after 2005.

O'Donnell and Schmitter's next category of political democracy, reflecting higher democratization and greater liberalization, appears to correspond to a number of western or OECD states but commonly is not reflected in developing countries' political systems. The use of the term polyarchy to describe this category is further developed by Dahl's seven attributes: elected officials, free and fair elections, inclusive suffrage, the right to run for office, freedom of expression, alternative information and associational autonomy (Dahl 1989: 221). Related to the form of polyarchy that is reflected in the political status of many OECD countries is the category of social democracy, implying higher democratization and high liberalization.

Assuming that authoritarianism and its variants have a negative normative value, this implies that the opposite has a positive normative value. Although perhaps reflecting the era in which it was written, O'Donnell and Schmitter's assessment of the positive is in contrast to even then more economic libertarian views. In this respect, they equate higher democratization and highest liberalization to welfare democracy (presumably of the type then found in Scandinavia and to a lesser extent Australia and New Zealand), and to socialist democracy (O'Donnell and Schmitter1986: 13), although it is unclear where such a socialist democracy actually exists, or has existed, other than in theory.

Assuming that much regime change will be opposed, and that transitions especially from authoritarian to democratic models require a shift in allegiance of the military, the military itself will often be politicized and divided between those who support regime change and those who oppose it. O'Donnell and Schmitter (1986: 15–17) characterize such military factions as 'hardliners' and 'softliners'. As these terms imply, hardliners oppose change, while softliners facilitate change, usually cautiously. Examples of successfully facilitated change by military softliners who have taken advantage of 'the military moment' (1986: 39) include Portugal and Greece in 1974, the Philippines in 1986, and Indonesia in 1998, although there are also numerous examples in Latin America. Moreover, limited liberalization away from a direct military rule while retaining a capacity for existing elite control or liberalization without introducing democracy may also be facilitated by such a softline military approach (for example, the removal of direct military rule in Indonesia 1986–8, and relative liberalization without democratization in 1991). Softliners, however, sometimes overestimate their popular support, and may engender a backlash that sets back movement towards liberalization (O'Donnell and Schmitter 1986: 58). For example, in Indonesia, President Habibie's decision to allow East Timor to vote on independence in 1999 resulted in his own political denouement just weeks later, with his liberal successor being ousted halfway through his presidential term. Softliners also encountered a backlash in the initial military-led steps of Portugal's 'Carnation Revolution' in 1974, and during Turkey's return to electoral politics in 1983.

As Dahl noted, a state is unlikely to quickly develop a democratic political system if it has had little or no experience of public contestation and competition, and lacks a tradition of tolerance towards political opposition (Dahl 1971: 208). That is, regime change in such a state is at least as likely to default to an alternative authoritarian government, or to partially do so. Similarly, although cautioning against political expectations arising out of such structural preconditions, Di Palma noted that economic instability, a hegemonic nationalist culture and the absence of a strong, independent middle class all impede transition from an authoritarian political model towards one that is more democratic (Di Palma 1991: 3).

There is debate in development politics over whether there is a structural or causal link between economic and political development. One view has it that societies need to reach a certain level of economic development before they can enjoy a similar level of political development (e.g. see Acemoglu and Robinson 2006: ch. 3). A competing view posits that a higher level of political development is possible without related economic development. This specific debate reflects a broader 'structure-agency' debate, in which there are competing views over whether material circumstances shape development outcomes or whether there is scope for human 'agency' or choice to determine how societies organize themselves.

In considering transitions from authoritarian to democratic models, there are a range of conditions that might be claimed to be essential for successful regime change. As noted by Dahl, these include control of the military and police by elected civilian officials; democratic beliefs and culture (Dahl 1989: 111) and no strong interference by foreign powers that are hostile to democracy (for example, the USSR in Eastern bloc countries). Further, Dahl identified conditions that were not absolutely necessary, but which were favourable for the establishment of democracy, including a modern market economy and society, and weak subcultural pluralism (or lack of opportunity for inter-ethnic conflict) (Dahl 2000: 147, see also Dahl 1989: ch. 8).

The incompletion of regime change can be demonstrated in the Philippines where, in 1986, the dictator Ferdinand Marcos lost the support of his US backers and, eventually, the country's oligarchic elite and sections of the military. In this respect, there appeared to have been an elite pact for careful change in the Philippines (O'Donnell and Schmitter 1986: 40–45). Capitalizing on the 'political moment', elites, with the support of mass mobilization, developed or reasserted political parties and organized political constituencies under a 'grand coalition'. In Indonesia in 1998, this also occurred, although rather than reflecting a more gradual economic decline and a sudden political incident, there was a more gradual political decline and a sudden economic incident, or 'economic moment'(O'Donnell and Schmitter 1986: 45–7) – the collapse of the Indonesian currency, followed by a sudden 'political moment' – the resignation of President Suharto after more than three decades in power. In the case of a sudden economic crisis, such as the 1997–8 financial collapse in Indonesia, there is an implied socio-economic pact between those who are most disaffected or economically disadvantaged and those who appear to be able to assume responsibility for alleviating the crisis (whether they are able to do so or not). In what Dahl has referred to 'the democratic bargain' of trust, fairness and compromise (1970), this pact normatively corresponds to a type of social contract.

The evolution of political forms from absolute autocratic rule towards civil government that encourage political participation, representation and accountability, require a type of social contract between citizens and its government. Under absolute rule, a sovereign monarch or tyrant is not party to any contract but rules with unlimited authority. This is not a form of civil government because there is no neutral authority to decide disputes between the ruler and the citizen. Under the 'social contract' model, however, the government accedes authority to the population, mediated by an independent authority (for example, an independent judiciary) in return for right to rule. This occurs on a sliding scale of a balance of authority until it is agreed that authority is ultimately vested in the citizens, is only held by the political leader or government on behalf of the citizens, and is able to be rescinded by the citizens in an agreed and orderly manner (that is, through regular elections).

In this, it is important that elites who intend to continue or expand their political rule are able to satisfy, or be seen to address, most outstanding demands while at the same time avoiding the strongest dissatisfactions from manifesting into collective action. As O'Donnell and Schmitter note, and which appears to be borne out by experience, transitional regimes from authoritarianism tend to be smoother and more successful if they promote essentially conservative or right-wing political outcomes, as this is seen as less threatening to out-going authoritarian elites. Democratic 'idealists', usually on the left and centre-left, are only given the opportunity to engage in transitional processes if elite survivors from the previous regime are willing to negotiate a mutually satisfactory set of rules of the new game (O'Donnell and Schmitter 1986: 70). Where such negotiations fail, more active, usually leftist, political actors may be rapidly marginalized, as occurred in post-1986 Philippines and in post-1998 Indonesia. In the latter case, those demanding total reform of the political system were quickly marginalized, resulting in the fragmentation of the reform movement (comprising in particular students, civil society and humanitarian NGOs and coalitions). The consequence of this leftist marginalization and fragmentation was that the political agenda quickly reverted to control by conservative elites, while the election as president of the reformist cleric

Abdurrahman Wahid by an oppositional if conservative coalition resulted in his own ousting by those same elites less than two years later.

In the case of the Philippines, public protest against then President Marcos and the blatant falsification of election results, backed by sections of the military, led to his ousting and replacement by his electoral opponent, Corazon Aquino, the widow of Marcos' murdered former opponent, Senator Benigno Aquino. While Corazon Aquino came to power on the back of a popular protest movement (known unreflectively as 'people power'), she in fact ushered in elite rule mirroring that of the oligarchic pre-dictatorship era. Under Aquino, the Philippines' elite structurally excluded genuine open participation in politics, despite it formally being an open electoral contest, and returned to squabbling over the spoils of state between them. In Indonesia, by comparison, the resignation of Suharto in 1998 and the weakening of the highly centralized state apparatus he and the military had constructed, led to a rash of genuine political reforms under his immediate successor, Habibie. A reconsolidating status quo elite and destabilization of the state under the reformist presidency of Abdurrahman Wahid partly contributed towards his ousting and replacement by pro-status quo elite/pro-military Megawati Sukarnoputri in mid-2001. Of particular transitional note, however, was the role played by military 'softliner', Susilo Bambang Yudhoyono, first as the leader of the reform faction of the Indonesian military in the early 1990s, following from dissent towards the then president and then as a political actor and finally as president himself.

One interesting aspect of regime transitions is the role played by external events. Although there are numerous exceptions, it appears that critical political shifts most often occur at times of pronounced social, economic and/or political dislocation. A range of pre-existing tensions or pressures must already exist in order to capitalize on the subsequent rupture, but the rupture itself appears to act as a catalyst for regime change. By way of illustration, the Russian Revolution took place after its disastrous involvement in the Great War. China's nationalist revolution was precipitated by colonial domination and its communist revolution came in response to Japanese occupation, while Portugal sloughed off dictatorship in the wake of economic collapse and failed colonialism. Similarly, Nicaragua deposed its dictatorship after a destructive earthquake, the Philippines and Indonesia removed dictators following the Asian economic crisis, Greece after the Turkish invasion of Cyprus and Argentina removed its military junta following its defeat in the Falklands War. In the two latter cases, democracy was achieved by stalemate and lack of consensus rather than by prior unity and consensus (see O'Donnell and Schmitter, 1986: 72). Indeed, virtually the whole post-Second World War decolonization period could be attributed, to a greater or lesser extent, to the direct and indirect economic, military and political effects of the war.

Foreign powers can also play a role in regime change by supporting various parties which might, at any given time, be in external exile or which may be underground within the country in question. It has been common practice for groups attempting to overthrow a particular regime to receive external assistance, by way of receiving sanctuary, training, logistical support and representation in international fora, a recent example of this being that of Libya in 2011.

Transitions born of crisis are, of course, not consistent in their outcomes, illustrated by the shifting contest between democracy and authoritarianism throughout Latin America and in countries such as Thailand and in much of sub-Saharan Africa. There are even cases of voluntary political redundancy, such as in Spain after Franco's death, although this too might be seen as a political 'shock'. In some cases, the 'shock' itself, though, is little more than an excuse to exercise an overdue necessity, where an ossified regime is aware of its redundancy, yet still requires an excuse to dignify and hence ease its own departure.

As noted, not all regime changes are towards democracy. Some changes may be partial (for example, Philippines post-1986, Indonesia post-1998) or lead to conflict (such as Cambodia 1975–98). Others simply revert from one type of authoritarianism to another, as has often been the case in sub-Saharan Africa. These different experiences of regime change invariably reflect competing views of what constitutes political progress; what is to some fairness is to others interference; what to some is freedom is to others disorder depending, as discussed earlier, on how one views the basic concepts of freedom and equality.

The state, society and democratization

Reflecting on the relationship between the state and society within the context of degrees of freedom, Stepan noted the putative if changing focus of the state from economic to political development:

> The assumptions of modernization theory that liberal democratic regimes would be inexorably produced by the process of industrialization was replaced by a new preoccupation with the ways in which the state apparatus might become a central instrument for both the repression of subordinate classes and the reorientation of the process of industrial development.   (Stepan 1985: 317)

The development of what have been called 'Bureaucratic Authoritarian regimes' that are associated with, if not necessarily responsible for, economic development (seen as industrialization) in a number of developing states, noted above as 'developmental states', has also fragmented and inhibited potential political opposition. The rise in relative authority of formal or recognized state institutions, and the non-negotiable imposition of their development programmes, has diminished other political institutions, including both the formal pluralist institution of 'Opposition' and the capacity of civil society (Stepan 1985: 317). That is to say, there can be and often is competition in developing countries between formal institutions, as well as between formal institutions and those institutions that are regarded as less formal. This in turn comes back to attempts to delegitimize political alternatives, and in particular, those that are necessary for a successful plural polity but which have an imposed reduced capacity that in turn delegitimizes them.

If there is a differentiation between early and more recent approaches in thinking about institutions, particularly as it applies to developing countries, it is in understanding institutions as not being just organizations of people with particular roles, but sets of rules or codes of behaviour that can include, for example, respect for the rule of law, notions of equality, and tolerance of or respect for alternative views (e.g. see Hall and Taylor 1996). The key distinctions here are between formal and informal rules or codes of behaviour, with greater emphasis being placed on important informal rules that nonetheless effectively play a formal role in political society. An example of an informal rule that might be considered critical is the opportunity for the creation and maintenance of civil society organizations, which have a central role in the open political function of developing states. The 'rules' by which such groups organize themselves are one way in which they constitute institutions, but the fact of their existence and their shifting social and political roles have also become institutionalized. That is, there is an expectation that such organizations will exist in a developing country, will be acknowledged as existing and will from time to time contribute to public debate and decision-making.

In circumstances where legitimacy implies consent to rule it is normative, in that it reflects a social value-judgement about whether or not a ruler or government has the 'right' to occupy that political position. This in turn opens up questions of moral authority and the extent of correspondence between such matters and between ruler and ruled. Positive legitimacy implies explicit agreement about the circumstances that confer legitimacy, such as compliance with equal and consistent rule of law, and the correspondence between the action of the ruler and such compliance. That is to say, legitimacy of rule derives from a sense of justice in social and political relations; where a sense of justice prevails, the social and political circumstances may be regarded as legitimate.

The relationship between civil society and government has been proposed as an indicator of the democratic health of the state, with the varying capacities of each institution being a key determinant. Stepan posits four sets of relationships between the state and civil society, which are characterized as the following:

1. Growth of state power and diminution of civil society power, which often occurs during the closure of political space by governments in developing countries.
2. Decline of state power and growth of civil society power, which is unusual in developing countries.
3. Growth of both state and civil society, which is again unusual in developing countries but may occur in democratic transitons.
4. Decline of both state and civil society (but with option of civil society growth outside the state), which tends to reflect failed state status. (Stepan 1985: 318)

Stepan was primarily concerned with the growth of state power in developing countries at the expense of civil society, or the imposition of bureaucratic authoritarianism with a parallel reduction in the capacity of non-state actors to compete with state power. While Stepan focused on Latin America, this situation could also characterize 'strong states' such as China, Vietnam or Syria in which an independent civil society is relatively weak. In the transitional phase away from bureaucratic authoritarianism, state power declines and civil society strengthens as a consequence of the opening of greater political space (for example, as military domination declined in Thailand). Civil society may also increase in its own right and therefore act as a contributor to declining state power (for example, Poland). Growth of both state and civil society power can be seen either in competition or as providing a balance for each other. With the former, the instability that derives from competition is unable to be sustained, and tends to either degenerate into internal conflict or the state or civil society fails to sustain its position and hence declines in power relative to the other. More positively, however, state power can be defined not only as bureaucratic authoritarianism (negative state power) but also as benign state capacity or an ability to resist the influence of vested interests (positive power). In such cases, where there is strong civil society and strong positive state power, the two are likely to interact together to increase their respective capacities. Perhaps the best examples of this can be seen in the Scandinavian states, and to a lesser extent in other plural democracies.

In cases where both state and civil society power decline, however, there is the possibility of state failure or reversion to pre-modern methods of state organization (ASC et al. 2003: 4), as neither institutional segment is available to compensate for the weakness of the other. Such a power vacuum often draws external actors into the collapsed political space. This could be seen in the case of Iraq during the insurgency against US intervention from 2003, where US intervention created the power vacuum and then led to the necessity of its continuing if increasingly troubled presence. Similarly, the political space collapsed in Afghanistan prior to the rise of the Taliban, and in East Timor from late April 2006 (see also FfP 2006). In studying the reduced autonomy of the Brazilian state in the early 1980s, Stepan noted the view of executive branch leaders that only the reduction of state autonomy relative to civil society through a process of liberalization could reign in the state's security apparatus. That is, if the state was weaker relative to civil society, then its institutional components would also be relatively weaker, including those that political leaders viewed as rather more malignant.

State institutions

Institutions, as they have been traditionally or narrowly understood (for example, Fukuyama 2004), tend to develop a quasi-independent capacity and sense of self. That is, in the search for meaning by the individuals who comprise such institutions, there is a tendency towards a higher level of self-regard which derives from a sense of institutional relevance and capacity. This sense of self-regard in turn derives from the necessity of institutional function, the usually internally defined level of quality that should be achieved, and the resources that are necessary in order to do that. As a consequence, the self-maintenance (and expansion) of institutions may take precedence over the function they were initially designed to undertake, especially where there are low levels of capacity, oversight or accountability. This is particularly the case concerning most classic institutions, especially the bureaucracy (see Weber 1946: 338–41). The key criterion for bureaucratic performance is performance assessment criteria set against 'stakeholder' interest – the interests of the main parties to the implementation of policy. But in spite of how stakeholders might view policy implementation, the self-referential character of many bureaucracies continues to slow or otherwise limit policy implementation.

While institutional self-affirmation – the process by which bureaucracies require an increasing series of often unresponsive checks and processes – can account for bloated and slow moving bureaucracies, it can also account for the political role of organizations such as the military, police or intelligence agencies, each of which tend to have a relatively more advanced or politically active role in developing countries. Having established themselves as relatively organizationally efficient, with the sole legal capacity to employ violence on behalf of the state, often economically self-benefiting and not infrequently having an over-developed self-regard, institutions also come to develop a 'culture' or world view which explains and rationalizes not just their continuing role but the orientation of such a role (for example, as reflected in the myth of the post-revolutionary 'people's army', public order, etc.). Given the economic benefit (employment and promotion, quasi-official business, corruption) that can accrue to institutions, they may be reluctant to adapt relative to changing circumstances, and can consequently be a considerable force for reaction.

The role of institutions has been identified by the World Bank, among others, as being central to the success or failure of development projects, particularly in their larger and more bureaucratic sense. That is, the capacity of states to make use of aid, to deliver its benefits and to sustain the process of development generally is seen by the World Bank, and many others, to be vested in the institutions of the state. This thesis was first developed by Huntington (1968) and later addressed by Fukuyama (2004).

After his earlier foray into determinist normative claims of the inevitability of democracy and free market capitalism in developing countries, Fukuyama appeared to recognize that liberal democratic capitalist outcomes in developing societies was not necessarily a given. Responding to his own country's assertion of military power, Fukuyama recognized two sets of closely related problems. The first was that the United States had intervened in the affairs of other states (most notably, Panama, Lebanon, Somalia, Afghanistan and Iraq) with the explicit intention of ending non-democratic regimes and in most cases, at least rhetorically, ending support for terrorist organizations and those countries' related military capacities (for example, 'weapons of mass destruction'). Such intervention was justified on the positive grounds that it was intended to bring democracy to these countries. However, local populations did not automatically see the benefits of a 'democratic' system of government when it appeared to be imposed and represented an alien ideology. More to the point, it was difficult to establish a democratic framework in states that did not enjoy the range of institutions that allowed democracy to exist, much less flourish. It was the lack of such institutions that was in most cases responsible for allowing particular states to degenerate to the point where they were unable to prevent or allowed the existence of terrorist organizations.

Second, it was a failure of state institutions more generally that provided fertile ground for the establishment of organizations that might be seen as antithetical to political development, e.g. the Taliban in Afghanistan, the Islamic Courts Union in Somalia. Beyond this, the lack of capacity or performance of state institutions was widely and increasingly seen as a key reason why such states remained mired in underdevelopment. This shift to an institution-focus began in organizations such as the World Bank following the collapse of the Soviet Union, and the shift from communitarian-bureaucratic systems of government (that is, 'communism') in a number of eastern European states towards a more free-market liberal democracy. The initial impediment in these regime transitions was a lack of institutional capacity. This was mirrored in the parallel transitions from authoritarian forms of government towards more open and, for a while at least, increasingly democratic forms in developing countries such as the Philippines, Thailand, Indonesia, Argentina, Nicaragua and Chile. Yet not all countries simply accepted a conventional democratic model and indeed some countries, or their leaders, sought to explain and legitimize their non-democratic rule by appealing to a competing set of values.

In such cases, claims to universalist legitimacy may be abandoned in favour of relativism, as exemplified by the 'deconstruction' of the universal to the particular of Derrida (1980), the anti-'grand narrative' approach of Lyotard (1984), and the micro-power structure focus of Foucault (1982). This translates as a preference for analysis of political outcomes based on claims to local traditional political methods in contradiction to wider and more consistent political methods, and is favoured by some political anthropologists and related social scientists (e.g. Grenfell 2007). In practice, this approach has been exercised in particular by Singapore's Lee Kwan Yew, Malaysia's Mahahir Mohamad and Indonesia's Suharto (all of whom have now, on way or another, left the active political scene).

Governance

Along with normative claims to democratic principles, the issue of 'governance' has become central to developing countries in the period since the end of the Cold War. No longer able to rely on the support of patron states under which there were few respected rules in exchange for strategic loyalty, developing countries have had to begin to order themselves in ways that conform to international standards. In particular, the issue of governance has come to the fore, in relation to organization efficiency and in particular corruption. The term 'governance' was originally used to imply fiscal probity, or the procedures by which institutions ordered their financial affairs. It has since come to take on a wider meaning, as used for example by the World Bank, of organizational probity or the procedures by which states order all of their affairs. Indeed, some practitioners now use the term 'governance' to imply the overall function of government, which is increasingly the case. The UN describes 'governance' as 'the process of decision-making and the process by which decisions are implemented (or not implemented)' (UNESCAP 2011). While this definition may seem in some contexts as anodyne, it is clarified by the qualification that 'Bad governance is being increasingly regarded one of the root causes of all evil within our societies' (UNESCAP 2011).

UNESCAP identifies good governance as accountable, transparent, responsive, equitable and inclusive, effective and efficient, follows the rule of law, participatory and consensus oriented (UNESCAP 2011). Each of these criteria accords with other general definitions, apart from that of being 'consensus oriented'. While consensus can be an important tool for resolving conflict and ensuring that no parties' fundamental interests are neglected, in traditional or developing societies it can also be used to impose the will of more powerful (and often self-interested) figures and may disempower the legitimate claims of less powerful groups. Moreover, consensus and rule of law do not sit easily together, especially where disputes arise over issues of law and equity.

Ideas of governance are closely related to institutional development, in particular regarding the capacity and probity of state institutions to undertake the functions that are allocated to them (World Bank 2011). In particular, the World Bank sees good governance linked to its anti-corruption activities as being important to its focus on alleviating poverty. The World Bank's Worldwide Governance Indicators (WGIs) project identifies aggregate and individual governance indicators for 213 economies over the period 1996–2009. Within the WGIs, the World Bank identifies six dimensions of governance, including 'Voice and Accountability', 'Political Stability and Absence of Violence', 'Government Effectiveness', 'Regulatory Quality', 'Rule of Law' and 'Control of Corruption'. Importantly, each of these criteria link with the others in constructing a political environment in which citizens (and investors) can expect a high degree of consistency in the political and economic environment, in which there are now off-budget 'surprises' and which provide mechanisms for accountability in cases where government institutions do not function appropriate to their brief.

The Asian Development Bank identifies a similar (but far from identical) set of criteria for 'governance', including accountability, predictability, participation and transparency. Its work in the governance field has been primarily in strengthening accountability institutions, including audit agencies, anti-corruption commissions and the judiciary. It notes that 'strengthening the rule of law... is crucial to encourage private sector investment and combat corruption' (ADB 2011). The ADB's criteria for governance differs in detail from those of the World Bank, but its basic goal of ensuring a safe, legal and consistent political and economic environment is consistent with that of the World Bank.

Notably, while both the World Bank and the ADB recognize there need to be different approaches to ensuring good governance in specific societies, both are equally strongly focused on combatting corruption in government institutions and agencies, as a primary means of ensuring the best possible environment for economic development. Increasingly, however, equal and consistent application of rule of law and ensuring a government that is open and responsive to citizens' needs, along with the other key qualities of good governance, is seen not just in instrumentalist terms of helping to ensure economic development. Like political development more generally, it is increasingly seen as a political good in its own right.

Legitimacy

A critical factor in the success or failure of states is the legitimacy of the government of the state or, in critical situations, of the state itself. In some cases, the legitimacy of the state can be determined by the legitimacy of the government, particularly in non-democratic environments that have less clearly sustainable claims to legitimate status.

The idea of legitimacy finds its origins in rule of law and assumes acceptance of rule under law as the most equitable form of government, which also complies with notions of good governance. However, in many developing states, faced with a limited capacity rationally to address dissent, they revert not to 'rule of law' by 'rule by law', or relatively arbitrary top-down political control.

According to Diamond, legitimacy is an outcome of causal factors, including the trajectory of historical legacy, the comparative values of regime systems within that historical legacy, the experience of positive social and economic results from the regime in question, efficacy of the regime and the way in which the regime conforms to political aspirations (1999a: 194–212). As outlined by Weber (1946), legitimacy may derive from a range of sources, depending on the political development of the social group in question, and may be normative or positive. In simple terms, Weber saw legitimacy as being derived either from charismatic leadership, traditional authority or a rational-legal structure, noting that all of these categories tended to reflect varying degrees or elements of the other. Weber's theory of legitimacy asserted that it either arose through acceptance of a precondition, imitation or rational belief in its value or its legality (Weber 1964: 130). In relation to developing country societies, many matched or still match each of these conditions to varying degrees among different groups of their citizens. Another set of criteria, however, might construe legitimacy as being composed of political structures built upon patron–client relations, or in a liberal-minimalist model characterized by the 'small state' approach of neo-liberalism, favoured by the IMF in its 'structural adjustment programmes'. They can also be located in a democratic-proceduralist model of agreement between (relatively) free and equal citizens, which implies a fair electoral system but which implies no further constraints on processes other than they derive from that initial system (Cohen 2003: 122). This is how many developing societies embarked on their political processes, satisfying the limited technical criteria of elections as the basis of democratic process yet often without other institutions such the judiciary being properly in place or being subsequently compromised (lacking autonomy from vested interests).

Conclusion

No two developing countries have identical political histories, systems or processes, but many do share some of a range of characteristics that help to explain why they often reflect particular outcomes that often appear to meet less than a normative standard. The way in which most developing countries have come into being, being physically shaped by their colonial experience, informed by their experience of colonialism and the wars that were often fought to end it. Having started from a low level of development in terms of economic and organizational capacity, many new states have subsequently slipped further, engendering disappointment and disenchantment with the independence process and tensions over the allocation of scarce resources. Very often, where different ethnic groups have been brought together in one state as a consequence of prior colonial incorporation, such tensions can take on a tribal or 'nationalist' hue and, in cases where the ethnic group has a specific territory, can lead to claims for separatism. These types of situations can become particularly problematic where states have limited capacity or skills to deal with such problems and, often through a military acculturation, respond with repressive measures, leading to a diminution of the legitimacy of the state.

Such states may liberalize over time, especially in light of a lack of support from other, more powerful states that might have had an interest in maintaining particular regimes. In some instances, popular revolts (e.g. Philippines, Thailand, Arab states) or the internal collapse of a prior regime (Indonesia) may also lead to democratic change. Too often, however, regime change is not permanent or even long-standing and collapses of government, coups and so on frequently lead to a cycle of authoritarian or military government, a process of liberalization and then a return to authoritarianism and so on.

One of the main problems that arises from such political instability and the lack of representative government and accountability that usually accompanies it is that the mechanisms of government intended to ensure good government are rarely in place. As a result, the overall development project tends to struggle under a burden of corruption, inefficiency and section self-interest. This then feeds into a sense of disillusionment with and the illegitimacy of the state, which leads to the predictable government response and the cycle referred to above. This is not the only reason why so many developing countries have failed to break out of the cycle of poverty, mismanagement and poor government, in some cases for over 60 years. But it has been and remains a common and significant contributing factor in the failure of the development process for many countries.

Note

1. Anderson's principal reference was to the use of print technology in the dispersal and standardization of language, but the principle of a common language applies regardless of the mechanism of its dispersal.

Chapter 8

Poverty Alleviation and Development

Matthew Clarke

Introduction

Poverty and development are intrinsically linked. Indeed, they can be considered two sides of the same coin. Those that have not experienced development experience poverty. It is through the process of development that poverty is reduced. Development seeks to improve the lives of the poor. Poverty is characterized by premature death, preventable illnesses, limited access to clean water and sanitation, economic insecurity and often illiteracy. Using the most common measure, 900 million of the world's population live in poverty existing on less than US$1.25 a day. Those who are interested in development and interested in improving the lives of the poor must therefore be primarily interested in ending poverty. The international community, as espoused by the Millennium Development Goals, committed to halving 1990 poverty levels by 2015. Recent estimates (Chandy and Gertz 2011) suggest that the last decade has seen substantial reduction in the number of people living in absolute poverty resulting in the 'early' achievement of the first MDG. According to these data, the number of people living in poverty fell from over 1.3 billion in 2005 to under 900 million in 2010, with an expectation that this number will further reduce to be less than 600 million by 2015. As Chandy and Gertz note, 'poverty reduction of this magnitude is unparalleled in history (p. 3). If this was to occur, Jeffrey Sachs' (2005) call for the world to end poverty completely within the next two decades would be realised.

Poverty, as discussed above, is assessed through per capita income levels. In this sense, poverty has been defined as living on less than US$1.25 per day. This is certainly a common definition and one that makes intuitive sense. However, it is not the only way to understand poverty. It is possible to define – and therefore measure – poverty in a variety of ways. This chapter will begin therefore with a review of how poverty is defined and describe the movement from the long-held approach of it being solely a function of income to its more recent multidimensional understanding best encapsulated by the Millennium Development Goals. An assessment of the recent changes in poverty will then be undertaken utilizing various poverty measures and data. The chapter will conclude with consideration of how poverty might be fully eradicated (or at least further reduced) through both micro (community) and macro (national and international) interventions.

What is poverty?

Prior to implementing poverty eradication interventions, it is necessary to define poverty. 'Clarification of how poverty is defined is extremely important, as different definitions imply the use of different indicators for measurement; they may lead to the identification of different individuals and groups as poor and require different policies for poverty reduction (Ruggeri Laderchi et al. 2006: 19). Thus, before we can eradicate poverty we clearly need to know what it is we are ending and who is experiencing it as only then can we determine what sort of development interventions will be most appropriate.

As already (inadvertently) demonstrated, the most common conceptualization of poverty is the lack of financial resources – in other words – how much money you have. If we determine that having greater than US\$1.25 a day is sufficient to meet basic needs, then the world has one billion people who do not have enough money and thus live in poverty. But there are other ways to define poverty (Ruggeri Laderchi et al. 2006). In addition to this common monetary approach, poverty can be understood in terms of capabilities, inequality and social exclusion, and participation.

Depending on which approach is used, those who are identified will differ, as will their number and most certainly so too will the development implementations needed to eradicate their poverty. It is useful to briefly discuss each approach before discussing some pertinent issues in greater detail.

Monetary poverty

Defining poverty as a lack of income is intuitively attractive. From our own personal experience, we know that money affords us the freedom to purchase most of our basic needs and nearly all our desired luxuries. Further, we know that having money allows us to make choices about those things we desire (whether they are good for us or bad for us). In economic jargon, we increase our utility or happiness) when we consume more by the simple fact that purchasing a particular commodity reveals our belief that this commodity will increase our utility. (If the commodity will not make us happy, why purchase it?) Thus the more we purchase, the greater our utility. As a human characteristic is holding unlimited desires, increasing income therefore increases our ability to maximize our utility (i.e., buy more stuff). Alternatively, having less money reduces our ability to consume and this lowers our utility. At the extreme, having income below a certain level means that even the basic needs (food, shelter and clothing) cannot be adequately met and an individual can be said to be experiencing poverty.

As stated, this approach to poverty is the most widely accepted within the development and economic literature. Other than its intuitive attractiveness discussed above, this is largely due to its long-standing application, dating back as it does to the earliest work on poverty in England during the nineteenth century (see Booth 1887; Rowntree 1902). This approach is still being used as is evidenced by the 2015 headline target of the Millennium Development Goals to *reduce by half the proportion of people living on less than a dollar a day*. The basic approach to eradicating poverty is simply to increase people's income. If poverty is defined as living on less than US$1.25, then increasing income above this figure will lift an individual out of poverty.

Capabilities approach

The second approach is a more recent understanding of poverty though it has ancient roots in Aristotle and more recently in Ruskin (1862), writing in the mid-nineteenth century. This approach focuses on defining well-being. Poverty in this sense is the absence of well-being. Well-being is not simply the measurement of economic possessions but the capability of utilizing them in an appropriate manner. Amartya Sen (1984, 1985a, 1987a, 1987b, 1993) provides the modern understanding and argues that well-being is not measured by the possession of a commodity, nor the utility of the commodity, but rather by what the person actually does with the commodity. Individuals who have low levels of functionings and capabilities can be said to be living in poverty.

For example, it has been found that resources are not related strongly to functionings and therefore the attainment of a high quality of life (functionings) is not dependent on high levels of material standard of living (resources) (Lovell et al. 1993). The key is the efficiency with which people use their resources (Denison 1971). Thus, efficiency or skills or social habit (Travers and Richardson 1993) allow 'people with relatively low levels of resources to lead a relatively high quality of life, and vice-versa' (Travers and Richardson 1993: 48). Other issues, such as personal circumstances (including health), the environment, social climate and social state, are all contingencies that 'can lead to variation in the "conversion" of income into the capability to live a minimally acceptable life' (Sen 1999b: 360). Exactly what is a minimally acceptable life has not been adequately defined.

Indeed, moving from theory to a practical application has proven difficult. In terms of empirical application, the Human Poverty Index (HPI) estimated by the UNDP (2006) is perhaps the most widely cited. As with the Human Development Index (HDI), the HPI is a composite indicator made up of three dimensions: (1) a long and healthy life; (2) knowledge; and (3) a decent standard of living. These dimensions are represented by corresponding indicators (with the last two both co-representing the decent standard of living): (1) percentage of people likely to die before 60; (2) percentage of adults who are functionally illiterate; (3) percentage of population without sustainable access to an improved water source; and (4) percentage of children under weight for age. No consideration of income is included.

Policies to increase capabilities (and thus reduce poverty) would include focusing on improving people's ability to function and achieve success in life. This includes improving literacy levels and health as well as allowing people to participate in the formal economy.

Inequality and social exclusion

Inequality is also an important aspect of poverty. The level of inequality within a society provides insights into the level of development experienced by that society. Income equality explores issues of distribution and access hidden within other discussions of poverty, such as the focus on average income or income per capita. It is possible that whilst average income, for example, is of a reasonable level a high level of disparity exists within that country due to the unequal distribution of that income. In the extreme instance, it is possible for a country of 100 people to have an average income of $1 (meaning that the total income for the whole country is also $100) but for 99 people to have zero income and the last person to have the full $100. Under these circumstances, understanding poverty requires understanding the divide between poor and non-poor.

The divide between poor and non-poor can be understood in both absolute and relative terms. The absolute gap is concerned with the actual circumstances of the poor and is best encapsulated by discussing monetary poverty. This gap is between these circumstances and what they require to achieve basic survival. Do they have enough income? Do they have enough freedom? Do they have enough access to a functioning environment? If the poor do not have 'enough', they can be said to be living in absolute poverty. The relative gap is concerned with the actual circumstances of the poor when compared with the actual circumstances of the non-poor. This gap is concerned with inequality. How much less income do the poor have than the non-poor? How much less freedom do the poor have than the non-poor? How much less access to a functioning environment do the poor have than the non-poor? If the poor have significantly less than the non-poor, a situation of inequality exists and there is relative poverty.

Within developing countries, emphasis is (rightly) placed on absolute poverty. In developed countries, whilst instances of absolute poverty may occur, greater emphasis is placed on relative poverty – or income inequality. For any number of reasons, there are individuals within wealthy countries that, when compared to the wider population, are excluded from experiencing the average standard of living enjoyed by the majority of that country. While they may not be considered poor when compared to those in developing countries, they are considered poor when compared to their own compatriots. Thus, this relative poverty (or income inequality) is often termed *social exclusion*.

For a number of reasons, certain individuals are excluded from participating in mainstream society. Indeed, much of the literature on exclusion focuses on social groups who are excluded (because of their membership of that group) more so than individuals who are excluded. 'This relational emphasis opens up a different policy agenda from the individualistic approaches: policies addressed to groups, such as eliminating discrimination and various forms of affirmative action' (Ruggeri Laderchi et al. 2006: 36).

As relativity is central to this conceptualization of poverty, empirical measurement is largely based on which experiences characterize the normal society and that which those who are not excluded cannot experience. As such, those who do not have access to the Internet, enjoy an inter-state holiday every two years, own a car (or the resources to own a car), ability to access $5,000 credit with a week's notice, etc. may be considered as being socially excluded. Such measures must naturally be constantly updated. For example, perhaps 30 years ago, the social expectation might be owning an electric fridge or having a black-and-white television, etc. As the quality of life increases in wealthy countries, so too do the expectations of what is required to be fully participating within that society. Interestingly, this is not a new idea at all and can be seen in the writings of Adam Smith, who noted the need for a day-labourer to wear a linen shirt so as not to be ashamed when in public. Determining levels of social exclusion therefore requires subjective estimates of what is required to participate in society and then (typically) household surveys to determine who is deprived of participation.

Participatory approaches

Thus far, the different concepts of poverty discussed have been determined by those other than the 'poor'. It indeed seems incongruent that, whilst the revealed preference approach (discussed above) gives primacy to the individual to determine what best enhances their own utility, such primacy is withheld when determining what poverty actually is.

Non-government organizations (NGOs) and community-based organizations (CBOs) have long understood the importance (if not necessity) of having communities participate and lead the development process. Such participation can be time-consuming and difficult to manage but sustainable outcomes require community ownership of any interventions if they are to have any lasting impact. This is because communities are experts on their own circumstances. By and large, communities know (with perhaps some guidance or facilitation) their strengths, weaknesses, resources and needs. Likewise, they are also very knowledgeable around issues of poverty. Utilizing this knowledge can provide useful insights into who the poor are and what they identify as their needs and desires for the future.

The largest international survey of this kind was undertaken by the World Bank in the late 1990s. In *Voices of the Poor,* over 40,000 people were interviewed in nearly 50 countries. Five key characteristics of poverty were found:

> First, poverty is multidimensional. Second, households are crumbling under the stresses of poverty. Third, the state has been largely ineffective in reaching the poor. Fourth, the role of NGOs in the lives of the poor is limited, and thus the poor depend primarily on their own informal networks. Finally, the social fabric, poor people's only 'insurance', is unravelling.   (Narayan-Parker and Patel 2000: 7)

Such insights would be unlikely under the previous approaches discussed because of the silence of the poor themselves within this analysis. There is great value therefore in including the poor in defining and measuring poverty. Indeed, when poverty is discussed with the poor, the actual term 'poverty' is sometimes considered inappropriate. For example, many Pacific countries prefer the term 'hardship' to poverty. Social networks often prevent hunger and outright destitution that are often associated with the term 'poverty' (IMF 2005). 'There is a social understanding in this community: nobody goes short of food; there's always somewhere to stay; the old and young are looked after; and the mentally ill, the disabled and the chronically sick are looked after' (Webber 1985: 45). Thus, the nature of poverty in the Pacific often relates to a lack of access to basic services and a lack of income earning opportunities rather than outright destitution (AusAID 2006a). The Asia Development Bank (ADB) has recently sponsored Participatory Assessments of Hardship (PAH) among communities in a number of Pacific countries. Results from these assessments indicate that poverty and hardship in Pacific countries are defined as 'inadequate levels of sustainable human development through access to essential public goods and services and access to income opportunities' (Abbott and Pollard 2004: xi).

The input this participation has had on policy though is less clear. Whether the international finance institutions or national governments have incorporated the understandings that grew from this participatory approach is yet to be seen.

Summary of different approaches

Defining poverty is contentious. Having diverse understandings of poverty is more than semantics because it has a practical effect. If we are interested in ending poverty, we must initiate policies that will directly and positively impact on those experiencing it. This can only be done if we can measure poverty, yet measuring poverty can only occur if it is clearly defined. Thus the different definitions and approaches discussed above will result in different measures, different individuals and groups being identified as living in poverty and different policies and remedies being proposed and implemented.

Each approach has its own strengths and weaknesses. The monetary approach is intuitive and easy to measure but very narrow. Policy outcomes are focused on the formal economy but this may overlook those whose participation in the formal economy is limited for any number of reasons. The capabilities approach presents a multidimensional view of poverty but there is ambiguity about exactly how to apply it empirically. The policy outcomes cut across economic, social and political spheres but, with limited resources (as a consequence of these countries being poor), the impact of such policies may be limited. Inequality provides a further level of understanding poverty but is limited to focusing on monetary measures of income. Social exclusion is more relevant to wealthier countries than developing countries. While offering flexibility, its subjective nature also hinders a policy focus. Policies that do emerge often focus on redistribution more so than on wealth creation. The final approach allows the voices of those we are concerned with – the poor themselves – to be heard. But the analysis and policy reaction still lie with the experts or non-poor and thus control at this important point is removed from the poor.

Measuring poverty

Having decided how to define poverty, it is then necessary to measure it empirically before any poverty reduction strategies can be implemented. Understanding who is experiencing poverty and the extent and depth of that poverty will inform anti-poverty policies. This knowledge will ensure that the correct programmes are designed and the correct people are targeted. Measuring poverty, however, is not without difficulties. There are both technical challenges and data constraints that must be addressed.

While each of the approaches to poverty discussed above are valid, discussion on measurement issues here will focus on the most common – monetary, capability and inequality. Social exclusion is less relevant for developing countries and the participatory approach has not been widely adopted by the international agencies (notwithstanding the World Bank's *Voices of the Poor* report).

Assessing monetary poverty

If poverty is to be defined as a level of income necessary to provide for certain basic necessities required for living, it is obvious that the primary data need to concern household income. Interestingly though, the World Bank prefer to use expenditure (on consumption) data rather than income data. First, expenditure on consumption more closely relates to having enough to meet basic needs as income itself is only the means of allowing consumption (income for instance doesn't necessarily consider access to or availability of goods and services). Secondly, consumption is more constant over time whereas income can vary seasonally or during times of harvest failure, for example. Even if income moves up and down, expenditure on consumption will remain fairly level as households either save excess income during boom times or access credit during bust times. Finally, expenditure on consumption is more accurately measured. Data collected through household surveys have shown that there is often a significant discrepancy between estimates of incomes and estimates of expenditure on consumption. This is largely explained through it being difficult correctly to estimate non-monetary income. For example, within the most recent Household income and expenditure surveys (HIES) completed in the Solomon Islands (SISO 2006), reported expenditure was considered more accurate than reported income as more than half of the surveyed households reported their household expenditure to be between 26 per cent and 200 per cent greater than their estimated income. Thus, data used to measure monetary poverty are generally household expenditure data.

The data are collected from household surveys. Again, in the case of the most recent HIES within the Solomon Islands, 3,822 separate households were surveyed (out of a possible 86,734 households across the Solomon Islands). The questionnaire focused on a number of areas but of most importance for measuring monetary poverty was total expenditure on consumption, divided into eight major categories composed of food and non-food items:

- food
- housing
- household operation
- clothing and footwear
- transport
- tobacco and alcohol
- payment of debt
- miscellaneous goods and services

Food expenditure itself consisted of food purchases, food given as gifts and the value of home-grown food consumption. The sub-categories of food include: (a) fruit; (b) dairy and milk products; (c) vegetables; (d) farm products, fats and oils; (e) meat and meat products; (f) non-alcoholic beverages; (f) poultry; (g) confectionery; (h) fish (including shellfish); (i) bread and biscuits; (j) takeaway and food eaten outside the products home; (k) cereal and cereal products; and (l) other foods. This is clearly quite comprehensive.

These data are then contrasted with data collected on income. In this survey, total household income included:

- annual wage/salary income
- annual income from self employment and related business activities
- annual income from previous job

- annual income from services
- annual income from benefits
- annual income from home production
- annual income from cash gifts
- annual income from goods received
- annual income from gambling
- annual income from rent
- annual loan income
- annual income from other sources

Data collection is a technical (and thus expensive) exercise. Often developing countries have neither the capacity nor the resources to undertake such surveys. Previous to the most recent HIES survey in the Solomon Islands, the last survey was in 1992. In this instance, this was largely an outcome of the civil unrest experienced during the interceding years. But such lengthy periods between data collection is not uncommon within poorer countries and this constrains analysis and thus policy formulation and implementation (such data constraints will be discussed in greater detail in the next section).

Having obtained reasonable data on consumption expenditure (and income), it is possible to then estimate poverty. There are a number of ways this can be done (ADB 2006; Coudouel et al. n.d.). The first step is to define the poverty line. This is an (arbitrary) estimate of what is required for an individual to meet the most basic of necessities. It can be estimated as 50 per cent of the country's average income (this is one component indicator used in the HPI discussed earlier), or it might be an estimate of the income required to purchase the minimum calorific requirements to survive, or it simply might be a common dollar amount for all countries, such as US$1.25 a day. Having nominated the poverty line, estimates of the experiences of poverty can be made.

The most straightforward estimate is the *headcount index*. Having determined the poverty line and now knowing the different expenditure (income) levels of the population, it is a simple exercise to simply rank those expenditure (income) levels from highest to lowest and count the number of people whose expenditure (income) falls below the nominated poverty line. The headcount index is simply the number of people whose income/expenditure is below the nominated poverty line compared to the whole population. This describes the number of people within the population experiencing poverty. Thus, it possible to say 20 per cent or 30 per cent and so on of the population are below the poverty line. This can be tracked over time to determine whether the incidence of poverty is increasing or decreasing.

However, the headcount index does not provide any indication of the depth of poverty: that is, how far below the poverty line the poor are. To determine this shortfall, it is necessary to subtract the income of each individual living in poverty from the poverty line and then add all these together. This sum is then divided by the poverty line and divided again by the total population. The result of this mathematical exercise is the total income shortfall or *total poverty gap*. This is also known as the Foster-Greer-Thorbecke poverty measure (Foster et al. 1984). Knowing the poverty gap is useful as it provides information on how much extra expenditure (income) is required to lift people out of poverty.

A third poverty line measure (related to the poverty gap) is *poverty severity*, which also considers inequality amongst the poor. This exercise is the same as the poverty gap, except that once the difference between the poverty line and the income of the poor has been divided by the poverty line, this result is multiplied by itself (or squared) before it is aggregated and divided by the total population. Intuitively it makes sense that the expenditure (income) distribution is uneven throughout all levels of society and so there will be inequality even amongst those below the poverty line. This measure considers this inequality and provides information therefore on not only the number of people below the poverty line and by what amount they are below it but also the distribution of incomes of those below it.

These three different measures provide different descriptions of the incidence of poverty and thus provide different priorities for policy-makers and practitioners interested in reducing poverty. Consideration to three aspects should be given when planning poverty reduction strategies as different interventions will impact on different groups and affect future measures of poverty in different ways.

Assessing poverty of capability

If poverty is to be considered more multidimensional than a narrowly focused monetary approach, it follows that its measurement must also consider a wider range of indicators. As discussed, for instance, the HPI is perhaps the most widely applied approach to measuring poverty and is based on three dimensions represented by four indicators:

- a long and healthy life: percentage of people likely to die before 60;
- knowledge: percentage of adults who are functionally illiterate;
- a decent standard of living: percentage of population without sustainable access to an improved water supply and percentage of children underweight for age.

On initial review, none of these indicators appear onerous in terms of data collection. Yet, in more than half of the developing countries to which the HPI was empirically applied (52 out 102) in 2006, data were either missing for at least one of the four indicators or were estimated based on outdated census or survey information or referred to periods other than that specified (UNDP 2006). If this estimate of poverty requires a number of assumptions and reliance on unreliable data, interpretation must be undertaken with great caution.

As with the HDI, the HPI is a composite indicator. This means that it combines four separate indicators into a single index. The benefit of this is that it allows a multidimensional representation of poverty to be presented as a single numerical index for ease of analysis. The shortcoming of this approach is that a composite indicator can also impede understanding of what is driving movements in the overall indicator (McGillivray 1991).

Having obtained data for each of the separate indicators, they must then be aggregated. As the third dimension itself comprises two indicators, these must first be aggregated and then divided by two to obtain an average measure. This 'average' measure of a decent standard of living can be then added to the remaining two indicators (percentage of people likely to die before 60 and percentage of adults who are functionally illiterate). Each of the three dimensions is equally weighted which means that each account for one-third of the final index. To ensure that the final index falls between 0 and 100, the sum of this aggregation is then divided by 3.

There are also limited policy implications flowing from the HPI as any concerted efforts to reduce it must be focused on its component indicators only. Whilst there are undoubtedly benefits to this, it does narrow the policy targets and moves this approach away from a multidimensional concept as is its intent.

Assessing poverty through inequality

Assessing inequality is generally limited to assessing income equality. There has been substantial debate within the development economic literature regarding income inequality. Initially, it was considered that increasing inequality was linked to economic growth and, as economic growth occurred, income inequality would increase. At a certain point, though, this increase would cease and inequality would fall. The implication for poverty reduction is that nations would have to expect relative poverty to initially increase (as income inequality increased) following periods of economic expansion prior to this very same eco-

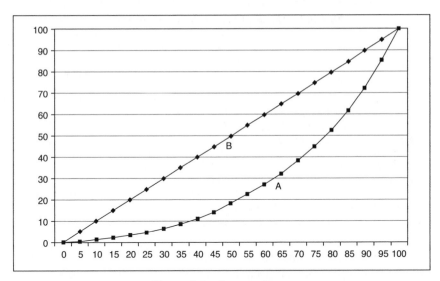

Figure 8.1 *Lorenz Curve*

importantly the issue of poverty and its eradication has assumed and sustained a prominence that will assist in increasing the visibility of the poor. This section will review poverty levels and trends focusing the monetary, capabilities and inequality approaches to poverty.

Monetary approach

The first MDG is to *eradicate extreme poverty and hunger*. Success against this Goal is to be assessed against the target of *reducing by half the proportion of people living on less than a dollar a day by 2015*. At the global level, it is probable that this target will be achieved but, when considered at the national level, there are many countries that will fail to achieve this target. The estimate of global poverty provided by Chandy and Gertz (2011) presents a very positive picture. Taking the most recent household survey data for 119 countries (which account for 95 per cent of the developing world's population), they use historical and forecast estimates of consumption growth per capita to estimate poverty levels. Their results suggest that global poverty – using the monetary approach based on $1.25 per day – has fallen from more than 1.3 billion people in 2005 to less than 900 million in 2010, and is likely to fall again to less than 600 million by 2015 (see Table 8.2). They argue therefore that the MDG target of reducing by half the proportion of people living in poverty in 1990 by 2015 was in fact achieved by 2008.

Table 8.2   *Number of people in poverty by region*

Region	Number of poor (millions)		
	2005	2010	2015
East Asia	304	140	53
Europe and Central Asia	16	8	4
Latin America and the Caribbean	45	35	27
Middle East and North Africa	9	7	5
South Asia	583	318	145
Sub-Saharan Africa	380	370	350
World	1338	878	585

Source: Adapted from Chandy and Gertz (2011).

While poverty remains clearly a south-Asian and sub-Saharan-African phenomena, unlike in past decades when poverty reduced in one region but grew in another region, poverty reduction in the first decade of the twenty-first century occurred across all regions. This is particularly good news for sub-Saharan Africa as for the first time, its poverty rate has fallen below 50 per cent and is projected to fall below 40 per cent by 2015. However, as poverty is falling more quickly elsewhere, the percentage of the world's poor living in Africa will actually increase from nearly 30 per cent to 60 per cent. Poverty in this sense will therefore be seen increasingly as an African problem. While in the past India had the largest number of the world's poor, it is expected that this dubious honour will fall to Nigeria.

It is of course the world's two populous nations, though, that have driven down the global poverty trends. China and India have been responsible for 75 per cent of the fall in people living in poverty across the globe. More than 350 Indians have been lifted out of poverty over the past decade and China may effectively eliminate its own absolute poverty by 2015.

The robustness of this poverty reduction is an important concern. While it is undoubtedly positive that people are being lifted out of poverty, it is also important that this improvement is not subject to shocks. In this regard, it is interesting to consider the 2008 global food crisis and the 2009 global financial crisis. Both these economic shocks had dramatic consequences around the world.

A lack of affordable food affects every aspect of a country's development. Rising costs of food undermine purchasing power of poor people and exacerbate the tragedy that is global hunger and malnutrition. It fuels civil unrest and further limits access to basic human rights. Food prices

Figure 8.3 shows the movements in the Gini coefficient for a random selection of developed countries. Figures 8.3, 8.4 and 8.5 show the movements in the Gini coefficient for a random selection of developing countries. What is most evident is the paucity of data around income inequality. There is a distinct lack of accurate and comparable data on inequality for most developing nations. This makes it difficult to track movements of inequality over time or compare inequality meaningfully between countries.

Within the selection of countries below, the common experience has been an increase in inequality (remembering that the higher the Gini coefficient, the greater the inequality), with Nigeria and Côte d'Ivoire being notable exceptions. Determinants of income inequality vary from country to country.

Interestingly, despite these general within-country increases in income inequality, it is more likely that overall global income inequality has fallen in recent decades, largely due to the economic growth in China (Sala-ì-Martin 2002). This is in line with other studies in which global income inequality was found to have risen from the 1820s to between 1980 and 1992, after which it stabilized (Bourguignon and Morrisson 2002). Sala-ì-Martin does caution though, that unless African countries increase their economic growth, global inequality will again begin to increase within the next two decades as the impact of China's 'upward pull' weakens.

Summary

It may be said that there is a poverty of data around poverty. It is very difficult to develop appropriate poverty interventions when basic data, such as the number of people living on less than a dollar a day, do not exist. Of course, the collection of data is an expensive exercise and removes potential resources from actual poverty alleviation programmes. However, such expenditure can be justified in terms of monitoring and evaluation. Ending poverty requires knowledge of the past as well as of current situations in order to determine what interventions are needed and whether these interventions have been successful.

Development interventions to end poverty

Ending poverty is clearly not an easy task. Indeed, that the international community can only seek to reduce by *half* the proportion of people living on less than a dollar a day suggests that complete eradication is perhaps impossible. If this MDG target is achieved, more than 700 million people will still be in poverty and perhaps a billion more living just above this level of miserable existence.

How then to proceed? Poverty is experienced by individuals. While countries may be considered poor (or wealthy), it is women, men and children who experience the harsh realities of poverty. Interventions intended to reduce poverty must be cognisant that the primary target must be individuals. However, that is not to say that all policies must be micro in nature. Pro-poor activities can thus be micro or macro in nature. It is therefore valuable to seek to increase foreign investment, increase trade and undertake infrastructure projects as these activities can also improve the lives of the poor by providing greater employment opportunities and access to markets. Any success in ending poverty is thus predicated on benefits flowing primarily to the poor.

Macro interventions

Sachs (2005) provides a 'roadmap for ending poverty' of what is required at the national level to improve the lives of the poor. He suggests investment in five key areas is required:

Agricultural inputs: food yields can increase (up to threefold) with fertilizers, improved fallows, green manures, crop covers, water-harvesting and farm-level irrigation and improved seeds. Having increased crop yields, farmers must also access improved storage facilities to store grain and release it slowly onto the market rather than flood the market immediately after harvesting which results in driving the price of their crop down.

Basic health: the majority of illnesses that affect those in poverty are treatable and preventable. The provision of free anti-malarial bed nets, anti-malarial medicines, treatment for opportunistic infections of those with HIV AIDS, anti-retroviral drugs for those with AIDS, and training for traditional birth attendants and reproductive health would reduce morbidity and increase the ability of the poor to work and feed their families. It would also remove the high (and often sudden) cost of health care when a family member falls ill, a life event that often precipitates a household falling under the poverty line.

Education: not only is there a need for increased investment in facilities and personnel, but the provision of meals for children attending school would simultaneously improve their health and their attendance and subsequent learning. Education could also expand to become more vocational so that modern farming, IT and engineering, etc. skills were also taught in both rural and urban areas. Schools could also become community hubs to provide adult education in a range of issues, including health, agriculture and water.

Power, transport and communications services: the International Energy Agency (2002) estimates that over 1.5 billion people do not have access to electricity and these are primarily the poor. Electricity powers lighting to allow night classes, computers for learning, pumps for safe-water wells, mills for food processing, refrigeration for food and medicine storage, etc. All-weather roads provide access to markets to sell surplus production and purchase other goods and services, health care, etc. Mobile phones (perhaps based on the Grameen Bank model where people are charged for individual calls) can link the poor to the wider community and assist in gathering information on market prices or weather emergencies, etc.

Safe drinking water and sanitation: The UNDP (2006) estimates more than one billion people do not have access to clean water and over 2.5 billion people lack adequate access to sanitation. Countless hours are spent each day by the poor carting water. Unsafe water facilitates increases in diseases and sickness. Poor sanitation exacerbates these illnesses.

Such simple investments though are beyond the affordability of the poor. Sachs (2005) argues that they are also beyond the capacity of national governments. Such activities though are not beyond the capacity of the international community to afford. The international community has long committed to providing 0.7 per cent of GNP to developing countries. Presently only Denmark, Luxembourg, Netherlands, Norway and Sweden provide aid to this level. (In 2005, all members of the European Union – except for newer members joining after 2002 – agreed to meet the target by 2015. This means that 16 of the 22 main aid-giving countries have committed to reach 0.7 per cent by 2015 or earlier. France, Germany, Italy and the UK are in this group, but Australia and the US are not.) The United Nations Millennium Project calculates that if countries follow through on their commitments to increase aid to this level of 0.7 per cent of GNP, all the MDGs (including halving extreme poverty) could be achieved by 2015.

Sachs (2005) also notes that interventions in different countries must be different and take into account the history, geography and issues specific to the poor in that country if interventions are to be successful and poor countries are able to properly absorb this additional aid. It requires for each country the following:

> A *Differential Diagnosis* that reflects the policies and investments that the country needs to achieve the MDGs.

> An *Investment Plan* that shows the size, timing and costs of the required investments.

> A *Financial Plan* to fund the Investment Plan, including the calculation of the MDG Financing Gap, the proportion of financial needs that the donors will have to fill.

> A *Donor Plan* that gives multi-year donor commitments for filling the MDG Financing Gap.

> A *Public Management Plan* that outlines the mechanisms of governance and public administration that will help implement the expanded public investment strategy. (Sachs 2005: 173–4)

Clearly, such plans and the proceeding interventions require substantial good will, co-operation and political will, something that has been demonstrably lacking in the past from both poor countries and wealthy countries. Thus, while it is possible that poverty be reduced in the coming years through macro interventions, it is still to be seen if this will occur.

Micro interventions

Individuals, households, local communities, CBOs and NGOs also have an important role in ending poverty. It is insufficient to simply wait for the international community to resolve poverty. Indeed, the lives of the poor have been improved at the micro level in spite of the macro interventions being imposed by national and international organizations from above. By focusing on local capacity building, grass-root interventions play a very important role in alleviating poverty. Perhaps the clearest examples of micro-level interventions impacting on poverty are those building local capacity.

The Solomon Islands provides some interesting examples of micro-interventions reducing poverty. The Solomon Islands has a dispersed rural population, most of which relies on subsistence agriculture for its livelihood. Given these characteristics, economic growth that most effectively reduces poverty is therefore growth of the agricultural sector (see

Feeny 2004; AusAID 2006a). The subsistence lifestyle of most Islanders means that, while they have sufficient access to local produce, they do not have access to money to pay for certain food items, such as rice and salt, nor services such as school fees, health care or intra-island transport (ADB 2005a). Economic progress that has occurred is primarily located in the few urban areas (but predominately Honiara) and is thus disconnected from the majority of the population. However, 'if growth can be widespread, geographically, its benefits will contribute to poverty reduction over a wider area' (ADB 2005b: 44). An alternative approach to development is therefore required within the Solomon Islands in order to address the poverty faced by the majority of its rural-based population (Oxfam 2006). Calls for such an alternative model that places people at the centre of the development (rather than economic outcomes) are not new (see Wallace 2002). Solomon Islanders own a wealth of natural resources. However, they require assistance to transform these natural resources into cash wealth that can be used to improve their material circumstances. Many opportunities exist in this regard. For example, on Simbo Island, local communities are harvesting eggs of the local megapode bird. The local communities manage this harvesting in a sustainable way so that the megapode population is not threatened. In other communities, butterflies are also now being raised and sold. Again, this community-based enterprise is being undertaken without affecting the balance of nature. Other income-generating schemes based on sustainable use of natural resources include 'harvesting tree wealth, making fibre paper, pressing ngali oil, planting coral and seaweed…(allowing) cash starved villagers to increase their earning capacity without destroying the very basis of these new industries' (Roughan 2002: 86). Within the Solomon Islands, it is more likely that communities as a whole, rather than individual families or households, will suffer poverty. Thus, interventions to alleviate poverty must also work with whole communities. For example, the Solomon Islands Development Trust worked with 18 village groups in central Makira to process ngali nut oil and establish international markets. These communities are now earning SI$30,000 per annum. Similarly, the community of Marovo Lagoon worked in partnership with the World Wide Fund for Nature to establish community-based eco-tourism, earning the community SI$60,000 per annum.

Conclusion

Regardless of how it is conceptualized, the reality of poverty should not be romanticized. It is harsh and inhumane. Children die unnecessarily, hunger is constant and basic needs go unmet. Those experiencing poverty lack freedom to determine their own lives and once in poverty it is often difficult for them to escape. If poverty is to end, it will require co-operation and good will at the international, national and local level. The international community has pledged to reduce poverty by half before 2015. Indeed, all regions have made improvements, though the driving force behind the significant reduction in global poverty levels is largely through the achievements in China and India. Sufficient resources exist at the international level to end poverty if wealthy countries met their commitments of providing less than 1 per cent of their GNP in overseas aid. Local organizations can also continue to play a vital role in facilitating individuals and local communities to build their capacity.

Interventions to end poverty rely on understanding the experience of poverty. It must be defined and measured before appropriate interventions can be planned and implemented at either the macro or micro level. It is precisely poverty's overwhelming nature that requires every effort to be made in order to eradicate it.

Chapter 9

Community Development

Damien Kingsbury

If development is intended to improve the lives of people, then there is a strong and logical case for development starting with people. Community development focuses on the development project as it relates to local, usually rural or small urban, communities, in particular addressing issues that are of immediate concern to communities that have the capacity to produce continuing localized results. It also reflects the notion that development, broadly conceived, is about the enhancement of the potential of people to emancipate themselves (see Sen 1999a). That is, it is intended to give them greater control over their own lives. This is usually referred to as 'empowerment'. This 'empowerment' approach to development 'places the emphasis on autonomy in the decision-making of territorially organized communities, local self-reliance, direct and inclusive (participatory) democracy, and experiential social learning' (Friedman 1992: vii). However, like many other good ideas that have been encapsulated in a single word or phrase, 'empowerment' has been used so widely and by so many people and organizations for so many different purposes that it has started to lose meaning: '[I]n some countries, governments talk glibly of empowerment of the poor in their development plans, having stripped the term of any real meaning' (Gardner and Lewis 1996: 118).

This chapter addresses some of the main issues in community development, looking at both the strengths and weaknesses of attempts to assist communities to empower themselves. Overall, the experience of community development has been positive but, as with the rest of the development process, it has not been immune to problems.

Like all ideas about development, what community development, or empowerment, means is contested, reflecting the range of interests that come into play when theory meets practice. There are two primary foci for community development, the first being encapsulated in the idea that it is about development of and for the 'community', and the second is about development via community decision-making processes. The 'community', in this instance, is usually defined as the local group or otherwise small groups of people, usually living in relative isolation, that are characterized by face-to-face relationships. In this, the 'community' size is determined by the needs of co-operation and consensus. To this end, the size of a viable community can vary from place to place, and is not able to be determined on a universal basis (Hodge 1970: 68). As a consequence, community development programmes must involve a capacity for modification according to local circumstances, according to local criteria of what constitutes the community, and to suit local needs. What should be noted is that both 'external' and 'internal' approaches to community development reflect a fundamental reorientation of development towards a grass-roots or localized process and outcomes, usually implying local participation in the process. This is in contrast to macro-level or infrastructure development projects that only indirectly affect people at the local level, and in which local communities have very little if any say, usually little or no participation, and almost always no control.

Bottom-up versus top-down

Community development processes have been shown, in a number of cases, to produce real, tangible and appropriate benefits for local people, as well as providing a greater sense of self-worth and empowerment. Such forms of development also work within and help preserve aspects of local culture that give meaning to community life and which assist in maintaining and enhancing the social cohesion that is necessary when engaging in a process of change.

While large-scale development projects can address macroeconomic or infrastructure requirements that can determine the parameters for more localized development, the failure of such 'top-down' projects and decision-making to deliver tangible benefits to many people, including the most marginalized, is common. Many large-scale projects not only fail but are not designed to meet the needs and preferences of people at the local level, are often not based on local experience and are frequently unsustainable once the aid provider has left. In all, such aid often benefits the aid provider, in that they are given a job and a social purpose, but has little, and sometimes negative, longer-term impact on the aid recipients. The adoption of 'bottom-up' or 'flat' local decision-making structures is thus seen as more responsive in addressing local needs. According to the World Bank:

> economic growth is necessary but by no means sufficient to achieve widespread poverty reduction in the world. The [World Development] Report [on Poverty] lists three essential pillars – opportunity, security,

and empowerment – to achieve a significant rate of sustained poverty reduction amongst the poorest population groups. By the same token, the recently released book on *The Quality of Growth*, published by the World Bank Institute, also clearly demonstrates the shift from a predominantly 'economic growth' development model to an approach in which the development of human and socio-cultural capital is deemed a sine qua non for achievement of balanced and sustainable development. For instance, the book demonstrates, using quantifiable indicators, that in countries with a relatively low level of inequality and a medium level of economic growth, the chances for large-scale poverty reduction are considerably greater than in countries with high economic growth and high levels of income inequality.   (World Bank 2001a; see also World Bank 2002a)

While local empowerment is important, not all decisions taken at a local level are appropriate. Some decisions are based in a sense of desperation and are, hence, very short-term or immediately focused, with little or no focus on longer-term sustainability. Other decisions can be based on a limited understanding of opportunities or of the consequence of such decisions, for example, taking out small loans to meet immediate needs but which create longer-term debt problems. In yet other circumstances, decisions can be taken or limited by traditional or recently established elites who retain power or influence in local settings, often in their own interests, or again, with a limited understanding of options or outcomes. Within many traditional societies, hierarchical power structures often removed from ordinary people not just the power to make larger decisions about their collective lives but constructed a social psychology of deference towards power holders. The issue of social power is a complex one and can be inconsistent across political and cultural contexts, despite what might otherwise be seen as commonalities of interest in particular strata of society, and very often the common material conditions applying to particular circumstances. As Weitz notes: 'when involving entire communities in development, the social planner must be capable of using existing social relations advantageously'. That is, a failure to recognize and sensitively employ traditional leaders and others can lead to development project failure (Weitz 1986: 167; see also Warren 1993).

External involvement

Assuming that local decision-making is most likely to produce results sensitive to local needs and desires, such decision-making may still require assistance, advice or information available primarily from external sources. However, outside aid providers can (sometimes unwittingly) shape local agendas or inappropriately insert themselves into local decision-making processes that may not be sustainable and that may destabilize local social relations. The issue of the role of the development worker is thus among the most difficult issue in community development, especially when it is focused on empowerment. In simple terms, while a situation might require the intervention of an external agent to create circumstances that allow change, that external intervention by definition must, at some stage, precede empowerment, and often displace it. Based on the assumption that if communities could change themselves they would have done so, it is a rare and extraordinarily sensitive community development project that is able to allow local people to lead.

In all discussion about community development, it must be noted that external factors, from the environment to government to broad material and economic conditions, will have a constraining influence on what is or is not achievable within a local context. According to Friedman: 'local action is severely constrained by global economic forces, structures of unequal wealth, and hostile class alliances' (1992: xii). If development is to look to communities as the source of change, they must also seek to transform social power into political power and engage in national and international issues (Friedman 1992: xii).

Yet, in helping to create an environment in which people can make decisions for themselves, decisions are often made for them. The first decision is whether or not they wish for such intervention in their lives. Further interventions tend to flow from that, including decisions about what aspects of community development are or should be available, what the priorities for community development are, the nature of local social and hierarchical relations and decision-making, and so on. This is especially the case if there is an explicit assumption on the part of development planners that there should be co-ordination between local and wider development goals (Weitz 1986: 79). This is despite acknowledging the necessity of recognizing the 'needs, beliefs and abilities of traditional peoples' (Weitz 1986: 78). However, as Freire (1985) noted: 'Attempting to liberate the oppressed without their reflective participation in the act of liberation is to treat them as objects which must be saved from a burning building, it is to lead them into the populist pitfall and transform them into masses which can be manipulated.'

In this, Freire implicitly opposed such populist manipulation and made it his project to assist with the creation of conditions that would allow people to 'liberate' themselves. Korten also notes that it is not really possible for one person to 'empower' another. People can only empower themselves (1989: 118–19).

Oliver recognized the potential conflict between the ideas of development planners and local people when he noted that it should be 'the first task of a voluntary organization...to encourage the people to speak up when aid projects go wrong' (Oliver 1983: 137). Weitz similarly noted that there needed to be an active 'feedback relationship' to allow constant revision of local development projects to fully take into account field realities (Weitz 1986: 174). In this, Weitz and Oliver were primarily referring to covering-up aid programmes that were failing or that had failed in order to save official embarrassment, but still allowing for such failure to be repeated. Similarly, Jain, Krishnamurty and Tripathi suggest that, 'the basic reason for the failure of rural development and poverty alleviation programmes is the exclusion of the people from participation in the development process and the abandonment of the institutions of democratic decentralization and the related electoral process' (Jain, Krishnamurty and Tripathi 1985: 15). Democratic decentralization, in this context, means 'recognizing multiple centres of power' (sometimes referred to as 'Public Interest Partnerships'), which assist in ensuring accountability, transparency, participation, equity, predictability and efficiency. In this sense, what is broadly referred to as governance becomes essential, reflecting the authenticity of local electoral democracy. In simple terms, 'good governance is good for development' (Gonzales, Lauder and Melles 2000: 165).

However, the principle of appropriate development programmes and the necessity for vocal local input remains valid. Weitz (1986: 174) similarly noted that there needed to be a bottom-up 'feedback relationship' to allow constant revision so that programmes could conform to local realities.

Background to community development

Ideas about community development were first commonly propagated in the early 1970s, following what was widely seen as the failure of the 'decade of development' of the 1960s in which decolonization did not automatically result in development and in which explicitly modernist or industrial policies were mistakenly regarded as the universal path to 'take-off'. What occurred instead, in many developing countries, was a mixture of semi-development, development experiencing losses and then gains in succession, or just simple underdevelopment, in which a number of countries increasingly went backwards. The overall result, at a time when the West remained optimistic, was an overall decline in developing countries and especially amongst the majority poor of developing countries. As Mortimer noted, this was in large part due to the blind faith held by western planners in the value of modernization and, consequently, in the lack of value accorded to 'peasants' (Mortimer 1984: ch. 3).

In response to continuing and increasing poverty in developing countries, then later as president of the World Bank, Robert McNamara outlined the Basic Needs, or 'redistribution with growth' approach to development, which focused development on local initiatives. McNamara's then groundbreaking view was that poverty alleviation for the world's poorest 40 per cent was of primary importance, although this should not be undertaken in ways that would damage prospects for economic growth (UNICEF 1996: ch. 3). In this, McNamara was influenced by the 'peripheral' work of NGOs, and thinking such as that expounded by British economist E. F. Schumacher in his seminal work *Small is Beautiful,* which turned away from large-scale industrialization and macroeconomics towards more appropriate medium levels of technology and local economics.

Yet, while this shift in focus was important, the origins of community development can be traced to some of the first thinking about development as a part of the process of decolonization, pre-dating the optimistic and sometimes grandiose ideas of the 1960s. The original United Nations position on community development, for instance, was that it 'is a technique for improving the levels of living, particularly in underdeveloped areas, community development being interpreted as a process creating conditions of economic and social progress for the whole community with its active participation and the fullest possible reliance upon the community's initiative' (UN 1958: 21). In this sense, the community may be relatively passive in the development process or the decision-making processes that are intended to lead towards development. In so far as there was a view that the community itself should be brought into the decision-making process, it was via what has been described as a methodology combining social work and public administration models (Ponsioen 1962). More recently, there has also been an increasing emphasis on local decision-making contributing to local employment and in the development of particular expertise.

Participatory democracy

One of the major criticisms of democratic processes has been that, through increasingly centralized representative processes, it has become too distant from the people being represented. Participatory democracy implies the greater direct participation of political constituents in political decision-making processes. Most common methods of participatory democracy are direct democracy, in which constituents vote directly on matters that affect them, primarily through local power structures or heavily decentralized political models. The advantage of this approach is the greater access to decision-making processes and potentially greater legitimacy of political outcomes. However, such systems do have limited application in large, complex societies that require broad decision-making affecting large populations. There are also questions around the extent to which voters might be familiar with the detail of all of the subjects they might be required to decide on, as well as the potential for short-term or narrowly focused decisions which could have longer-term or wider negative consequences.

One increasingly popular mechanism developed to address the sense of distance in political decision making, and which has also been applied in limited ways in non-democratic states such as China and Laos, has been that of 'deliberative democracy', sometimes also referred to as 'discursive democracy'. This model of decision-making combines elements of representative as well as direct democratic processes, with constituent members of a political group (e.g. village, town) discussing political decisions or laws with representatives and having a consensus view of their deliberations reflected in political action. An alternative to this approach is deliberative polling, in which participants do not meet directly. The deliberative democracy model was initially developed in the 1980s but has since seen its widespread theoretical adoption and, in some cases, practical use (e.g. see discussion by He 2010 of its application in China).

The principal benefit of deliberative democracy is intended to be, through being able to trace their origins, as with other participatory forms, an increased sense of legitimacy in political decisions. There is also a sense in which, through widespread consultation, there is a higher degree of impartiality, rationalist and knowledge of relevant facts in decision-making (Bessette 1994). Some negative consequences of this process, however, include the argument that the process inhibits rather than helps rational decision-making, that it is ideologically biased in favour of liberalism and republican models over parliamentary ones, that, like other participatory methods, it can too readily reflect self-interest and that it promotes a division between the state and society (see Blattberg 2003).

Given that decisions on spending usually limited income is key in political processes, participatory budgeting is a key element of participatory democracy. This process usually involves the public identification of spending needs, their prioritization, the public decision-making process and, finally, its implementation via public officials. While this process can have some of the shortcomings of more general participatory decision-making, it does increase equity and the transparency and accountability of financial decision-making. In Porto Alegre, Brazil, since 1989 this process has led to direct improvements in water and sanitation and access to public education (Lewit 2002). Since this beginning, the process has spread elsewhere in Latin America, to Asia, Europe and North America. Despite positive outcomes, the actual rate of participation in the process has been proportionately low, with some 50,000 people in Porto Alegre participating from a population of 1.5 million. Further, some experiences have shown that participation rates decline after initial needs have been met. The process has, however, increased in popularity and provided a real mechanism for addressing needs as understood at the community level.

Education as development

Even though the use of education was an early approach to community development, its history dates back even further, being first conceived of by the British Colonial Office in the 1920s, although it was not applied, in Africa, until the 1940s. Ghana launched its first mass literacy and education campaign in 1951, which was soon after adopted by the nearby French colonies (Manghezi 1976: 41). In this, community development was seen as 'a vehicle for progressive evolution of the peoples to self-government in the context of social and economic change' (Manghezi 1976: 39–40). The idea of community development was not well developed initially, although even at this stage it was recognized that education was a critical component which found translation as the opening of 'development area schools' and similar projects (Manghezi 1976: 41). The idea of education generally and literacy in particular was later seized upon as a critical factor in community development, both for broader utilitarian purposes and to directly enhance the knowledge base (and hence capacity for decision-making) of individuals.

In the sense that education allows participation and opens opportunities, community development is seen to be about enhancing local decision-making processes via the 'empowerment' of people who are the targets of development projects and to give them more practical political power over the goals and outcomes of the development process. The idea of empowerment, in this context, is reflected in the ideas of Paulo

Freire (1976, 1985), based on the need to develop people's abilities to understand, question and resist structural conditions for their poverty and to have the capacity to change those conditions. In this, education generally, and literacy in particular, are seen as critical criteria for individual and group development (see also Rensberg 1980). Freire's critique was essentially derived from a 'bottom-up' perspective of social and economic relations and was predicated upon the idea of reflection (via education) leading to action (praxis) (Freire 1985: Ch. 3). Perhaps the biggest difference between Freire's revolutionary pedagogy and the role of education in a more contemporary community development is that the latter is based upon a more localized and, hence, contained basis, and that it seeks to allow its recipients to participate in wider economic and political spheres, rather than to overthrow them.

Freire's work can be understood as a basic principle of 'capacity building', in which local communities not only have opportunities to make decisions but have developed an enhanced capacity to be able to do so. Discussion about capacity-building has been a significant feature of development discourse since the mid-1990s, yet there are few clear definitions about its meaning. One interpretation has capacity-building as equivalent to developing social capital (CVCB 2007), while others have it as the development of practical skills. According to the UNDP, capacity-building is 'the creation of an enabling environment with appropriate policy and legal frameworks, institutional development, including community participation (of women in particular), human resources development and strengthening of managerial systems, adding that UNDP recognizes that capacity building is a long-term, continuing process, in which all stakeholders participate' (cited in Walker 2007).

Of these attributes at a community level, literacy, as the most fundamental aspect of education, has thus remained a key issue in empowerment and participation of local communities and remains both an obvious means to individual and local development, as well as feeding in directly to the capacity of the state, via its constituents, proactively to pursue its own wider development goals. Literacy can also be argued to be an end in itself, in terms of enhancing the scope of individuals to participate in a literate world.

In a not dissimilar fashion, literacy has been cited as being useful to individuals as well as for 'development' in Bangladesh (although this nominally assumes the questionable distinction between the welfare of individuals and 'development'). A literacy programme was developed by the Friends in Village Development Bangladesh for landless men and women, which was based on small groups and was combined with organizational support, savings and credit schemes, technical assistance for income generation and the rebuilding of a sense of self-worth. 'Literacy is therefore linked to generating local group structures and capacity-building', not least of which is the capacity to participate in the development process (Gardner and Lewis 1996: 117). It is worth noting here that those developing countries that have performed best, such as the 'newly industrialized countries' of east Asia, invested heavily in education as a precondition for their growth. In particular, the centrality of education to Confucian thinking resulted in massive investment in education in Singapore, Taiwan and South Korea, in each case with dramatic results.

While literacy has been identified by most governments of developing countries as a – probably *the* – critical development issue, it has not been free of problems, both internally and externally. One of the internal problems with education campaigns is that they do not necessarily address the educational imbalance that can occur between people with and without power. That is, a person with power who is probably already literate may have their literacy enhanced, while an illiterate person may achieve only a basic level of literacy and, in terms of complex written information, still be at a significant disadvantage (especially if their literacy is tested, for example, via a contract or other complex device). Literacy is also most useful when combined with other technical support or enhancement. Literacy alone has the capacity, too, to breed resentment through a greater awareness of structural imbalances or other unfairness or enhanced expectations that cannot be changed in the short term. Indeed, this has been a major problem in places where literacy and structural unemployment are both relatively high, such as independent East Timor (e.g. see UNMIT 2006). General estimates of unemployment in East Timor in 2002 were in the order of 75–80 per cent, although dropping to still over 40 per cent among urban youth and 20 per cent in rural areas by 2006 (World Bank 2006a). The earlier figure did not take account of the subsistence nature of much rural employment, although it was a fair reflection of the extent of the non-cash economy. By 2011, education in East Timor had improved significantly and literacy had increased more widely, but unemployment, especially among younger people, remained problematically high. The events of 2006 in which gangs of youths formed political alliances and went on a rampage of violence and destruction, almost bringing the fledgling state to its knees, continuing high youth unemployment and the heightened expectations that literacy can bring, constituted a double-edged sword for the future.

From an external perspective, education campaigns have often been amongst the first to be affected by externally imposed 'structural adjust-

organization requiring leadership can be difficult to obtain. In a different cultural context, there is a widespread view that village office should neither be coveted nor too highly rewarded. One consequence of this, though, is that 'villagers might content themselves with mediocre leadership for long periods without concerted attempts at replacement' (Warren 1993: 123).

Notions of authority and hierarchy vary from context to context, and the role of authority in local decision-making and how that is employed is not consistent. In some cases, authority is a capacity not to be trusted or to be used with caution. Warren noted that in Bali, members of the traditional aristocracy, civil servants, and agents of political parties who were seen to have status, office or wealth (that is, traditional patrons) had difficulty in presenting their views publicly in what was seen to be the disinterested manner that is otherwise regarded as a cultural ideal. Hence, orators without such *manjar* significance, but who have influence based on personal qualities, including knowledge of local *adat* (customary law) and skills in public speaking, are often in as strong or a stronger position to persuade local people of the value of an idea.

As a consequence of this public distinction between formal and informal authority figures, a dual leadership pattern can emerge. However, within this, while corporate ideals were supposed to predominate, formal or traditional decision-makers still exercise informal influence on orators. 'Although close association with patrons would compromise an orator's credibility, covert alliances develop and orators are able to use their skills to frame factional interests of powerful patrons in terms of principles acceptable in the public forum.' This presentation of a shadow leadership pattern, allied to formal and informal political arenas and codes of expression, shares certain features with Bloch's proposition (1975: 6, 12) that formalized rules and speech forms are essentially vehicles of traditional authority and established power relations. That is to say, even though this social environment might portray itself as formally egalitarian and moral, it actually remains hierarchic and instrumental (Warren 1993: 73). In such cases, deeply ingrained notions of structural hierarchy mean that it may be difficult to achieve local development projects without the consent or participation of local authority figures, or that their involvement will more likely guarantee the success of a project.

In other cases, it can be difficult to achieve successful local projects without the support of local leaders. Warren has noted that the Indonesian family planning project, which has been generally regarded as successful, achieved its greatest success on the island of Bali. This has been identified as being a direct consequence of what was called the

Sistem Banjar (Neighborhood Association System), in which the village community was a conduit for family planning. By way of illustration of its success, in 1985 Bali had the highest rate for use of contraceptives (74.5 per cent) in Indonesia, compared with the national 52.2 per cent average (Arifin 2010; Warren 1993: 217). This use of contraceptives was directly linked to the highest decline in the fertility rate, by almost half. In order to achieve this level of contraception usage, heads of *banjar* (neighbourhood or hamlet associations) were sent to training seminars and liaised with district family planning field workers to provide information and contraceptives. *Banjar* heads were also responsible for registering eligible couples, compiling statistics on contraceptive use and motivating acceptance in communities (Warren 1993: 218). According to Warren, the *klian* (head) of Banjar Tegah said the contraceptive campaign 'would not ever have succeeded if it hadn't gone through the *banjar*. Before everyone was embarrassed to talk about such matters. Now it is normal. At each assembly meeting we discussed family planning until everyone understood sufficiently' (Warren 1993: 218). This conformed to Weitz's view that, 'when involving entire communities in development, the social planner must be capable of using existing social relations advantageously' (Weitz 1986: 167). However, this also reflected the broad interests, and reinforced the status of, the local elite.

Apart from local elite input, Warren said there was no difference in contraceptive use based on social or economic status, although there was variance between *banjar* (between 30 and 60 per cent acceptance) which correlated to the distance between *banjar* and the local family planning clinic (Warren 1993: 219) and between support or otherwise of *klian* for the programme (Warren 1993: 220). Proximity to both the source of the programme and the motivator for the programme was critical to the success of a local programme. Warren noted that while local leadership was important, and was influenced by proximity, discussion of leadership or local institutions also needed to take account of Balinese conceptions of the 'popular' which were unquestionably influenced by modern ideas about democracy as well as traditional practices and status orientation (Warren 1993: 123).

Social organization

Even in local projects, in which autonomy is meant to be paramount, there can continue to be a heavy reliance upon external agencies for assistance in which the local community provides only part of the total requirement to undertake a local project. One such illustration of this, co-operative finance, there was 'no evidence to suggest default is more frequent among small farmers than among large farmers' (Jain, Krishnamurthy and Tripathi 1985: 57).

In principle, co-operatives can and often do give greater productive capacity and greater independence to local farmers or other groups of small-scale workers. And in forming what amounts to small companies, they do return the benefits of their joint labour to the 'shareholders' – the co-operative members themselves. But questions of adequate or appropriate management, equity, and so on, all need to be addressed in a co-operative enterprise. Perhaps the most successful co-operatives are those that pool resources, and in some cases labour, for certain aspects of a co-operative project but which retain independence of co-operative stakeholders in terms of clearly delineating inputs and, hence, proportionate outcomes. This 'reward for effort' is perhaps the key formal distinction between a co-operative enterprise and a communal enterprise. The point, however, is that community development is most enhanced when local people voluntarily come together around a local project which is to the benefit of all. In making a decision to work co-operatively towards a shared goal and then by undertaking the work, people in the local context combine practical resources and skills, potentially increase their efficiency through specializing tasks and achieve economies of scale not available to individuals. However, at least as important, by doing so local people also take their material circumstances into their own hands and, by forming what amounts to a political collective, empower themselves in terms of what they can achieve, but also through increasing their economic and political autonomy for their own benefit.

Expecting the unexpected

Anthropologists have noted that one of the most critical factors affecting development programmes, especially those that are located within and run by the local community, is the impact of development on local patterns of behaviour and economic, social and political relations. That is, development programmes that alter a local environment are not free from flow-on effects, nor are they free of importing external values (such as consumer materialism), despite the implied belief that all societies can potentially adopt with relatively little disruption to the development paradigm. In seeking the advantages of development and in focusing on its potential for positive contribution, there is frequently too little concern for potential negative consequences, meaning that 'unexpected' problems can and do arise, sometimes to the extent of derailing the development process. That is 'social change often entails costs that are neither expected nor planned for' (Appel 1990: 271).

In recognizing that there are impacts from the local development process that are often not planned for, Appel noted seven principles of social change within the development context. They are:

1. Every act of development or modernization necessarily involves an act of destruction.
2. The introduction of a new activity always displaces an indigenous activity.
3. The adaptive potential of a population is limited, and every act of change temporarily reduces this potential until such time as that change has been completely dealt with.
4. Given such reduction, each act of change has the potential to cause physiological, psychological, and/or behavioural impairment in the subject population (such as stress or 'social bereavement').
5. Modernization erodes support and maintenance mechanisms for managing social stress.
6. Change always produces psychological loss, as well as compensation for such loss.
7. Change threatens the nutritional status of a population, and there is often disruption to traditional nutrition patterns. (Appel 1990: 272)

In identifying these factors, Appel also notes that they are all exacerbated by the speed of change. That is, the speed of change might not just have a quantifiable impact – that twice the rate of change will produce twice the potential problems, but that the quality of the impact can increase disproportionately to the rate of change – that twice the rate of change could lead to a greater multiplier of related problems (1990: 273). The encouragement given to a shift to cash cropping, for instance, can damage local ecology and lead to a loss of subsistence crops. The loss of access to locally sourced food can and often does have a direct impact on the nutritional status of local communities (Appel 1990: 273–4). Not only is the variety of nutritional sources not always available in a purely cash context within a local community at the lower end of the development scale but cash crops may be subject to total failure (mixed crops tend to be subject to partial failure), hence depriving the grower of access to any return. Further, the trajectory of prices for cash crops, on the whole, declined in real terms between the late 1970s and around 2006, with regular dips in pricing depending on the extent of oversupply and relative competition on global markets. This then reduced the potential income to a subsistence crop grower until the more recent price increase and, hence, their capacity to secure adequate supplies of food. Even when the sale price of agricultural commodities increased, this was often at the wholesale and retail end of the market, with little of the benefit being passed on to growers. This then returns to the observations made by Weitz, Warren, Friedman and Oliver: that in any community development process, there needs to be primary recognition given to the knowledge, values, needs and desires of the local people, which is what, at base, community development is supposed to be about.

Community development at work: the East Timor experience

In assessing the practical potential for community development, the most recent significant programme (at the time of writing), East Timor's Community Empowerment and Local Governance Project (CEP), stands as a useful illustration. The CEP in East Timor showed what was available through community development but it also pointed up some of the problems that continue to trouble local development projects. The CEP was a World Bank-funded project intended to stimulate community level development projects and to encourage democratization at a local level in a society that prior to its commencement, apart from one violent and externally organized election, had never previously experienced the democratic process.[1]

The formative stages of the CEP came into being soon after the UN returned to East Timor in late September 1999, following the Indonesian army's 'scorched earth' policy in response to the UN-supervised ballot in which East Timorese voted to separate from Indonesia. Already the equal poorest province in Indonesia, East Timor had more than 70 per cent of its buildings and infrastructure destroyed by the retreating Indonesian army and its militia proxies. Prior to the vote, East Timor had been under Indonesian occupation since late 1975, during which time there were limited attempts to introduce literacy and centrally planned development programmes, the latter mostly contributing to larger Indonesian-owned enterprises. Development at the local level was decided upon by Indonesian government appointees (sometimes through a nominal electoral process) and, if at a lower level of implementation, followed a standardized Indonesian model, with even less functional democracy than existed in most of the rest of Indonesia under that country's decidedly authoritarian New Order government.

After the first year of the incipient CEP, in November 2000, the US$21.5 million programme largely shifted from the control of foreign employees to an indigenous management team. From this time, the small management team in Dili supported 60 sub-district facilitators, more than 800 village facilitators, and one district project accountant and a district monitor in every district, all of whom were East Timorese.

Recognizing East Timor's history of not having experienced democracy, the key CEP objective was to introduce and establish transparent, democratic, and accountable local structures in rural areas to make decentralized decisions about development projects. While providing the opportunity for local communities to rehabilitate basic infrastructure and revive local economies, the local councils established under CEP were intended to be a vehicle for the local expression of development needs and desires, and for implementing projects. This was, at the time, regarded as a good example of 'bottom-up' development planning and as representing a new policy direction by the World Bank, which funded the project. The former UN Transitional Authority in East Timor head of District Administration, Jarat Chopra, described the CEP as 'an introduction to local democracy, as well as a functioning form of self-determination in the reconstruction process' (La'o Hamutuk 2000).

After its first 12 months, the CEP had funded over 600 sub-projects and supported the formation of 57 sub-district councils. More than 400 village development councils were founded in all districts, between them accounting for a total of 6,270 representative council members. One notable aspect of this programme was that the council positions were equally divided between men and women (World Bank 2000; TFET 2000). This was in contrast to East Timor's deeply entrenched culture of male domination. However, while this division of representation by sex was broadly regarded as appropriate (not least by many East Timorese women), it was a very clear example of the imposition of external values on a sometimes reluctant indigenous society:

> In many ways, the CEP councils are creations of the 'international community' – albeit with the expressed support of the CNRT [Timorese National Resistance Council]. In this regard, they are not as legitimate and vibrant as socio-political structures that have emerged out of local, long-term processes. As the 'Joint Donor' report noted, '[A]t present the talent and energy at village level is more likely to be found around the chief and the old clandestine structures than within the council.' It is such structures that the

report contends 'must be built upon if the country's urgent rural development problems are to be solved.' What the report calls their 'control mentality and gender bias,' however, run counter to international notions of democracy, as well as to the official positions of the CNRT. How the CEP will reconcile its praiseworthy principles with the need to respect indigenous beliefs, practices, and structures is an ongoing challenge, In this regard, working more closely with local and national organizations – such as East Timorese women's groups, for example – might go a long way toward realizing many of the CEP's goals. (La'o Hamutuk 2000)

As a result of the post-ballot destruction, local communities largely chose to invest CEP funds in rebuilding or repairing community and personal infrastructure. Some 43 per cent of funding was allocated for the construction of community meeting halls, a quarter for small roads linking up to larger ones and for the repair of agricultural infrastructure, 15 per cent for the restoration of household assets (such as pots, pans, plates, cups, and/or spoons shared by villagers) and productive equipment (such as simple, communally owned farm equipment, lathes, or saws), 10 per cent for repair of water supply infrastructure (wells and pipes), and 7 per cent for schools or clinics. 'Vulnerable groups' and others, such as orphans and widows, were targeted for CEP support, as were local NGOs and the development of community radio (La'o Hamutuk 2000; Estefa 2001). (It has been common experience in developing countries since the advent of transistorization that radios are the cheapest and most accessible form of mass communication). As noted by a then senior CEP manager, Chris Dureau, reflecting on the programme a decade later, it was a priority for traumatized communities that had lost everything to re-establish a sense of normality, by replacing some of that which had been destroyed, rather than embark on what were perceived as ambitious small business projects.[2]

While the CEP was seen as relatively successful in introducing democratization to East Timor, and in improving the social, economic and political position of women, it also had some failures. The introduction of localized democratization necessarily led to tension with traditional power structures and, in cases where traditional leaders prevailed, it served to strengthen their political position, as well as offering them the chance to exploit economic opportunities offered by the projects. Similarly, although the CEP served to strengthen and, in principle, democratize local decision-making, there was an initial lack of co-ordination between villages, and between villages and the district level administrations. This was, in large part, resolved through the establishment of District Advisory Boards providing such linkages. The position of women in such CEPs was also less successful, with a continuing 'culture of silence' on the part of many women (and expected by many men), and otherwise a lack of active participation on the part of many women. Further, not all CEP elections were as democratic as intended, with some 30 per cent of elections undertaken by 'acclamation' of candidates who had been chosen by local leaders. Villagers were also frequently inactive, in part due to a lack of training, in part due to lack of reward and in part due to concern over introducing opportunism to impoverished environments. According to Dureau, the CEP's project of dispersing money to districts initially undermined democratic principles, mostly because the processes intended to ensure participation were in many cases short-circuited to ensure the efficient dispersal of funds (Dureau 2003).

On balance, however, the CEP was widely regarded as having achieved a number of its goals, not least of which was the locally directed repair of the physical fabric of East Timorese society, as well as wider social and government capacity building (World Bank 2006b). Between the CEP and externally supervised elections for the legislature and the presidency (and following the vote for independence), notions of participatory and representative democracy were overwhelmingly enthusiastically received, and were becoming ingrained into the thinking of many, perhaps most, local people as a desirable and legitimate means of decision-making. The biggest threat to this process related not to the success or otherwise of the CEP but to the broader economic conditions of the fledgling state, and the social dislocation caused by unmet economic expectations, militant conflict between senior political actors and their proxies (leading to a political crisis in 2006), and the social trauma of a quarter century of brutalization that, pro rata, was on a scale equivalent to that of Cambodia under the Khmer Rouge. Set against this backdrop, the CEP functioned to restore or establish some order of normality and, broadly conceived, 'progress'. However, as a programme with a finite tenure for external funding, there was real concern about its viability after its external sources of funding ended. When that time came, the real test of the success of the programme could be measured.

The purpose of the CEP was to provide funding to communities for infrastructure and social activities. While the World Bank ran with the idea, the Asian Development Bank preferred an emphasis on governance. Communities that were funded tended to use the funds available to restore a sense of normality rather than thinking about long-term development strategies. It was initially a puzzle as to why communities opted for 'normalization' rather than development, but the pattern of recurrence showed that the message from communities in post-disaster or conflict places such as Aceh, Afghanistan, Laos, Bougainville and the Solomon Islands was that communities initially needed small scale activities of limited duration. Efforts to establish 'proper' development activities in most cases were not successful. According to Dureau, 'We now know that in these situations the communities fall into the category of recovery rather than development (personal communication 4 May 2011).

A decade on from the CEP, the evolved model is widely regarded to have worked well, if with some qualifications, and has become the benchmark model of community empowerment projects in a number of other countries. Indonesia followed with similar initiatives, such as with the evolution of the National Program for Community Empowerment which became the Kecamatan Development Program, reflecting an increased menu of social activities and longer-term involvement consultation, and the Musrenbang (*Musyawarah Rencana Pembangunan* – Multi Stakeholder Consultation Forum for Development Planning) offered progress in community involvement in local decision making, which led to the establishment of locally determined projects including new roads, potable water, irrigation, health clinics and schools (World Bank 2010).[3] Similar projects were also developed in a number of other developing countries across Asia and Africa.

Local versus global

Regardless of the value attached to it, there is little doubt that the world is in many ways becoming a smaller, more connected and integrated place. Interestingly, however, while the world grows smaller, local cultures are increasingly asserting themselves in ways that were initially unnecessary and then, for a while, difficult if not impossible. That is, as remote corners of the globe are increasingly exposed to the glare of international exposure, the people within them are seeing themselves as a separately identifiable component of a diverse and otherwise overwhelmingly culturally heterogeneous global population. This is nowhere more pronounced than in relation to states, many of which as developing countries have only made the transition to statehood in a qualified manner, perhaps reflecting the specific historical and material origins of the world's first (and to date more successful) states. The failure of many states to meet, or be able to meet, the needs of many of their citizens, and the broad sweep of globalization, has meant that many communities have turned back to themselves for development, if in fact many of them ever ceased to do so.

For many in developing countries, what is called 'development' but which in other contexts might just be a simple, perhaps minor improvement in standard of living, is the product of local conditions, effort, imagination and capacity. Governments can and do develop major infrastructure projects and sometimes these have a direct positive benefit on local people. But very often they do not and in too many cases the effects are deleterious, or are simply not sustained and, hence, become a larger economic burden. Yet, there is no quality of government that exceeds its desire to involve itself down to the most local level of its population, in part certainly to be able to claim some equality of care of its citizens but, almost as surely, to regulate and control them as well. It is at this point that exists the juncture between state and local aspirations for development.

There is no doubt that some local development projects have to fit into a wider development scheme. For example, and other than for initial educational purposes, it would be rather pointless developing a local educational facility if the language being taught was not consistent with a wider literacy programme: so too a road project, in which roads to a proposed bridge faced each other at points that did not correspond. Equally, however, the one-size-fits-all model of development can also fail to address specific local needs, impose inappropriate development and silence the voice of the local community. Even with the best of intentions, external authorities can only rarely presume to know how people think without actually asking them. Added to this are all the usual inefficiencies of a larger hierarchical or bureaucratic structure, the continuation of patron–client relations, modified forms of economic status and deference, and the consequent potential for corruption and reduction of service at the final point of the process.

It is not accurate to say that all the problems of development decision-making can be resolved by devolving responsibility for such decisions to the local level. Even amongst local communities, there are specific interests, conflicts and tensions that can and do derail local decision-making processes, or which default to traditional, often non-representative and usually exclusive power structures. There are also problems with awareness, education and technical competence. Yet, in acknowledging such issues, the legitimacy of direct representation in local decision-making remains valid, the sensitivity and awareness to local needs, concerns and values is most acute at the local level. So too is the capacity for inclusiveness in and, hence, ownership of the development process is greatest at the local level. Development is not just about the accumulation of material resources but about the allocation of such resources. In societies that have less than perfectly representative political systems, the process that determines such allocation is most sensitive to local needs when decisions are taken at the local or community level.

Notes

1. Much of the information regarding East Timor is taken from the author's direct experience of regular visits since the country voted for independence in 1999.
2. Discussion with Chris Dureau, Baucau, Timor-Leste, April 2011.
3. The Kecamatan Development Program was run between 1998 and 2009 by the Ministry of Home Affairs in conjunction with the World Bank. Its key principles included being a decentralized, participatory and transparent programme in which residents could suggest their own local spending priorities. See www.worldbank.org/id/kdp.

Chapter 10

Gender and Development

Janet Hunt

Whatever the prevailing trend in development, one thing remains constant. Gender implications of development processes are neglected. In the early post-war years, when the concept of 'development' evolved, issues of gender equity were not even considered relevant to the economic development of third-world countries. Today, after much debate about approaches to development, significant advances have been made through the United Nations Decade for Women 1975–85, and the UN World Women's Conference in Beijing in 1995. Yet following the impacts of debt and adjustment in the eighties and nineties and the multiple crises of finance, food and energy in the first decade of the twenty-first century, and despite a global commitment to the MDGs, the challenge of making development gender-equitable remains a very significant one. The issue that emerged from feminist analysis of, and activism about, development has become 'diluted, denatured and depoliticised, included everywhere as an afterthought' (Cornwall, Harrison and Whitehead 2004: 1). Indeed, "Gender" is something 'everyone knows they are supposed to do something about' but 'everyone sighs' (Cornwall, Harrison, and Whitehead 2004: 1).

Yet gender inequality remains a feature of every region, though it is most pronounced in south Asia, sub-Saharan Africa and the Middle East. Women are underrepresented in governmental decision making in most countries, with only about 17 per cent of all parliamentary seats in the world's national parliaments; across the world, we earn only 70–90 per cent of male earnings in the formal employment sector. There is not a single developing country in which women and men enjoy equal rights under the law. In particular women are discriminated against in areas relating to financial and economic resources, such as their right to land and property and their right to conduct business independently (World Bank 2001b; UNDP 1995; UNIFEM 2000; UN 2009, 2010). Thus women are more vulnerable to poverty than men, especially as a result of widowhood, separation or divorce, and the consequent loss of access to productive assets, although equating all women-headed households with poverty is oversimplistic, as Chant (2004, 2010b) emphasizes. Furthermore, the way development agencies and governments have responded to the 'feminization of poverty' argument, which strongly links poverty with women, may not have assisted them in dealing with their burden of work which results from their poverty (Chant 2008).

The future will remain unequal in many parts of the world. Girls represent 54 per cent of all children not enrolled in school worldwide (UN Millennium Project 2005: 42; UN 2010: viii). In sub-Saharan Africa, the gender gap in school enrolment remained much the same for the 20-year period 1970–90, but in the last 20 years, progress towards gender parity in primary school enrolment has been significant, although a considerable gender gap remains at secondary level. For example, across Africa, there was a 16 per cent increase in girl's enrolment in primary school between 1999 and 2007. Gender parity in enrolment in primary education has been reached in 117 of 163 countries for which data is available, however, there remain 38 countries where disparities which favour boys persist (UN 2010: 52–4).[1]

Sex and gender: what are we talking about?

In raising the issues of gender inequality, early writers focused on *women* in development. A shift in emphasis to *gender* in the last decade of the twentieth century signalled a change in perspective and approach. While women and men differ biologically – that is their *sex* is different – the behaviour and socially learned characteristics associated with their maleness or femaleness, is their *gender*. The learned behaviours and roles associated with being male and female may vary from culture to culture. For example, in one culture males take care of money. In another, it is the women who control the purse strings. Thus roles associated with each gender may vary from place to place, as well as over time. In the economic sphere, men and women often undertake different activities. Women may plant certain crops; men may plant others. Harvest work may be gender-specific. In each setting, we have to be clear what the roles are and how they interrelate.

A study of rural households in Vietnam, for example (Kabeer and Anh 2000) noted that Vietnamese women have always been active traders, making up half the trading labour force in the 1960s unlike their counterparts in south Asia and the Middle East, who comprised only about 10 per cent of traders at that time. By the late 1990s in Vietnam, some 90 per cent of men and women were involved in income-earning economic activities, but women were more likely than men to be found in 'catering, food and beverage manufacturing, wholesale and retail trade, and garment and leather industries. Men predominated (80 per cent) in storage and transport services, mining and fishing' (Kabeer and Anh 2000: 11). In terms of agricultural labour, Kabeer and Anh cite research from the Red River Delta which indicates that women alone were

> largely responsible for sowing, transplanting and weeding; both men and women were active in soil preparation and in harvesting. Animal husbandry was women's responsibility in about 50 per cent of households and a joint activity in 33 per cent. Homestead gardening was done solely by women in 30 per cent of households and jointly in 43 per cent. (Kabeer and Anh 2000: 12)

Such detailed and localized analysis is required to identify gender roles and responsibilities, and thus to identify appropriate development strategies.

Early development workers, however, made false assumptions, largely based on their own experience of male and female roles in Europe and North America in the early 1900s. It was assumed that women's roles were largely as mothers and 'housewives' in the European sense. Their extremely significant *economic* roles in the household or as farmers were entirely overlooked. As early as 1929, Nigerian women were resisting their loss of land and their reduced status as farmers, as a result of colonists' efforts to 'modernize' agriculture (Boserup 1970; Mies 1986).

Thus early development projects ignored women and neglected to understand the diverse roles they were playing in social and economic life. As a result, some projects made life worse for women, depriving them of land which was taken over for the development project's crops, denying them access to technical assistance, providing resources, training and education to men, and often, unknowingly adding to women's work burden (Dey 1982; Rogers 1980). Any income from the 'development' activities went straight to the men, creating wider inequalities than already existed.

Where there were development activities for women, they were generally either mother–child health projects (generally with more focus on the child than the mother) or family planning projects to encourage women to adopt family planning methods to reduce population growth (Rogers 1980). Women were seen only as mothers, often of too many children! Such projects did nothing to enhance women's status or promote their equality, although they may have been of some practical support.

Integrating women into development

Ester Boserup's seminal work, *Women's Role in Economic Development* (1970), challenged all this. The book documented different household and farming systems in Asia and Africa, pointing out that there were vast differences between the social and economic arrangements in the various household types, and in what she termed male and female farming systems. She observed that women played a very active role in agriculture in Africa, particularly in areas of extensive farming and shifting cultivation. In Asia, on the other hand, in intensive, settled agriculture where the plough was used, women took a far lesser role and their labour was replaced by male landless labourers. She drew attention to the significance of land tenure arrangements and stimulated a plethora of empirical research to explore these issues in many different contexts. Boserup also drew attention to the economic significance of polygamous households where extra wives provided a source of free agricultural labour to the household. The European nuclear family model was shown to be a context-specific arrangement, not a universal model. Furthermore, she argued that women could play a much more active role in industrial development and the modern sector and that economic growth would be enhanced if this were encouraged. Her view was that, contrary to popular belief, women would not take jobs from men but would expand the available labour force and hence the opportunities for economic growth (Boserup 1970).

Boserup's work stimulated the emergence of the Women In Development (WID) movement (Moser 1993), a movement that was gaining strength at the same time as the movement for the New International Economic Order, in the mid-1970s. While the latter movement argued for a redistribution of the world's resources in favour of developing countries, women argued for a redistribution to balance gender inequalities.

The WID movement embraced modernization and argued that women should be 'integrated' into development. If there was to be economic growth, women were to contribute to it and get their fair share of its benefits: women's subsistence farming should be given access to credit and extension services equally with men; women should have equal access to educational opportunities to give them the opportunity to participate in the modern sector. The language of 'efficiency' was adopted by the WID advocates, to convince development planners to involve women in development. It was a language the latter understood, although it was clear they had little idea how to implement the approach (Rogers 1980; Moser 1993).

Early efforts to respond to WID advocates resulted in the establishment of Women's Projects and Women's Desks in development agencies. They tended to be peripheral to the main development effort going on which simply remained unchanged. Thus projects for women were supported in areas such as 'home economics' and traditional crafts, as well as credit for income generation. The theory was that women's poverty resulted from their underdevelopment, and all that was required for development to occur was to increase their productivity through provision of credit (Moser 1991). Many of the credit programmes were poorly conceived and managed and they often turned into welfare-type projects that avoided any resource competition with men (Buvinic 1986).

The mainstream of development was barely touched. Even as late as 1995, a study of four major donors and two southern aid-recipient countries found that the donor agencies had taken the easy path and avoided hard choices, 'creating underfunded mandates, adding a few projects to their existing portfolios, and supporting research, training and the development of operational tools and techniques' (Jahan 1995: 126). WID had become a technical fix, not an agency for empowering women and genuinely transforming development (Jahan 1995). The fundamentally gendered development theories on which the whole development 'project' rested were not up for question.

Women and development: a new critique

While modernization was being critiqued by the school of dependency theorists, feminists were developing their own Marxist-based critique of modernization. Marxist feminists saw that the accumulation of capital resulted not simply from the exploitation of 'peripheral' countries, but from the free subsidy of women's unpaid reproductive and subsistence labour. Maria Mies argued that capitalism could not spread without the subjugation and exploitation of women (Mies 1986). Her research found that, contrary to former belief that men were the preferred labour force, women were being employed in some key areas at lower wages and in poor conditions. She found that poorly paid 'compliant' women were the labour force of choice in many multinational companies, particularly in the electronics, textile and garment industries in free trade zones (FTZs), and in large commercial agricultural companies. Their work was seen as 'supplementary' to the male 'breadwinner' so they were typically paid only 50–70 per cent of male wages in FTZs, and their generally casual employment arrangements made them vulnerable. Long hours and poor working conditions affected their health, particularly in the electronics industry (Mies

1986; Pyle and Dawson 1990; Pearson 2001). Women had indeed been integrated into development, comprising 60–90 per cent of FTZ workers in Asia by 1986, but in such a way as to perpetuate inequality and their own subordination (Mies 1986: 114). Mies' case that low-paid women were being exploited for capitalist development seems borne out by the evidence of the FTZ experience – a significant part of such countries' export-oriented national development policies (Pyle and Dawson 1990).

Mies' work was published a year after the Nairobi Women's Conference to mark the end of the UN Decade for Women. At Nairobi, a new 'southern' women's network, 'DAWN' (Development Alternatives for Women in a New Era), also made a strong critique of current development approaches. Sen and Grown (1987) explain DAWN's view that implicit in many of the activities and discussions about women and development it is assumed that,

> women's main problem in the Third World has been insufficient participation in an otherwise benevolent process of growth and development. Increasing women's participation and improving their shares in resources, land, employment and income relative to men were seen as necessary and sufficient to effect dramatic changes in their economic and social position. Our experiences now lead us to challenge this belief … A development process that shrinks and poisons the pie available to poor people and then leaves women scrambling for a relatively larger share is not in women's interest … Equality for women is impossible within the existing economic, political and cultural processes that reserve resources, power and control for small sections of people. But neither is development possible without greater equity for and participation by women.   (Sen and Grown 1987: 11, 15)

Thus the DAWN women were also challenging the WID approach and its assumption that modernization just needed to incorporate women.

DAWN, and many women working in non-government development organizations around the world, recognized that to challenge this development orthodoxy, women needed to be mobilized and empowered to realize a different development vision.

Gender and development

The focus on women's empowerment became one thread in the next phase of work to promote gender equity in development. But the main thrust was to shift attention from women themselves to the *relations between men and women* and particularly to analyze the unequal power relations between them at every level, from the household to the national economy. Gender workers recognized that all social, political and economic structures needed to be examined in this light, with the intention of transforming development to become a more gender-equitable process (UN 1999). Development organizations replaced their Women in Development policies with Gender and Development policies, guidelines and procedures in an attempt to achieve 'Gender Mainstreaming' across the institutions (Rathgeber 1990; Ostergaard 1992; Moser 1993).

An important contribution to the analytical work was made by Caroline Moser (Moser 1993). She distinguished between women's 'practical' and 'strategic' needs, and highlighted the interrelationships between women's different roles – reproductive, productive and community managing. Women's 'practical needs' were those which resulted from their current subordinated position and might include assistance in areas such as education, improved health care, agricultural advice, etc. But their strategic needs are those that might help to transform their situation. These might include legal reform to remove gender discrimination; an end to violence against women; and more politically active and better organized women. Such changes would contribute to an end to women's subordination. Moser challenged development programmes to address women's strategic gender needs, not just their practical ones. Her call for better understanding of women's triple roles would also help shape development programmes to avoid increasing women's workload, and focus on improving their lives.

At the same time feminist economists were trying to deal with economic models of the household that were still far from accurate. In general, development economists have treated the household as a single unit and much data collected at the household level is not gender-disaggregated. Bina Agarwal (1997a) has developed a gendered 'bargaining model' of the household which explores how men and women interact within households to meet their subsistence needs, have access to necessary resources and frame the 'social norms' within which such bargaining takes place. In addition she outlines the external factors in the market, the community and the state, which shape the bargaining power available to different household members. Thus a woman's ability to bargain favourably to have equal access to resources for subsistence, such as land, may be affected by laws relating to inheritance, her access to government officials who deal with land registration matters, her educational level and legal literacy, the community's view about the legitimacy of her claim (whatever its legal merits) and her ability to support herself independent of counter-claimants (such as brothers or uncles) (Agarwal 1997a: 14). Greater attention is now being given to these institutional factors and societal gender norms that Agarwal also highlighted, indicating the power they have in shaping gender relations within the household (Mabsout and van Staveren 2010). Tripathy (2010), however, challenges Agarwal's model of the developing world's household as a site of conflict, arguing that families are also sites of co-operation; through these ideas of intra-household struggles, she says, gender and development theorists have perpetuated the victimhood of the third-world woman. Rather, she says, we should understand that 'masculinity and femininity ... are not something which men or women have, but are constantly re-constructing themselves in a context of shifting priorities' (Tripathy 2010: 120). Whilst Tripathy may be right about the mutability of gender relations, neverthless, Agarwal's approach of detailed analysis of gender at the household level and its interaction with wider societal factors – which has been underlined by Mabsout and van Staveren's work – presents a challenge to development planners to check their assumptions, carry out their prior research and pay greater attention to the gendered effects of different policies and programmes. However, the real world may be more complex than our gender analysis models suggest and there is scope to develop approaches that will capture a less essentialized reality, recognize co-operation as well as conflict in gender relations, and take account of multiple sources of inequality (Woodford-Berger 2007).

Gender and adjustment

While efforts were under way to make development policies and programmes more gender-sensitive, many countries were facing enormous problems of indebtedness. From the early 1980s, the Philippines, Mexico and many African countries were soon undergoing the rigours of structural adjustment. Governments had to reduce spending, currencies were devalued and there was a strong push to trade more and open the economies to foreign investment (Beneria 1999).

As the DAWN women explained in Nairobi, women became the 'shock absorbers' in this process. In the name of 'economic efficiency', the policies shifted a considerable burden onto women to make up for the austerity measures that were imposed. At the household level, women's workloads increased as they struggled to provide for their families.

The effects on women of structural adjustment programmes have been well documented (see, for example, Commonwealth Expert Group 1989; Elson 1991; Sparr 1994; Beneria 1999; de Pauli 2000; Floro and Schaeffer 2001). As formal sector employment shrank for both men and women, women increased their activity in the informal sector, working long hours in petty trading, selling sweets and drinks, cooked food, handcrafts and the like, as well as making clothes and other small items such as purses, bags and baskets. The informal sector workforce in Zambia almost doubled in the period 1986–96 during Zambia's adjustment process, with women comprising over two-thirds of the 3.4 million informal sector workers in 1996 (Floro and Schaeffer 2001).

The cutbacks in public expenditure on food subsidies, health care and education hit women too. As income fell, food prices rose for many staples, such as maize in Africa, rice in Asia, and oil and cooking fuel. Women were faced with trying to provide for their families on less. They extended their food growing to try to overcome the impact of reduced household income. But even those who grew food were not immune from the crisis. Zambia, for example, deregulated the price of maize, which tripled in cost. However, the increase in income for women maize farmers was insufficient to offset a sevenfold increase in the price of fertilizers. Many small maize farmers (mostly women) went out of business and maize output fell by 46 per cent (Floro and Schaeffer 2001).

The reduced health services meant that mothers with sick children might have to walk much further than before for any medical help, the cost of drugs increased, and generally health suffered, particularly as women often ate less and anaemia increased. The introduction of user-pays fees in education often meant that the girl children of the family dropped out of school, leaving boys to continue (Sparr 1994).

Not all women were affected negatively. The employment effects of export promotion varied from place to place, with some women gaining employment and increased status. In the Philippines there was a growth in urban industrial employment, especially for young women, but this was mainly focused in the garment and electronics industries in the free trade zones. However, in the rural areas the shift from maize for home consumption to sugar for export displaced women agricultural workers as men were hired to cut the sugar cane (Floro and Schaeffer 2001).

Overall, though, it became widely recognized that the gender impacts of structural adjustment policies had been overlooked and women were bearing the brunt of them. This experience highlighted the need for women to focus on macroeconomic policies rather than just development programmes, since the gender impacts of these policies could be significant and widespread.

Gender and the environment

By the early 1990s, global attention shifted to the environment. Women became actively involved in lobbying around the 1992 Earth Summit, as it offered another opportunity for women to mobilize globally to have an impact on policies and programmes in an area of deep concern.

Women have been intimately concerned with environmental problems in many parts of the world, often being the ones who felt the effects of environmental destruction most keenly. In Kenya, the Green Belt Movement, a national women's movement, has had a massive impact through its collection of indigenous seeds, development of tree nurseries and tree-planting programmes across the country (Rodda 1991). In North India, the 'Chipko' movement of women made world news by hugging trees to stop them being felled (Shiva 1989). In Papua New Guinea, women have actively opposed logging operations that have affected their environment and their livelihoods.

At the Rio Earth Summit, women's advocacy led to recognition of women's role as environmental managers and gained government commitments for women to participate more in environmental decision-making. However, the central assumption of the final statement, that more economic growth is needed to provide the resources to solve the world's environment problems, is seen as an inherent contradiction by many feminists (Braidotti et al. 1997). Indeed, writers and activists such as Vandana Shiva see this approach as nothing less than destructive maldevelopment.

Shiva's ecofeminist views derive from her experience working with Indian peasant women farmers coupled with her intellectual critique of western science. Shiva says that western patriarchal science is reductionist – that is, it reduces everything to its parts. It achieved dominance as a mode of thinking by: 'excluding other knowers and ways of knowing... in contrast to the organic metaphors, in which concepts of order and power were based on interconnectedness and reciprocity, the metaphor of nature as a machine was based on the assumption of separability and manipulability' (Shiva 1989: 22). Shiva contrasts this mode of thinking with the Indian cosmology that is holistic, creative, dynamic and integrated. The relational aspects of all parts of life and nature are understood. She contrasts the way women have traditionally managed food, water and forest resources in a sustainable manner, and how new approaches (e.g., the 'Green Revolution') have damaged the ecology and undermined women's traditional methods of nurturing their environment. One example she cites is the introduction of high yielding, short-stalked strains of irrigated sorghum in south Asia. These were grown alongside local drought-resistant sorghum varieties traditionally interspersed with other crops such as pulses and green leafy vegetables, including the highly nutritious *bathua* and a drought-resistant crop called *save*. The new high-yield varieties of sorghum needed large quantities of water and pesticides. The latter then destroyed the predators of a pest, the *midge*, which attacked the local sorghum, eventually wiping it out. This led to a severe reduction in sorghum straw, an important fodder crop for the livestock, leading to a reduction in the number of animals a family could keep. This in turn reduced the natural fertilizer available. Thus, in Shiva's view, the scientists and agricultural 'experts' who focused on increasing the output of one crop, sorghum, neglected to recognize that the traditional farming system was a complex and ecologically balanced one, with multiple produce that withstood drought conditions and provided good nutrition for growers' families. There was no miracle of high yields in the new system when the total production of the old one was taken into account. In fact, the new varieties left people far more vulnerable to crop failure in drought conditions (Shiva 1989: 122–31).

Wee and Heyzer (1995) recognize that some women have benefited from prevailing patterns of growth but their concern, like Shiva's, is the depletion of the natural resource base on which rural women in particular, but in the end all of us, depend. The issue of shrimp farming in Asia illustrates their point that a few companies can deplete global resources, enriching themselves and impoverishing others. Several Asian countries have provided favoured sites for aquaculture farms that produce tiger prawns and other marine produce for export, particularly to the USA, Europe and Japan. These are huge commercial ventures, quite different from traditional aquaculture that has been practised sustainably for generations. The new systems destroy wetlands and mangroves and displace traditional fisherfolk; they create huge amounts of waste and draw not only on seawater but on large quantities of ground water as well, depleting the water sources for local people. In India, scientists found that the new systems caused many

> serious social and ecological effects, including the spread of salt water over farms (causing a loss of agricultural lands and drinking water): loss of mangrove ecosystems; loss of landing grounds for traditional fishermen; increased health ailments of people living nearby due to pollution; increased unemployment due to displacement of livelihood in surrounding communities.   (Wee and Heyzer 1995: 114–15)

Wee and Heyzer argue that what is required is that the many realities experienced by different people need to be reflected in development decision-making. The current development paradigm, based as it is on a single world view that makes others' views invisible, has to be challenged by alternative realities. The empowerment of poor women, so that their reality can count as much as anyone else's, is critical to this transformation of development. They suggest that the efforts to make visible (and to place a value on) women's unpaid work, and the hidden free subsidies which the natural environment provides to development, is an important part of the process of making alternative realities visible.

In line with this, Marilyn Waring (1988) has developed a pithy critique of the United Nations System of National Accounts (UNSNA), the system used by all countries to establish their economic results. As she so clearly demonstrates, women's unpaid work and the 'free' contribution of nature is never valued, and hence not recognized in the national accounts of nations. This results from a series of gender-blind bureaucratic definitions of what is measured that exclude a huge amount of women's reproductive work. If such services were provided commercially – water and fuel purchased from utility companies, food bought in the market, meals purchased in a restaurant and childcare provided in a childcare centre – all this would be included in the national accounts. But when a woman provides it herself, she is deemed economically inactive! Despite detailed proposals about how women's work could be valued and counted for national statistics (Lewenhak 1992), no country has yet adopted such an approach, although some are developing 'satellite accounts' instead (UN 1995). Hoskyns and Rai believe that developing measures is urgent as women's ability to do this unpaid work 'is currently being affected across North and South by the globalisation of production, the move of women into paid work, the commercialisation of services and the changing functions of the state' (Hoskyns and Rai 2007: 297). They argue that it is essential to understand how this capacity is being depleted and the consequences it might have for development policy.

The most recent debates about gender and the environment now relate to the gender-specific impacts of climate change and how to respond to them. The 1992 United Nations Framework Convention on Climate Change (UNFCCC) makes no reference to gender and women have been scarce in decision-making around this issue. Yet climate change has the potential to exacerbate gender inequalities, and increase women's work burden in a number of ways. For example increasing extreme weather events will impact on women's agricultural activities, but their poor asset base and their difficulty in accessing credit may make climate change adaptation strategies difficult to implement; however there may be possibilities that climate change mitigation strategies, such as the introduction of bio-gas cookers, could benefit women (Demetriades and Esplen 2008; Oxfam and United Nations Vietnam 2009; Smyth 2009).

Postmodernism and difference

The postmodernist school of thought, which questions the 'grand theories' of the past and the idea that rational thinking and technological solutions will bring 'progress' to the world, reinforces Wee and Heyzer's view that what is needed to transform development is to open it up to different voices, different meaning systems and different realities.

Postmodernists draw attention to how the category 'woman' or 'man' is constructed, and how particular categories of women (poor women, third-world women, Asian women, Muslim women) are created, and by whom. Mohanty has been particularly critical of western feminists who have presented the 'third-world woman' as implicitly, if not explicitly, 'ignorant, poor, uneducated, tradition-bound, domestic, family-oriented, victimised, etc.', in contrast to western women 'as educated, as modern, as having control over their own bodies and sexualities, and the freedom to make their own decisions' (Mohanty 1997: 80). Such categorization has colonialist overtones and is firmly (and correctly) rejected by feminist writers from the developing world. The 'women in development' literature has unfortunately been the most prevalent source of such representation of women in the developing world.

Parpart's 'feminist postmodern critique' of much development discourse highlights the significance of 'difference' in gender debates. As she explains, the practical implications of this critique are to get planners to take seriously the realities of women's lives, especially to explore different women's views about what changes they want from development: 'this approach to development recognizes the connection between knowledge, language and power, and seeks to understand local knowledge(s), both as sites of resistance and power' (Parpart 1995: 264).

It is this perspective that demonstrates the importance of women being organized, documenting their own lives from their own perspectives as subjects, not objects, of research (validating their own knowledge), and having a key role in development decision-making. This is particularly important for minority women, indigenous women, women who are old, or who have disabilities, or who may be particularly marginalized in development planning.

However, the global political climate of recent years, with its emphasis on 'identity politics', is at the same time a troubling development for women's rights and women's voices. Attacks on women's rights have 'resulted from the resurgence of religious identities that include the assertion of "traditional" gender roles and systems of authority' (Molyneux and Razavi 2005: 1000). Some women align themselves with such movements in the face of powerful actors – national or foreign – as part of a backlash against globalization and 'modernity', consumerism and excessive libertarianism. Women may wear the hijab, for example, as a deliberate act, to assert identity or to shield themselves from men. Feminists, particularly those in the Muslim world, have promoted alternative interpretations of religious texts which support gender equity to counter this trend but the political environment is not always safe for debate and dialogue of this nature. Similarly, framing equality issues in terms of human rights is often too risky, as it is perceived as a western imposition. Development actors concerned to promote gender equity confront significant challenges in such contexts where power is held by fundamentalists of any religion, or where women and their identities become pawns in complex tribal, political and religious conflicts or global power plays (Hopkins and Patel 2006; Kandiyoti 2007, 2011; Shepherd 2006; Tadros 2011). Balchin (2010) however lays out many strategies that can be used to challenge any religious fundamentalisms that may oppress women, and both Kandiyoti and Marchand suggest ways to move beyond the binaries of religious/secular or western/other to unpack 'actors, interests and practices' (Kandiyoti 2011:13). Unpacking gender relations in Bangladesh, Ahmed suggests that many Muslim women draw on feminist Muslim spirituality to help them improve their lives (Ahmed 2008), thus more nuanced understandings of Islam are required if gender equity is to be achieved in Muslim settings. Marchand (2009) seeks to explore the concept of the 'Global South' (which embraces poverty in developed as well as developing countries) and 'in between' sites such as transnational migrant communities, to help rethink the sharp distinction between first and third worlds embedded in development discourse.

The focus on gender, combined with the whole focus on how categories and meanings are constructed which is now coming to the fore, has also led to some focus on men and 'masculinity' in development (Bannon and Correia 2006). An important issue to explore is how men contribute to reproducing inequalities in gender relations, and how they can help transform the situation (Greig et al. 2000). There are complex issues involved, as all men benefit from their gender privilege in relation to women, but recent work is suggesting that, as some men's traditional roles disappear or change following economic restructuring, they are left with very low self-esteem which manifests itself through their descent into alcoholism and increased violence and abuse towards women (Snyder and Tadesse 1997; Narayan et al. 2000; Silberschmidt 2001). Their definitions of 'masculinity' appear to be challenged by their new circumstances.

Other writers recognize that men themselves are caught within the dominant definitions of masculinity and argue that it is in many men's interests to promote different masculinities and challenge the dominant gender norms that constrain them (Ruxton 2004; Karkara et al. 2005; Esplen 2006). Ahmed (2008) suggests that Muslim men in Bangladesh, widely seen as opposed to women's empowerment, express different masculinities, some of which can be mobilized to support female empowerment. From a development perspective, it seems critical to engage with men, particularly young men, if gender inequalities are to be reduced. Issues such as HIV AIDS, reproductive health and violence against women cannot be resolved unless men are engaged and change their behaviours. Various strategies and programmes are now under way which encourage men to play positive roles in sexual relationships, fathering and family care, and preventing violence and conflict, with some clear lessons emerging. These generally indicate that successful approaches draw on men's sense of responsibility, their power to contribute to change for the better, and are built on positive behaviours rather than attributing blame (Ruxton 2004; Esplen 2006).

Overall, the lesson from postmodern thinkers is that rather than focusing on predefined categories such as male/female, ethnic or not, western/non-western or any other binary, we should focus on the processes which produce these identities and categories and understand the interplay for these identities in human lives. We should be asking who creates them, how they are used, and whose interests they advance.

Community development approaches

Since the 1990s, approaches to development have inclined to be more participative and inclusive than in the past but we have to ask what happens in gender terms when participative methodologies are used. It is not at all clear that gender equity will result from more community participation, particularly unless special measures are put in place to give voice to the views and wishes of women, especially women who may be more marginal in the community (Gujit and Shah 1998).

Community participation approaches can easily lead to a false consensus being derived from the views of those with power and influence in a community. Thus the views of the most significant problems and

the agricultural export sector lengthened. (Fontana et al. 1998). Jobs in the textile and apparel industries increased but women's proportion of those jobs reduced, and they are overwhelmingly represented in the low-skilled, low-paid positions. Men are three times more likely to be in technical or managerial positions. Many of the new jobs for women are in small enterprises where conditions are poor (Cardero 2000).

In South Africa trade liberalization favoured urban and male-headed households in relation to rural and female-headed households (Cockburn et al. 2007) while in three different African countries it widened the gender gap in wages (Cockburn et al. 2008). Across six countries – Ghana, Uganda, Sri Lanka, Pakistan, Bangladesh and Jamaica – Fontana et al. (1998) found that trade liberalization had different impacts for men and women in different contexts and these were related to factors such as 'gendered patterns of rights in resources, female labour force participation rates, education levels and gaps by gender and patterns of labour market discrimination and segregation, as well as socio-cultural environments' (Fontana et al. 1998: 2).

In many African countries, women have not generally benefited from increased agricultural export production, as they have limited land rights and their unpaid labour is used without them gaining control of the income. Worse, their labour may be diverted from subsistence crop production and the nutritional status of the household may suffer, or girls may be kept out of school to take up that work (Fontana et al. 1998: 48; Fontana 2009). They suggest that in countries where female participation in wage labour in export industries is high, emphasis should be on reducing labour market discrimination and promoting worker's rights, especially in the informal sector; and in countries where agriculture is the main focus of export activity, it is important to strengthen and enforce women's property rights in land (Fontana et al. 1998: 48).

To summarize, as these examples have illustrated, trade liberalization policies can have three effects on gendered poverty: 'changes in employment structures and wages; changes in prices and their impact on consumption patterns; and changes in financing for social expenditure' (ODI 2008: 2) as government income may reduce due to tariff reductions.

However, rather than trade expansion envisaged through trade liberalization, declining global trade due to the 2008 GFC is also having gender-differentiated effects; for example in Central Asia, the GFC led to reduced demand for textiles in importing countries. This export industry is dominated by women, so they have experienced increased job insecurity and reduced income, making them more vulnerable to gender discrimination in employment (Raaber 2010: 15).

Until the GFC, financial liberalization was a macroeconomic area with little understood gender effects. Prior to the GFC, Singh and Zammit (2000) studied the gender implications of rapid movements of capital, and the extent to which such movements plunge economies (such as Indonesia's in 1997) into crisis. They found that the effects are likely to be differentiated by gender, with women suffering more, particularly if the downturn is long and deep. Stotsky (2006) also drew attention to the gendered effects of exchange rate depreciations, which may differ according to whether women are largely engaged in subsistence agriculture (in which case it may push costs up and have negative effects) or in export industries which may benefit from new jobs. In 2011, the gender inequity implications of the GFC are still being analysed (Elson 2010; Jones et al. 2009), but early indications are that the impacts will vary significantly according to pre-existing gender inequities, gender segregation in the economy and each country's specific contexts and policies. Poor and marginalized women will be particularly affected, and the financial crisis will exacerbate the pre-existing food and fuel crises. Women's informal sector work and unpaid caring work is likely to expand. Sadly, with families under greater stress, violence against women and children is also likely to increase (King and Sweetman 2010; Raaber 2010). In response to this crisis, feminists are highlighting again the need for more women to be involved in macroeconomic decision-making (Seguino 2010). They are calling for a new approach to economics that recognizes the invisible 'care economy', and is based on human rights (Raaber 2010; Razavi 2009); they are promoting a 'social economy' designed to achieve an equitable distribution of wellbeing (Randriamaro 2010). In the short term, there are many policy prescriptions required to provide for greater economic security and gender equity (Seguino 2010), among them better social protection policies, and gender-sensitive stimulus packages (King and Sweetman 2010: 12). As Kabeer notes, most workers in developing countries are found in 'part-time, irregular and unstable forms of work with little or no social protection' (Kabeer 2008: 15) and women are most numerous and vulnerable among them; hence social protection policies are needed which are designed with full appreciation of these gender issues.

Gender and governance

Thus at the global level, the effects of global economic restructuring and crises over the past decade or two is threatening gains made through the system of human rights instruments, and 'soft law' agreements negotiated through the series of United Nations Conferences throughout the 1980s and 1990s aiming to achieve gender equity. The 1997 Convention for the Elimination of All Forms of Discrimination Against Women (CEDAW) and the 1995 Beijing Platform for Action are the key documents within this system. In contrast, the system of rules for trade and financial services that is increasingly brought under the oversight of the World Trade Organization has far more impact due to its tough penalty regime. This system operates without any serious consideration of gender equity concerns. Sadly, there is no connection between these two rules systems. This suggests a need for reform of global governance structures to bring these systems into alignment and ensure that trade and financial liberalization takes place within a framework whose goals are the achievement of human rights and gender equity, as well as environmental sustainability. Worse still, the UN's own MDG framework seriously neglects a number of aspects of the Beijing Platform for Action in relation to gender equality as a goal, indicating a lack of coherence even within the more gender-sensitive system.

However, to date, the interest in 'governance' has been largely focused at a national level and has been largely gender blind. Governance in development jargon generally refers to economic management, public sector reform, legal reform and civil society programmes. The examples above suggest that gender considerations rate very low in economic governance priorities at a global level. At the national level, the picture is equally biased. The economic governance agenda is clearly about the promotion at national level of the global economic orthodoxy already discussed (Taylor 2000).

One valuable economic governance initiative is the concept of gender-responsive budgeting (GRB). As Budlender remarks, the budget 'is in many respects the single most important policy or law passed by any government, determining the resources to be allocated to its policies and programmes' (Budlender 2001: 323). In South Africa, for example, a Women's Budget Initiative has had a remarkable impact. Unlike the original Australian exercise, in which the analysis was undertaken within the bureaucracy, this initiative was a collaboration of women's NGOs, women researchers and women parliamentarians. Its success in generating a debate about budget impact on women, boosting funding allocations in some key areas for women and inspiring other African countries to undertake a similar exercise has been important. Budlender feels, however, that the greatest effect is opening up budget discussion, formerly the preserve of white, male businessmen, to women of all races across South Africa and bringing gender issues, including the unpaid work of women, into economic debates in South Africa. Gender-responsive budgeting ideas are spreading rapidly, with diverse interpretations of the idea and variable results in countries as diverse as India and Timor-Leste; whilst not a panacea, GRB is one strategy to contribute to reducing women's poverty (Costa et al. 2009; Elson and Sharp 2010; Jhamb and Sinha 2010).

The second area of governance is the public sector reform agenda that has been associated with the economic restructuring taking place in many countries. Public sectors have been 'downsized' and privatized with little consideration for the gender effects, both in terms of women's employment and the provision of essential social and other services. The privatization of water is particularly contentious from a gender perspective, with evidence from a number of countries indicating negative impacts on women through high prices and reduced access, and low priority given to improving access to water in rural areas. Privatization has done little or nothing to address women's human rights to water (Brown 2010; Laurie 2011). A similar story of failure to improve the lives of the poorest women and contribute towards the MDGs is true of electricity privatization, at least in sub-Saharan Africa (Bayliss and McKinley 2007). And the lack of publicly-provided infrastructure and services in a range of areas increases women's unpaid work burden (Budlender 2008).

Legal reform, the third area, may include incorporation of the CEDAW's provisions into national law and reform of laws to eliminate gender discrimination through the statutes but Das Pradhan (2000) points out that there are many difficulties associated with attaining gender inclusion in legal development programmes and projects. However, this aspect of the 'governance' agenda is potentially a very useful one.

Fourth, civil society programmes may include support for women's organizations, an essential factor if gender equity is to be achieved; however, studies of civil society programmes to date have rarely focused on their gender aspects, so it is unclear how much these may have contributed to gender equity. Support to strengthen women's groups, especially those involved in promoting women's human rights and empowerment, could undoubtedly be enhanced.

However, the general principles of governance agenda – especially transparency, accountability, efficiency, equity and participation – *in theory* should provide a useful set of principles on which gender advocates can base their case. But to do so, they will clearly need to challenge orthodox assumptions about these concepts. At what level and for whom is efficiency to be judged, for example, when it seems to mean shifting care and responsibility from the public sector increasingly to

throughout an organization, but as Tiessen observes, rather than being everywhere, it ends up nowhere, because responsibility for ensuring that it is happening is too dispersed (Tiessen 2007). Tiessen argues that addressing gender in development agencies is not simply about gender inequality in developing countries – it requires attention to and changes in gender structure and organizational processes to overcome an inaccurately assumed 'gender neutrality' in development organizations themselves as well as overcoming the idea that attention to gender is additional to core development work, rather than central to it (Tiessen 2007). However, other writers caution about the expectations feminist advocates may have of bureaucracies as potential agents of social transformation as a result of poor theorizing about policy and its implementation, and the low status of women's agencies and units within them (Goetz and Sandler 2007; Mukhopadhyay 2007; Standing 2007). Some argue that trying to mainstream gender in the context of a violent and insecure world, with policy increasingly framed through a security lens, is contradictory, and that we need to deepen our understanding of women's responses to violent situations and masculinist hierarchies and foster human security (Leckie 2009).

New aid instruments such as Sector Wide Approaches (SWAPs) have also required innovative thinking by gender advocates, with mixed results. For example, Theobold et al. (2005) suggest that mainstreaming in the health sector presents major challenges as it remains poorly understood and is bedevilled by human capacity and resource constraints. Standing (2004, 2007) bemoans the weakness of a strategy that relies on bureaucratic transformation to achieve social transformation. Yet Rao and Kelleher (2005), like Tiessen (2007), argue that genuine institutional transformation is what is required. The 'deep structures' of organizations, the 'taken-for-granted values, and ways of thinking and working that underlie decision-making and action' have to change (Rao and Kelleher 2005: 64). These include the cultural and accountability systems in which gender bias is embedded. However, international experience indicates that reinvigorating gender advocacy as a political force is a necessary factor to generate institutional changes (True 2003).

The changing nature of aid, following the Paris Declaration on Aid Effectiveness, may also make mainstreaming more difficult to achieve, notwithstanding the release of the OECD Development Assistance Committee's new 'Guiding principles for aid effectiveness, gender equality and women's empowerment' (OECD DAC 2009). The overarching principles underlying the new aid arrangements include greater developing-country ownership of development and alignment of aid with national development strategies, greater harmonization of donor support and greater mutual accountability through managing for results. As UNIFEM (2006) comments, women will not benefit unless gender equality is seen as 'a key component of poverty reduction and national development' (UNIFEM 2006: 3).[2] At present, there is usually limited priority given to gender equality in development plans and budgets, donors may struggle to harmonize around gender as a priority and the proposed results to be measured usually neglect gender equity. Ironically, measures to enhance aid effectiveness may fail to do so where gender is concerned.

These recent developments also highlight the urgent need to bring gender considerations into macroeconomic institutions, policies and programmes. Feminist economists are making an important contribution at an academic level. Their impact at policy level has so far led to greater visibility of women's work in national accounts, promoting more gender-sensitive alternatives to orthodox adjustment policies for indebted countries (Beneria 1995). Serious efforts are now underway to develop a dialogue about how to 'engender macro-economic and international trade models' (Grown et al. 2000) and to undertake training that brings gender experts and macroeconomists together (Pearson 1995). However, most mainstream economists would not recognize or accept that gender equity should be a deliberate goal of economic policy. They usually argue that it will result from greater economic growth (World Bank 2001b) and achieving that is their primary objective. However, a survey of research on gender and macroeconomics (Stotsky 2006) draws attention to the fact that, while this is true, gender *inequalities* also *reduce* economic growth. She urges recognition that 'systematic differences in the behavior [sic] of men and women may lead to different macroeconomic outcomes...and different public choices with regard to the composition of expenditures' (Stotsky 2006: 48). Unless economic policies at all levels explicitly try to support gender equity, they may well undermine it, and the development policy goals embraced at Beijing will mean little in practice (Molyneux and Razavi 2005).

Finally, while development planners and economists pursue the development model which feminists like Wee and Heyzer, Shiva and the DAWN network roundly condemn as unsustainable and unjust, the question of the sustainability of the current development path refuses to go away. This is a critical question. How significant will it be to have gender equality on a development path that is utterly unsustainable? How can women and men concerned about the nature of development that we are pursuing work in a gender-equitable way to turn it around and make it sustainable for generations? If we seriously assess development to date, this is the fundamental challenge ahead – and it is a truly global challenge, for the developed nations as much as for developing ones, and for market actors as much as state and community sector ones.

Notes

1. There are eight countries in which the disparities in primary school enrolment favour girls.
2. UNIFEM was merged into a new agency 'UN Women' in 2010, bringing together a number of small agencies dealing with women's affairs within the UN.

Chapter 11

Environment and Development

Damien Kingsbury

It is a truism to say that without the environment there can be no development. Any capacity to develop, no matter how it is defined, must occur within its physical context and ultimate limitations; land to grow food on, water to drink and air to breathe. The global rush to achieve and expand material development has been predicated on the capacity of the physical environment to support it. In some cases the environment has been despoiled and in others it is simply running out of resources. Care for the environment and its use in a sustainable and affordable manner, for present and future generations, are critical issues in the development process.

The rise in importance of the environment in developing countries reflects a growing awareness of such issues in developed countries and, hence, among many bilateral and multilateral aid agencies and aid organizations. This has, in turn, been communicated to developing countries, although in many developing countries awareness of environmental issues has also come from direct experience with environmental problems. The growth of industrialization, often quickly and with few if any environmental safeguards, and populations swelling on the back of the 'green revolution', has had a real and substantial impact on many developing countries.

In particular, arguably the world's most important and potentially most devastating environmental problem – global warming – is a direct result of global industrialization's emission of carbon dioxide and other 'greenhouse' gases into the atmosphere (Stern 2007). As well as carbon dioxide, greenhouse gases include methane, nitrous oxide, hydrofluorocarbons, perfluorocarbons and sulphur hexafluoride that also contribute directly to both building a cloud of gases which trap heat, thus increasing global temperatures with a wide range of negative consequences, including destroying the atmosphere's ozone layer, which increases penetration of biologically harmful ultraviolet rays. As the 'Stern Report' notes, the economic impact of global warming alone could shrink the global economy by up to 20 per cent if not acted upon;

such action would cost around 1 per cent of global GDP per year (Stern 2007: ch. 2).

In this, all industrialized and industrializing countries are responsible for greenhouse gas emission and this includes all developed countries as well as many developing countries. This indicates two related points; that environmental degradation does not recognize borders and is ultimately a global problem affecting all peoples, if in some cases disproportionately; and that all countries have a responsibility to actively reduce or eradicate environmentally unsustainable practices. The signing of the Kyoto Protocols by all countries except the United States and Australia was recognition of both this impact and their responsibility to address the problem (even if developing countries are largely exempted from the provisions of the protocols).

Set against such recognition, it is little surprise that, to date, the development process' environmental record has been poor. Environmental degradation has continued at a pace that has had a major impact on the capacity of some societies to continue to function (e.g., South Korea, see Cho 1999), while building a global problem that may not be reversible. Similarly in China, its coal-fuelled rapid industrialization has led to among the world's worst air pollution along most of the eastern coast, while substantially contributing to the wider global problem. Although most developing countries have not yet reached such a devastating level of industrial development, the industrialization process in the vast majority were also showing serious signs of failing to implement environmental safeguards, the rationale being that as developing countries they could not 'afford' such safeguards. This environmental failure did not to begin to include over-logging and deforestation, land degradation and desertification, and run-off from herbicides, insecticides and human waste pollution that not only reduces supplies of potable water but also damages the wider environment.

Part of the reason for continued unsustainable ecological practices derives from there being little or no consensus about the range of meanings of sustainability or the terminology that is used to denote it. Moreover, since the release of the Brundtland Report in 1987, there has continued to be debate about what does or does not constitute sustainable practice and the range of or limitation on options about addressing environmental challenges.

In particular, there are extensive debates about whether there is a need for continued economic growth and over the lead-times for introducing adequate and sustainable energy sources. This is set against further debates about population growth and what constitutes a sustainable population, how to best manage the environment not just

for the present generations but for future generations, possible technological options for supporting population growth (or not, as the case
may be), patterns of consumption and the culture of consumerism. One
part of the debate around 'sustainable development' even suggests that
the term is internally contradictory (e.g. see Ferry 2009), in that development by its nature consumes finite resources. Brundtland's classical
definition of sustainable development meeting 'the needs of the present
without compromising the ability of future generations to meet their
own needs' (1987) is a case in point; it does not appear to be possible to
meet present and future needs on the basis of existing and projected
populations. Brundtland's own, more complete, definition was more
sophisticated than this simple rebuttal might imply, and she acknowledged the range of competing and contradictory forces at play in the
development process. There have also been criticisms of sustainable
development on the basis of unknown or unintended consequences, particularly economic consequences.

Within the global environmental debate, there are increasingly questions about how long current development processes can continue
before ecological systems collapse as, in some cases, they have already
done. Within the global warming debate, there is now widespread
global acceptance, as indicated by the signing of the Kyoto Protocols,
on the need to curb the emission of carbon dioxide and other greenhouse gases. There is also related concern about the effects of industrialization on global ecological systems. Environmental damage may
occur in one country and be a consequence of that country's policies but
environmental degradation, such as acid rain, does not respect arbitrary
state divisions. Damage in one country can easily impact upon another
country, or many countries, and widespread environmental collapse is
no longer a matter of if, but when and where, should there not be a fundamental shift in development thinking, planning and implementation.

Global warming

Although recognized in some sectors as a major climatic issue for many
years, the issue of global warming has only recently been taken seriously
as the world's biggest environmental problem. This is now accepted as
scientific fact by the scientific societies and academies of science in all
industrialized countries. In 2010 alone, of 74 countries measured, 21
recorded their highest ever temperatures, with a further 15 countries
recording their highest temperature in the previous ten years.[1] Even the
American Association of Petroleum Geologists, which has a vested inter-

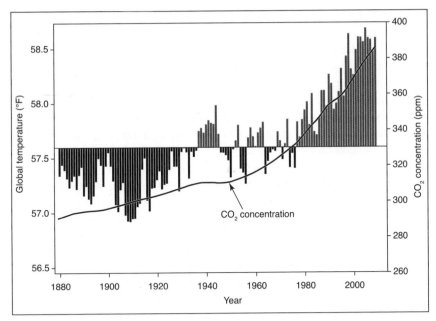

Source: National Climatic Data Center, US Department of Commerce.

Figure 11.1 *Global temperature and carbon dioxide presence*

est in continuing fossil fuel production, has modified its position from rejecting the science to being non-committal. According to the Stern Report, commissioned by the British government, global temperatures have already risen, if by a small margin, over the previous century, but are likely to rise between 2°C and 3°C, and with an even chance of rising by up to five degrees, over the next 50 years (Stern 2007; see also Hansen et al. 2006). The Intergovernmental Panel on Climate Change (IPCC) has predicted a slightly smaller rise in global temperatures, of 1.1 to 6.4°C, depending on greenhouse gas emission and climate sensitivity, between the start of the twentieth and end of the twenty-first centuries. As noted by the Labor Environment Action Network, total global carbon dioxide emissions increased by 70 per cent between 1970 and 2004 and continued to rise at an increasing rate. The annual increase of total global carbon dioxide emissions jumped from an average 1.1 per cent over 1990–99 to more than 3 per cent between 2000 and 2004. This growth rate of emissions since 2000 has exceeded even the most pessimistic projections of the IPCC (LEAN 2011).

In short, global warming has already begun fundamentally to shift the balance of the planet's water, from reduced polar ice caps and lost permafrost to flooding of low-lying lands. This is expected to affect some 200 million people, to lead to increases in tropical areas as well as turning once fertile lands into arid areas, thus decreasing food production, to alter the habitat and survivability of up to 40 per cent of the earth's species and to generate unexpected and increasingly volatile weather 'events', including both extended drought and flood. As with other negative impacts, those people already living closest to absolute poverty and with little or no capacity to absorb such impact will be most affected by such change.

> The effect that increased droughts, extreme weather events, tropical storms and sea level rises will have on large parts of Africa, on many small island states and coastal zones will be inflicted in our lifetimes. In terms of aggregate world GDP, these short term effects may not be large. But for some of the world's poorest people, the consequences could be apocalyptic. In the long run climate change is a massive threat to human development and in some places it is already undermining the international community's efforts to reduce extreme poverty.　(UNDP 2008: 3)

The main approaches to limiting further climate change include greater restrictions on the production of carbon dioxide waste and tradable carbon emissions; the creation of a global carbon market, in which the production of carbon is taxed; further development and expansion of non-carbon sources of energy (such as solar and wind power); the preservation and expansion of 'carbon-sinks' – large forests such as those found in Brazil and Borneo and the creation of new forests; and a reduction of overall consumption. However, there remains considerable debate about how to resolve the global warming problem. Developing countries, such as China and India, have been exempted from the Kyoto Protocols, which has enhanced their industrial capacity in contrast to industrial countries that have committed to limiting greenhouse gas emissions. This has led the US to refuse to ratify the protocols on the grounds that it would unfairly limit its own economies (Australia also refused to ratify the protocols until 2007).

Population reduction

In terms of reducing overall consumption and assuming that people will not volunteer to significantly alter their consumption behaviour, one of the critical and most controversial issues in environmental development revolves around the capacity of the earth to sustain existing numbers of people. There are those who believe that the earth has greater capacity to sustain people than currently exists (Simon 1994) and those who believe that the earth is already being taxed beyond up to or beyond its capacity (e.g., UNEP 1999; Varfolomeyev and Gurevich 2001).

Even where the earth has shown that it has a high carrying capacity, this is usually enhanced by the use of fertilizers, pesticides and high-energy transport, all of which add a cost that is not often factored into economic assessments (see Milbrath 1996: ch. 10). That is, the full cost of industrialization or other forms of production and energy consumption rarely accounts for 'off-book' expenses such as to the environment. For example, the use of agricultural pesticides can and often does enhance productivity but it also has implications for water quality (UNCSD 2002b), while transport and manufacturing costs rarely incorporate costs to the atmosphere. In this respect, the full cost of economic growth is usually greater than the simple single bottom-line formula used by most accountants in that it also uses 'public good' (clean air, water, habitat, other amenity) that is not properly, or often at all, costed. In particular, there is conflict over the notion of 'public' or shared resources, especially where this 'free' resource (e.g., water, air) is used excessively or unwisely and impacts on 'non-market' activities (Portney 1982: 4). In this sense, private markets may allocate resources inefficiently and the 'externalities' generated by private development may impact on a wider 'public good' (Portney 1982: 6). In one sense, the over-exploitation of some resources by some parts of the earth's population, or 'resource capture', produces a structural imbalance in access to resources (Homer-Dixon 1999: 15–19) and potential for conflict.

There are significant parts of the world that have a very limited carrying capacity and are vulnerable to degradation due to over-exploitation. These marginal areas, such as Africa's Sahel, are growing in size and their capacity to support life is reducing. And apart from the consumption of non-renewable resources, it would appear that at some point there must, logically, be a limit to the carrying capacity of the earth, regardless of how sensitively and wisely it is used.

There have been, as Homer-Dixon has noted (1999: 53) distinct physical trends in global change, and while these have occurred over varying timescales and in different locations, their effects have become increasingly global and interrelated. Homer-Dixon noted an interconnectivity between, for example, human population growth, rising energy consumption, global warming, ozone depletion, rising cropland scarcity, tropical deforestation, rising scarcity of free water, declining fish stocks and a more general loss of biodiversity.

In particular, the sheer increase in the global population, the consumption of natural resources implied by such growth and the human and industrial pollution that has been produced, is perhaps the single most important issue. Of the world's 7 billion people at 2011, more than 5 billion live in developing countries and about 3 billion live in rural areas and depend largely on agriculture for their income or subsistence. Korten notes that while the world's poor only add marginally to environmental degradation, if they were to achieve higher levels of development the already unsustainable consumption of natural resources would quickly move into the critical zone. Yet, the alternative is to condemn the poor to underdevelopment in perpetuity (Korten 1989: 166). And there is also a view that suggests poverty actually increases environmental degradation through more desperate use of resources, such as forest depletion for fuel wood. The only way to raise global standards of living to a higher, more equitable level is to reduce global consumption, most readily through reducing the global population.

Assuming no change in behaviour, away from a global tendency increasingly to consume natural resources, or the adoption of less resource-reliant technologies, it would appear there needs to be a considerable reduction in the world's population in order to accommodate limited natural productive capacity and to find alternative and more sustainable finite natural resources. However, the only signs of absolute population reduction, apart from natural or human calamities, has been amongst the most developed societies (although many countries have reduced the rate at which they are increasing their population). This implies that global society will have to develop significantly further before there is any in-built tendency towards population reduction and, frankly, all indicators are that there is not time for this 'natural' process to take place before environmental catastrophe. The argument that suggests there are limits to the earth's capacity to sustain an increasing population is sometimes referred to as Malthusianism, or neo-Malthusianism, a later version of which posited that as resources are finite, and larger families in any case contributed to poverty, birth control and subsequent population reduction were necessary conditions for sustainable development.

The world's total population was about 1.65 billion in 1900; by 2011 it had grown to 7 billion, representing a more than fourfold increase. The annual growth rate, while slowing since the late 1960s to just over 1 per cent in the early twenty-first century, had peaked at 88 million a year in 1989, reduced to around 74 million a year by 2003, went up to 75 million in 2006 but was expected to continue to decline to around

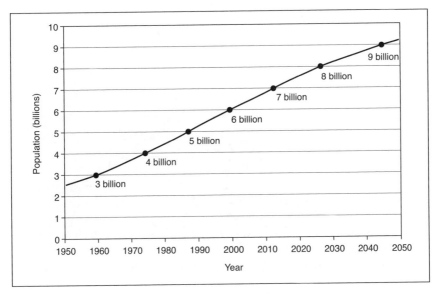

Source: USCB, *International Data Base*, December 2010 Update.

Figure 11.2 *World population, 1950–2050*

40 million over the coming four decades, to reach just over 9 billion people (USCB 2011).

Added to this has been a massive shift in consumption patterns over the 100 years, currently doubling each 30 years, notably in industrialized countries but also in developing countries. The massive increase in hydrocarbon (oil and gas) consumption and its consequences for the environment (e.g. greenhouse effect, enhancing desertification), is one illustration of the shift in consumption. 'Peak oil', in which the maximum rate of oil extraction is reached, was expected to occur around 2010–12. This meant that while current oil reserves would last until around 2040, accessing such oil would become increasingly difficult and hence more expensive, especially against increasing levels of consumption, thus pushing up the price of oil and oil-based products such as petrol (gasoline).

One short-term consequence of this 'peak oil' phenomenon was that oil companies were increasingly pushing to explore for oil in wilderness heritage sights, such as the Arctic region. Another was that they were attempting to cut exploration and production costs, leading to short cuts that resulted in environmentally damaging spills, for example in Nigeria, the Amazon basin and the Gulf of Mexico. Another, more pos-

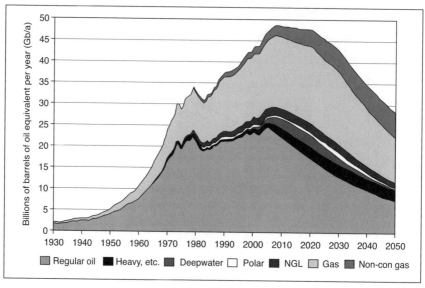

Source: www.aspo-ireland.org.

Figure 11.3 *Global oil and gas production profiles*

itive, consequence was that, slowly, a number of oil-dependent companies were exploring alternative energy sources, if often in hybrid forms
with oil-based energy. Similar to the global consumption of oil, the
world's increasing demand for timber and timber products, including
paper, which is leading to increased deforestation as well as forest
reduction more quickly than forests can regenerate (Tscharnthe et al.
2010; Dangwal 2005).

The main criticism of neo-Malthusianism derives from governments
and policy-makers who claim that large populations sustain markets
that are necessary to increased growth, and are also capable of caring
for increasingly larger older populations, which are especially noticeable
as a consequence of fertility 'booms' such as those following the Second
World War and the 'Green Revolution'. Some governments also continue to argue that a large population is necessary for defence purposes,
although the linkage between the two rather more reflects a pre-modern
view of strategic advantage. And apart from cultural traditions, in
which larger families are regarded as a safeguard against abandonment
in old age, some religions (such as Roman Catholicism) actively encourage propagation to increase the numbers of their followers. The ration-
alization of this position is that the earth is intended for the

consumption of humanity, and that it has the capacity to sustain a much greater overall consumption. Many policy-makers (including the Catholic Church) also argue that the earth's problems less reflect overall consumption and more reflect the unequal distribution of consumption (see Homer-Dixon 1999: 35–7).

Having noted this, by the 1960s the governments of some of the more heavily populated countries decided that their population 'bomb' was already ticking and took steps to limit population growth (see Ehrlich 1969, for one of the first, most critical, though somewhat alarmist discussions on the subject). The 1960s were critical in this respect, as not only had a number of countries recognized that there was about to be a major problem with excessive population but at the same time fertility rates were growing, to peak at 2.1 per cent a year between 1965 and 1970 (Homer-Dixon 1999: 13). Nowhere was population growing more quickly than in Asia, with Korten notes that population growth in developing countries was at an average of 2.5 per cent (Korten 1989: 11).

As a consequence, in Asia, by 1966, 12 of 22 states had taken measures to curb fertility (Ness and Ando 1984: 18). The world's first, second and fourth most populous countries, China, India and Indonesia, are three prominent examples of countries that have active population control policies and, while the heavy-handedness of these policies in India and particularly in China have given ammunition to the 'pro-fertility' lobby, they have served as recognition that population growth has costs as well as benefits. However, the success or otherwise of these programmes was less the issue than a recognition of the basic problem. And not all countries with large populations, high population densities, or limited environmental capacities support the idea of limiting their populations. Ness and Ando noted that contrasting with the Asian experience, only four of 26 Latin American countries, three of 40 African states and three of 18 Mediterranean states had adopted fertility control measures (1984: 19). This reflected the Asian lead in the fertility control field that was itself predicated on a public recognition that median and mean populations densities were generally higher in Asian countries, and tended to be higher in other countries that also adopted fertility control programmes (Ness and Ando 1984: 22–3). The success of those programmes further reflected the actual strength of implementation of the programme (Ness and Ando 1984: 132–9). Not surprisingly, the timing of the move towards controlling fertility rates corresponded with more localized policy planning as a result of independence, rapidly increasing populations as a consequence of the 'Green Revolution', and access to new and more widely available methods of contraception.

Deforestation

The impact of population spread and consumption is perhaps most visible in terms of loss of forests and associated desertification and is equally the world's most significant environmental problem. Such deforestation has a number of implications, including soil erosion, land degradation (in particular degradation of arable farmland) and desertification, loss of habitat for various animal species and reduction in other biodiversity, the absorption of carbon dioxide (with a resulting increase in global warming) and a reduction in the production of oxygen, upon which all animal (and human) life depends (FAO 2001). Estimates vary but, at the current rate of deforestation, some of the world's major forests, such as those in Indonesia/Borneo, Papua New Guinea and the Amazon Basin, will be completely eradicated within 30 years, and possibly sooner. Chile, with approximately one-third of the world's temperate rainforest, at current rates of logging, could be completely deforested by 2022. Holy Shit

Brazil contains the world's single largest forest, in the Amazon Basin, but existing logging, which has been driven by the timber industry and new settlements and farmland, has depleted the forest at an unsustainable rate. Between 1978 and 1996, some 52 million hectares, or 12.5 per cent of the total forest, was cleared, representing a loss of around 2.9 million hectares a year. Logging, continuing at the rate of 13,000 hectares a day, or 4.75 million hectares a year, received renewed impetus at the beginning of the twenty-first century as Brazil struggled to meet external loan repayments. The president of the Amazon Working Group (representing some 350 regional NGOs), Claudionor Barbosa da Silva, said that 90 per cent of funding to Amazon conservation programmes had been cut to meet IMF loan schedules, along with two-thirds of rainforest protection capacity and demarcation of lands belonging to indigenous peoples. Austerity measures resulting from the IMF programme encouraged illegal logging of the forest (Knight and Aslam 2000). Other countries looking to address critical economic problems through increased excessive logging of old-growth forests included Russia and Indonesia, which, along with Brazil, were home to just under half of the world's old-growth rainforests.

While environmental policies in Indonesia were always very poor, the decentralization of government following the end of the New Order in 1998 further impacted on the environment, in particular exacerbating the loss of Indonesia's tropical rainforests. Already very poor, local environmental protection has slid further, due to less central control over logging, short-term local government economic priorities and the decentralization of corruption. The annual deforestation rate between 1985 and 1997 was estimated to be 1.7 million hectares (Resosudarno 2002). Since 1998, that level has increased significantly. A 2007 UN report estimated that illegal logging in Kalimantan accounted for three-quarters of all logging in Indonesia, which made the single largest contribution to Indonesia becoming the third largest greenhouse gas emitter in the world. At recent rates of deforestation, Indonesia may lose 98 per cent of all its forests by 2020 (UNCTSD 2007).

In other areas in Kalimantan and in northern Sumatra, in the face of a larger economic collapse, illegal logging has increased dramatically, although local governments have turned less than a blind eye towards it, by taxing the logs that are illegally taken to continue to raise revenue: 'In the months of April, May and June 2000 alone, the district [of Kotawaringin] raised 24 billion rupiah by taxing illegal timber coming out of [East] Kotawaringin...This initiative is effectively "legalizing" illegal timber' (Resosudarno 2002: 8). And as Resosudarno notes, much illegal logging has taken place in protected and conservation areas (2002: 9–10). This type of experience is common in many developing countries, where forests have been seen as a resource with almost unlimited exploitable potential.

In some areas, it can be simple government policy that leads to excessive logging. In Burma, between 40 and 50 per cent of the state remained under forest cover by 1995. Between 1990 and 2005, the country lost 18 per cent of its forests (Htaw 2008). However, Burma's military government remains desperate for hard currency to finance its military following the long-term collapse of its economy. The international community has condemned its opium/heroin trade so it has increasingly turned to logging. At the same time, anti-government guerrilla groups have also engaged in logging to support their campaigns while allowing corrupt Thai generals and Chinese and Thai businessmen also illegally to log or buy logs from across the border (KNG 2011). Where once forests covered around 55 per cent of Thailand, they now cover around 5 per cent, with half of that remaining being held in reserves. Thailand, once a wood exporter, now imports timber and paper (similarly to Nigeria). In this, Thailand has been effectively logged out and further logging is now banned there (Gallasch 2001: 8–9, 11, see also Bryant in Hirsch and Warren 1998). Similarly, logging is also banned in Yunnan Province. China theoretically banned the import of timber in 2005. However, an extensive black market operated by the Kachin Independence Organisation with the blessing of the Burmese government continues to ship illegal logs across the border (KNG 2011).

Interestingly, while developed countries have called on developing countries to preserve their forests, in particular rainforests, some leaders of developing countries have pointed out that such calls are somewhat hypocritical, given that most developed countries almost completely depleted their own stands of forests in the process of industrialization. More positively, on World Environment Day in 2007 the recently elected governor of the heavily forested Indonesian province of Aceh, Irwandi Yusuf, banned logging entirely.[2] At the tip of Sumatra, Aceh contained considerable first growth triple canopy rainforests and was home to wild elephants and Sumatra's remaining tigers. Despite some shortcomings with the logging ban, including continued illegal logging, the move was short listed for a Future Policy Award by the Hamburg-based World Future Council.

Desertification

Drought and desertification, resulting from global climate change and direct human activity, threaten the livelihoods of more than 1.2 billion people across 110 countries. Around 2 billion people live in 'drylands', which occupy around 40 per cent of the earth's land surface, while 90 per cent of people who live in drylands are from developing countries. Of the earth's dry lands, up to 20 per cent is already degraded and desertification shows no signs of abatement (Holtz 2007). Drought is a generally natural variation towards lower rainfall in what are already low rainfall areas. However, rainfall patterns can also be affected by changed global weather patterns (such as the 'El Niño' effect), global warming due to the emission of 'greenhouse' gases and the removing of forests and other ground cover.

Desertification, or the degradation of drylands, involves the loss of biological or economic productivity and complexity in croplands, pastures and woodlands. Desertification occurs mainly as a consequence of climate variability and unsustainable human activities, with the most commonly cited forms of unsustainable land use being over-cultivation, over-grazing, deforestation and poor irrigation practices. Of the world's drylands (excluding hyper-arid deserts), 70 per cent, or some 3,600 million hectares, is degraded. Excessive use of lands generally and drylands in particular is allowed by unregulated access which is usually driven by economic necessity, or desperation. In many cases, even where people know their practices are not sustainable, they are looking to survive to next week, rather than next year. The future of the environment can, in such circumstances, start to look like a luxury many people cannot

access to potable water in the last two decades of the twentieth century, by 2011 just under a billion people still did not have access to safe drinking water. People must have potable water in order to survive. But what is less appreciated is that the often poor quality of available water continues to be the single biggest contributing factor to general illness, notably through nutritional and fluid loss (primarily through diarrhoea), a situation which is reflected in infant mortality rates (Fordham 2002). That is, lack of access to potable water not only directly impacts upon the health of people who have no choice but to drink unsuitable water but this, in turn, limits their capacity to work and consequently has a direct economic impact on their capacity for development (see Whittington and Swarna 1994; also Latham 2000; and Strauss, especially p. 168, in Pinstrup-Andersen 1993 for discussion on nutrition and development).

The combination of industrial waste, increased use of herbicides, insecticides, growth promoters, deforestation and human population growth have all impacted negatively on the world's supply of potable water. As Baur and Rudolph (2001) have noted, the simple question of whether there is enough fresh water for each person is already a critical issue. Around 3,800 cubic km of fresh water is now withdrawn annually from the world's lakes, rivers and aquifers, about twice the amount extracted in the mid-twentieth century. Agriculture uses around two-thirds of available water, industry uses almost one-fifth, and municipal and domestic use accounts for slightly less than 10 per cent. The world's population of almost 7 billion people is expected to reach close to 10 billion before it stabilizes or falls. Each person requires up to 50 litres of water a day for drinking, food preparation, sanitation and bathing (with around 20 litres considered a practical minimum). Yet at the turn of the century, more than a billion people did not have access to potable water (Kothari 2002) – despite previous improvements, a situation unimproved five years later – or had access to less than the required amount (Baur and Rudolph 2001). By 2011, this situation had improved, but not by much. Not surprisingly, access to water is not evenly distributed, with a number of countries occupying what are considered 'water stressed' (semi-arid and arid) zones. One-third of these countries are expected to face severe water shortages this century. By 2025, there will be approximately 3.5 billion people living in water-stressed countries, a situation that appears to be exacerbated by global warming. In simple terms, there are more people than there is available water, especially in less supportive environments. Where the environment has a greater capacity to support higher populations, those populations are placing such stresses on water supplies that its supportive capacity is diminishing.

The imbalance in water supply has been most notable in the increasing swings between drought and floods. Flooding in Jakarta in February 2007 not only led to more than 30 deaths, it also led to a widespread range of infections caused by industrial and human pollution of the city's canals being mixed with water that swamped large sections of the city. Other problems with water pollution, primarily of rivers but also of paddies, affects much of Indonesia (see Lucas in Hirsch and Warren 1998). And in many rural areas where there remains no access to running water, water drawn from wells or ground pumps is increasingly affected by chemical and human pollution seeping into the water table. Australia, East Timor and parts of eastern Indonesia, by contrast, underwent more than 10 years of drought from the mid-1990s but faced extensive flooding in 2010–11.

Loss of potable water, due to inadequate or failing waterways is a significant factor in the development profile of a number of cities in developing countries. In Pakistan, almost a half of the country's 135 million people (44 per cent) and up to 90 per cent in rural areas do not have access to drinkable water, primarily due to industrial waste and agricultural run-off (Rosemann 2005: 3; Yes Pakistan 2002). Infrastructure projects, often funded by multilateral lending agencies such as the Asian Development Bank, are being undertaken in places like Karachi and Manila, to reduce this unnecessary loss of drinking water. However, the extent of the problem, the rate at which it continues to grow worse, and the cost involved in fixing it, as well as ensuring the reliable supply of potable water to urban systems, means that the larger problem is expanding faster than it can be addressed.

While many developing countries do have restrictions on pollution, these restrictions are very commonly observed in the breech. And in any case, governments of developing countries are more inclined to go softly on such industry, as they cite economic inability to provide alternative means of waste disposal while pointing out the contribution of industrial development and enhanced food production to self-sufficiency, employment and economic development.

One suggested answer to declining water stocks is the privatization of water. That is, water should cease to be (in principle) a generally freely available resource and should become a commodity like any other. The case for privatizing water is that it will reduce wastage while encouraging private companies to secure greater potable water supplies for further sale (Segerfeldt 2005). While most countries do charge for water access, they do so through the provision of water as a government service as a broad social responsibility. The World Bank has estimated that the world water market was worth almost 1 trillion dollars at the beginning of the twenty-first century, although that only accounted for the approximately 5 per cent of the world's water consumers who obtained water through corporations. Two of the world's major private water suppliers, Suez Lyonnaise des Eaux (SLE) and Vivendi SA, own or control water companies in 120 countries, with each distributing water to more than 110 million people (Ondeo 2002; Vivendi 2002). However, the privatization of water assumes two points. The first point assumed is a capacity to pay, although it is likely that when there is no choice people will, if they can, pay for water as a primary necessity. However, many of the world's most poor would be unlikely to be able to pay for privatized water while there are questions about the benefit to those who can do so. The second point is that everything can be commodified and that what has for most people traditionally been an assumed public right, somewhat like breathing air, can or should be regarded as the preserve of private interest. Regardless of private business's poor record on environmental issues, there are deep philosophical questions attached to the idea that what was once a common public good is available for private ownership. However, in principle, such questions go to the core of the nexus between humankind and the environment, and how human affairs are organized in ways that are equitable or otherwise, and which are sustainable or otherwise.

Political economy of the environment

Although it is sometimes posited in these terms, environmental degradation is not just a consequence of people mindlessly destroying the world they live in. For many people, notably the most poor in developing countries, drawing down on environmental resources is a matter of survival. Logging to clear land can occur because of population pressure or displacement, the need to earn cash income or the provision of fuel wood for cooking. Washing clothing and bathing in streams is a common practice in developing countries but adds detergent and soap to waterways that not only deplete fish stocks and other species but which also reduce their use for drinking water. Yet there appear to be few alternatives to people without access to other sources of water. Similarly, even where people construct toilet facilities away from waterways (and they are often close), seepage through ground water can and does lead to a high level of bacteria in streams and wells, with negative consequences for the health of people who use such sources. In some cases, environmental degradation is a consequence of a lower level of awareness or lack of education. But in most cases, poor people engage in such practices not through choice but through sheer necessity. For other communities, unsustainable resource exploitation is a consequence of living in marginal environments, or environments that are unable to comfortably sustain growing populations. However, many people who had previously come from subsistence societies have increasingly been encouraged to participate in monoculture cash cropping. With world commodity prices falling between the 1970s and the early 2000s (non-energy commodity prices falling by about half between 1980 and 2000 (GCM 2000), increased prices and food scarcity after 2006 and increasing tariff barriers to value-added food products, cash cropping required more exploitation of a given area to produce the same income (or what is most often in reality less real income) or, more recently, to make up for higher priced foodstuffs.

In most developing countries, the quickest and most lucrative wealth is to be made by selling off resources, usually without value-adding (e.g., saw-minerals, raw logs, wood-chips), or by cutting costs such as those expended on environmental safeguards (e.g., dumping pollutants into waterways). While local exploiters often operate for personal profit at the expense of their fellows and the environment, the wider relationship between the local and the global comes into play in determining which resources are in demand, how much is to be paid for them, what alternatives a local economy might have for income generation and, arguably, the direction in which local economies can operate. The price of commodities alone can determine environmental impact, not through steering providers away from lower-priced commodities but through increasing production to make up for shortfalls in prices or to undercut competition. That is, if a product, say saw-logs, is reduced in price by half, at least twice as many logs (due to higher marginal costs) will need to be produced to return equivalent levels of income. The reduction in the price of saw-logs can be a consequence of simple reduced demand but at least as likely it will be a consequence of major buyers pitting primary commodity producers against each other to bargain down prices. Where prices for particular commodities fall to levels that become socially or environmentally unsustainable, the option is often to increase production to produce more profit, rather than to seek alternatives.

Beyond the rapaciousness of international carpetbaggers and their proxy comprador elites, there is some awareness of the problems caused by the iniquity of global allocation of resources. In a world that continues to be dominated by a version of *Realpolitik*, state leaders are only answerable to their constituents, amongst whom are international businesses. They are not answerable to the citizens of other countries, nor is there any agreed global regulatory system that apportions wealth on the basis of effort or need (see Morgenthau 1978). As a consequence, if the benefits to their own citizens are at the expense of another's citizens then, in simple terms, it is the citizens of the other state that are disadvantaged. The primary consequence of this is that states that have less advantage in international relations tend to be exploited, or at best not have their interests considered, in the arranging of international trade, with the consequence that if they are not further impoverished in absolute terms then they are at least allowed access to fewer opportunities to relative development. This, then, relates to the earlier mentioned desperation that many people in developing countries find themselves facing, meaning they are often forced into environmentally unsustainable practices to survive, or that pressures to retain 'comparative advantage' comes to include a disregard for the environment or environmental regulations.

One response to this state of affairs, primarily from more developed countries, is that developing countries must implement a range of practices to ensure that they escape from the trap of economic underdevelopment and desperation. However, the policies that are recommended to implement are, at best, often environmentally damaging and, at worst, only replicate the cycle of poverty that led to them in the first place (see GE 2002). In reality, those countries that control large proportions of the world's economy have the capacity to direct global pricing by driving up or down world prices for key commodities, and resource management, through demand. Where, in rare circumstances, a country does manage to escape from this structural imbalance in capacity to determine prices and hence opportunity for development, it can find itself on the receiving end of anti-competitive tariffs, an economic embargo or blockade, or direct intervention. As a consequence, in a bid to engage in the global economy and seek the benefits that it can offer, many impoverished countries continue to be structurally obliged to engage in environmentally unsustainable economic practices.

Alternatives

Recognition of environmental problems stemming from and hindering development had become, by the beginning of the twenty-first century, a fundamentally uncontested issue. There continues to be debate about the extent of environmental degradation, the capacity of natural resources and the possibility of technological 'fixes'. But there is little argument that the global climate is changing, that forests – and their capacity to produce oxygen – are disappearing at a rate that is unsustainable, that deserts are growing rather than shrinking, and that, despite exceptions, air, water and land pollution continue to constitute major and unsustainable problems. There is also debate about the contribution of absolute population size to environmental degradation, the imbalance in resource distribution, the symbiotic relationship between scarcity and conflict and the necessity of moving towards environmental sustainability.

Environmentally related conflict is identified by Dabelko (1996) as falling into two broad resource categories; renewable and non-renewable. Dabelko regards conflict over non-renewable resources as being more conventional conflict, focused on economic benefit. Examples of such conflict include Iraq's invasion of Kuwait, the subsequent US-led attack on Iraq and 2003 invasion (oil), Morocco's conflict with the Polisario Front (phosphate), South Africa's occupation of Namibia and conflict in Angola (diamonds), the Khmer Rouge's occupation of western Cambodia (gems, timber), Burma's conflict with separatists (gems, timber, opium), Nigeria (oil), Russia and Chechnya (oil), Indonesia and West Papua (oil, liquid natural gas, copper, gold), and many others.

Conflicts related to renewable resources, and more from particular resource scarcity, tend to operate from a less naked desire for economic control. Conflicts may arise is relation to losses of renewable resources in one area and availability in another, or through over-population relative to available resources. But one less clear source of renewable resource conflict is relative to population growth, in which there is chronic poverty, or in which there is a pointed lack of consensus about the legitimacy of common political organization via the distribution of resources within it (especially if that is understood as related to ethnic identity). In such cases, resultant institutional weakness can lead to a breakdown in authority and civil conflict. This relates to Homer-Dixon's proposition that environmental 'stress' has 'social effects, that lead to conflict both within and between states' (Homer-Dixon 1991: 76–7).

Where internal 'stress' can and often does manifest is in abuses of the human rights of people protesting about the degradation of their land in various ways. Importantly, where human rights defenders often try to support such protesters, or to protect them from attack, they themselves are victims of attack and human rights abuses, including arbitrary arrest and detention, torture and extra-judicial killing. In this there is a clear link between environmental and human rights issues – over the capacity of ordinary people to be able to speak freely when things directly, negatively, affect their own lives.

As a consequence of the high costs of development, in environmental as well as other terms, there has increasingly been discussion about 'appropriate development' and 'sustainable development', two ideas that often overlap. What is commonly referred to as 'appropriate development' is where the level of technology is suitable for the needs and conditions of the area undergoing the process of development and does not require environmentally destructive or economically unsustainable industry. Sustainable development similarly means the idea that development can be sustained, primarily in ecological terms but also economically, politically, and socially.

'Appropriate development' and 'sustainable development' include a capacity to be locally operated and sustained without requiring either external expertise or capital. In this respect, sophisticated technology is regarded as far less important than technology that works, can be maintained at little or no expense and has few environmental side effects. An example of inappropriate development, for example, is the use of diesel-powered electric generators in poor, oil-importing countries. Appropriate development might rely on solar, wind, geothermal or water (stream-, dam-, wave- or tidal-generated) power (Dunkerley et al. 1981), while there has been development of alcohol and oilseed (such as rapeseed) as a replacement for petrol and diesel as transport fuels. Solar power is also advancing quickly and, while it might remain a relatively capital-expensive form of energy, its cost is quickly reducing while its practicability is increasing through the use of photo-voltaic cells that can provide power on a cloudy day or by moonlight. They are a lot cheaper than similar cells were a few years ago and have effectively no running or environmental costs. However, in the shorter term, there might simply have to be, in some cases, an acceptance that such sources of power are not available, economically affordable or suitable to a particular environment.

The issue of access to energy, in particular electricity, is the source of considerable tension in environmental debates. Up to 2 billion people in developing countries do not have access to electricity. Even in countries that currently employ fossil fuels as their primary energy source, prices will continue to increase and, for many, become prohibitively expensive, a situation that has arguably already happened with the passing of peak oil and the projected consumption of all current oil stocks by 2040. As a consequence, there will be an increasing economic necessity to consider alternative forms of energy-producing technology. That is, while there has been some move towards exploring alternative forms of energy, the major research and development will only occur when fossil fuels become prohibitively expensive which they are expected to do by the end of the first quarter of the twenty-first century. However, while this applies to developed countries, and countries that produce, subsidize or have low taxes on oil products, there are many countries that already struggle to meet their fuel import bill. The environmental issues related to fossil fuel use are increasingly critical, not least of which is the air pollution in many of the world's major developing cities. In particular, with an increasingly urbanized population, Asia has some of the world's most polluted cities, including Beijing, Tianjin, Shanghai, Jakarta, Bangkok, Manila, Mumbai, Calcutta and Delhi (Haq et al. 2002: chs 1–7), although urban sprawls such as Mexico City have also recorded dangerously high air pollution levels.

One energy proposal that received renewed impetus in the early twenty-first century, after a couple of decades of being sidelined, was nuclear energy. Despite having high establishment costs and long lead times, once established, nuclear energy is a relatively efficient energy producer and the material reserves it relies on are relatively substantially available. Despite earlier failures, such as at Chernobyl disaster in the Ukraine and Three Mile Island in the US, by the early twenty-first century nuclear energy was again being promoted as a 'clean' and efficient energy production method. Debate about the safety of nuclear energy resumed again, however, with the failure of 'fail-safe' mechanisms and subsequent large-scale radiation leaks at the Tokyo Electric Power Company (TEPCO) plant at Fukushima following a massive earthquake and tsunami in March 2011. The Fukushima disaster led to a 40 kilometre radius exclusion zone and the dumping of radioactive water into the ocean. As a result the nuclear industry was pushed back by two decades and established, again, that the real issue with this form of power production was that, despite some claims to the contrary, it could not be absolutely guaranteed as safe and that the risks of it not being safe were too high.

Following the Fukushima disaster, a nuclear plant project scheduled for development in the southern US state of Texas was shelved, while violent protests met continuing plans to develop a nuclear power plant in India's earthquake-prone western state of Maharashtra. Indonesia similarly said it would continue to develop its own plans for nuclear power, despite being in one of the world's most tectonically active regions. The Indonesian nuclear development was pronounced as *haram* (forbidden) by the country's largest Islamic organization, the Nahdlatul Ulama, marking the first time an Islamic organization had become directly embroiled in the nuclear debate. Even assuming that safeguards against failure, leakage and waste disposal were mostly overcome in developed countries (and this remains a hotly contested claim, not least in light of the Fukushima disaster), technical imprecision, tectonic instability and related problems do not augur well for its use by developing countries. Given the half-life of nuclear radioactivity (between 65,000 and 24,000 years, depending on type), problems in one part of the world have great capacity to eventually negatively affect all parts of the world.

Renewable energy

Renewable energy has been noted as one means of retaining existing energy consumption levels while maintaining relatively high levels of environmental sustainability. There is, not surprisingly, some debate about the ecological credentials of all renewable fuels, especially hydro-electricity, which was the most widespread form of renewable energy in use at the time of writing. About one-fifth of the world's agricultural land is irrigated, and irrigated agriculture accounts for about 40 per cent of the world's agricultural production. Half the world's large dams were built exclusively or primarily for irrigation and an estimated 30 to 40 per cent of the 271 million hectares of irrigated land worldwide (around 15 per cent of the total) rely on dams. Dams producing hydro-electricity also produce close to 20 per cent of the world's total electric supply, with 24 countries depending on hydroelectricity for 90 per cent of their power supply. Dams also inhibit flooding which between 1972 and 1996 affected around 65 million people, which is more than war, drought or famine combined (Baur and Rudolph 2001).

Less positively, however, large dams have proven to be only marginally cost-effective. The main problems with large dams have been cost over-run, a tendency to fall short of projected power targets and a return of less revenue than anticipated. Dams also impact upon fish stocks, floodplain agriculture and reduce habitat through flooding. It is worth noting that less than half of the dams commissioned during the 1990s had environmental impact assessments (WCD 2000; Baur and Rudolph 2001). Dams have also been shown to have a high social cost, especially in terms of displacing local peoples. Baur and Rudolph (2001) suggest that between 40 and 80 million people have been displaced by dam construction, with more than half of those coming from India and China (see Fuggle and Smith 2000). The Narmada River dam project in India, which includes some 30 large dams and 3,000 small dams, has been highly controversial and the site of resistance by local people opposed to being removed from their homes. There has also been extensive criticism of the project over inaccurate costing, benefits and returns (see Rangachari et al. 2000). (On large dams in Indonesia, see Aditjondro in Hirsch and Warren 1998.) The Three Gorges Dam on

China's Yangtze River (originally conceived in 1999) was, upon its completion in 2006, the world's largest dam, generating a projected 22,500 megawatts of electricity. Construction of the dam, however, displaced 1.3 million people, destroyed historic artefacts and substantially changed the region's ecology. More positively, the dam was expected to reduce coal-fired electricity production by 31 million tonnes a year, saving approximately 100 million tonnes of greenhouse gas emissions, helping to establish China as one of the global environment leaders if also as its biggest energy consumer (passing the United States in 2008) (IEA 2010).

While some developed countries such as Norway have fully developed hydroelectric schemes, others, such as Australia, discovered that the headlong rush towards hydroelectricity had become self-perpetuating, regardless of energy needs, while itself having a significant environmental impact yet not meeting energy or consumption needs. In land-locked Laos, which has least-developed (LLDC) status, a major hydroelectric project on the Theun River (Nam Theun) was intended to produce sustainable energy for both consumption in Laos and for selling-on to Thailand (which, at least in the short to medium term, had reduced its electricity demand due to the Asian economic crisis of the late 1990s). The project was heavily criticized for saddling Laos with international debt and for flooding a significant forest area. However, the Lao government agreed that the area to be flooded be logged first and has restricted legal logging in much of the rest of its forests. With around half the country under forest cover, Laos arguably remains among the most densely forested countries in the world. (There is debate about this – the government claims it is 55 per cent forested, while the World Rainforest Movement says that it is now less than 40 per cent forested, down from 70 per cent in 1940 (WRM 2000).) While the Nam Theun II dam project has been subjected to international scrutiny, due to local deforestation, social displacement and questions about the demand for the power it will generate, such controversy has at least ensured that the project has been closely monitored, with an eye to ensuring it proceeds according to agreed criteria (Iverach, in Stensholt 1997: 69–70, 76). Large dams required to generate hydroelectricity have also been highly controversial in many other cases, in Latin America, across Asia and throughout Africa. Up to 10 million people are said to have been displaced by large dam development since 1948, with most not returning to their former standard of living, while many older dams are now beginning to silt up, reducing their capacity and future potential (IRN 2001). By the end of the twentieth century, there were over 45,000 large dams in over 150 countries, with an average age of 35 years which meant they were mostly coming to the end of the useful water storage life (Baur and Rudolph 2001).

Support for large dam projects, which has cost some 125 billion dollars in multilateral and bilateral aid since 1950 (although as little as 15 per cent of total costs), has been challenged on the grounds of cost efficiency. Especially with the advent of micro-turbines, there is greater consideration being given to smaller, cheaper and more environmentally friendly forms of hydroelectricity.

Wind power is also becoming an increasing common form of energy, with wind turbines making appearances on windswept landscapes in a number of countries. However, while wind turbines are non-polluting, energy production relative to initial cost is relatively low. However, long-term benefits of wind turbines include reducing relative costs and high levels of sustainability.

Beyond those forms noted above, there is also what its supporters are fond of calling 'the fifth fuel' – energy conservation. Consumption drives resource exploitation and is in turn driven by two criteria. The first is that the world's population continues to grow, in simple terms providing a multiplier effect for existing consumption. The second criterion is that technological development has led many and perhaps most of the world's population to, if not expect, then at least to want more of almost everything, as the developed world has and continues to do. For example, chlorofluorocarbons (CFC) are internationally recognized as depleting the earth's ozone layer and manufacturers of refrigerators that use CFCs have been banned by most countries. However, CFC refrigerators are cheaper to produce than non-CFC refrigerators so when China embarked on a programme to ensure that each family has a refrigerator, it initially turned to the cheaper CFC refrigerators. The international community expressed its dismay at the prospect of tens of millions of CFC-producing refrigerators that would be added to the world's total but the Chinese government replied that its people could not afford non-CFC refrigerators, and yet it was not prepared to deny them the right to preserve food. Similarly, when the international community condemned the Malaysian government for unsustainable logging of old-growth tropical forests in northern Borneo, it replied that it would not be denied the right to also achieve developed status, to which such logging would contribute. And, it pointed out, that the West in particular had developed in part through deforesting its own lands and that it was hypocritical for it to now tell other states they could not do the same.

What this implied was that industrialized states were beginning to be forced to reconsider their own patterns of consumption and to look at ways of modifying and ultimately reducing them. The Kyoto Protocols, for example, intended to reduce greenhouse gas emissions by 8 per cent of 1990 levels by 2012. However, the December 2009 Copenhagen talks on climate change failed to craft a successor to the Kyoto Protocols, with China, followed by India and other developing countries, insisting on greenhouse gas emission differentials in favour of developing countries over developed countries. At the end of the talks, greenhouse emission targets were lowered or dropped – initial plans to limit global greenhouse emissions to limit warming to two degrees by 2020 were replaced by 'as soon as possible'. The talks were widely considered to have been a failure, despite the pressing importance of addressing climate change and attendant global warming.

One means of encouraging more environmentally friendly practices has been the policy of 'greenhouse trading'. Greenhouse trading is essentially a credit system by which industries that emit greenhouse gases are encouraged to reduce emissions by being able to claim reductions against taxation or other methods of payment, e.g. one tonne of greenhouse gas could be worth, for instance, US$2. The savings (or payments) would then be invested in seeking non-polluting means of industrial capacity. However, while greenhouse trading was emerging as one means to resolve greenhouse gas emissions problems, its emergence was fitful and unco-ordinated (Pew Centre 2002). However, by 2010, a version of this carbon taxation and trading plan was adopted by the European Union and some other states.

The world's largest mining company and indirectly one of the greatest contributors to greenhouse gas emissions, BHP-Billiton, 'acknowledge[d] that the mainstream science is correct' on climate change and that while 'We have historically expressed our preference for a unified global solution but recognize that local action is more likely in the short term' (Kloppers 2010). The company's head, Marius Kloppers, also accepted that reducing CO^2 emissions is a complex task requiring a mix of strategies including the enhancement of renewable energy, standards and regulations, taxes and market based measures (Kloppers 2010). A part of the BHP-Billion proposal included an emissions trading scheme, in which emissions trading works on the basis that a limited number of permits are available to emit carbon, that there can be a trade in permits and that such a trade would put a price on the emission of carbon in ways that should encourage emitters to seek alternative or cleaner methods of production.

Appropriate development usually (although not always) posits that social and ecological outcomes have precedence over economic outcomes and that development should, and indeed must, occur at the local level, relying on renewable, local inputs with little or no negative impact

Chapter 12

Security and Development

John McKay

general things mentioned, incorrect grammar, idiots
*some

It has long been recognized that violence, warfare and various kinds of instability represent one of the major obstacles to development and prosperity. But in the modern world it is also painfully apparent that there is now a wide range of threats to human life and welfare, and indeed to the broader ecosystem upon which human life depends, that includes but goes beyond warfare. With modern military technologies now capable of massive destruction, traditional conflicts – and most of all nuclear warfare – still represent perhaps the most potent threat but other kinds of danger are also attracting more and more attention. The threat of the spread of various kinds of diseases is one example. Even though the First World War caused massive losses of life on both sides, the outbreak of Spanish influenza that quickly followed resulted in a far greater number of deaths. Thus, current fears of the spread of any new strain of influenza or any other virus are now seen as a major threat to global welfare. Similarly, the environmental consequences of continued global warming are seen as having devastating consequences.

These are just two examples of concerns in the burgeoning field of human security which have been responsible for a radical rethinking and broadening of the older concepts. This process has been under way for a number of years but was given much impetus after the terrorist attacks on New York and Washington in September 2001, an event now known universally as 9/11. This chapter explores the serious and multi-faceted implications of these security concerns for the entire development agenda and, in particular, evaluates the costs and opportunities for developing countries of the new security agenda.

It has often been argued that the modern field of development studies was born in the immediate aftermath of the Second World War, and in particular with the urgent concerns to rebuild nations that had suffered major devastation and to stimulate growth in the newly independent former colonies that began to emerge from the late 1940s. The desire was to ensure that the destruction resulting from major war should never return but to use the technologies and new planning techniques that were the direct result of the war effort to achieve this new and more prosperous world. Such optimism was of course cut short by the rapid onset of the Cold War and this had important implications for the developing world. A new emphasis on the creation of ever more deadly weapons absorbed vast amounts of finance that might have been used for development. This diversion of funds became even larger as more nations beyond just the principal protagonists sought to guarantee what they saw as their legitimate security interests. Each side in the Cold War sought to build alliances with a wide range of countries, however small, and this provided some opportunities as well as costs. Some nations were drawn into destructive conflicts that were essentially proxy wars, since a full conflict between the US and the Soviet Union was too destructive to contemplate. Wars in Korea and Vietnam were prime examples but there were also bloody and long-running regional conflicts in various parts of Asia, Africa and Latin America. However, some countries also benefited from large-scale development assistance that was given for essentially security reasons, and some in particular were able to demand particularly favourable treatment by threatening to move over to the other side. Also, the very concept of the third world, aligned with neither the first world of the US and its allies nor the second world of the Soviet empire, dates from this period and has generated a sense of co-operation and mutual assistance that has been helpful in part.

Some of these essentially Cold War conflicts – notably those in Korea and across the Straits of Taiwan – have never been resolved and are still among the most serious threats facing the global community. However, with the fall of the Berlin Wall in 1989 and the subsequent collapse of communist rule in Russia, there was some optimism that the age of conflict was over. Francis Fukuyama (1992) famously declared 'the end of history', in that the old basis for conflict had disappeared with the complete triumph of liberal democracy as the clearly superior system. The developing world was seen as the major beneficiary of the expected 'peace dividend' that was to follow.

The reality has turned out to be very different. Not only did some of the old conflicts persist but new threats began to be seen even in the more traditional security realm. Rapid economic growth in China, followed by large investments in modernizing its military capability, has been seen by many US security analysts as representing a new threat to American strategic dominance, and attitudes in Washington to the problem of Taiwan partly reflect this thinking. But, importantly from a developing country perspective, the peace dividend was never distributed. Small countries that had never been important economically were now not even seen as being strategically significant and could safely be ignored.

But soon there was no peace dividend even for the United States. In the place of the old ideological contest between capitalism and communism, new fault lines appeared leading to new kinds of conflicts. Samuel Huntington (1996) portrayed this as a new 'clash of civilizations' with broad cultural and religious divides at the epicentre and the renewal of the centuries-old contest between Christianity and Islam as the most dangerous element. While this view generated much criticism as well as support, the events of 9/11 added a new urgency to what had until then been largely an academic debate. Terrorism is not a new phenomenon and there had been a series of attacks on US interests in the lead-up to 9/11 but it was a strike at the centre of American power that finally produced a massive change in thinking about the whole question of security. From the very first day, issues of development were to the fore. In one enduring image, the television cameras recorded a speech by the then president of the World Bank, James Wolfensohn. Standing in front of the smouldering ruins of the World Trade Center, he urged the global community to now take issues of poverty more seriously and to avoid the conflicts and terrorism that deprivation inevitably engenders.

Since then, any hope of a peace dividend has been replaced by massive spending in the name of the 'war on terror'. The attack on Afghanistan to replace the Taliban regime that had provided shelter for the Al-Qaeda terrorists responsible for 9/11 was followed in 2003 by the invasion of Iraq, with the aim of removing Saddam Hussein and to provide the first stage of what was hoped would be a complete transformation of the Middle East and the rest of the Muslim world. One result has been a massive increase in US military spending and hence in its budget deficits.

To some extent, the consequences of the 'war on terror' are similar to those of the Cold War, and the recent tenth anniversary of 9/11 has increased debate about these policies. Massive sums are being spent on security, money that could have been spent for more productive purposes. Repression and torture are again being justified in the name of security and rather dubious regimes around the world are given support because of their role in the fight against terrorism. Anti-terrorism measures are also imposing some significant costs. For example, new rules designed to protect shipping containers and other cargoes from terrorists are resulting in significant extra costs for exporters and transport companies. But again, as in the Cold War period, some countries are able to leverage their positions: the US has brought out its old slogan that 'you are either with us or against us' and some leaders have pointed out that such support demands something in return.

However, the new security agenda includes much more than the fight against terrorism. In the post-Cold War period, much more attention has had to be given to new kinds of transnational crime, including illegal population movements and people-smuggling. Agricultural methods, especially in various parts of Asia, have been widely blamed for outbreaks of new kinds of diseases, and especially those involving cross-infections from animals to humans. Increased population pressures and the frantic pursuit of industrial growth have resulted in serious environmental damage, with real fears of irreversible climate change. Once again such threats bear down particularly on the poorer nations. Countries like Bangladesh are predicted to face very serious threats from flooding, while a number of Pacific nations may disappear completely as sea levels rise.

These are the themes explored in this chapter, with a particular focus on the period since 9/11. In the first part, the redefinition and broadening of the whole concept of security is explored, and especially research on the numerous implications for development. It is argued that while this emphasis on a number of new kinds of threat is to be welcomed, we must not lose sight of the continued menace of old-fashioned security concerns either. Indeed, some of best new studies are explicitly concerned with the interrelationships between traditional and new concepts of security. Some of the policy responses, many of them involving innovative forms of international co-operation that have been suggested to deal with these complex dangers, are evaluated.

The second part of the chapter looks in more detail at terrorism and related forms of violence. This is of course only one aspect of the human security debate but it is a very topical issue and has dominated many of our discussions of international problems, particularly since 9/11. Here several key issues are explored. First, we ask whether the kind of violent act that was perpetrated on 9/11 can be considered as a completely new kind of phenomenon. Terrorism has been with us for centuries in one form or another but some analysts have suggested that we have now witnessed the birth of the 'new terrorism'. Second, and most importantly here, the immediate and wider development costs associated with the 'war on terror' and similar attempts to counter such violence in various regions are considered. Finally, the discussion focuses on particular outcomes for some of the most vulnerable members of society and considers the whole relationship between violence and development.

Revisiting the concept of security: linking security and development

The current debate about the redefinition of the whole concept of security is based around three separate but related threads. First, the scope of what constitutes the security domain is under question, with a number of writers arguing that we must look at definitions that are much broader than have been conventionally used. Second, the place of economic relations within the security domain forces us to think directly about the centrality of developmental issues within this agenda. It has often been contended that trade and other economic linkages play a positive role in the development of stable and productive links between nations but this has been challenged in a number of recent studies. Third, even those writers who still concern themselves with the traditional concerns of security studies now argue that new kinds of threats to stability must be included in our analyses and there is much to be gained from exploring the complex interactions between the traditional and the newer security factors as well as their overall relationship with the development agenda.

Broadening the security agenda

A basic conceptual problem concerns the changing nature of international relations and the consequent focus of concern for states. During the Cold War, there was a simple and overriding imperative for survival and defence and this is still true for relations between the two Koreas, for example. But in many other domains, the very concept of security has been extended to include many topics central to the development agenda, ideas of *economic security, environmental security* and *food security* as well as concerns with international crime, illegal migration and various pandemics. Some would argue that the most useful new overarching concept is that of *human security,* which reflects many of the concerns of traditional security but with a wider concern for the individual as the object of security and for the ways in which increasingly global systems impact on the family and other small local groups. It also looks at 'structural violence' emanating from non-territorial threats (Tow, Thakur and Hyun 2000; McRae and Hubert 2001). The emphasis on human security received much initial impetus from a UNDP report (UN 1994) which proposed that two forms of security are vital for the individual: *freedom from want* and *freedom from fear,* and this formulation is still very influential in most accounts of the concept.

Alan Dupont (2001) argues, for example, that a new class of non-military threats has the potential to destabilize East Asia and reverse decades of economic and social progress. Here he includes issues such as overpopulation, pollution, deforestation, unregulated population movements, transnational crime and HIV AIDS. This broadening of the scope of security issues to include, at the very least, questions of national priorities in areas such as trade and economic priorities has a number of important consequences: the traditional separation of international relations from defence studies is no longer valid, indeed any meaningful study must also include a broad range of other viewpoints and disciplines. Similarly, at the level of government, ministries of foreign affairs, trade and health, at the very least, all need to make policy inputs to security questions, something which simply does not happen in most countries.

The gathering pace of globalization is also adding a number of complications. Actors at a range of scales, from local communities through cities to regions of various kinds, are now part of global networks in their own right. In many countries, the nation state is no longer the sole arbiter of policy, even of policies that have implications for security, especially if one accepts the new, broader concept of security discussed above. The entire post-war security system has been built around relations and treaties between sovereign states, but this concept looks rather shaky.

Economic growth, trade and security

In the literature on international relations and security, there has been a long-running debate about the relationships between economic change and the degree of resultant stability or instability in the security environment. On the one hand, some analysts have argued that economic growth will inevitably lead to greater interdependence between nations and a general desire to avoid any conflict that might interrupt economic progress. Hence, economic growth and change lead to regional stability. Also, as growth proceeds, there has been a tendency in many countries for more democratic forms of government to emerge and some commentators have gone on to argue that two democracies will never go to war – the so-called democratic peace theory (Richardson 1997). This view has been put very strongly by Kishore Mahbubani (1998), who has argued that one of the major reasons for Asia's economic dynamism is that a tidal wave of common sense has hit the region: it is accepted that Asia's success must not be jeopardized by any petty, nationalist squabbles.

In a controversial theoretical analysis by Etel Solingen (1998), the themes of democracy and peace have also been linked to the possible relationship between economic liberalization and regional stability. She argues that the architecture of regional order depends upon the construction of various kinds of coalitions. Basically, two forms of coalition are possible. *Internationalist coalitions, made up of supporters of economic liberalization,* usually create co-operative regional orders that encourage peace and stability. On the other hand, opponents of economic liberalization give rise to *statist/nationalist coalitions* that are prone to create and reproduce zones of wars and militarized disputes. Thus, the fostering of economic reform can be regarded as a major contribution to regional security.

In marked contrast, some analysts have argued that the process of growth itself can lead to instability, especially in the current phase of capitalist development in which there have been marked shifts in power distribution between nations as well as a seemingly inevitable widening of the gap between rich and poor both between and within nations. The intense competition that now characterizes the world economy can lead to serious rivalries and disputes that can escalate into armed conflicts. At the same time, the increased national wealth that has resulted from rapid growth can be used to purchase ever more sophisticated and destructive weapons, intensifying the damage resulting from any conflict. Few if any nations in a region such as Asia can be regarded as supporters of the status quo, especially in the economic realm, and intense competition has been an inevitable consequence of the greater integration into global markets. Zysman and Borrus (1996), for example, have argued that there are several important lines of fracture that result from economic competition. Efforts by middle-power and mid-technology countries such as Korea to break loose from the existing hierarchy of economic power by moving towards higher value and higher technology products could create serious rivalries of development strategies. China and India may in turn provide alternative and competing lines of development, making economic competition within Asia into a form of security competition. Also, there is always a danger that Asia may be transformed into a more self-contained economic bloc competing with the US and Europe (see also Friedberg 1993; Betts 1993).

These old debates have taken on new forms and increased relevance in the period following the Asian financial crisis of 1997–8 and the recent (and perhaps ongoing) GFC. The Asian crisis, and the role of the West and IMF in its management and seeming resolution, created in some Asian minds a new sense of vulnerability and, for some, a blaming of the United States in particular, and US-dominated institutions such as the IMF, for these problems. The 'politics of resentment' (Higgott 2000) have created a new and more unstable environment in the region, compounding the already serious security issues facing Asia. The rapid recovery of Asia from its crisis and the rapid growth of China re-ignited debate over the Asian Century and the potential for conflict between a rising China and a declining United States, and more generally a marked acceleration of the return of Asia as the centre of the global economy. This issue has already been discussed at length in Chapter 6, but we need to stress here the potential for conflict in key regions such as the Indian Ocean that are also central to global development concerns (Kaplan 2010).

These theoretical controversies are crucial to those organizations set up to foster regional co-operation, economic progress and more general dialogue. If economic prosperity leads automatically to a more peaceful region, regional trade organizations by themselves make a significant contribution to peace and security. If, on the other hand, economic growth is rather more problematic in its security implications, then a rather more complex set of policy and institutional solutions need to be designed (McKay 2003b).

Linking traditional and newer security agendas

Some of the best literature on human security is not arguing that traditional security concerns have become obsolete; this is clearly not the case. Rather there is a search for conceptual linkages between the old issues and the new ones. Tow and Trood (2000) have suggested four potential linkages between the two schools of thought:

1. *Conflict prevention.* Traditional security studies have spent much time dealing with the ways in which conflict can be prevented and these are very much at the centre of the debate about human security. Co-operative security arrangements, and a broader sensitivity to the interests and priorities of other nations or peoples, can be much more cost-effective than waging war and prevent large-scale human suffering.
2. *Reducing vulnerability.* Traditional studies have dealt with the nation state as the subject of security, and have employed concepts of state sovereignty and social contract to deal with overriding issues of order. Human security stresses human welfare goals and sees the state only as a means to achieving these goals, and only one means among many. A meeting point between these concepts can be the use of various instruments such as collective security to overcome behaviour that could threaten states, communities or groups.
3. *Who is to be governed and secured?* A number of recent studies have argued that security is a civilizational problem. This acknowledges

that fault lines do exist between peoples, an area of concern in traditional security as well as human security analysis.

4. *Collective security.* Both traditional and new concepts of security concede that there is a crisis of collective security at regional international levels and the development of new institutions and mechanisms is regarded by both as a high priority.

Attempts to push the new agenda of human security have met some strident criticisms. Some critics have seen the human security agenda as yet another example of western models of economic and political development being foisted on developing countries. The emphasis in much of this new agenda on the individual is seen as potentially undermining the jurisdiction and power of the nation state. In some versions of the human security blueprint, for example that put forward by the Canadian government, options for humanitarian intervention in crisis-ridden countries are left open, something which is vehemently opposed by many countries. Most governments, notably that of Japan, favour an emphasis on 'freedom from want' rather than 'freedom from fear', and this brings the debate very close to traditional concepts of development. Still others have questioned just how much the idea of human security adds to the much older formulations of *comprehensive security*. For example, Japan as long ago as 1980 put forward a policy of comprehensive security to safeguard the economic livelihood of the Japanese people, protect vital markets and sources of raw materials, and guarantee Japanese investments. The idea was taken up in a number of South East Asian countries, including Singapore, which proposed a concept of *total security*. Acharya (2002) has attempted to answer these criticisms, arguing that many of the basic ideas of human security were in fact first articulated by Asian scholars. He also stresses some important differences between the formulations of human security and comprehensive security. However, he concedes that the basic unit of analysis in human security has shifted to the individual and the community, away from the emphasis on state security and regime stability that is central to comprehensive security. This is its strength, he argues, and forges a direct link to development concerns but this is bound to cause suspicion in many regional governments.

Exploring the complex interaction between security and development

Defining the nexus between security and development is now one of the important and complex tasks within the overall field of international development. As has been noted in an important recent study from the International Peace Institute (Tschirgi et al. 2010) all the statistics point to some obvious connections: since the 1980s some 80 per cent of the poorest nations have been wracked by violent conflict of some kind. Similar relationships are highlighted in the *World Development Report 2011* (World Bank 2011). About 1.5 billion people – some 25 per cent of the global population – live in situations of conflict and violence, and the gap in poverty is increasing between stable nations and those affected by violence. No fragile or conflict-ridden nation has yet achieved a single Millennium Development Goal. But the nature of violence has undergone a profound change – in this respect the new millennium is radically different from the previous one. Both inter-state conflict and civil war have declined in total, but a number of nations have suffered from repeated violence. In the last decade, 90 per cent of countries enduring civil wars have had one or more such conflicts in the last 30 years, and in many cases this kind of instability has been ongoing. New forms of instability, such as organized crime and other kinds of criminal violence, have also emerged, but the basic causal mechanisms seem to be constant. Stresses resulting from internal and international conditions are unable to be contained by weak and often corrupt institutions resulting in rapid loss of development momentum, which in turn fuels new rounds of violence and breeds new kinds of criminal behaviour. Nations that in the past were devastated by civil war – such as Mozambique and Rwanda – have made good progress recently, but in many conflict situations such as the Democratic Republic of Congo anything resembling an effective government has ceased to exist.

But moving beyond these obvious relationships to explore some key causal relationships is proving to be much more challenging. Fukuda-Parr (2010) has stressed that the links between poverty and conflict are complex and two-way. Civil war hampers development, reducing GDP and government revenues. Administrative capacity is reduced along with expenditures for productive and social sectors. Social institutions, social networks and trust are all seriously eroded, incomes fall, nutrition declines and diseases increase along with child and infant mortality. Women and children are particularly vulnerable to all these effects. In such situations people may feel they have little to lose by continuing conflict, and young men – well represented in most developing countries' demographic structures – are easily persuaded to join rebel armies (Cincotta 2010). Conflict seems particularly common in situations of marked inequalities between community groups, particularly ethnic groups, and when countries are dependent on particular commodities with high returns available to those who control high value products such as diamonds. The struggle over resources may also be magnified when environmental deterioration puts pressure on increasingly scarce resources. Many people may be forced to migrate, bringing them into conflict with other groups. Conflict may also spill over from neighbouring countries – for example it is estimated that in recent years Tanzania's GDP has been reduced by 0.7 per cent per year as the result of conflict in adjoining nations (World Bank 2011).

One area that has received increased attention in recent years is the growing evidence that pressures on the environment and its resources are an important source of conflict. A much discussed case here is the ongoing conflict in the Darfur region of Sudan where rapid population growth and declining rainfall have placed impossible pressures on the predominantly farming and herding communities, and adding to the existing ethnic rivalries and the problems created by a corrupt and ineffective government (Matthew 2010). Recently there has also been much discussion of the potential for conflict that can result from global climate change: problems of competition for food and water could have serious consequences for security in many parts of the world (Chellaney, 2011; McKay, 2009). But there is a danger that many potential conservation measures can have particularly detrimental effects on some poorer communities and actually enhance the possibilities for even greater conflict. Thus, as Matthew has argued, planners need to search for conservation strategies that are pro-poor and thus pro-stability. 'Peace parks' along the borders of two formerly warring neighbouring countries or regions have been suggested as part of such an approach.

Similar policy imperatives are also apparent in many areas of conflict that are at least in part related to widespread poverty. Fukuda-Parr (2010) suggests that many aid programmes in fact exacerbate existing conflict situations or create the potential for new conflagrations that can have disastrous consequences for progress: the development planning process needs to be redefined to include assessments of security risks for all aid programmes. She supports the idea of creating some Millennium Security Goals (MSGs) to bring development and security agendas more into harmony. Such an approach is based on the work of Picciotto and others (see, for example, Picciotto et al. 2006; Picciotto et al. 2009) who have suggested eight MSGs as an agenda for a more balanced approach to development:

1 reduce the number, length, and intensity of conflicts between and within states;
2 reduce the number and severity of attacks;
3 reduce the number of refugees and displaced persons;

4 regulate the arms trade;
5 reduce the extent and severity of core human rights violations;
6 protect civilians and reduce women's and children's participation and victimization in war;
7 reverse weapons proliferation and achieve progress toward nuclear, radiological, chemical, and biological disarmament; and
8 combat transnational crime and illegal trafficking.

These goals are easy to enumerate but extremely difficult to achieve, but we will return to this idea of human security as a new focus for the entire development agenda.

The nature and costs of terrorism

The 'new terrorism'

Alvin Buckelew (1984: 18) has defined terrorism as 'violent, criminal behaviour designed primarily to generate fear in the community, or in a substantial segment of the community, for political purposes'. Such activity is certainly not new, with examples of terrorist groups identified for at least 2,000 years. However, a number of commentators have argued that the 9/11 attacks on the United States have heralded the emergence of what is being called *the new terrorism* (see, for example, Ramakrishna and Tan 2002; Hoffman 2002). Hoffman has identified a series of features that set this new phenomenon apart from earlier terrorist attacks:

- The 9/11 attacks killed an unprecedented number of victims. No previous terrorist act had ever killed more than 500 persons.
- The event consisted of a co-ordinated series of spectacular and simultaneous attacks.
- The attacks showed a new level of patient and detailed planning.
- The hijackers showed a willingness to kill themselves as well as their victims.
- The hijackers had a relatively high level of education, and contrary to popular stereotypes they were not drawn from the ranks of the mentally unstable, the poor or the isolated loners.

To this list could be added the dominantly religious dimension of the terrorist organizations (Ramakrishna and Tan 2002) and the distinctively networked nature of their operational procedures (O'Brien 2002).

Some of these individual features are not entirely new – for example suicide bombers had been used earlier by the Tamil Tigers in Sri Lanka and by a number of Palestinian groups – but it is the integration of all of these elements into a new and distinctive strategy that is important. All of these researchers argue that a clear understanding of this new phenomenon must be central to any strategy to deal with these terrorist threats.

Hoffman has also drawn our attention to the sheer audacity and imagination involved in the 9/11 attacks. Most earlier assumptions about the nature of likely targets and the methods that could be employed were shattered and this is turn has created a great deal of community unease – one of the key aims of terrorism for centuries – as possible new kinds of targets and new kinds of vulnerabilities are identified. He poses a list of potential targets that have not yet been attacked simply to highlight that the list of possible terrorist acts is almost limitless and certainly impossible to totally guard against. Perhaps here we come to the real core of the threat posed by the 'new terrorism'. Within governments and the population at large there is now an acceptance that there is nothing that the new breed of terrorist is not capable of. The recent tenth anniversary of 9/11 has seen a number of important re-evaluations of the policy responses to that attack (for example, Jenkins and Godges 2011) but even after the death of Osama bin Laden and the appearance of a number of commentaries predicting the demise of Al Qaeda especially in the light of the new wave of democratization now sweeping the Middle East and North Africa (for example, McCants 2011) nothing now seems safe, and there is no limit to the precautions that might and should be taken. The cost implications are of course enormous.

Calculating the costs of terrorism

The events of 9/11 and the responses to this tragedy have engendered a number of studies that have tried to quantify the costs of terrorism, and of armed conflict more generally. Gupta et al. (2002) and others have attempted to put the impacts of the 'new terrorism' within the broader historical literature on the consequences of conflicts of various kinds. This suggests that conflicts such as terrorism lower growth, both directly and indirectly in various ways:

- the process of financial deepening is adversely affected by the undermining of confidence in the domestic currency due to fears of inflation and depreciation;

- funds tend to move away from productive assets to non-productive ones, notably gold;
- the supervision of the financial system is neglected;
- the transaction costs of doing business increase sharply;
- additional security precautions can impede the flow of goods and services;
- fiscal accounts can be disrupted through the erosion of the tax base, the lowering of efficiency in tax administration and the distortion of public spending;
- military expenditure tends to increase dramatically, and historically has remained high even after the end of conflict;
- the destruction of infrastructure and human capital, plus the indirect effects such as reductions in trade, tourism or business confidence, all weaken the fiscal position of the nation involved in conflict. (See also Addison et al. 2002)

Other authors have concentrated on the more specific impacts of terrorism in the post-9/11 environment. The OECD in its *Economic Outlook* of 2002 attempted to evaluate the economic consequences of terrorism (OECD 2002). Usefully, the authors try to separate the short-term impacts from those of a medium- and longer-term nature. They argue that the short-term consequences of the attacks were limited by some swift policy responses. Short-term loans and guarantees were put in place, for example. The insurance industry raised its premiums, reduced its coverage and called on governments to step in and cover risks deemed too difficult for the private sector, but private sector initiatives soon emerged to provide coverage for these kinds of risks. However, they concede, in the longer term tighter border controls may well have a detrimental impact on trade. One result of globalization and the introduction of just-in-time supply chain management systems is that companies depend to an increasing extent on efficient border-crossing systems. Long delays that result from enhanced security precautions can have serious consequences for the efficiency of manufacturing systems. It is suggested that these new security measures have added 1–3 per cent to total trading costs. They also suggest that spending on homeland security and military operations, especially in the United States, as well as private spending on the security of premises, employees and information, may crowd out accumulation in directly productive capacity. This finding contradicts the opinions expressed by Hobijn (2002), who in response to the question of what homeland security in the US would cost, answered 'not much'.

More detailed modelling work on the trade impacts of terrorism has been undertaken by Nitsch and Schumacher (2002) and Walkenhurst and Dihel (2002). Nitsch and Schumacher analyzed data on trade flows between some 200 countries from 1960 to 1993, concluding that a doubling in the number of terrorist incidents is associated with a decrease of bilateral trade by around 6 per cent. Walkenhurst and Dihel, by contrast, attempted to disaggregate the impacts of the various factors leading to increased costs:

- *Air transport.* Given the methods used in the 9/11 attacks, it was natural that air services should be given particular attention in the attempt to counter increased terrorist threats. Tighter screening of passengers and their luggage was introduced, cockpit access was restricted, and on a number of flights armed air marshals were introduced. Training of personnel was increased at all levels. Insurance premiums increased sharply. Similar measures were introduced to protect air cargo services. Many airlines passed on these costs to passengers in the form of 'security surcharges'.
- *Maritime transport.* Before September 2001, only 2 per cent of the 72 million containers moved annually were screened in any way but a whole range of safety checks was quickly introduced. For example, documents for all shipments going to the US must now be lodged with US authorities before the ship leaves the port of origin, all ships must now travel at very low speeds within US harbours, insurance premiums have increased sharply and a range of war-risk surcharges have been introduced in particular regions.
- *Road and rail transport.* Delays on land-crossing into the US, for example from Mexico, have increased markedly. Freight yards have been fenced in a more secure way and sensors have been introduced to alert operators to any interference with cargoes. Inspections of train lines, bridges and tunnel have increased.
- *Customs.* Increased inspections of various kinds have undone the efficiency gains from simplified and automated procedures introduced over the last few years, although much work is now going on to develop new systems that can again reduce costs.

The authors developed a model to evaluate the real global costs of these enhanced security measures. They conclude that total world welfare has declined by a staggering $US75 billion per year as a direct result of the attacks of 9/11. The largest losses were estimated to be in Western Europe, North America and North Asia, but in relative terms the economies of South Africa, North Africa and the Middle East were even more seriously affected. The authors note that, in an increasingly integrated global economy, even small changes in trade costs can have a significant impact on trade flows and economic welfare. Even countries not directly involved in conflict can suffer serious losses as the result of enhanced security concerns and higher frictional costs of trade.

Many costs associated with countering terrorism are predominantly faced by the rich countries – for example the naval operations to counter piracy of the Horn of Africa and in the Indian Ocean is estimated to cost around $2 billion per year, but many small companies in poorer countries – for example 30 per cent of firms in Africa – are seriously affected by crime and violence (World Bank 2011).

It should be noted that some commentators believe that the costs associated with precautions against terrorism need not be permanent. In fact, it has been argued that once new technologies are fully developed, the efficiencies achieved might mean that the actual costs of processing cargoes and passengers, for example, may be even less than they were before 9/11. Advance passenger information systems and other electronic innovations at airports should in time result in faster passenger movements. Similarly, new standardized manifest systems at all ports may in time cut costs and reduce handling times. The US Customs' Automated Commercial Environment (ACE) project, developed to identify high-risk cargo, may eventually reduce costs to business and facilitate the faster processing of trade. It has been estimated that over the next 20 years the ACE system will save US importers around $US22.2 billion and save the US government $US4.4 billion in administrative costs over the same period (Raby 2003).

Facing the basic causes of terrorism and other human security issues

The basic argument in this last major section of this chapter is that we need to move beyond considerations of the costs of human insecurity, and certainly beyond the simplistic sloganizing that has characterized much of the recent debate. In the case of terrorism, for example, while direct security efforts to safeguard aircraft, ships, trains and other possible targets are necessary and laudable, rather more has to be done. Essentially, this involves taking a much longer-term view of the phenomenon of terrorism, trying to understand what motivates the terrorists and attempting to deal with the underlying causes. This is the only real and constructive way to manage the problem. This also brings the discussion directly into the domain of development and what might be involved is nothing less than the creation of a new agenda for development studies.

But it is necessary at this point to make one important thing very clear. There has been a tendency in the press and in some political circles to equate any call for understanding terrorism with some kind of tacit support for terrorist causes, or at least with a 'soft' approach to the problem. Jessica Stern (2003) in her landmark study of religious terrorism, has done us all a favour in this regard, by firmly demolishing all of these kinds of spurious and anti-intellectual arguments. As Stern notes, empathy and understanding do not necessarily imply sympathy or support. She argues that it is important to look behind the slogans and stereotypes and try to gain deeper insights into motivations.

AMEN.

In the current situation, such analysis and search for understanding are absolutely essential. It may be that at the end of such a programme of intense work many of the 'causes' of terrorism that we identify may be dismissed as unworthy, absurd or not to be tolerated. But clearly the methods we are currently adopting are not working and are unlikely to produce viable long-term answers to the problem; hence we must embark on quite a new agenda. There are at least four major arguments to support such a position.

First, it now seems clear that by themselves conventional strategies are unlikely to be effective. However well thought out and executed these plans may be, there are just too many trains, bridges, airports or whatever to guard all day every day. Even if the precautions are effective for 99 per cent or more of the time, some terrorist event will take place somewhere – and people will die. Also, much of our thinking about what terrorists will target next has been based on what their targets were last time around. Certainly transport and trade are the most obvious areas to be threatened but, as Hoffman suggests, the range of possible targets is almost endless. If we cannot guard all the obvious targets, how can we deal with all those extra possibilities of which we are only dimly aware?

Second, many of the methods that have been used in the recent past to limit the activities of terrorist groups may in fact have made the problem worse by fuelling resentment. Many programmes have been poorly thought through and relied on simple stereotypes and prejudices. In turn, they have served to simply reinforce the stereotypes and prejudices held about the West. The thwarting of some terrorist activities may in fact have come at the cost of boosting the recruitment of the next generation of terrorists. Kumar Ramakrishna (2002: 208) has set out the dangers very clearly – the emphasis on military solutions and coercion can be very counterproductive and should be replaced by a series of indirect strategies that can deal with the problem of terrorism without making the problem worse, and in particular without generating the kind of 'civilizational conflict' that a number of authors, notably Huntington (1996), have warned us about.

Third, in many parts of the world protests have been raised about the impact of what many people see as severe anti-terrorism regulations on the rights of the bulk of the population. Once sacrosanct civil and political rights, such as freedom of expression, freedom of association, protection from arbitrary detention and the right to independent legal advice, have been tossed aside in the name of the 'war on terror'. Importantly Hocking (2004) and others have asked whether we can ever protect ourselves by removing the very freedoms that define us as a democracy. Similarly, arguments have been put forward in a number of publications coming out of Asia. Notable here is a volume edited by Johannen, Smith and Gomez (2003) in which several contributors argue that in Asia a number of authoritarian regimes have seized the opportunity to emphasize that their continued concerns for national security have been vindicated, and that the crushing of political dissent is essential.

Fourth, the ongoing costs of these measures in purely economic terms are enormous, as we have seen, and the developmental impacts may be quite severe. Various links between poverty and terrorism have been made yet terrorism and counterterrorism measures seem to be having a relatively much larger impact on low-income countries, and the costs of terrorism and anti-terrorism now constitute a major new handicap to development (Gupta et al. 2002). Yet it is precisely the lack of development that is one of the major underlying factors in the growth of terrorism in many countries (World Bank 2011).

Thus, there are some important reasons to take a much longer-term view of the issue of terrorism rather than simply relying on the direct, military and quasi-military tactics now being employed. But these are complex and heavily contested issues and there is little consensus in the literature on the mix of factors that has led to the emergence of terrorism, hence the development of more sophisticated policy initiatives is made more difficult. As a next step here, we draw out some of the lessons or at least identify the major schools of thought on the causes of terrorism and insecurity.

Old versus new: the fear of modernity

A number of political leaders, notably former president George W. Bush, are fond of saying things like 'terrorists want all of us to return to a mediaeval way of life', or 'what terrorists hate about us is our freedom and our way of life'. Thus the 'war on terror' for them is a struggle for the defence of modernity against the primitive tenets of a tribal, desert society. This position is also based on a specific view of Islam that is portrayed as having progressed hardly at all since the death of the Prophet.

Such attitudes have flourished in the general spirit of self-confidence, or even triumphalism, that has pervaded much of the West since the end of the Cold War. Francis Fukuyama, in an article published soon after 9/11 (*Guardian*, 11 October 2001) defended his assertions against those who saw terrorism as a new 'clash of civilizations', arguing that western liberal democracy remains the only system that will dominate world politics and terrorism represents only a rearguard action by those societies whose very existence is threatened by modernization.

Such ideas have been rejected by Stuart Sim (2004) who has argued that we now live in a new age of dogma and fundamentalism, and western belief in the unchallenged superiority of its political and economic system is but one aspect of 'political fundamentalism'. The entire world, apart from a few who have not yet seen the light, is assumed to be only too anxious to join the 'born-again liberal democrats' (p. 152). This, he suggests, parallels a strong element of market fundamentalism, which is a modern and more intense version of the protestant work ethic. Like all fundamentalisms, there are strong theological overtones and it is no accident that the religious right in the US is closely linked to a form of market fundamentalism that stresses the purity of its principles, even if the social impact of its policy outcomes can be very damaging to the social fabric. He also notes that, for every fundamentalism, there grows up an equally dogmatic opposing fundamentalism and in this case it is the growth of the anti-globalization movement that is particularly instructive.

Even more vehement comments along these general lines have been made by John Gray (2003) who argues that, far from being mediaeval in nature, Al Qaeda and other radical Islamic organizations are essentially modern.

> Western societies are governed by the belief that modernity is a single condition, everywhere the same and always benign. As societies become more modern, so they become more alike. At the same time they become better. Being modern means realising *our* values – the values of the Enlightenment, as we like to think of them. (Gray 2003: 1)

The reality is rather different, he suggests. Al Qaeda is very much a by-product of globalization, and like the Soviet Union and Nazi Germany, it sees history as a mere overture to a brave new world. All such move-ments, including the Enlightenment itself, are convinced that it is possi-ble to transform the human condition, the myth that is at the centre of modernity. In this sense, radical Islam and neo-liberal orthodoxy are very similar, even though their goals seem so different.

This kind of analysis, which defines modernity as a form of funda-mentalism, is very challenging for many practitioners of development, who have often seen development itself as a process of modernization, and I will return to these emerging notions below.

Religion and holy war

One current belief shared by many in the West is that Islamic and other recent forms of terrorist movements reflect a fanaticism and fundamen-talism that comes directly out of notions of *jihad.* After 9/11, there appeared a large number of books attempting to elucidate the meaning of such fundamentalism and the precise nature of 'holy war' (see for example, Ruthven 2002, 2004; Kepel 2002). Ruthven has chronicled the origins and development of the term 'fundamentalism', arguing that it is extremely slippery and paradoxical and has outgrown much of its origi-nal meaning. It was first coined with reference to a particularly zealous protestant movement in the United States, which stressed that all impor-tant truths could only be found in the Bible; hence the path to wisdom depended on a willingness to undertake detailed analysis of this one true source. The Bible was revealed truth and hence should be interpreted lit-erally. Since then, the use of the term has been widened to include many kinds of religious, economic and political belief systems, all of which make some claim to an exclusive pathway to true enlightenment or per-fection. Ironically, Ruthven suggests, the replacement in at least some areas of western thought of modernity with newer post-modern concepts has provided some important space for various kinds of thought systems. If, as the postmodernists argue, the validity of any overarching meta-nar-rative is no longer tenable, then all theories and world views become equally valid. But, and here is the irony, each of these new fundamental-ist stories is not only asking for equal recognition but in fact claims to be the single source of truth and salvation. Hence, the postmodern world might be characterized as a 'clash of fundamentalisms'. Others have also suggested that, in the uncertain or even chaotic world that has resulted from the postmodern or globalized condition, unerring faith in the one true source provides some certainty and comfort.

Islamic fundamentalism is often portrayed in just these terms. While the adherence to the revealed truth of the Koran and the demands for the establishment of Islamic states based on *sharia* law provide an immediate identification with fundamentalism, many commentators have argued that the sense of extreme uncertainty or even shame prevalent in the Middle East in particular has provided a fertile breeding ground for broader and more politically based notions of Islamic fundamentalism.

Closely related to these ideas is the notion of *jihad*. The original meaning of this word is simply 'struggle' but it has come to be seen as a struggle or holy war on behalf of Islam to defend this one true religion against attacking infidels. As Kepel (2002) has suggested, the term is now used in some quarters as the ultimate justification for what might seem unacceptable violence and terrorism. Kepel goes on to argue that 9/11, however spectacular it may seem, should not be interpreted as a sign of growing Islamic strength and influence. In fact, the triumph of the revolution in Iran and the Taliban in Afghanistan should be seen as the highpoint of success, and since then there have been a series of important reverses. In order to reverse this trend, Osama bin Laden sought to bring off a spectacular attack aimed not at what had been his prime target – what he portrayed as the corrupt, anti-Islamic and pro-western regime in Saudi Arabia – but at the more general evil of western hegemony. The West, and the US in particular, would be seen by ordinary Muslims as weak and impotent and this would trigger a much wider *jihad*. But, Kepel stresses, such mobilization can only be achieved by long-term political action reaching down to the grass roots, not through one act of terrorism, however daring. However, the importance of Osama bin Laden as a symbol of just struggle should not be underestimated, especially since he demonstrated a real genius in harnessing the media to get his message across.

The home-grown terrorists

Closely related to these ideas of fundamentalism and *jihad* is the important work that has been done trying to explain why many terrorist acts that have been perpetrated in the West have been undertaken by Islamic immigrants, or more usually the children of immigrants actually born in the country of the attack – the so-called 'home-grown terrorists'. In fact, a number of commentators have suggested that this now represents one of the most important fronts in the 'war on terror'.

Two very important studies – by Gilles Kepel (2004) and Olivier Roy (2002) – have done much to shape how we think about such issues. Roy notes that one of the key results of globalization has been the international migration of large numbers of people. No fewer than one-third of the world's Muslims now live as minorities in other countries. Many members of these communities, and in particular younger Muslims, feel alienated and rootless. This should not be seen as a backlash against westernization, he suggests, but one of its outcomes. What he terms 'neo-fundamentalism' is fuelling a new kind of radicalism that embraces the leadership of Al Qaeda and often includes rejection of integration into western societies. This Islamic revival, or what he calls 're-Islamization', is an attempt by westernized Muslims to reassert their identities. Importantly, this is not manifested as a yearning for a lost homeland or nation but a declaration of a more general affinity with a universal religious identity or community, often represented by an imaginary *ummah* or Muslim community. Thus, echoing many of the arguments of John Gray already presented, Islamic fundamentalism in this context is not simply a reaction against westernisation but a product of the multiple forces we call globalization.

Kepel (2004), though, presents a further complication to this already sophisticated analysis. He argues that a fierce contest is being waged between two elements of the Islamic youth communities in western nations. One group consists of the disillusioned and angry group identified by Olivier Roy. But there is another, more positive segment that is optimistic about the future and sees itself as the bearer of a new westernized and more democratic ideology that can be passed back to the countries from which their families emigrated. The clash between these two views is really about the right of self-definition, Kepel contends, and constitutes a vital 'battle for Europe'. The issue of identity has also been taken up by Amartya Sen (2007), who suggests that in the current phase of globalization identity can be a source of strength, linking people into support networks of various kinds, but it can also be the source of violence, since by identifying membership of any community one is also defining an outgroup. The answer, he contends, is to give people the freedom to develop multiple, overlapping identities, including a global identity.

Reactions to US imperialism and the wars in Iraq and Afghanistan

In considering various contending theories on the causes of terrorism, one must acknowledge a number of writings that suggest that the lack of progress in solving the Palestine question, the close identification in the Muslim world of the US with the Israeli cause and the wars in Iraq and Afghanistan are all major contributors to the spread of terrorism (Freedman 2008). At first sight, these sorts of arguments have very limited relevance to the kinds of themes being addressed in this chapter but some recent commentary would suggest otherwise.

John Gray (2007) sees in the war in Iraq a struggle over several of the issues that are central to the future direction of global development. There is of course the question of resources, and oil in particular, and he evaluates the extent to which a desire to secure supplies of this key commodity led to the decision to invade Iraq. But there is also the broader question of how power and states are to be defined in this new age. Echoing the views of Bobbitt (2002), he suggests that for neo-liberals at least the old state system is being replaced by a concept of the 'market state', in which the aim of policy is no longer to reflect the views of citizens but to satisfy the demands of the global economy. The crusade to spread democracy in the Middle East and beyond undertaken by the 'armed missionaries of liberalism' is part of a broader view that everything must be done to speed up the transition to a brave new world in which there is no place for evil – a utopian and apocalyptic project of the kind that has, he suggests, failed so many times in the past.

Poverty, globalization and insecurity

Finally, the importance of poverty as a driver of terrorist activity and a major contributor to all kinds of conflict and human insecurity must be reiterated, along with some of the claims that the particular kind of global economy that is emerging is a major contributor to a range of disputes. In attempting this synthesis, it is also important to review some of the arguments that have been put forward in various chapters of this volume.

Brainard, Chollet and LaFleur (2007: 1) have set out in a very concise manner the complex linkages that exist between poverty and insecurity:

> Extreme poverty exhausts governing institutions, depletes resources, weakens leaders, and crushes hope – fueling a volatile mix of desperation and instability. Poor, fragile states can explode into violence or implode into collapse, imperilling their citizens, regional neighbors, and the wider world as livelihoods are crushed, investors flee, and ungoverned territories become a spawning ground for global threats like terrorism, trafficking, environmental devastation, and disease. Yet if poverty leads to insecurity, it is also true that the destabilizing effects of conflict and demographic and environmental challenges make it harder for leaders, institutions, and outsiders to promote human development.

Some political leaders have questioned role of poverty as a motivator for terrorists, pointing out that almost all of the perpetrators of the 9/11 attacks were well educated and from relatively affluent middle-class families. However, as part of a massive research study seeking to understand the mind of the terrorist (Stout 2004), a number of contributing authors presented a very different picture. Staub (2004), for example, argues that poverty – and in particular the constant confrontation with people who are better off – magnifies a sense of hopelessness and lack of power and may result in a turning to extreme forms of ideology. In addition, many people find it difficult to pursue education and newer forms of employment in a situation that increasingly requires a fruitful integration of the old and the new. In societies undergoing change, this will often result in confusion over identity, an issue I have already introduced. But more generally within the research community there has been an acceptance that poverty and failed states are important contributors to the problem of terrorism.

Poor or failing states face a wide array of serious problems that contribute to instability and violence. Poverty is itself a factor, but so is environmental degradation and the particular demographic structure of many developing countries in which there are large numbers of young people who often feel that their life chances are very limited and are able to compare their lot with the western affluence portrayed in the media (Rice 2007). In a similar vein, Miguel (2007) considers two competing theories as to the central causes of violent conflict in developing countries. One theory focuses on the impact of political repression, while the second views economic conditions as being of prime importance, and the author comes down firmly in favour of the explanatory power of poverty. For unemployed young people with little hope of advancement through formal channels, joining an armed group can be very attractive. Apart from meeting a range of psychological needs, such involvement can provide a number of opportunities for significant income from activities such as looting, drug running, extortion and various forms of smuggling. He does point out that the political repression and poverty theories need not be mutually exclusive, and one factor may feed off the other, which raises the issue of how important the fostering of democracy can be to reducing violence and the chances of terrorism. The Bush administration in the US has often been criticized for giving too much attention to its 'freedom agenda' rather than devoting more resources to poverty alleviation programmes. This issue is taken up directly by Windsor (2007) who argues that democratic systems can produce much greater advances in development than can authoritarian regimes; hence the fostering of democracy deals simultaneously with the issue of repression and that of poverty. However, this is a very contentious finding.

Conclusions: human security as a focus for development studies

This chapter began with a general review of the concept of human security and then, to illustrate some major points and approaches, looked at the very topical issue of terrorism and its multifaceted connections with a range of development concepts and policy dilemmas. By way of conclusion, we broaden the discussion again and suggest ways in which the study of problems of human security can provide a very innovative and productive focus for the whole field of development studies.

There can certainly be no doubting the seriousness of the challenges posed to developing nations by violent conflict, terrorism and other issues of human security, and as we have noted, almost all of the countries that score lowest on the UN's Human Development Index have suffered from some kind of conflict since 1990 and their populations suffer from extremely high levels of child mortality and low life expectancies (UN 2005; World Bank 2011). Conflict has resulted in the destruction of food systems, basic services and health facilities, and there is clear evidence that the harshest burdens fall on the poor and the marginal, the women and children most of all. Populations have been displaced on a massive scale, and in conflict situations there is an added risk of the spread of HIV AIDS. In such situations, leadership and the basic institutions of governance are often destroyed, making it much more difficult to end conflicts and initiate programmes of reconstruction. Thus, the scale and importance of these tragic events is quite clear.

But, as we have also seen, the causes of violence and terrorism are complex and far-reaching and to truly understand what is going on we need to go back to the basic dynamics of global development. This point has been made very strongly by Caroline Thomas (2007) who contends that a human security approach offers some important advantages for our analysis. The inbuilt focus on the individual rather than the nation state is essential in dealing with issues of vulnerability and threat. It also forces us to think through the interconnected forces operating at various geographical scales to produce particular outcomes and this is also helpful in the design of appropriate policy responses. Human security also provides normative power and a strong moral justification for transformative action. If development is about power and the politics of its appropriation, then this approach leads us immediately to ask the appropriate but often uncomfortable questions about just what is going on in the world, and also leads us to the design of the reforms in global and local governance that are essential. But here we are faced with some stark policy choices. As Menkhaus (2010) has argued in relation to the disastrous situation in Somalia, the usual assumption that state structures and governance need to be strengthened is problematic, at least in the short term. State building and peace building are seen as antagonistic enterprises by groups that feel they may be excluded from the rewards associated with a new state.

If this book has any single theme, it is to support the idea of development as freedom. The challenges we face are enormous and, as we have seen, some severe doubts have been expressed about the ability of studies of development to rise to this immense task. If we need a new mandate for the subject, human security might just fit the bill: the ideas of *freedom from want* and *freedom from fear* are both noble and essential for our collective survival.

References

Abbott, D. and Pollard, S. (2004) *Hardship and Poverty in the Pacific: Strengthening Poverty Analysis and Strategies in the Pacific* (Manila: Pacific Department, Asian Development Bank).

Acemoglu, D. and Robinson, J. (2006) *Economic Origins of Dictatorship and Democracy* (Cambridge: Cambridge University Press).

Acharya, A. (2002) 'Human Security: What Kind for the Asia-Pacific?', in D. Dickens (ed.), *The Human Face of Security: Asia-Pacific Perspectives* (Canberra: Strategic and Defence Studies Centre, Australian National University), Papers on Strategy and Defence, no. 144.

Acharya, A., de Lima, A. F. and Moore, M. (2004) *Aid Proliferation: How Responsible are Donors?*, IDS Working Paper no. 214 (Sussex: Institute of Development Studies).

Adade, C. (1991) 'Cut: Drastic Reductions Likely in Soviet Support', *New Internationalist*, 216.

ADB (Asian Development Bank) (2005a) *Asia Development Outlook 2005* (Manila: Asian Development Bank).

——(2005b) *Private Sector Assessment for Solomon Islands* (Manila: Asian Development Bank).

——(2006) *Poverty Handbook Analysis and Processes to Support ADB Operations: A Working Document* (Manila: Asia Development Bank).

——(2011) 'Governance', in *Sectors and Themes*, Asian Development Bank, 12 August 2011.

Addison, T. (2000) 'Aid and Conflict', in F. Tarp (ed.), *Foreign Aid and Development: lessons Learned and Directions for the Future* (London: Routledge), pp. 392–408.

Addison, T., Chowdhury, A. and Murshed, M. (2002) 'By How Much Does Conflict Reduce Financial Development?', WIDER Discussion Paper no. 2002148 (Helsinki: World Institute for Development Economic Research, United Nations University).

Adelman, I. and Taft Morris, C. (1973) *Economic Growth and Social Equity in Developing Countries* (Stanford, CA: Stanford University Press).

Agarwal, B. (1997a) '"Bargaining" and Gender Relations: Within and Beyond the Household', *Feminist Economics*, 3(1), pp. 8–9.

——(1997b) 'The Gender and Environment Debate: Lessons from India', in N. Visvanathan, L. Duggan, L. Nisonoff and N. Wiegersma (eds), *The Women, Gender and Development Reader* (London: Zed Books), pp. 68–74.

Agarwala, A. N. and Singh, S. P. (eds) (1958) *The Economics of Underdevelopment* (Oxford: Oxford University Press).

Agenor, P.-R., Miller, M., Vines, D. and Weber, A. (eds) (1999) *The Asian Financial Crisis: Causes, Contagion and Consequences* (Cambridge: Cambridge University Press).

Ahamed, L. (2009) *Lords of Finance: The Bankers Who Broke the World* (London: Penguin).

Ahlburg, D. et al. (1994) *Independent Enquiry Report into Population and Development* (Canberra: AGPS/ADAB).

Ahmed, F. E. (2008) 'Hidden Opportunities: Islam, Masculinity and Poverty Alleviation', *International Feminist Journal of Politics*, 10(4): 542–62.

Alkire, S. (2002) 'Dimensions of Human Development', *World Development* 30(2): 181–205.

Amacher, R. D., Haberler, G. and Willett, T. D. (eds) (1979) *Challenges to a Liberal International Economic Order* (Washington, DC: American Enterprise Institute).

Amin, S. (1976) *Unequal Development* (London: Monthly Review Press).

—— (1977) *Imperialism and Unequal Development* (Hassocks: Harvester).

——(1978) *Some Thoughts on Self-Reliant Development, Collective Self-Reliance and the NIEO* (Stockholm: Institute for International Economic Studies).

Amsden, A. (1989) *Asia's Next Giant: South Korea and Late Industrialization* (New York: Oxford University Press).

——(2001) *The Rise of 'The Rest': Challenges to the West from Late-Industrializing Economies* (Oxford: Oxford University Press).

Anand, S. and Sen, A. (2000) 'Human Development and Economic Sustainability', *World Development*, 28(12): 2029–49.

Anderson. B. (1990) *Language and Power: Exploring Political Cultures in Indonesia* (Ithaca, NY: Cornell University Press).

——(1991) *Imagined Communities*, 2nd edn (London: Versa).

Anderson, J. (1985) *Research and Agricultural Progress* (Armidale: University of New England).

Anderson, J., Herdt, R. and Scobie, G. (1986) *Science and Food: The CGIAR and its Partners*, vols 1–4 (Washington, DC: CGIAR).

Anderson, M. (1999) *Do No Harm: How Aid Can Support Peace – or War* (Boulder, CO: Lynne Rienner Publishers).

Antrobus, P. (n.d.) 'MDGs – the Most Distracting Gimmick. Contextualising the MDGs. Seeking Accountability on Women's Human Rights: Women Debate the Millennium Development Goals', *Women's International Coalition for Economic Justice*. Available at: www.wicej.addr.com/mdg/toc.html (accessed 1 March 2011).

Appel, G. (1990) 'Costing Social Change', in M. Dove (ed.), *The Real and Imagined Role of Culture in Development: Case Studies from Indonesia* (Honolulu: University of Hawaii Press).

Ariff, M. (ed.) (1998) *APEC and Development Cooperation* (Singapore: Institute of South East Asian Studies).

Arifin, E. (2010) 'Contraceptive Discontinuation in Bali, Indonesia'. Available at: www.blisstiger.com/topic/view/id-17266 (accessed 16 April 2011).

Aristotle (1997) ed. and trans. P. Simpson, *The Politics of Aristotle* (Charlotte: University of North Carolina Press).

Arrighi, G. (2002) 'The African Crisis: World Systemic and Regional Aspects', *New Left Review* 15: 5–38.

Arrighi, G. (2005) 'Hegemony Unravelling', *New Left Review* 32, 33.

ASC, TI, CSS, PRC (2003) *Failed and Collapsed State in the International System*. The African Studies Center (Leiden: The Transnational Institute; Amsterdam: The Center for Social Studies; Coimbra University, the Peace Research Center-CIP-FUHEM), December 2003.

Aspinall, E. and Mietzner, M. (eds) (2010). *Problems of Democratisation in Indonesia* (Singapore: Institute of Southeast Asian Studies Press).

Atkinson, A. (2006) 'Funding the Millennium Development Goals: A Challenge for Global Public Finance', *European Review* 14(4): 555–64.

AusAID (Australian Agency for International Development) (2001) Budget Summary 2001–02, available at www.ausaid.gov.au/budget/ summary (accessed 22 May 2001).

——(2006a), *Pacific 2020: Challenges and Opportunities for Growth* (Canberra: AusAID).

——(2010a) 'Cairns Compact on Strengthening Development Coordination: What is the Cairns Compact?' Available at: www.ausaid.gov.au/country/pacific/cairnscompact.cfm (accessed 1 March 2011).

——(2010b) *Women, Peace and Security AusAID's Implementation of United Nations Security Council Resolution 1325* (Canberra: AusAID).

Avonius, L. and Kingsbury, D. (2008) *Human Rights in Asia: A Reassessment of the Asian Values Debate* (London: Routledge).

Ayers, J. and Huq, S. (2009) 'Supporting Adaptation to Climate Change: What Role for Official Development Assistance?' *Development Policy Review*, 27(6): 675–92.

Ayres, R. (1983) *Banking on the Poor: The World Bank and World Poverty* (Cambridge, MA: MIT Press).

Baek, S.-W. (2005) 'Does China Follow "The East Asian Development Model"?', *Journal of Contemporary Asia*, 35: 485–98.

Bain, I. (1996) 'The China Country Program', in P. Kilby (ed.), *Australia's Aid Program: Mixed Messages and Conflicting Agendas* (Melbourne: Monash Asia Institute and Community Aid Abroad).

Balassa, B. (1971) *The Structure of Protection in Developing Countries* (Baltimore, MD: Johns Hopkins University Press).

Balchin, C. (2010). *Towards a Future without Fundamentalisms: Analyzing Religious Fundamentalist Strategies and Feminist Responses* (Toronto: AWID).

Bannon, I. and Correia, M. C. (eds) (2006) *The Other Half of Development: Men's Issues in Development* (Washington, DC: World Bank).

Barton, C. and Pendergast, L. (n.d.) 'Seeking Accountability on Women's Human Rights: Women Debate the Millennium Development Goals. Debates on Gender and the MDGs', (Women's International Coalition for Economic Justice. Available at http://www.eldis.or/assets/Docs/14154.html

Barr, M. (2000) 'Lee Kuan Yew and the "Asian Values" Debate', *Asian Studies Review*, 24(3), 1 June 2000: 309–34.

Bass, T. A. (1990) *Camping with the Prince and Other Tales of Science in Africa* (New York: Penguin).

Bates, R. (2001) *Prosperity and Violence* (New York and London: W. W. Norton).

Battaile, W. (2002) *ARDE 2001: Making Choices* (World Bank Annual Review of Development Effectiveness).

Bauer, J. and Bell, D. (1999) *The East Asian Challenge for Human Rights* (Cambridge: Cambridge University Press).

Bauer, P. (1971) *Dissent on Development* (London: Weidenfeld & Nicolson).

Bauer, P. (1993) *Development Aid: End it or Mend It*, Occasional Papers No. 43 (San Francisco: International Center for Economic Growth/ICS Press).

Baulch, B. (2004) 'Aid Distribution and the MDGs', *World Development*, 34(6): 933–50.

Baur, J. and Rudolph, J. (2001) 'Water Facts and Findings on Large Dams as Pulled from the Report of the World Commission on Dams', *Development and Cooperation*, no. 2.

Bayliss, K. and McKinley, T. (2007) 'Privatising Basic Utilities in Sub-Saharan Africa: The MDG Impact', *Policy Research Brief* (Brasilia, International Poverty Centre, UNDP).

Bebczuk, R. and Gasparini, L. (2000) 'Globalization and Inequality: The Case of Argentine', paper in *Poverty and Income Inequality in Developing Countries: A Policy Dialogue on the Effects of Globalization* (Paris: OECD, 30 November–1 December 2000).

Beck, U. (2000) *What is Globalization?* (Cambridge: Polity).

Beeson, M. and Islam, I. (2005) 'Neo-Liberalism and East Asia: Resisting the Washington Consensus', *Journal of Development Studies*, 41: 197–219.

Bell, D. (2000) *East Meets West: Human Rights and Democracy in East Asia* (Princeton, NJ: Princeton University Press).

——(2008) *China's New Confucianism: Politics and Everyday Life in a Changing Society* (Princeton: Princeton University Press).

Belshaw, H. (1947) 'Observations on Industrialization for Higher Incomes', *Economic Journal* (September): 379–87.

Ben-David, D., Nordstrom, H. and Winters, L. (1999) *Trade, Income Disparity and Poverty Special Studies 5* (Washington, DC: World Trade Organization).

Beneria, L. (1995) 'Toward a Greater Integration of Gender in Economics', *World Development*, 23(11): 1839–50.

——(1999) 'The Enduring Debate over Unpaid Labour', *International Labour Review*, 138(3): 287–309.

——(2001) 'Structural Adjustment Policies', in L. Beneria and S. Bisnath (eds), *Gender and Development: Theoretical, Empirical and Practical Approaches* (London: Elgar Publishing), pp. 419–27.

Beneria, L. and Bisnath, S. (2001) *Gender and Development: Theoretical, Empirical and Practical Approaches,* vols 1 and 2 (London: Elgar Publishing).

Beneria, L. and Permanyer, I. (2010) 'The Measurement of Socio-economic Gender Inequality Revisited', *Development and Change*, 41(3): 375–99.

Berger, M. and Borer, D. (eds) (1997) *The Rise of East Asia: Critical Visions of the Pacific Century* (London: Routledge).

Berlin, I. (1958) *Two Concepts of Liberty* (Oxford: Oxford University Press).

Bessell, S. (2010) 'Methodologies for gender-sensitive and pro-poor poverty measures', in S Chant (ed.) *The International Handbook of Gender and Poverty: Concepts, Research, Policy* (Cheltenham, UK, and Northampton, MA, USA: Edward Elgar) pp. 59–64.

Bessette, J. (1994) *The Mild Voice of Reason: Deliberative Democracy and the American National Government* (Chicago, IL: University of Chicago Press).

Betts, Richard K. (1993) 'Wealth, Power and Instability: East Asia and the United States After the Cold War', *International Security*, 18(3): 34–77.

Bhagwati, J. (2004) *In Defense of Globalization* (New York: Oxford University Press).

Bhagwati, J. and Desai, P. (1970) *India – Planning for Industrialization* (London: Oxford University Press).

Bilgin, P. and Morton, A. (2002) 'Historicizing Representations of "Failed States": Beyond the Cold War Annexation of the Social Sciences?', *Third World Quarterly* 23(1).

Birdsall, N. (2011) 'The Global Financial Crisis: The Beginning of the End of the "Development" Agenda', in N. Birdsall and F. Fukuyama (eds), *New Ideas on Development After the Financial Crisis* (Baltimore, MD: Johns Hopkins University Press), pp. 1–26.

Black, M. (1992) *A Cause for Our Times: Oxfam the First 50 Years* (Oxford: Oxfam).

Blair, H. (1997) *Success and Failure in Rural Development: A Comparison of Maharasthra, Bihar and Bangladesh,* paper presented to Peasant Symposium, Bucknell University, 10 May 1997.

Blattberg, C. (2003) 'Patriotic, Not Deliberative Democracy', *Critical Review of International Social and Political Philosophy*, 6(1): 155–74.

Bloch, M. (ed.) (1975) *Marxist Analyses and Social Anthropology* (New York: Wiley).

Bobbitt, P. (2002) *The Shield of Achilles: War, Peace and the Course of History* (London: Allen Lane).

Boff, L. and Boff, C. (1984) *A Concise History of Liberation Theology* (New York: Orbis Books).

Booth, C. (1887) 'The Inhabitants of Tower Hamlets (School Division Board), Their Condition and Occupations', *Journal of the Royal Statistical Society* 50: 326–40.

Booth, D. (2011) 'Aid, Institutions and Governance: What Have We Learned?' *Development Policy Review* 29: s5–s26.

Borer, T. A. (2009) 'Gendered War and Gendered Peace: Truth Commissions and Postconflict Gender Violence: Lessons From South Africa', *Violence Against Women*, 15(10): 1169–93.

Boserup, E. (1970) *Women's Role in Economic Development* (New York: St Martin's Press).

Bourdieu, P. (1977) *Outline of a Theory of Practice*, trans. Richard Nice (Cambridge: Cambridge University Press).

Bourguignon, F. and Morrisson, C. (2002) 'Inequality Among World Citizens: 1820–1992', *American Economic Review*, 92(4): 727–44.

Bouta, T. and Frerks, G. (2003) *Women's Roles in Conflict Prevention, Conflict Resolution and Post-Conflict Reconstruction: Literature Review and Institutional Analysis* (The Hague: Netherlands Institute of International Relations).

Boyce, J. (2002) 'Unpacking Aid', *Development and Change* 33(2): 329–46.

Boyer, R. and Hollingsworth, J. (1997) 'The Variety of Institutional Arrangements and their Complementarity in Modern Economies', in J. R. Hollingsworth and R. Boyer (eds), *Contemporary Capitalism: The Embeddedness of Institutions* (Cambridge: Cambridge University Press), pp. 49–54.

Brabant, J. van (1990) *Remaking Eastern Europe— On the Political Economy of Transition* (Dordrecht: Kluwer Academic Publishers).

Braidotti, R., Charkeiwicz, E., Hausler, S. and Wieringa, S. (1997) 'Women, the Environment and Sustainable Development', in N. Visvanathan, L. Duggan, L. Nisonoff and N. Wiegersma (eds), *The Women, Gender and Development Reader* (London: Zed Books), pp. 54–61.

Brainard, L., Chollet, D. and LaFleur, V. (2007) 'The Tangled Web: The Poverty-Insecurity Nexus', in L. Brainard and D. Chollet (eds), *Too Poor for Peace? Global Poverty, Conflict, and Security in the 21st Century* (Washington, DC: Brookings Institution Press), pp. 1–30.

Bremmer, I. (2010) *The End of the Free Market* (New York: Portfolio).

Brenner, R. (2006) *The Economics of Global Turbulence* (London: Verso).

Broadman, H. (2007) *Africa's Silk Road: China and India's New Economic Frontier* (Washington, DC: World Bank).

Brown, R. (2010). 'Unequal Burden: Water Privatisation and Women's Human Rights in Tanzania', *Gender and Development*, 18(1): 59–67.

Brundtland, G. (1987) *Our Common Future* (Oxford: Oxford University Press).

Buckelew, A. (1984) *Terrorism and the American Response* (San Rafael, CA: Mira Academic Press).

Budlender, D. (2001) 'The South African Women's Budget Initiative: What Does it Tell Us about Poverty Alleviation?' (ch. 15) in F. Wilson, K. Nazneen and E. Braathen (eds), *Poverty Reduction: What Role for the State in Today's Globalised Economy?* (Cape Town: CROP International Studies on Poverty, NAEP).

——(2008) 'Why Care Matters for Social Development', *UNRISD Research and Policy Brief* no. 9 (Geneva: UNRISD).

Bulír, A., Gelb, A. and Mosley, P. (2008) 'Introduction: The Volatility of Overseas Aid', *World Development*, 36(10): 2045–47.

Burkey, S. (1988) *People First: A Guide* (London and New Jersey: Zed Books).

Burki, T. (2010) 'Aid Slows to a Trickle as Pakistan Crisis Enters a New Phase', *The Lancet* 376(9746): 1041–42.

Burnside, C. and Dollar, D. (1997) *Aid, Policies and Growth*, Policy Research Working Papers 1777 (Washington, DC: World Bank).

Burton, M., Gunther, R. and Higley, J. (eds) (1992) *Elites and Democratic Consolidation in Latin America and Southern Europe* (Cambridge: Cambridge University Press).

Bush, G. W. (2002) The National Security Strategy of the United States of America, available at: www.whitehouse.gov/nsc/nss/html (accessed 23 October 2002).

Bussolo, M. and De Hoyos R. (2009). 'Introduction and Overview', *Gender Aspects Of The Trade And Poverty Nexus: A Macro-Micro Approach* (Washington, DC: World Bank).

Buvinic, M. (1986) 'Projects for Women in the Third World: Explaining their Misbehavior', *World Development*, 14(5): 653–64.

Buxton, J. and Phillips, N. (eds) (1999) *Developments in Latin American Political Economy* (Manchester: Manchester University Press).

Bytown Consulting and C.A.C. International (2008) *Evaluation of CIDA's Implementation of its Policy on Gender Equity. Executive Report*, presented to Evaluation Division, Canadian International Development Agency.

Cagatay, N. (2003) 'Gender Budgets and Beyond: Feminist Fiscal Policy in the Context of Globalization', *Gender and Development*, 11(1): 15–24.

Cairncross, A. (1962) *Factors in Economic Development* (London: Allen & Unwin).

Camilleri, J. (1994) 'Reflections on the State in Transition', *Arena* (Melbourne).

Camilleri, J. and Falk, J. (1992) *The End of Sovereignty? The Politics of a Shrinking and Fragmented World* (London: Edward Elgar).

Campbell, T. (1983) *The Left and Rights* (London: Routledge & Kegan Paul).

Cardero, M. (2000) 'The Impact of NAFTA on Female Employment in Mexico', in L. de Pauli (ed.), *Women's Empowerment and Economic Justice: Reflecting on Experience in Latin America and the Caribbean* (New York: UNIFEM).

Cardoso, F. (1982) 'Dependency and Development in Latin America', in H. Alavi and T. Shanin (eds), *Introduction to the Sociology of Developing Countries* (New York: Monthly Review Press), pp. 112–27.

Cardoso, F. and Faletto, R. (1979) *Dependency and Development* (Berkeley: University of California Press).

Cassen, R. and Associates (1994) *Does Aid Work?*, Report to an Intergovernmental Task Force (Oxford: Clarendon Press).

Cassidy, J. (2010) *How Markets Fail: The Logic of Economic Calamities*. New York: Picador.

Cassity, E. (2010) 'New Partnerships and Education Policy in Asia and the Pacific', *International Journal of Educational Development*, 30: 508–17.

Cernea, M. (ed.) (1985) *Putting People First*, 1st edn (New York: Oxford University Press/World Bank).

Cernea, M. (ed.) (1991) *Putting People First*, 2nd edn (New York: Oxford University Press/World Bank).

CCSBT (Commission for the Conservation of Southern Bluefin Tuna) (2002) *Origins of the Convention* (Canberra: Commission for the Conservation of Southern Bluefin Tuna).

CGIAR (Consultative Group on International Agricultural Research) (1978) *Farming Systems Research at the International Agricultural Research Centers* (Rome: FAO).

——1985) *Summary of International Agricultural Research Centers: A Study of Achievements and Potential* (Washington, DC: CGIAR Secretariat).

Chambers, R. (1980) *Rural Poverty Unperceived: Problems and Remedies* (Washington, DC: World Bank).

——(1983) *Rural Development: Putting the Last First* (Harlow: Longman).

Chan, S. (2002) *Liberalism, Democracy and Development* (Cambridge: Cambridge University Press).

Chandler, D. (2010) *International Statebuilding: The Rise of Post-Liberal Governance* (London: Routledge).

Chandy, L. and Gertz, G. (2011) 'Poverty in Numbers: The Changing State of Global Poverty from 2005 to 2015', *Brookings Global Views Policy Brief 2011–01* (Washington, DC: The Brookings Institute).

Chang, H.-J. (1999) 'The Economic Theory of the Developmental State', in M. Woo-

Cumings (ed.), *The Developmental State* (Ithaca, NY: Cornell University Press) pp. 182–99.

——(2002) *Kicking Away the Ladder: Development Strategy in Historical Perspective* (London: Anthem Press).

——(2007a) *The East Asian Development Experience: The Miracle, the Crisis and the Future* (London: Zed Books).

——(2007b) *Bad Samaritans: The Guilty Secrets of Rich Nations and the Threat to Global Prosperity* (London: Random House).

——(2010) *23 Things They Don't Tell You About Capitalism* (London: Allen Lane).

Chant, S. (2004) 'Dangerous Equations? How Female-headed Households became the Poorest of the Poor: Causes, Consequences and Cautions', *IDS Bulletin*, 35(4): 19–26.

——(2007) 'Gender, Cities, and the Millennium Development Goals in the Global South', *New Working Paper Series*, LSE Gender Institute.

——(2008) 'The "Feminisation of Poverty" and the "Feminisation" of Anti-Poverty Programmes: Room for Revision?' *Journal of Development Studies*, 44(2): 165–97.

——(2010a) 'Gendered Poverty Across Space and Time: Introduction and Overview', in S. Chant (ed.) *The International Handbook of Gender and Poverty: Concepts, Research, Policy* (Cheltenham, UK, and Northampton, MA, USA: Edward Elgar), pp. 1–26.

——(2010b) 'Towards a (Re) Conceptualisation of the "Feminisation of Poverty": Reflections on Gender-differentiated Poverty from The Gambia, Philippines and Costa Rica', in S. Chant (ed.) *The International Handbook of Gender and Poverty: Concepts, Research, Policy* (Cheltenham, UK, and Northampton, MA, USA: Edward Elgar), pp. 111–16.

Chellaney, B. (2011) *Water: Asia's New Battleground* (Washington, DC: Georgetown University Press).

Chenery, H. (1955) 'The Role of Industrialization in Development Programmes', *American Economic Review*, 45(2), May.

—— (ed.) (1971) *Studies in Development Planning* (Cambridge, MA: Harvard University Press).

——(1979) *Structural Change and Development Policy* (London: Oxford University Press).

Chenery, H., Ahluwalia, M. S., Bell, C. L. G., Duloy, J. H. and Jolly, R. (1974) *Redistribution with Growth* (Oxford: Oxford University Press).

Chenery, H. and Syrquin, M. (1975) *Patterns of Development, 1950–70* (London: Oxford University Press).

Chibba, M. (2011) 'The Millennium Development Goals: Key Current Issues and Challenges', *Development Policy Review*, 29(1): 75–90.

Chirot, D. (2011) 'A Turning Point or Business as Usual?' in C. Calhoun and G. Derluguian (eds) *Business as Usual: The Roots of the Global Financial Meltdown* (New York: New York University Press), pp. 113–36.

Chirzin, H. (2002) *Globalization, Development and Liberation in the Third Millennium: An Islamic Perspective,* available at: www.202.64.82.162/daga/ds/dsp00/dl3m-h.htm (accessed 24 December 2002).

Cho, K. (1999) *Pollution Statistics in Korea in Relation to 1993 SNA* (Seoul: Bank of Korea Research Department).

Chomsky, N. (1994) *Media Control: The Spectacular Achievements of Propaganda* (New York: Open Media/Seven Stories Press).

Chomsky, N. and Herman, E. (1988) *Manufacturing Consent: The Political Economy of the Mass Media* (New York: Pantheon Books).

Chun, H, Munyi, E., and Lee, H. (2010) 'South Korea as an Emerging Donor: Challenges and Changes on its Entering OECD/DAC', *Journal of International Development*, 22(6): 788–802.

Churchill, W. (1947) Speech to House of Commons, London, 11 November 1947. CIDA Review, Ottawa 1995.

Cincotta, R. (2010) 'Demographic Challenges to the State', in N. Tschiri, M. Lund and F. Mancini (eds) *Security and Development: Searching for Critical Connections* (Boulder, CO: Lynne Rienner), pp. 77–98.

Clague, C. (ed.) (1997) *Institutions and Economic Development: Growth and Governance in Less-Developed and Post-Socialist Countries* (Baltimore, MD: Johns Hopkins University Press).

Clapham, C., Herbst, G. and Mills, G. (eds) (2006) *Big African States* (Johannesburg: Wits University Press).

Clark, C. (1940) *The Conditions of Economic Progress* (London: Macmillan).

Clark, J. (1991) *Democratizing Development* (London: Earthscan).

Clarke, M. (2006) 'Assessing Well-Being Using Hierarchical Needs', in M. McGillivray and M. Clarke (eds), *Understanding Human Well-Being* (Tokyo: United Nations University Press).

Clarke, M. and Paech, S. (2004) 'The Measurement of Well-being Based on Hierarchical Needs: A Multidimensional Approach Applied to South-east Asia', paper to the 28th General Conference of the International Association for Research in Income and Wealth, Cork, 22–28 August.

Clarke, M., Islam, S. and Paech, S. (2006) 'Measuring Australia's Well-being Using Hierarchical Needs', *Journal of Socio-Economics*, 35(6): 933–45.

Clay, E., Geddes, M., and Natali, L. (2009) *Untying Aid: Is it working? An Evaluation of the Implementation of the Paris Declaration and of the 2001 DAC Recommendation of Untying ODA to the LDCs* (Copenhagen: Danish Institute for International Studies).

Club of Rome (1972) *Limits to Growth* (Rome).

——(1974) *Mankind at the Turning Point* (Rome).

Cockburn, J., Fofana, I., Decaluwe, B., Mabugu, R. and Chitiga, M. (2007) 'Gender-Focused Macro-Micro Analysis of the Poverty Impacts of Trade Liberalization in South Africa', in Peter J. Lambert (ed.) *Equity (Research on Economic Inequality)*, Emerald Group Publishing Limited, 15: 269–305.

Cockburn, J., Decaluwé, B., Fofana, I.,Robichaud, V. (2008) *Trade, Growth and Gender in Developing Countries:A Comparison of Ghana, Honduras, Senegal and Uganda*, Poverty and Economic Policy (PEP) Research Network and CIRPÉE (Université Laval).

Cohen, J. (2003) 'For a Democratic Society', in S. Freeman (ed.) *The Cambridge Companion to Rawls* (Cambridge: Cambridge University Press).

Colclough, C. and Manor, J. (eds) (1991) *States or Markets? Neo-Liberalism and the Development Policy Debate* (Oxford: Oxford University Press).

Cole, M. and Neumayer, E. (2003) 'The Pitfalls of Convergence Analysis: Is the Income Gap Really Widening?' *Applied Economic Letters*, 10(6): 355–57.

Coleman, J. (1990) *Foundations of Social Theory* (Cambridge, MA: Harvard University Press).

Collier, D. and Levitzky, S. (1997) 'Democracy with Adjectives: Conceptual Innovation in Comparative Research', *World Politics* 49(3).

Collier, P. (1998) 'The Political Economy of Ethnicity', paper to the Annual World Bank Conference on Development Economics, Washington, DC, 20–21 April.

——(2009) *Wars, Guns and Votes: Democracy in Dangerous Places* (New York: Harper-Collins).

Collinson, S. Elhawary, S. and Muggah, R. (2010) 'States of Fragility: Stabilisation and its Implications for Humanitarian Action', *Disasters*, 34: S275–S296.

Commonwealth Expert Group (1989) *Engendering Adjustment for the 1990s: Report of a Commonwealth Expert Group on Women and Structural Adjustment* (London: Commonwealth Secretariat).

Considine, M.-L. (2010) '*REDD alert*' *ECOS: Towards a Sustainable Future,* CSIRO Publishing, available at: www.ecosmagazine.com/paper/EC10047.htm (accessed 1 March 2011).

Conway, G. R., McCracken, J. A. and Pretty, J. N. (1987) *Training Notes for Agroecosystem Analysis and Rapid Rural Appraisal,* 2nd edn (London: IIED).

Coote, B. (1992) *The Trade Trap: Poverty and the Global Commodity Markets* (Oxford: Oxfam).

Cornia, G., Jolly, R. and Stewart, F. (eds) (1987) *Adjustment with a Human Face,* vols 1 and 2 (Oxford: Clarendon Press).

Cornwall, A. (2001) 'Making a Difference? Gender and Participatory Development', *IDS Discussion Paper,* no. 378 (Brighton: Institute of Development Studies).

Cornwall, A., Harrison, E. and Whitehead, A. (eds) (2007) *Feminisms in Development: Contradictions, Contestations and Challenges* (London: Zed Books).

Cornwall, A., Harrison, E. and Whitehead, A. (2004) 'Introduction: Repositioning Feminisms in Gender and Development', *IDS Bulletin,* 35(4): 1–10.

Cornwell, R. (1999) 'The End of the Post-Colonial State System in Africa?', *African Security Review* 8(2).

Costa, M., Sharp, R., Elson, D. (2009) 'Gender Responsive Budgeting in the Asia Pacific Region: Democratic Republic of Timor-Leste', available at: www.unisanet.unisa.au/genderbudgets (accessed 27 January 2011).

Coudouel, A., Hentschel, J. and Woden, Q. (n.d.), 'Poverty Measurement and Analysis', in World Bank (ed.), *Poverty Reduction Strategy Sourcebook,* vol. 1: *Core Techniques and Cross-Cutting Issues,* available at: www.worldbank.org/poverty/strategies/chapters/data/pdtn0509.pdf (accessed 22 February 2007).

Cowen, M. and Shenton, R. (1996) *Doctrines of Development* (London: Routledge).

Cox, R. (1996) 'A Perspective on Globalization', in J. Mittelman (ed.), *Globalization: Critical Reflections* (Boulder, CO: Lynne Rienner Publishers).

Crone, P. (1986) 'The Tribe and the State', in J. Hall (ed.), *States in History* (Oxford: Basil Blackwell).

Crouch, C. (2011) *The Strange Non-Death of Neoliberalism* (Cambridge: Polity).

CVCB (Co-operative Venture for Capacity Building) (2007) *About Capacity Building,* available at www.rirdc.gov.au/capacitybuilding/about.html (accessed 28 April 2007).

Dabelko, G. (1996) *The Environment and Conflict in the Third World: Examining Linkage, Context and Policy,* Occasional Paper no. 12, Harrison Program on the Future Global Agenda, January 1996.

Dahl, R. (1970) *After the Revolution: Authority in Good Society* (New Haven, CT: Yale University Press).

——(1971) *Polyarchy and Opposition: Participation and Opposition* (New Haven, CT: Yale University Press).

——(1986) *Democracy, Liberty and Equality* (Toyen: Norwegian University Press).

——(1989) *Democracy and Its Critics* (New Haven, CT: Yale University Press).

——(2000) *On Democracy* (New Haven, CT: Yale University Press).

Dains, R. (2004) 'Lasswell's Garrison State Reconsidered: Exploring a Paradigm Shift in US Civil–Military Relations', PhD thesis, University of Alambama, Tuscaloosa.

Dangwal, D. (2005) 'Commercialisation of Forests, Timber Extraction and Deforestation in Uttaranchal, 1815–1947', *Conservation and Society,* 3(1): 110–33.

Danielson, A. (1982) *The Evolution of OPEC* (New York: Harcourt, Brace, Jovanovich).

DARA (2010) 'The Humanitarian Response Index 2010: The Problems of Politicisation. Executive Summary' (Madrid: DARA).

Darling, M. L. (1925) *The Punjab Peasant* (London).

Das, S. (2006) *Traders, Guns and Money: Knowns and Unknowns in the Dazzling World of Derivatives* (London: Prentice Hall).

——(2011) *Extreme Money: The Masters of the Universe and the Cult of Risk* (London: Penguin).

Das Pradhan (2000) 'Engendering Good Governance in Practice', *Development Bulletin* 51: 6–9.

Davies, J. B., Sandstrom, S., Shorrocks, A. and Wolff, E. N. (2006) 'The World Distribution of Household Wealth', *World Institute for Development Economics Research* (Helsinki), December 2006.

Davis, K. and Dadush, S. (2010) 'The Privatization of Development Assistance: Symposium Overview', NYU *Journal of International Law and Politics,* vol. 42.

de Bary, W. (1998) *Asian Values and Human Rights: A Confucian Communitarian Perspective* (Cambridge, MA: Harvard University Press).

de Pauli, L. (ed.) (2000) *Women's Empowerment and Economic Justice: Reflecting on Experience in Latin America and the Caribbean* (New York: UNIFEM).

de Rivero, O. (2001) *The Myth of Development: The Non-Viable Economies of the 21st Century* (London: Zed Books).

de Silva, D. (1990) *Against All Odds: Breaking the Poverty Trap* (London: Panos).

de Soto, H. (1989) *The Other Path,* trans. J. Abbott (New York: Harper & Row).

——(2000) *The Mystery of Capital: Why Capitalism Triumphs in the West But Fails Everywhere Else* (London: Bantam Press).

de Ste Croix, G. (1987) *The Class Struggle in the Ancient Greek World from the Archaic Age to the Arab Conquests* (London: Duckworth).

de Waal, A. (1989) *Famine that Kills* (Oxford: Clarendon Press).

——(1998) *Famine Crimes: Politics and the Disaster Relief Industry in Africa* (Indiana: Indiana University Press).

Deininger, K. and Squire, L. (1998) 'New Ways of Looking at Old Issues: Inequality and Growth', *Journal of Development Economics* 57: 259–87.

Demetriades, J. and E. Esplen (2008) 'The Gender Dimensions of Poverty and Climate Change Adaptation' *IDS Bulletin,* 39(4): 24–31.

Denison, E. (1971) 'Welfare Measurement and the GNP', *Survey of Current Business* 51: 13–16,39.

Derrida, J. (1980) *Writing and Difference* (Chicago, IL: University of Chicago Press).

Desai, R. and Kharas, H. (2010) 'Democratizing Foreign Aid: Online Philanthropy and International Development Assistance', *International Law and Politics,* 42(4): 1111–42.

Desch, M. (1999) *Civilian Control of the Military: The Changing Security Environment* (Baltimore, MD: Johns Hopkins University Press).

Dey, J. (1982) 'Development Planning in the Gambia: The Gap between Planners and Farmers' Perceptions, Expectations and Objectives', *World Development,* 10(5).

DFID (Department for International Development) (1997) *Eliminating World Poverty: A Challenge for the Twenty-First Century,* White Paper (London: DFID).

——(2000) *Making Globalization Work for the World's Poor: An Introduction to the UK Government's White Paper on International Development* (London: DFID).

——(2010) *Eliminating World Poverty: Building our Common Future* (London, DFID).

Diamond, J. (1999a) *Guns, Germs and Steel: The Fates of Human Societies* (New York: W. W. Norton).

Diamond, L. (1999b) *Developing Democracy Toward Consolidation* (Baltimore, MD: Johns Hopkins University Press).

DiMarco, L. (ed.) (1972) *International Economics and Development: Essays in Honour of Raul Prebisch* (London: Academic Press).

Di Palma, G. (1991) *To Craft Democracies: An Essay on Democratic Transition* (Berkeley: University of California Press).

Dodd, C. (1972) *Political Development* (London: Macmillan).

Dollar, D. and Kraay, A. (2002) 'Spreading the Wealth', *Foreign Affairs* 81(1): 120–33.

Dollar, D and Levine, V. (2006) 'The Increasing Selectivity of Foreign Aid' 1984–2003', *World Development*, 34(12): 2034–46.

Domar, E. (1957) *Essays in the Theory of Economic Growth* (New York: Oxford University Press).

Dore, R. (1986) *Flexible Rigidities: Industrial Policy and Structural Adjustment in the Japanese Economy, 1979–80* (London: Athlone Press).

Downie, S. and Kingsbury, D. (2001) 'Political Development and the Re-emergence of Civil Society in Cambodia', *Contemporary Southeast Asia* 23.

Downs, A. (1957) *An Economic Theory of Democracy* (Harper: New York).

Doyal, L. and Gough, I. (1991) *A Theory of Human Need* (London: Macmillan).

Drechsler, D. and Jütting, J. (2010) 'Why is Progress in Gender Equality so Slow? An Introduction to the "Social Institutions and Gender" Index', in S. Chant (ed.) *The International Handbook of Gender and Poverty: Concepts, Research, Policy* (Cheltenham, UK and Northampton, MA, USA: Edward Elgar), pp. 77–83.

Duffield, M. (2002) 'Social Reconstruction and the Radicalization of Development: Aid as a Relation of Global Liberal Governance', *Development and Change* 33(5): 1049–71.

——(2005) 'Social Reconstruction: The Reuniting of Aid and Politics', *Development*, 48(3): 16–24.

Duménil, G. and Lévy, D. (2011) *The Crisis of Neoliberalism* (Cambridge, MA: Harvard University Press).

Duncan, R. (2000) *Globalization and Income Inequality: An International Perspective*, Conference on International Trade Education and Research: Managing Globalization for Prosperity, Victorian Department of State and Regional Development, Melbourne, 26–7 October.

Dunkerley, J., Ramsay, W., Gordon, L. and Cecelski, E. (1981) *Energy Strategies for Developing Nations* (Baltimore, MD, and London: Johns Hopkins University Press).

Dupont, A. (2001) *East Asia Imperilled: Transnational Challenges to Security* (Cambridge: Cambridge University Press).

Dureau, C. (2003) Address to 'Working Together for East Timor' Conference, Darebin City Council, Melbourne, 4–5 April.

Dutt, A. (ed.) (2002) *The Political Economy of Development*, vols 1–3 (Cheltenham: Edward Elgar).

——(2005) 'International Trade in Early Development Economics', in K. S. Jomo and Erik Reinert (eds), *Development Economics: How Schools of Economic Thought Have Addressed Development* (London: Zed Books), pp. 99–127.

Dymski, G. (2010) 'Why the Subprime Crisis is Different: A Minskyian Approach', *Cambridge Journal of Economics*, 34: 239–55.

Easterly, W. (2001) *The Elusive Quest for Growth* (Cambridge, MA: MIT Press).

——(2006) *The White Man's Burden: Why the West's Efforts to Aid the Rest have Done So Much Ill and So Little Good* (New York: Penguin Press).

——(2010) 'Foreign Aid for Scoundrels', *The New York Review of Books*, November 25. Available at: www.nybooks.com/articles/archives/2010/nov/25/foreign-aid-scoundrels (accessed 1 March 2011).

Ehrlich, P. (1969) *The Population Bomb* (New York: Ballantyne Books).

Eichengreen, B. (1999) *Toward a New International Financial Architecture: A Practical Post-Asia Agenda* (Washington, DC: Institute for International Economics).

——(2007) *Global Imbalances and Lessons of Bretton Woods* (Cambridge, MA.: MIT Press).

Eichengreen, B. and Fishlow, A. (1998) 'Contending with Capital Flows: What is Different about the 1990s?' in M. Kahler (ed.), *Capital Flows and Financial Crises* (Manchester: Manchester University Press), pp. 23–68.

Eicher, C. K. and Staatz, J. M. (eds) (1990) *Agricultural Development in the Third World,* 2nd edn (Baltimore, MD: Johns Hopkins University Press).

Elkington, J. (1999) *Cannibals with Forks: The Triple Bottom Line of 21st-Century Business* (Oxford: Capstone).

Elliott, C. (1987) *Comfortable Compassion* (London: Hodder & Stoughton).

Elliot, L. and Denny, C. (2002) 'Top 1% Earn as Much as the Poorest 57%', *The Guardian,* 18 January.

Ellis, H. S. (ed.) (1961) *Economic Development for Latin America* (London: Macmillan).

Elson, D. (1991) 'Structural Adjustment: Its Effect on Women', in T. Wallace and C. March (eds), *Changing Perceptions: Writings on Gender and Development* (Oxford: Oxfam), pp. 39–59.

——(2010) 'Gender and the Global Economic Crisis in Developing Countries: A Framework for Analysis', *Gender and Development,* 18(2): 201–12.

Elson, D. and Sharp, R. (2010) 'Gender-responsive Budgeting and Women's Poverty', in S. Chant (ed.) *The International Handbook of Gender and Poverty: Concepts, Research, Policy* (Cheltenham, UK, and Northampton, MA, USA: Edward Elgar), pp. 522–7.

Ely, R. T. (1903) *Studies in the Evolution of Industrial Society.* (New York, The Macmillan Company; London, Macmillan & Co. Ltd). Available at http://www. archive.org/details/studiesinevolut00elygoog.

Emmanuel, A. (1972) *Unequal Exchange* (London: Monthly Review Press).

Englebert, P. (2000) 'Pre-Colonial Institutions, Post-Colonial States, and Economic Development in Topical Africa', *Political Research Quarterly,* 53(1): March, 7–36.

Eriksen, T. (2002) *Ethnicity and Nationalism,* 2nd edn (London: Pluto Press).

Escobar, A. (1995) *Encountering Development: The Making and Unmaking of the Third World* (Princeton, NJ: Princeton University Press).

Espino, M. (2000) 'Women and Mercosur: The Gendered Dimension of Economic Integration', in L. De Pauli (ed.), *Women's Empowerment and Economic Justice* (New York: UNIFEM).

Esplen, E. (2006) *Engaging Men in Gender Equality: Positive Strategies and Approaches – Overview and Annotated Bibliography* (Brighton: BRIDGE, Institute of Development Studies).

Estefa (2001) *Evaluating the World Bank's Community Empowerment Project,* 7(2).

Evans, P. (1995) *Embedded Autonomy: States and Industrial Transformation* (Princeton, NJ: Princeton University Press).

Evans, P, Rueschemeyer, D., and Skocpol, T. (eds) (1985) 'On the Road Towards a More Adequate Understanding of the State', in *Bringing the State Back In* (Cambridge: Cambridge University Press).

Eyben, R. (2008) 'Power, Mutual Accountability and Responsibility in the Practice of International Aid: A Relational Approach', *IDS Working Paper* (Brighton: Institute of Development Studies at the University of Sussex).

Faber, M. and Seers, D. (eds) (1972) *The Crisis in Planning* (London: Chatto & Windus).

FAO (Food and Agriculture Organization) (2001) *State of the World's Forests 2001* (Rome: Food and Agriculture Organization of the United Nations).

——(2006) *State of the World's Fisheries and Aquaculture* (New York: FAO, United Nations).

——(2010) *State of the World's Fisheries and Aquaculture* (New York: FAO, United Nations).

Feeny, S. (2004) 'The Impact of Foreign Aid on the Rural Sector in Melanesia', *Report Prepared for the Australian Agency for International Development* (Melbourne: RMIT University Press).

Feeny, S. and Clarke, M. (2006) 'Will the MDGs be Achieved in the Asia-Pacific

Region?', presented at the *Education for the End of Poverty Conference,* Melbourne, 28 April.

Feith, H. (1962) *The Decline of Constitutional Democracy in Indonesia* (Ithaca, NY: Cornell University Press).

Fengler, W. and Kharas, H. (eds) (2010) *Delivering Aid Differently: Lessons from the Field* (Washington, DC: Brookings Institution Press).

Ferguson, N. (2005) 'Sinking Globalization', *Foreign Affairs,* 2005 (2): 64–77.

——(2011) *Civilization: The West and the Rest* (London: Allen Lane).

Ferry, L. (2009) 'Sustainable Development in the Context of Globalization', speech to French Senate, 1 October.

FfP (Fund for Peace) (2006) *Failed State Index 2006,* available at: www.fundforpeace. org/programs/fsi/fsindex2006.php.

Firth, R. (1927) 'The Study of Primitive Economics', *Economica,* December: 312–35.

Fishlow, A. (1985) 'Lessons from the Past: Capital Markets in the 19th Century and the Interwar Period', in M. Kahler (ed.), *The Politics of International Debt* (Ithaca, NY: Cornell University Press), pp. 37–94.

Florini, A. (2000) 'Who does What? Collective Action and the Changing Nature of Authority', in R. Higgott, R. Underhill and A. Bieler (eds), *Non-State Actors and Authority in the Global System* (London: Routledge).

Floro, M. and Schaeffer, K. (2001) 'Restructuring of Labour Markets in the Philippines and Zambia: The Gender Dimension', in L. Beneria and S. Bisnath (eds), *Gender and Development: Theoretical, Empirical and Practical Approaches,* vol. 2I (London: Elgar Publishing), pp. 393–418.

FOE (Friends of the Earth) (2002) *Friends of the Earth WTO Scorecard: WTO and Free Trade vs. Environment and Public Health,* available at: www.foe.org/camps/intl/green-trade/scorecard.pdf.

——(2005) 'WTO GM trade war – has Europe lost the case?'(London: Friends of the Earth).

Fontana, M. (2009) Gender Justice in Trade Policy: The Gender Effects of Economic Partnership Agreements – Synthesis Report. (London: One World Action and the Commonwealth Secretariat) http://www.genderandtrade.org/files/219947/FileName/GENDER_TRADE_REPORT_FINAL_V2_lo-res.pdf Accessed 19 December 2011.

Fontana, M., Joekes, S. and Masika, R. (1998) *Global Trade Expansion and Liberalisation: Gender Issues and Impacts* (Brighton: BRIDGE, Institute of Development Studies).

Fordham (2002) 'Scatter Plot: Infant Mortality versus Access to Safe Water', *Stabilization Policy in Developing Countries, Political Economy and Development* (New York City: Fordham University).

Forsberg, K. (2011) 'Spending cuts Shortsighted: Bad for America's Future', Media Release, 15 February (Washington, DC: Interaction).

Foster, J., Greer, J. and Thorbecke, E. (1984), 'A Class of Decomposable Poverty Measures', *Econometrica,* 52(3): 761–6.

Foster, M. and Leary, J. (2001) *The Choice of Financial Aid Instruments,* Working Paper no. 158 (London: Overseas Development Institute).

Foucault, M. (1976) *Society Must Be DefendedLectures at the College de France 1975–76,* trans. D. Macey (London: Allen Lane).

——(1982) *The Archeology of Knowledge and The Discourse on Language,* trans. R. Swyer (New York: Pantheon Books).

Fox, J. (2009) *The Myth of the Rational Market: A History of Risk, Reward, and Delusion on Wall Street* (New York: Harper).

Fox, J. and Brown, D. L. (1998) *The Struggle for Accountability: The World Bank, NGOs and Grassroots Movements* (Cambridge, MA: MIT Press).

Frank, A. G. (1966) 'The Development of Underdevelopment', *Monthly Review*, 18: 17–31.

Frank, A. G. (1967) *Capitalism and Underdevelopment in Latin America* (London: Monthly Review Press).

Frank, A. G. (1980) *Crisis in the World Economy* (New York: Holmes & Meier).

Frank, A. G. and Gills, B. (1992) 'The Five Thousand Year World System: an Interdisciplinary Introduction', *Humboldt Journal of Social Relations*, 19(2): 1–80.

Frank, A. G. and Gills, B. (1993) *The World System: Five Hundred Years or Five Thousand* (London: Routledge).

Frank, A. G., Chew, S., and Denemark, R. (eds) (1996) *The Underdevelopment of Development: Essays in Honor of Andrew Gunder Frank* (Thousand Oaks and London: Sage Publications).

Freedman, L. (2008) *The Choice of Enemies: America Confronts the Middle East* (London: Weidenfeld & Nicolson).

Freedom House (2002) *Freedom in the World Country Ratings, 1972–3 to 2001–2* (New York).

Freire, P. (1976) *Education: The Practice of Freedom* (London: Writers and Readers Publishing Cooperative).

——(1985) [1970] *Pedagogy of the Oppressed* (Harmondsworth: Pelican Books).

Friday, L. and Laskey, R. (1989) *The Fragile Environment: The Darwin College Lectures* (Cambridge: Cambridge University Press).

Friedberg, A. (1993) 'Ripe for Rivalry: Prospects for Peace in a Multipolar Asia', *International Security*, 18(3): 5–33.

Frieden, J., Pastor, M. and Tomz, M. (eds) (2000) *Modern Political Economy and Latin America: Theory and Policy* (Boulder, CO: Westview).

Friedman, E. (2009) 'How Economic Superpower China Could Transform Africa'. *Journal of Chinese Political Science*, 14: 1–20.

Friedman, J. (1992) *Empowerment: The Politics of Alternative Development* (Oxford: Blackwell Publishing).

Fritz, V. and Cammack, D. (2006) 'State-building and Fragile States. Development Horizons: Future Directions for Research and Policy Seminar', 15 December (London: Overseas Development Institute).

Fritz, V. and Menocal, A. R. (2006) '(Re)building Developmental States: From Theory to Practice', Working Paper no. 274 (London: Overseas Development Institute).

Fromm, E. and Maccoby, M. (1970) *Social Character in a Mexican Village: A Sociopsychoanalytic Study* (Englewood Cliffs, NJ: Prentice-Hall).

Frost, Ellen (2008) *Asia's New Regionalism* (Boulder, CO: Lynne Rienner).

Frot, E. and Santiso, J. (2010) 'Crushed Aid: Fragmentation in Sectoral Aid', *OECD Development Centre Working Paper* (Working Paper no. 284).

Fuggle, R. and Smith, W. (2000) *Experience with Dams in Water and Energy Resource Development in the People's Republic of China* (Cape Town: World Commission on Dams).

Fuglesang, A. and Chandler, D. (1986) *Participation as Process: What We Can Learn from Grameen Bank, Bangladesh* (Oslo: NORAD).

Fukuda-Parr, S. (2010) 'Reducing Inequality – The Missing MDG: A Content Review of PRSPs and Bilateral Donor Policy Statements' *IDS Bulletin*, 41(1): 26–35.

Fukuyama, F. (1992) *The End of History and the Last* Man (London: Verso).

——(2004) *State Building* (London: Profile Books).

Furnival, J. S. (1939) *Netherlands India: A Study of a Plural Economy* (Cambridge: Cambridge University Press).

Furtado, C. (1964) *Development and Underdevelopment* (Berkeley: University of California Press).

Furtado, C. (1965) *Diagnosis of the Brazilian Crisis* (Berkeley: University of California Press).

——(1969) *Economic Development in Latin America* (Cambridge: Cambridge University Press).

Gagne, G. (2000) 'International Trade Rules and States: Enhanced Authority for the WTO?', in R. Higgott, R. Underhill and A. Bieler (eds), *Non-State Actors and Authority in the Global System* (London: Routledge).

Galati, G. and Melvin, M. (2004) 'Why has Foreign Exchange Trading Surged? Explaining the 2004 Triennial Survey', *BIS Quarterly Review*, December.

Galbraith, J. K. (1979) *The Nature of Mass Poverty* (Cambridge, MA: Harvard University Press).

Galbraith, J. and Berner, M. (2001) *Inequality and Industrial Change* (Cambridge: Cambridge University Press).

Gallasch, D. (2001) *Taking Shelter Under Trees* (Chiang Mai: Friends without Borders).

Galtung, J. (1997) 'Grand Designs on a Collision Course', *Development* 40(1): 71–5 (reprinted from *International Development Review* (1978): 3–4).

Gamble, C. (1986) 'Hunter-gatherers and the Origins of the State', in J. Hall (ed.), *States in History* (Oxford: Basil Blackwell).

Gao Bai (2001) *Japan's Economic Dilemma: The Institutional Origins of Prosperity and Stagnation* (Cambridge: Cambridge University Press).

Gardner, K. and Lewis, D. (1996) *Anthropology, Development and the Post-Modern Challenge* (London: Pluto Press).

Garrett, G. (2004) 'Globalization's Missing Middle', *Foreign Affairs* 83(6): 84–96.

Gaye, A., Klugman, J., Kovacevic, M., Twigg, S. and Zambrano, E. (2010) 'Measuring Key Disparities in Human Development: The Gender Inequality Index', *Human Development Research Paper*, UNDP.

GCM (Global Commodity Markets) (2000) 'Summary', *Global Commodity Markets* (Washington, DC: World Bank).

GE (Global Economy) (2002) *Global Economy: World Bank and IMF* (San Francisco: Global Exchange).

Gellner, E. (1964) *Thought and Change* (London: Weidenfeld & Nicolson).

——(1983) *Nations and Nationalism* (Ithaca: Cornell University Press).

George, S. (1998) *A Fate Worse than Debt* (London: Penguin).

Gereffi, G. and Wyman, D. (eds) (1990) *Manufacturing Miracles: Paths to Industrialization in Latin America and East Asia* (Princeton, NJ: Princeton University Press).

German, T. and Randel, J. (2002) 'Never Richer, Never Poorer', part 4, World Aid Trends, in *The Reality of Aid: An Independent Review of Poverty Reduction and Development Assistance* (Manila: IBON Books), pp. 145–57.

Gerschenkron, A. (1962) *Economic Backwardness in Historical Perspective* (Cambridge, MA: Harvard University Press).

GHI (Global Humanitarian Initiative) (2010) *GHA Report 2010* (Somerset: Global Humanitarian Assistance, Development Initiatives).

Ghosh, B. N. (ed.) (2001) *Global Financial Crises and Reforms* (London: Routledge).

Gibb, R., Hughes, T., Mills, G. and Vaahtoranta, T. (eds) (2002) *Charting a New Course: Globalization, African Recovery and the New Africa Initiative* (Johannesburg: South African Institute of International Affairs).

Giddens, A. (1990) *The Consequences of Modernity* (Stanford, CA: Stanford University Press).

——(1991) *Modernity and Self-Identity* (Cambridge: Polity).

——(1995) *Beyond Left and Right* (Cambridge: Polity).

Gill, I. and Kharas, H. (2007) *An East Asian Renaissance: Ideas for Economic Growth* (Washington, DC: World Bank).

Gill, I., Huang, Y. and Kharas, H. (2007) *East Asian Visions: Perspectives on Economic*

Development (Washington, DC: World Bank; and Singapore, Institute of Policy Studies).

Glewwe, P. and van der Gaag, J. (1988) 'Confronting Poverty in Developing Countries: Definitions, Information and Policies', *Living Standards Measurement Study,* Working Paper no. 48 (Washington, DC: World Bank).

Global Witness (2007) 'Hot Chocolate: How Cocoa Fuelled the Conflict in Côte d'Ivoire' (Washington, DC: Global Witness).

Goertz, A.-M. and Sandler, J. (2007) 'Swapping gender: from cross-cutting obscurity to sectoral security?', in A. Cornwall, E. Harrison and A. Whitehead (eds) (2007), *Feminisms in Development: Contradictions, Contestations, and Challenges* (London, Zed Books), pp. 161–73.

Gonzalez, J., Lauder, K. and Melles, B. (2000) *Opting for Partnership: Governance Innovations in Southeast Asia* (Ottawa and Kuala Lumpur: Institute on Governance).

Gonzalez-Vicente, R. (2011) 'China's Engagement in South America and Africa's Extractive Sectors: New Perspectives for Resource Curse Theories', *The Pacific Review,* 24: 65–87.

Goulet, D. (1971) *The Cruel Choice: A New Concept in the Theory of Development* (New York: Atheneum).

Gowan, P. (1999) *The Global Gamble: Washington's Faustian Bid for World Dominance* (London: Verso).

Gramsci, A. (1971) *Selections from Prison Notebooks,* ed. and trans. Q. Hoare and G. Smith (London: Lawrence & Wishart).

Grant, J. A. and Taylor, I. (2004) 'Global Governance and Conflict Diamonds: The Kimberley Process and the Quest for Clean Gems', *The Round Table,* 93(375): 385–401.

Grawert, E. (2009) *Departures From Postcolonial Authoritarianism* (Frankfurt am Main: Peter Lang).

Gray, J. (1998) *False Dawn: The Delusions of Global Capitalism* (London: Granta).

——(2003) *Al Qaeda and What it Means to be Modern* (London: Faber & Faber).

——(2007) *Black Mass: Apocalyptic Religion and the Death of Utopia* (London: Allen Lane).

Green, R. H. (1978) 'Basic Human Needs: Concept or Slogan, Synthesis or Smokescreen?', *IDS Bulletin* 9(4): 7–11.

Greenpeace (2001) *Safe Trade in the 21st Century: The Doha Edition,* Greenpeace Comprehensive Proposals and Recommendation for the 4th Ministerial Conference of the World Trade Organization (Amsterdam: Greenpeace International).

Greig, A., Kimmel, M. and Lang, J. (2000) 'Men, Masculinities and Development: Broadening our Work towards Gender Equality', *Gender in Development Monograph Series* 10 (New York: UNDP).

Grenfell, D. (2007) 'Reconstituting the Nation: Reconciliation and the National Community in Timor-Leste', *Occasional Papers in Justice and International Studies,* School of International and Community Studies, RMIT University.

Griffin, K. and Kahn, A. R. (1978) 'Poverty in the Third World: Ugly Facts and Fancy Models', *World Development,* 6(3), March: 295–304.

Griffiths, M. (2003) 'Self-determination, International Society and World Order', *Macquarie Law Journal,* vol 3.

Groves, L. and Hinton, R. (eds) (2004) *Inclusive Aid: Changing Power and Relationships in International Development* (London: Earthscan).

Grown, C., Elson, D. and Cagatay, N. (2000) 'Introduction', *World Development,* 28(7): 1145–56.

Grugel, J. (2002) *Democratization: A Critical Introduction* (Basingstoke: Palgrave Macmillan).

Guillen, M. (2001) 'Is Globalization Civilizing, Destructive, or Feeble? A Critique of Five Key Debates in the Social-Science Literature', *Annual Review of Sociology,* 27.

Gujit, I. and Shah, M. K. (1998) *The Myth of Community: Gender Issues in Participatory Development* (London: Intermediate Technology Publications).

Gupta, S., Clements, B., Bhattacharya, R. and Chakravartiv, S. (2002) 'Fiscal Consequences of Armed Conflict and Terrorism in Low- and Middle-Income Countries', IMF Working Paper no. 142 (Washington: International Monetary Fund).

Gupta, S., Pattillo, C. and Wagh, S. (2009) 'Effect of Remittances on Poverty and Financial Development in Sub-Saharan Africa', *World Development*, 37 (1):104–15.

Gurtov, M. (1994) *Global Politics in the Human Interest,* 3rd edn (Boulder, CO: Lynne Rienner).

Gusfield, J. (1976) 'Tradition and Modernity: Misplaced Polarities in the Study of Social Change', *American Journal of Sociology*, 72.

G77 (2002) *Final Communique Adopted by the Thirty-Second Meeting of the Chairmen/Coordinators of the Chapters of the Group of 77,* Geneva, 14–15 February.

Haber, S. (ed.) (2000) *Political Institutions and Economic Growth in Latin America: Essays in Policy, History and Political Economy* (Stanford, CA: Hoover Institution Press).

Haberler, G. (1948) 'Some Economic Problems of the European Recovery Program', *American Economic Review* (September): 495–525.

Habermas, J. (2001a) 'A Constitution for Europe?', *New Left Review*, 11: 5–26.

——(2001b) *A Postnational Constellation* (Cambridge, MA: MIT Press).

Hadjimichael, M. (1996) *Adjustment for Growth: The African Experience,* Occasional Paper (Washington, DC: International Monetary Fund).

Hadjimichael, M. T., Ghura, D., Muhleisen, M., Nord, R. and Ucer, E. M. (1995) *Sub-Saharan Africa: Growth, Savings and Investment 1986–93,* Occasional Paper no. 118 (Washington, DC: International Monetary Fund).

Haggard, S. (2000) *The Political Economy of the Asian Financial Crisis* (Washington, DC: Institute for International Economics).

Haggard, S., Lim, W. and Kim, E. (eds) (2003) *Economic Crisis and Corporate Restructuring in Korea* (Cambridge: Cambridge University Press).

Hall, P. and Taylor, R. (1996) 'Political Science and the Three New Institutionalisms', *Political Studies*, 44(5): December, 936–57.

Halper, S. (2010) *The Beijing Consensus: How China's Authoritarian Model Will Dominate the Twenty-First Century* (New York: Basic Books).

Hameiri, S. (2008) 'Risk Management, Neo-liberalism and the Securitisation of the Australian Aid Program', *Australian Journal of International Affairs,* 62(3): 357–71.

Han, F, Fernandez, W and Tan, S. (1998) *Lee Kuan Kuan Yew: The Man and His Ideas* (Singapore: Times Editions).

Hancock, G. (1989) *Lords of Poverty* (London: Macmillan).

Hannig, A. and Jansen, S. (2010) 'Financial Inclusion and Financial Stability: Current Policy Issues', ABDI Working Paper no. 259 (Tokyo: Asian Development Bank Institute).

Hansen, A. H. (1941) 'The Stagnation Thesis', in *Fiscal Policy and Business Cycles,* reprinted in A. Smithies and J. K. Butters (eds) (1955), *AEA Readings in Fiscal Policy* (Homewood, IL: Richard D. Irwin), pp. 540–57.

Hansen, H. and Tarp, F. (2000) 'Aid Effectiveness Disputed', in F. Tarp (ed.), *Foreign Aid and Development: Lessons Learned and Directions for the Future* (London: Routledge), pp. 103–28.

Hansen, J., Ruedy, R., Sato, M. and Lo, K. (2006) *GISS Surface Temperature Analysis, Global Temperature Trends: 2005 Summation* (New York: Goddard Institute for Space Studies, National Aeronautics and Space Administration).

HAP International (2008) *The Guide to the HAP Standard: Humanitarian Accountability and Quality Management* (Oxfam GB for HAP International).

Haq, G., Han, W. and Kim, C. (eds) (2002) *Urban Air Pollution Management and Practice in Major and Mega Cities of Asia* (Seoul: Korea Environment Institute).

Harrison, L. and Huntington, S. (eds) (2000) *Culture Matters: How Values Shape Human Progress* (New York: Basic Books).

Harrod, R. (1948) *Towards a Dynamic Economics* (London).

Harvey, D. (2003) *The New Imperialism* (Oxford: Oxford University Press).

——(2010) *The Enigma of Capitalism and the Crises of Capitalism* (Oxford: Oxford University Press).

Haynes, J. (ed.) (2000) *Democracy in the Third World* (London: Routledge).

HDR (2006) *Human Development Report 2006: Beyond Scarcity: Power, Poverty and the Global Water Crisis* (New York: United Nations Development Program).

He, B. (2010) 'Participatory and Deliberative Institutions in China', in E. Leib and B. He (eds), *The Search for Deliberative Democracy in China* (London: Palgrave Macmillan).

Healey, D. (1973) 'Development Policy: New Thinking about an Interpretation', *Journal of Economic Literature*, 10.

Hegel, G. (1967) *Hegel's Philosophy of Right,* trans. T. M. Knox (Oxford: Oxford University Press).

Heinonen, P. (2006) 'Changing Perceptions: Globalization, Women and Development', International Women's Congress, Women's Role in the Alliance of Civilizations, Istanbul, 28–9 January.

Held, D. (1996) *Models of Democracy,* 2nd edn (Cambridge: Polity).

Held, D. and McGrew, A. (2007) *Globalization/Anti-globalization: Beyond the Great Divide* (Cambridge: Polity Press).

Held, D. and Young, K. (2011) 'Crises in Parallel Worlds: The Governance of Global Risks in Finance, Security and the Environment', in C. Calhoun and G. Derluguian (eds) *The Deepening Crisis: Governance Challenges After Neoliberalism* (New York: New York University Press), pp. 19–42.

Held, D., McGrew, A., Goldblatt, D. and Perraton, J. (1999) *Transformations* (Cambridge: Polity).

Hellinger, S., Hellinger, D. and O'Regan, F. (1988) *Aid for Just Development* (London: Lynne Rienner).

Herbst, G. (2000) *States and Power in Africa: Comparative Lessons in Authority and Control* (Princeton, NJ: Princeton University Press).

Herfindahl, O. and Brooks, D. (eds) (1974) *Resource Economics: Selected Works of Orris C. Herfindahl* (Baltimore, MD: Resources for the Future).

Herman, E. and McChesney, R. (2000) 'The Global Media' in D. Held and A. McGrew (eds), *The Global Transformations Reader* (London: Polity).

Hettne, B. (1995) *Development Theory and the Three Worlds,* 2nd edn (London: Longman).

Hickey, S. and Mohan, G. (2005) 'Relocating Participation within a Radical Politics of Development', *Development and Change*, 36(2): 237–62.

Hicks, N. (1980) 'Is there a Trade-off between Growth and Basic Needs?', *Finance and Development*, 17(2): 17–20.

Hicks, N. and Streeten, P. (1979) 'Indicators of Development: The Search for a Basic Needs Yardstick', *World Development* 7: 567–80.

Higgins, B. (1958) *Economic Development: Principles, Problems, and Policies* (London: Constable).

Higgott, R. (2000) 'The International Relations of the Asian Economic Crisis: A Study in the Politics of Resentment', in R. Robison, M. Beeson, K. Jayasuriya and H.-R. Kim (eds), *Politics and Markets in the Wake of the Asian Crisis* (London: Routledge), pp. 261–82.

Hill, S., Elsom, J., Stewart, J. and Marsh, K. (1981) *Development with a Human Face* (Canberra: AGPS).

Hillar, M. (1993) 'Liberation Theology: Religious Response to Social Problems – A Survey', in M. Hillar and H. R. Leuchtag (eds), *Humanism and Social Issues: An Anthology of Essays* (Houston, TX: American Humanist Association), pp. 35–52.

Hinsley, F. (1978) *Sovereignty*, 2nd edn (Cambridge: Cambridge University Press).

Hiro, D. (1995) *Between Marx and Muhammad: The Changing Face of Central Asia* (London: HarperCollins).

Hirsch, P. and Warren, C. (eds) (1998) *The Politics of Environment in Southeast Asia: Resources and Resistance* (London: Routledge).

Hirschman, A. (1958) *The Strategy of Economic Development* (Yale, CT: Yale University Press).

Hirschmann, D. (1987) 'Early Post-Colonial Bureaucracy as History: The Case of the Lesotho Central Planning and Development Office, 1965–1975', *International Journal of African Historical Studies*, 20(3): 455–70.

Hirst, P. and Thompson, G. (1996) *Globalization in Question* (London: Polity).

HM Treasury (2004) 'International Issues: International Finance Facility'. PDF file of International Finance Facility Proposal, available at: www.hm-treasury.gov.uk/medi/D64/78/IFF_propsal_doc_080404.pdf.

——(2006) 'International Issues. International Finance Facility', available at: www.hm-treasury.gov.uk/documents/international_issues/int_gnd_intfinance.cfm.

Hobijn, B. (2002) 'What Will Homeland Security Cost?', Paper presented to the German Institute of Global Research (DIW) workshop on 'The Economic Consequences of Global Terrorism', Berlin, available at www.diw.de/deutsch/service/veranstaltungen/ws_consequences.

Hobsbawm, E. (1983) in Hobsbawm, E. and Ranger, E. (eds) *The Invention of Traditions* (Cambridge: Cambridge University Press).

——(1998) 'Introduction' to a modern edition of Karl Marx and Frederick Engels, *The Communist Manifesto* (London: Verso), pp. 1–29.

——(2004) *Nations and Nationalism since 1870: Programme, Myth, Reality* (Cambridge: Cambridge University Press).

Hocking, J. (2004) *Terror Laws: ASIO, Counter-Terrorism and the Threat to Democracy* (Sydney: University of New South Wales Press).

Hodge, P. (1970) 'The Future of Community Development', in A. Robson and B. Crick (eds), *The Future of Social Services* (Harmondsworth: Penguin Books).

Hoffman, B. (2002) 'The Emergence of the New Terrorism' in A. Tan and K. Ramakrishna (eds), *The New Terrorism: Anatomy, Trends, and Counter-Strategies* (Singapore: Eastern Universities Press), pp. 30–49.

Hoffman, P. (1997) 'The Challenge of Economic Development', *Development* 40: 19–24.

Holtz, E. (2007) 'Implementing the United Nations Convention to Combat Desertification from a Parliamentary Point of View: Critical Assessment and Challenges Ahead', Seventh Parliamentarians Forum of the United Nations Convention to Combat Desertification (New York: United Nations).

Homer-Dixon, T. (1991) 'On the Threshold: Environmental Changes as Causes of Acute Conflict', *International Security*, 16: 76–116.

Homer-Dixon, T. (1999) *Environment, Security, and Violence* (Princeton, NJ: Princeton University Press).

Hopkins, A. and K. Patel (2006) 'Reflecting on Gender Equality in Muslim Contexts in Oxfam GB', *Gender and Development*, 14(3): 423–35.

Hopkins, M. (1991) 'Human Development Revisited: A New UNDP Report', *World Development* 19(10): 1461–73.

Hopkins, R. F. (2000) 'Political Economy of Foreign Aid', in F. Tarp (ed.), *Foreign Aid and Development: Lessons Learned and Directions for the Future* (London: Routledge).

Hopkins, T. and Wallerstein, I. (1982) *World-Systems Analysis: Theory and Methodology* (Beverly Hills, CA: Sage).

Hoppe, H. (2001) *Democracy: The God That Failed* (Rutgers, NJ: Transaction Publishers).

Horowitz, D (1985) *Ethnic Groups in Conflict* (Berkeley, CA: University of California Press).

Hoskyns, C. and Rai, S. M. (2007) 'Recasting the Global Political Economy: Counting Women's Unpaid Work', *New Political Economy*, 12(3): 297–317.

Hossain, M. (1988) *Credit for Alleviation of Rural Poverty: The Grameen Bank in Bangladesh,* Research Report no. 65 (Washington, DC: International Food Policy Research Institute).

Howard, R. (1983) 'The Full-Belly Thesis: Should Economic Rights Take Priority over Civil and Political Rights? Evidence from Sub-Saharan Africa', *Human Rights Quarterly* 5(4): November, 467–90.

Howell, J. (2006) 'The Global War on Terror, Development and Civil Society', *Journal of International Development*, 18: 121–35.

Howlett, D. (2010) '"Please Keep Pushing on the Financial Transaction Tax" G20 Sherpa Tells Civil Society', Make Poverty History Canada, available at: www.robinhoodtax.ca/story/please-keep-pushing-on-the-financial-transaction-tax-g20-sherpa-tells-civil-society (accessed 1 March 2011).

Htaw, L. (2008) 'Burma Tops List in Deforestation', Independent Mon News Agency (USA), 6 June.

Huang, Y. (2008) *Capitalism with Chinese Characteristics: Entrepreneurship and the State* (New York: Cambridge University Press).

Hudson Institute (2010) *The Index of Global Philanthropy and Remittances* 2010, available at: www.hudson.org/files/pdf_upload/Index_of_Global_Philanthropy_and_Remittances_2010.pdf. (Washington DC: Hudson Institute Center for Global Prosperity) (accessed 22 December 2010).

Hulme, D. and Shepherd, A. (2003) 'Conceptualizing Chronic Poverty', in D. Hume and A. Shepherd (eds), *Chronic Poverty and Development Policy, World Development* Special issue (Oxford: Pergamon), pp. 403–23.

Human Rights Watch (2002) 'Bush Should Urge Democratic Reforms in Pakistan', Press Release, 12 September.

Hundt, D. (2005) 'A Legitimate Paradox: Neo-liberal Reform and the Return of the State in Korea', *Journal of Development Studies*, 41: 242–60.

Hunt, D. (1989) *Economic Theories of Development: An Analysis of Competing Paradigms* (New York: Harvester Wheatsheaf).

Hunt, J. (1996) 'Women's Vision of a Just World Order', in *Towards Sustainable Livelihoods: Report of 1994–95 SID PIED Workshops on Civil Society and Sustainable Livelihoods, held in Asia, Sub-Saharan Africa, Latin America and North America* (Rome: Society for International Development).

Huntington, S. (1957) *The Soldier and the State: The Theory and Politics of Civil–Military Relations* (Cambridge, MA: Belknap Press).

——(1968) *Political Order in Changing Societies* (Cambridge, MA: Yale University Press).

——(1971) 'The Change to Change: Modernization, Development, and Politics', *Comparative Politics*, 3: 283–328.

——(1987) 'The Goals of Development', in M. Weiner and S. Huntington (eds), *Understanding Political Development* (Boston, MA: Little, Brown), pp. 4-28.

——(1993a) The Clash of Civilizations', *Foreign Affairs* 72(3): 22–50.

——(1993b) 'Democracy's Third Wave', *Journal of Democracy* Vol 2, No. 2. Spring 1991, pp 12–34.

——(1996) *The Clash of Civilizations and the Remaking of the New World Order* (New York: Simon & Schuster).

Hurley, D. (1990) *Income Generation Schemes for the Urban Poor*, Development Guidelines no. 4 (Oxford: Oxfam).

Hutchcroft, P. (1998) *Booty Capitalism: The Politics of Banking in the Philippines* (Ithaca, NY: Cornell University Press).

IBT (International Business Times) (2001) 'What is Foreign Exchange?', *International Business Times*, available at: www.au.ibtimes.com/articles/110821/20110210/what-is-foreign-exchange-currency-conversion-financial-markets-forex-foreign-exchange-markets.htm (accessed 31 March 2011).

IEA (International Energy Agency) (2002) *World Energy Outlook, 2002* (Paris: OECD and IEA).

——(2010) 'World Energy Outlook 2010 Factsheet' (Paris: International Energy Agency).

ILO (International Labour Organization) (1976) *Employment, Growth and Basic Needs* (Geneva: International Labour Organization).

——(1977) *Employment, Growth and Basic Needs: A One World Problem* (New York: Praeger).

IMF (International Monetary Fund) (2002) *Globalization: A Framework for IMF Involvement* (Washington, DC: International Monetary Fund).

——(2005) 'Solomon Islands: 23005 Article IV Consultation', Staff Report and Public Information Notice on the Executive Board Discussion, IMF Country Report no. 365 (Washington, DC: IMF).

——(2007) *Global Financial Stability Report, April 2007*, International Monetary Fund (Washington, DC: International Monetary Fund).

——(2009) *World Economic Outlook* (Washington, DC: International Monetary Fund), April.

Inglehart, R., Basanez, M., Moreno, A. and Mendozo, M. (1998) *Human Values and Beliefs: A Cross-Cultural Sourcebook* (Ann Arbor: University of Michigan Press).

INGO (International Non-government Organizations) (2006) Accountability Charter, available at: www.ingoaccountabilitycharter.org/wpcms/wp-content/uploads/ingo-accountability-charter-eng.pdf (accessed 1 March 2011).

IRN (International Rivers Network) (2001) *Manibeli Declaration* (International Rivers Network).

Isbister, J. (1991) *Promises Not Kept* (West Hartford, CT: Kumarian Press).

Ivanic, M. and Martin, W. (2008) 'Implications of Higher Global Food Prices in Low-Income Countries', *World Bank Policy Research Working Paper 4594* (Washington, DC: World Bank).

Jackson, B. (1990) *Poverty and the Planet: A Question of Survival* (London: Penguin).

Jackson, K. (ed.) (1999) *Asian Contagion: The Causes and Consequences of a Financial Crisis* (Boulder, CO: Westview).

Jackson-Preece, J. (2000) 'Self-Determination, Minority Rights and Failed States', paper presented to the Failed States Conference, Florence, 7–10 April.

Jacoby, T. and James, E. (2010) 'Emerging Patterns in the Reconstruction of Conflict-affected Countries', *Disasters*, 34: S1–S14.

Jaguaribe, H. (1968) *Economic and Political Development* (Cambridge, MA: Harvard University Press).

Jahan, R. (1995) *The Elusive Agenda: Mainstreaming Women in Development* (London: Zed Books).

Jain, L., Krishnamurty, B. and Tripathi, P. (1985) *Grass Without Roots: Rural Development Under Government Auspices* (New Delhi: Sage Publications).

Jefferess, D. (2008) *Post-Colonial Resistance: Culture, Liberation and Transformation* (Toronto: University of Toronto Press).

Jefferys, A. (2002) 'Giving Voice to Silent Emergencies', *Humanitarian Exchange* 20: 2–4.

Jenkins, B. and Godges, J. (2011) *The Long Shadow of 9/11: America's Response to Terrorism* (Santa Monica, CA: Rand).

Jhamb, B. and N. Sinha (2010) *Millennium Development Goals and Gender Budgeting: Where does India stand?* (New Delhi: Centre for Budget and Governance Accountability).

Johannen, U., Smith, A. and Gomez, J. (2003) *September 11 and Political Freedom: Asian Perspectives* (Singapore: Select Publishing).

Johnson, C. (1987) 'Political Institutions and Economic Performance: The Government Business Relationship in Japan, South Korea and Taiwan', in F. Deyo (ed.), *The Political Economy of the New Asian Industrialism* (Ithaca, NY: Cornell University Press), pp. 136–65.

——(2000) *Blowback: The Costs and Consequences of American Empire* (New York: Little, Brown).

Johnsson-Latham, G. (2010), 'Power, Privilege and Gender as Reflected in Poverty Analysis and Development Goals', in S. Chant, S. (ed), *The International Handbook of Gender and Poverty* (Cheltenham: Edward Elgar Publishing Inc.), pp. 41–6.

Jolly, R. (1999) 'New Composite Indices for Development Cooperation', *Development*, 42(3): 36–42.

Jomo, K. S. (ed.) (1998) *Tigers in Trouble: Financial Governance, Liberalisation and Crises in East Asia* (London: Zed Books).

Jomo, K. and Nagaraj, S. (2001) *Globalisation Versus Development* (Basingstoke: Palgrave).

Jomo, K. S. and Rodriguez, F. (2011) 'Structural Causes and Consequences of the 2008–2009 Financial Crisis', in C. Calhoun and G. Derluguian (eds), *Aftermath: A New Global Economic Order* (New York: New York University Press), pp. 97–118.

Jones, N., Harper, C., Pantuliano, S. and Pavanello, S. (2009) 'The Global Economic Crisis and Impacts on Children and Caregivers: Emerging Evidence and Possible Policy Responses in the Middle East and North Africa', Background note (London: ODI).

Jones, N., Harper, C., and Watson, C. with Espey, J., Wadugodapitiya, D., Ella Page, Stavropoulou, M., Presler-Marshall, E. and Clench, B. (2010) *Stemming Girls' Chronic Poverty: Catalysing Development Change by Building Just Social Institutions* (Manchester: Chronic Poverty Research Centre).

Jones, N., Holmes, R. and Espey, J. (2010) 'Progressing Gender Equality Post-2015: Harnessing the Multiplier Effects of Existing Achievements', *IDS Bulletin,* 44(1): 113–22.

Juara, R. (2000) 'Experts Seek Ways to Combat Desertification', *Third World Network.*

Jupp, J. (1968) *Political Parties* (New York: Routledge & Kegan Paul).

Kabeer, N. (1999) *The Conditions and Consequences of Choice: Reflections on the Measurement of Women's Empowerment,* UNRISD Discussion Paper no. 108 (Geneva: UNRISD).

——(2005) 'Gender Equality and Women's Empowerment: A Critical Analysis of the Third Millennium Development Goals', *Gender and Development*, 13(1): 13–24.

——(2006) ' Poverty, Social Exclusion and the MDGs: The Challenge of "Durable Inequalities" in the Asian Context', *IDS Bulletin,* 37(3): 64–78.

——(2008) *Mainstreaming Gender in Social Protection for the Informal Economy* (London: Commonwealth Secretariat).

Kabeer, N. and Anh, T. T. V. (2000) 'Leaving the Ricefields, but not the Countryside: Gender, Livelihood Diversification and Pro-poor Growth in Rural Viet Nam', *UNRISD* Occasional Paper no. 13 (Geneva: UNRISD).

Kamal-Chaoui, L. (2000) 'Halving Poverty', *OECD Observer,* 17 April.

Kanbur, R. (2000) 'Aid, Conditionality, and Debt in Africa', in F. Tarp (ed.), *Foreign Aid*

——(1972) *Capital,* vol. III (London: Lawrence & Wishart).

——(1973) *Grundrisse* (Harmondsworth: Penguin Books).

Marx, K. and Engels, F. (1967) *Manifesto of the Communist Party* (Moscow: Progress Publishers).

Maslow, A. (1970) *The Farther Reaches of the Human Mind* (New York: Viring Press).

Mason, P. (2009) *Meltdown: The End of the Age of Greed* (London: Verso).

Matthew, R. (2010) 'Environment, Conflict, and Sustainable Development', in N. Tschiri, M. Lund and F. Mancini (eds) *Security and Development: Searching for Critical Connections* (Boulder, CO: Lynne Rienner), pp. 47–75.

Mattick, P. (2011) *Business as Usual: The Economic Crisis and the Failure of Capitalism* (London: Reaktion Books).

McCants, W. (2011) 'Al Qaeda's Challenge: The Jihadists' War with Islamist Democrats', *Foreign Affairs,* 90(5): 20–32.

McCracken, J. A., Pretty, J. N. and Conway, G. (1988) *An Introduction to Rapid Rural Appraisal for Agricultural Development* (London: LIED).

McGillivray, M. (1991) 'The Human Development Index: Yet Another Redundant Composite Development Indicator?', *World Development,* 19(10): 1461–8.

McGillivray, M., Feeny, S., Hermes, N. and Lensink, R. (2006) 'Controversies over the Impact of Development Aid: It Works; It Doesn't; It Can, but That Depends...', *Journal of International Development,* 18: 1031–50.

McGillivray, M., Dutta, I. and Markova, N. (2009) 'Health Inequality and Deprivation', *Health Economics,* 18(S1): 1–12.

McGregor, R. (2010) *The Party: The Secret World of China's Communist Rulers* (London: Allen Lane).

McKay, J. (2003a) 'The Restructuring of the Korean Economy since 1986 and the Onset of the Financial Crisis: The Industrial-Financial Nexus', in Moon Joong Tcha (ed.), *The Economic Crisis and the Korean Economy at the Crossroads* (London: Routledge).

——(2003b) 'APEC's Role in Political and Security Issues', in R. Feinberg (ed.), *APEC as an Institution: Multilateral Governance in the Asia-Pacific* (Singapore: Institute of Southeast Asian Studies), pp. 229–66.

——(2009) 'Food and Health Considerations in Asia-Pacific Regional Security' *Asia Pacific Journal of Clinical Nutrition,* 18(4): 654–63.

McKenzie, J. (2000) *Oil as a Finite Resource: When is Global Production Likely to Peak?* (Washington, DC: World Resources Institute).

McNamara, R. (1981) *The McNamara Years at the World Bank* (Baltimore, MD: Johns Hopkins Press).

McPhail, T. (2010) *Global Communication: Theories, Stakeholders and Trends,* 3rd edn (Chichester: Wiley-Blackwell).

McRae, R. and Hubert, D. (eds) (2001) *Human Security and the New Diplomacy: Protecting People, Promoting Peace* (Montreal: McGill-Queen's University Press).

Mehotra, S. (2002) 'International Development Targets and Official Development Assistance', *Development and Change,* 33(3): 529–38.

Meier, G. (1995) *Leading Issues in Economic Development* (Oxford: Oxford University Press).

Meier, G. and Seers, D. (1984) *Pioneers in Development* (New York: Oxford University Press for the World Bank).

Menkhaus, K. (2010) 'Beyond the Conflict Trap in Somalia', in N. Tschiri, M. Lund and F. Mancini (eds) *Security and Development: Searching for Critical Connections* (Boulder, CO: Lynne Rienner), pp. 135–70.

Michel, S. and Beuret, M. (2009) *China Safari: On the Trail of Beijing's Expansion in Africa* (London: Nation Books).

Michels, R. (1959) *Political Parties: A Sociological Study of the Oligarchical Tendencies of Modern Democracy* (New York: Dover).

Mies, M. (1986) *Patriarchy and Accumulation on a World Scale: Women in the International Division of Labour* (London: Zed Books).

Miguel, E. (2007) 'Poverty and Violence: An Overview of Recent Research and Implications for Foreign Aid', in L. Brainard and D. Chollet (eds), *Too Poor for Peace? Global Poverty, Conflict, and Security in the 21st Century* (Washington, DC: Brookings Institution Press), pp. 50–59.

Milbrath, L. (1996) *Learning to Think Environmentally while there is Still Time* (Albany, NY: State University of New York Press).

Milburn, S. (1954–5) *A Study Prepared for the UN*, UN Series on Community Organisation and Community Development, no. 21 (New York: United Nations).

Mill, J. (1910) *Utilitarianism, Liberty, Representative Government* (London: J. M. Dent).

Miller, D. (1993) 'In Defence of Nationality', *Journal of Applied Philosophy*, 10(1): 3–16.

——(1995) *On Nationality* (Oxford: Oxford University Press).

Milliken, J. and Krause, K. (2002) 'State Failure, State Collapse, and State Reconstruction: Concepts, Lessons and Strategies', *Development and Change*, 33(5): 753–74.

Mills, G. (2002) *Poverty to Prosperity: Globalization, Good Governance and African Recovery* (Johannesburg: Tafelberg Publications and the South African Institute of International Affairs).

——(2010) *Why Africa is Poor: And What Africa Can Do About It* (Johannesburg: Penguin).

Mills, C. Wright (1956) *The Power Elite* (New York: Oxford University Press).

Ministerial Review Team (2001) *Report of the Ministerial Review Team: Towards Excellence in Aid Delivery: A Review of New Zealand's Official Development Assistance Programme* (Wellington).

Minsky, H. P. (1986) *Stabilizing an Unstable Economy* (New Haven: Yale University Press).

Mitchell, S. (2006) 'Not Everything that Counts can be Counted', *Development Bulletin*, 71: September, 20–2.

Mohanty, C. (1997) 'Under Western Eyes: Feminist Scholarship and Colonial Discourses', in N. Visvanathan, L. Duggan, L. Nisonoff and N. Wiegersma (eds), *The Women, Gender and Development Reader* (London: Zed Books), pp. 79–85.

Molyneux, M. and Razavi, S. (2005) 'Beijing Plus Ten: An Ambivalent Record on Gender Justice', *Development and Change*, 36 (6): 983–1010.

Montes, M. Popov, V. (2011) 'Bridging the Gap: A New World Order for Development?' in C. Calhoun and G. Derluguian (eds), *Aftermath: A New Global Economic Order* (New York: New York University Press), pp. 119–48.

Moon, S. and Mills, Z. (2010) 'Practical Approaches to the Aid Effectiveness Agenda: Evidence in Aligning Aid Information with Recipient Country Budgets' (London: Overseas Development Institute).

Moore, M. and Unsworth, J. (2006) 'Britain's New White Paper: Making Governance Work for the Poor', *Development Policy Review*, 24(6): 707–15.

Morganthau, H. (1978) *Politics Among Nations: The Struggle for Power and Peace*, 5th edn (New York: Alfred A. Knopf).

Morris, C. (1998) *An Essay on the Modern State* (Cambridge: Cambridge University Press).

Morris, I. (2010) *Why the West Rules – For Now* (London: Profile Books).

Morris, M. D. (1979) *Measuring the Condition of the World's Poor: The Physical Quality of Life Index* (New York: Pergamon).

Morris-Suzuki, T. (1989) *A History of Japanese Economic Thought* (London: Routledge).

Morrissey, O. (2000) 'Foreign Aid in the Emerging Global Trade Environment', in F. Tarp (ed.), *Foreign Aid and Development* (London: Routledge), pp. 375–90.

Mortimer, R. (1984) 'Stubborn Survivors: Dissenting Essays on Peasants and Third World Development', in H. Feith and R. Tiffen (eds), *Monash Papers on Southeast Asia, no. 10* (Melbourne: Centre for Southeast Asian Studies, Monash University).

Mosca, G. (1939) *The Ruling Class*, trans. A. Livingstone (New York: McGraw-Hill).

Moseley, P. and Eeckhout, M. (2000) 'From Project Aid to Programme Assistance', in F. Tarp (ed.), *Foreign Aid and Development* (London: Routledge), pp. 131–53.

Moser, C. (1991) 'Gender Planning in the Third World: Meeting Practical and Strategic Gender Needs', in T. Wallace and C. March (eds), *Changing Perceptions: Writings on Gender and Development* (Oxford: Oxfam), pp. 158–71.

——(1993) *Gender Planning and Development: Theory, Practice and Training* (London: Routledge).

Moss, T. (2007) *African Development: Making Sense of the Issues and Actors* (Boulder, CO: Lynne Rienner).

Moyo, D. (2009) *Dead Aid: Why Aid is not Working and How There is Another Way for Africa* (New York: Farrar, Strauss & Giroux).

Mukhopadhyay, M. (2007) 'Mainstreaming Gender or "streaming" Gender Away: Feminists Marooned in the Development Business', in A. Cornwall, E. Harrison and A. Whitehead (eds), *Feminisms in Development: Contradictions, Contestations, and Challenges* (London, Zed Books), pp. 135–49.

Mussa, M. (2002) *Argentina and the Fund: From Triumph to Tragedy* (Washington, DC: Institute for International Economics).

Myrdal, G. (1957) *Economic Theory and Underdeveloped Regions* (London: Duckworth).

Narayan, D., Chambers, R., Shah, M. K. and Petesch, P. (1999) 'Global Synthesis: Consultations with the Poor', paper presented at *Global Synthesis Workshop,* World Bank, Poverty Group, 22–3 September, Washington, DC.

Narayan, D., Chambers, R., Shah, M. K. and Petesch, P. (2000) *Voices of the Poor: Crying Out for Change* (New York: Oxford University Press).

Narayan-Parker, D. and Patel, R. (2000) *Voices of the Poor: Can Anyone Hear Us?* (Oxford: Oxford University Press).

Natsios, A. (2006) 'Five Debates on International Development: The US Perspective', *Development Policy Review* 24(2): 131–9.

Nayyar, N. (ed.) (1977) *Economic Relations between Socialist Countries and the Third World* (London: Macmillan).

Nehru, J. (1950) *Independence and After* (New York: John Day).

Nelson, H. (2006) 'Governments, States and Labels', *State, Society and Governance in Melanesia,* Discussion Paper no. 1, Research School of Pacific and Asian Studies (Canberra: Australian National University).

Ness, G. and Ando, H. (1984) *The Land is Shrinking: Population Planning in Asia* (Baltimore, MD: Johns Hopkins University Press).

Nettl, J. (1969) 'Strategies in the Study of Political Development', in C. Leys (ed.), *Politics and Change in Developing Countries* (Cambridge: Cambridge University Press): 13–30.

Nisbet, R. (1969) 'The Metaphor of Growth', in *Social Change and History – Aspects of the Western Theory of Development* (Oxford: Oxford University Press).

Nitsch, Volker and Schumacher, Dieter (2002) 'Terrorism and Trade', paper presented to the German Institute of Global Research (DIW) workshop on 'The Economic Consequences of Global Terrorism', Berlin, available at www.diw.de/deutsch/service/veranstaltungen/ws_consequences).

Nkrumah, K. (1957) *The Autobiography of Kwame Nkrumah* (London: Thomas Nelson).

Noland, M. and Pack, H. (2003) *Industrial Policy in an Era of Globalization: Lessons from Asia* (Washington, DC: Institute for International Economics).

Norman, D. (1974) 'Rationalizing Mixed Cropping under Indigenous Conditions: The Example of Northern Nigeria', *Journal of Development Studies*, 11: 3–21.

——(1980) 'Farming Systems Approach: Relevance for the Small Farmer', *Rural Development Paper no. 5* (East Lansing: Michigan State University).

Nurkse, R. (1952) *Problems of Capital Formation in Developing Countries* (New York: Oxford University Press).

Nussbaum, M. (2000) *Women and Human Development: The Capabilities Approach* (Cambridge: Cambridge University Press).

O'Brien, K. (2002) 'Networks, Netwar and Information-Age Terrorism', in A. Tan and K. Ramakrishna (eds), *The New Terrorism: Anatomy, Trends, and Counter-Strategies* (Singapore: Eastern Universities Press), pp. 73–106.

O'Donnell, G. (1996) 'Illusions and Conceptual Flaws', *Journal of Democracy*, 7(4): October, 160–8.

O'Donnell, G. and Schmitter, P. (1986) *Transitions from Authoritarian Rule: Tentative Conclusions about Uncertain Democracies* (Baltimore, MD: Johns Hopkins University Press).

OAU (Organization of African Unity) (1981) *The Lagos Plan of Action for the Economic Development of Africa 1980–2000* (Geneva: OAU).

Ober, J. (2000) 'Quasi-rights: Political Boundaries and Social Diversity in Democratic Athens', *Social Philosophy and Policy*, 17(1): 27–61.

Ocampo, J. (2010) 'Latin American Development after the Global Financial Crisis', in N. Birdsall and F. Fukuyama (eds), *New Ideas on Development after the Financial Crisis* (Baltimore, MD: Johns Hopkins University Press), pp. 133–57.

ODI (Overseas Development Institute) (2008) 'Untangling Links Between Trade, Poverty and Gender: Latin American Experience shows Women need Support to Benefit from Trade Liberalisation', *Briefing Paper* (London: ODI).

—— (2010) 'Brazil: An Emerging Aid Player. Lessons on Emerging Donors, and South-South and Trilateral Cooperation', Briefing Paper (London: ODI).

OECD (Organization for Economic Cooperation and Development) (1989) *Development Cooperation in the 1990s: Efforts and Policies of the Members of the Development Assistance Committee* (Paris).

——(2002) 'Economic Consequences of Terrorism', *OECD Economic Outlook*, 71 (Paris: OECD), 117–40.

OECD (2010a) *Development Co-operation Report Summary 2010* (OECD DAC).

——(2010a) *Arab Development Assistance: Four Decades of Cooperation* (Washington: World Bank).

——(2010b) *Development Co-operation Report 2010* (OECD DAC).

——(2010c) *Development Co-operation Report 2010 Statistical Annex*.

——(2010d) *2010 DAC Report on Multilateral Aid*.

——Development Cooperation Directorate (DCD-DAC) (n.d.) The Paris Declaration and the Accra Agenda for Action, available at: /www.oecd.org/document/18/0,3343, en_2649_3236398_35401554_1_1_1_1,00.html (accessed 1 March 2011).

OECD DAC (Organization for Economic Cooperation and Development, Development Assistance Committee) (2006) 'Statistical Annex of the 2006 Development Co-operation Report, Table 18 Major Aid Uses by Individual DAC Donors'; Table 19 Aid by Major Purposes in 2005, available at: www.oecd.org/document/9/0,2340, en_2649_34485_1893129_1_1_1_1,00.html (accessed 28 February 2011).

——(2007) Development Co-operation Report 2006 Summary, available at: www.sourceoecd.org/developmentreport (accessed 28 February 2011).

and G. Derluguian (eds), *Aftermath: A New Global Economic Order* (New York: New York University Press), pp. 97–118.

Save the Children (2010) *At A Crossroads: Humanitarianism for the Next Decade,* (London: Save the Children).

Schauer (1982) *Free Speech: A Philosophical Inquiry* (Cambridge: Cambridge University Press).

Schultz, T. (1962) 'Reflections on Investment in Man', *Journal of Political Economy,* Supplement (October): 1–8.

——(1964) *Transforming Traditional Agriculture* (New Haven, CT: Yale University Press).

——(1980) 'The Economics of Being Poor', *Journal of Political Economy*, August.

Schumacher, E. (1973) *Small is Beautiful: A Study of Economics as if People Mattered* (London: Blond & Briggs).

Schumpeter, J. (1934) *The Theory of Economic Development* (Cambridge, MA: Harvard University Press).

——(1976) *Capitalism, Socialism and Democracy.* (New York: Harper & Row).

Schure, T. (2010) 'Conflict Minerals: The New Blood Diamonds', available at: www.worldpress.org/print_article.cfm?article_id=3834&dont=yes (accessed 17 December 2010).

Schuurman, F. (2001) *Globalisation and Development Studies: Challenges for the 21st Century* (London: Sage).

Scully, G. (1988) 'Institutional Framework and Economic Development', *Journal of Political Economy*, 96: 622–62.

Seabrook, J. (1993) *Victims of Development* (London: Verso Press).

Security Council Report (2010) *Cross-Cutting Report on Women, Peace and Security* (New York: Security Council Report).

Seers, D. (1972) 'The Meaning of Development', in N. Baster (ed.), *Measuring Development: The Role and Adequacy of Development Indicators* (London: Frank Cass).

Segerfeldt, F. (2005) 'Private Water Saves Lives', *Financial Times*, 25 August.

Seguino, S. (2010) 'The Global Economic Crisis, its Gender and Ethnic Implications, and Policy Responses', *Gender and Development, 18(2)*: 179–99.

Seligson, M. A. and Passe-Smith, J. T. (1998) *Development and Under-Development* (London: Lynne Rienner).

Sen, A. (1980) 'Equality of What?', in S. McMurrin (ed.), *Tanner Lectures on Human Values* (Cambridge: Cambridge University Press).

——(1981) *Poverty and Famine: An Essay on Entitlement and Deprivation* (Oxford: Clarendon Press).

——(1983) 'Development: Which Way Now?', *Economic Journal*, 93: December, 754–7.

——(1984) *Resources, Values and Development* (Oxford: Basil Blackwell).

——(1985a) *Commodities and Capabilities* (Amsterdam: North Holland).

—(1985b) 'Well-being Agency and Freedom', *Journal of Philosophy*, 82: 169–221.

——(1987a), 'The Standard of Living: Lecture 1, Concepts and Critiques', in G. Hawthorn (ed.), *The Standard of Living* (Cambridge: Cambridge University Press).

——(1987b) 'The Standard of Living: Lecture 2, Lives and Capabilities', in G. Hawthorn (ed.), *The Standard of Living* (Cambridge: Cambridge University Press).

——(1990) 'Development as Capability Expansion', in K. Griffin and J. Knight (eds), *Human Development and the International Development Strategy for the 1990s* (London: Macmillan).

——(1992) *Inequality Re-examined* (Oxford: Clarendon Press).

——(1993) 'Capability and Well-Being', in M. Nussbaum and A. Sen (eds), *The Quality of Life,* (Oxford: Clarendon Press).

——(1999a) *Development as Freedom* (New York: Alfred A. Knopf).

——(1999b) 'The Possibility of Social Choice', *American Economic Review*, June: 349–78.

——(2000) *Development as Freedom* (London: Oxford University Press).

——(2007) *Identity and Violence: The Illusion of Destiny* (London: Allen Lane).

Sen, G. and Grown, C. (1987) *Development Crisis, and Alternative Visions: Third World Women's Perspectives* (New Delhi: DAWN).

Seymour, M. (2000) 'On Redefining the Nation', in N. Miscevic, (ed.), *'Nationalism and Ethnic Conflict. Philosophical Perspectives* (La Salle and Chicago: Open Court).

Shah, A. (2002) *Structural Adjustment – A Major Cause of Poverty,* available at: www.globalissues.org/TradeRelated/SAP.asp. (August).

Shah, M. and Strong, N. (2000) *Food in the 21st Century* (Washington, DC: CGIAR/World Bank).

Shari, I. (2001) 'Globalization and Economic Disparities in East and Southeast Asia: New Dilemmas', in J. Mittelman and N. Othman (eds), *Capturing Globalization* (London and New York: Routledge).

Sharp, J. and Briggs, J. (2006) 'Postcolonialism and Development: New Dialogues?' *Geographical Journal*, 172: 6–9.

Sharp, J, Briggs, J. Yacoub, H. and Hamed, N. (2003) 'Doing Gender and Development: Understanding Empowerment and local Gender Relations', in *Transactions of the British Institute of Geographers*, n.s. 28: 281–95.

Sheehan, N. (1988) *A Bright Shining Lie: John Paul Vann and America in Vietnam* (New York: Random House).

Shepherd, L. J. (2006) 'Veiled References: Constructions of Gender in the Bush Administration Discourse on the Attacks on Afghanistan post-9/11', *International Feminist Journal of Politics,* 8(1): 19–41.

Sherman, A. (1992) *Preferential Option* (Grand Rapids, MI: Eerdmans Publishing).

Shiller, R.J. (2009) *Irrational Exuberance* (New York: Broadway Books).

Shirk, S. (2007) *China: Fragile Superpower* (New York: Oxford University Press).

Shiva, V. (1989) *Staying Alive: Women, Ecology and Development* (London: Zed Books).

——(2000) BBC Reith Lecture, Radio 4.

Silberschmidt, M. (2001) 'Disempowerment of Men in Rural and Urban East Africa: Implications for Male Identity and Sexual Behaviour', *World Development,* 29(4): 657–71.

Sim, S. (2004) *Fundamentalist World: The New Dark Age of Dogma* (London: Icon).

Simon, D. (2006) 'Separated by Common Ground? Bringing (Post) Development and (Post) Colonialism Together', *Geographical Journal*, 172: 10–22.

Simon, Julian L. (1994) 'More People, Greater Wealth, More Resources, Healthier Environment', *Economic Affairs: Journal of the Institute of Economic Affairs,* April.

Simons, P. et al. (1997) Committee to Review the Australian Overseas Aid Program, *One Clear Objective: Poverty Reduction Through Sustainable Development,* Report of the Committee of Review (Canberra: AusAID).

Singer, H. (1950) 'The Distribution of Gains Between Investing and Borrowing Countries', *American Economic Review Papers and Proceedings* (May) pp. 473–85, reprinted in A. Dutt (ed.) (2002), *The Political Economy of, Development,* vols 1–3 (Cheltenham: Edward Elgar), pp. 19–205.

Singer, H. (1993) *Economic Progress and Prospects in the Third World* (Aldershot: Edward Elgar).

Singh, A. and Zammit, A. (2000) 'International Capital Flows: Identifying the Gender Dimension', *World Development,* 28(7): 1249–68.

SISO (Solomon Islands Statistical Office) (2006) *Household Income and Expenditure Survey 2005/6–- Provincial Report* (Honiara: Department of Finance and Treasury).

Siwakoti, G. (2002) 'Who's Aiding Whom? Poverty, Conflict and ODA in Nepal', in J. Randel, T. German and D. Ewing (eds), *The Reality of Aid,* pp. 81–97.

Skidelsky, R. (2009) *Keynes: The Return of the Master* (London: Allen Lane).

Slater, D. and Bell, M. (2002) 'Aid and the Geopolitics of the Post-colonial: Critical Reflections on New Labour's Overseas Development Strategy', *Development and Change*, 33(2), April: 335–60.

Smillie, I. (1995) *The Alms Bazaar: Altruism under Fire – Non-profit Organisations and International Development* (London: Intermediate Technology Publications).

——(1999) 'Public Support and the Politics of Aid', *Development*, 42(3): September, 71–6.

Smith, A. (1986a) 'State-Making and Nation-Building', in J. Hall (ed.), *States in History* (Oxford: Basil Blackwell).

——(1986b) *Nationalism and Modernism* (London: Routledge).

——(1986c) *The Ethnic Origins of Nations* (Oxford: Blackwell Publishing)

—— (1998) *Nationalism and Modernism* (London: Routledge).

Smith, B. (1996) *Understanding Third World Politics: Theories of Political Change and Development* (Bloomington and Indianapolis: Indiana University Press).

Smith, M. (2010) *Global Capitalism in Crisis: Karl Marx and the Decay of the Profit System* (Halifax, Nova Scotia: Fernwood).

Smyth, I. (2009) 'Gender in Climate Change and Disaster Risk Reduction, Manila, October 2008', *Development in Practice*, 19(6): 799–802.

Sneyd, A. (2006) 'Jeffrey Sachs: Rolling Back Neo-liberalism through Neo-modernisation?', *IPEG Papers in Global Political Economy*, no. 23, Working Draft. June.

Snyder, M. and Tadesse, M. (1997) 'The African Context: Women in the Political Economy', in N. Visvanathan, L. Duggan, L. Nisonoff and N. Wiegersma (eds), *The Women, Gender and Development Reader* (London: Zed Books), pp. 75–78.

Solingen, E. (1998) *Regional Orders at Century's Dawn: Global and Domestic Influences on Grand Strategy* (Princeton, NJ: Princeton University Press).

Solow, R. (1956) 'A Contribution to the Theory of Economic Growth', *Quarterly Journal of Economics* 70: 65–94.

South Centre, The (1998) *Statement to the Second WTO Ministerial Conference by the South Centre* (Geneva: The South Centre).

——(2008) 'Analysis of Lamy's Special Safeguard Mechanism Numbers (of 25 July 2008)', *South Centre's Analysis and News of the WTO's Mini-ministerial*, 4: 7 July 2008.

Spanger, H.-J. (2000) 'Failed State or Failed Concept? Objections and Suggestions', paper presented to the *Failed States Conference*, Florence, 7–10 April.

Sparks, C. (2007) *Globalization, Development and the Mass Media* (London: Sage Publications Ltd).

Sparr, P. (1994) *Mortgaging Women's Lives: Feminist Critiques of Structural Adjustment* (London: Zed Books).

Sphere Project, The (2004) *Humanitarian Charter and Minimum Standards in Disaster Response* (Geneva: The Sphere Project).

Spillane, S. (2004) 'Governance and Poverty: Can the Goals Get Donors Back on Track?' in J. Randal, T. German and D. Ewing (eds), *The Reality of Aid* (London: Zed Books), pp. 165–71.

Standing, H. (2004) 'Gender, Myth and Fable: The Perils of Mainstreaming in Sector Bureaucracies', *IDS Bulletin*, 35(4): 82–8.

Standing, H. (2007) 'Gender, Myth and Fable: The Perils of Mainstreaming in Sector Bureaucracies', in A. Cornwall, E. Harrison and A. Whitehead (eds), *Feminisms in Development: Contradictions, Contestations, and Challenges* (London: Zed Books), pp. 101–11.

Staub, E. (2004) 'Preventing Terrorism: Raising "Inclusively" Caring Children in the Complex World of the Twenty-First Century', in C. Stout (ed.), *Psychology of Terrorism: Coping with the Continued Threat* (Westport, CT: Praeger), pp. 199–244.

Stedman Jones, G. (2002) 'Introduction' to new edition of Karl Marx and Frederick Engels, *The Communist Manifesto* (London: Penguin), pp. 3–187.

Stensholt, R. (1997) *Developing the Mekong Subregion* (Melbourne: Monash Asia Institute).

Stepan, A. (1985) 'State Power and the Strength of Civil Society in the Southern Cone of Lain America', in P. Evans, D. Rueschemeyer and T. Skocpol (eds), *Bringing the State Back In* (Cambridge University Press: Cambridge).

Stern, J. (2003) *Terror in the Name of God: Why Religious Militants Kill* (New York: HarperCollins).

Stern, N. (2007) *The Economics of Climate Change* (Cambridge: Cambridge University Press).

Stewart, F. (1985) *Basic Needs in Developing Countries* (Baltimore, MD: Baltimore University Press).

Stewart, F. (2001) 'Horizontal Inequality: a Neglected Dimension of Development', 2001 WIDER Annual Lecture (Helsinki: World Institute for Development Economics Research of the United Nations University).

Stiglitz, J. (2000) 'The Insider: What I Learned at the World Economic Crisis', *The New Republic*, available at: www.tnr.com/041700/ stiglitz041700.html.

Stiglitz, J. (2002) *Globalization and its Discontents* (New York: W.W. Norton).

Stiglitz, J. (2006) *Making Globalization Work: The Next Steps to Global Justice* (London: Allen Lane).

Stiglitz, J. (2010) *Freefall: Free Markets and the Sinking of the Global Economy* (London: Allen Lane).

Stiglitz, J. and Yusuf, S. (2001) *Rethinking the East Asian Miracle* (Oxford: World Bank and Oxford University Press).

Stotsky, J. G. (2006) 'Gender and Its Relevance to Macroeconomic Policy: A Survey', *IMF Working Paper* (Washington, DC: International Monetary Fund).

Stout, C. (ed.) (2004) *Psychology of Terrorism: Coping with the Continued Threat* (Westport, CT: Praeger).

Strange, S. (1986) *Casino Capitalism* (Oxford: Basil Blackwell).

——(1998) *Mad Money* (Manchester: Manchester University Press).

Streeten, P. (1979) 'Basic Needs: Premises and Promises', *Journal of Policy Modeling*, 1(1): 136–46.

Streeten, P., Burki, S. J., ul Haq, M., Hicks, N. and Stewart, F. (1981) *First Things First: Meeting Basic Human Needs in Developing Countries* (Oxford: Oxford University Press).

Stubbings, L. (1992) 'Look *What You Started, Henry': A History of the Australian Red Cross, 1914–1991* (Australian Red Cross).

Subrahmanian, R. (2007) 'Making Sense of Gender in Shifting Institutional Contexts: Some Reflections on Gender Mainstreaming', in A. Cornwall et al. (eds), *Feminisms in Development: Contradictions, Contestations, and Challenges* (London: Zed Books), pp. 112–21.

Subrahmanian, A. (2011) 'The Crisis and the Two Globalization Fetishes', in N. Birdsall and F. Fukuyama (eds), *New Ideas on Development After the Financial Crisis* (Baltimore, MD: Johns Hopkins University Press), pp. 62–82.

Suhrke, A. (2006) 'The Limits of Statebuilding: The Role of International Assistance in Afghanistan', paper presented to the International Studies Association annual meeting San Diego, 21–4 March.

Supachai, P. (2002) 'Director-General Supachai Welcomes Agreement Streamlining LDC Membership' (press release) (Geneva: World Trade Organization), 3 December.

Sylvester, C. (2006) 'Bare Life as a Development/Postcolonial Problematic', *Geographical Journal*, 172: 66–78.

——(2009) 'From Global Imbalances to Global Reorganisations', *Cambridge Journal of Economics*, 33: 539–62.

Walkenhurst, P. and Dihel, N. (2002) 'Trade Impacts of the Terrorist Attacks of 11 September 2001: A Quantitative Assessment', paper presented to the German Institute of Global Research (DIW) workshop on The Economic Consequences of Global Terrorism', Berlin, available at www.diw.de/deutsch/service/veranstaltungen/ws_consequences.

Walker, R. (2007) 'Capacity Building and Cookie Enabling', *Christian Science Monitor*, 19: April .

Wallace, H. (2002) 'Community Development Strategies and their Role in Promoting an Alternative Development Approach in the South Pacific Region', *Development Bulletin*, 58: 56–9.

Wallace, T. and March, C. (eds) (1991) *Changing Perceptions: Writings on Gender and Development* (Oxford: Oxfam).

Wallerstein, E. (2006) 'The Curve of American Power', *New Left Review*, 40.

Wallerstein, I. (1974) *The Modern World System* (New York: Monthly Review Press).

——(1979) *The Capitalist World Economy* (Cambridge: Cambridge University Press).

—— (1984) *The Politics of the World Economy* (Cambridge: Cambridge University Press).

——(2011) *Centrist Liberalism Triumphant, 1789–1914* (Berkeley, CA: University of California Press).

Wang Hui (2009) *The End of the Revolution: China and the Limits of Modernity* (London: Verso).

Waring, M. (1988) *Counting for Nothing: What Men Value and What Women are Worth* (Wellington: Allen & Unwin).

Warren, B. (1980) *Imperialism: Pioneer of Capitalism* (London: Verso).

Warren, C. (1993) *Adat and Dinas: Balinese Communities in the Indonesian State* (Oxford: Oxford University Press).

Washington State (2002) *Best Export Prospects 2002: Pollution Control Equipment* (Taiwan: Washington State).

WB-GNI (2002) *GNI Per Capita 2000, Atlas Method and PPP,* World Development Indicators Database (Washington, DC: World Bank).

WBPNL (World Bank Poverty Net Library) (2001) 'Cultural Capital and Educational Attainment', *Social Capital,* World Bank Poverty Net Library (Washington, DC: World Bank).

WCD (World Commission on Dams) (2000) 'Executive Summary', *Large Dams Cross Check Survey* (New York: World Commission on Dams).

Webber, R. (1985) 'Health and Development', in B. Kinika and S. Oxenham (eds), *The Road Out: Rural Development in Solomon Islands* (Suva: University of South Pacific).

Weber, C. and Bierstaker, T. (eds) (1996) *State Sovereignty as Social Construction* (Cambridge: Cambridge Studies in International Relations).

Weber, M. (1946) *Social and Economic Organization*, ed. T. Parsons (New York: Oxford University Press).

——(1964) *The Theory of Social and Economic Organization* (New York: Free Press).

—— (1968) [1922] *Economy and Society,* tr. and ed. G. Roth and C. Wittich (New York: Bedminster Press).

——(2006) *The Protestant Ethic and the Spirit of Capitalism* (Oxford: Routledge Classics).

Wee, V. and Heyzer, N. (1995) *Gender, Poverty and Sustainable Development: Towards a Holistic Framework of Understanding and Action* (Singapore: ENGENDER).

Weiner, M. (ed.) (1966) *Modernization: The Dynamics of Growth* (New York: Basic Books).

Weinstock, D. and Nadeau, C. (2004) *Republicanism: History, Theory and Practice* (London and Portland: Frank Cass).

Weiss, L. (2003) 'Guiding Globalization in East Asia: New Roles for Old Developmental States', in L. Weiss (ed.), *States in the Global Economy: Bringing Domestic Institutions Back In* (Cambridge: Cambridge University Press), pp. 245–70.

Weiss, L. and Hobson, J. (1995) *States and Economic Development* (Cambridge: Polity).

Weissman, S. et al. (1975) *The Trojan Horse: A Radical Look at Foreign Aid* (Palo Alto, CA: Ramparts Press).

Weitz, R. (1986) *New Roads to Development* (New York: Greenwood Press).

Wheen, F. (2006) *Marx's Das Kapital: A Biography* (London: Atlantic Books).

Whittington, D. and Swarna, V. (1994) *The Economic Benefits of Potable Water Supply Projects to Households in Developing Countries,* paper no. 53 (Manila: Asian Development Bank, Economic and Development Resource Centre).

WHO/UNICEF (2006) 'Joint Monitoring Program for Water Supply and Sanitation', available at: www.wssinfo.org/en/40_mdg2006.html (accessed 26 April 2007).

——(2008) 'Progress in Drinking Water and Sanitation', WHO/UNICEF Joint Monitoring Programme for Water Supply and Sanitation, New York, 17 July.

Wigg, D. (1993) *The Quiet Revolution,* World Bank Development Essay, no. 2 (Washington, DC: World Bank).

Williams, M. (1997) 'The 1970s: A Need for Reappraisal', *Development*, 50(1).

——(2002) 'Gender and Governance in the Multilateral Trading System: Critical Areas of Decision-making and Global Responses', GERA Mid-term Review Workshop, 25–9 November 2002, Milkin Hotel, Accra, Ghana.

——(2005) 'Tensions between the Role of Trade, Development and Gender Equality', paper presented to 'WTO After 10 Years: Global Problems and Multilateral Solutions', 22–5 April WTO Public Symposium (Geneva, Switzerland: WTO).

Williamson, J. (1994) *The Political Economy of Policy Reform* (Washington, DC: Institute for International Economics).

——(2000) 'What Should the World Bank Think about the Washington Consensus?', *World Bank Research Observer,* 15(2): 251–64.

——(2002) *Is Brazil Next?* (Washington, DC: Institute for International Economics).

——(2004) 'The Years of Emerging Market Crises', *Journal of Economic Literature*, 42: 822–37.

Williamson, J. and Mahar, M. (1998) *A Survey of Financial Liberalization*, Princeton Essays in International Finance no. 211.

Windsor, J. (2007) 'Breaking the Poverty-Insecurity Nexus: Is Democracy the Answer?', in L. Brainard and D. Chollet (eds), *Too Poor for Peace? Global Poverty, Conflict, and Security in the 21st Century* (Washington, DC: Brookings Institution Press), pp. 153–62.

Winters, A. and Yusuf, S. (2007) *Dancing with Giants: China, India and the Global Economy* (Washington, DC: World Bank).

Wittfogel, K. (1957) *Oriental Despotism* (New Haven, CT: Yale University Press).

WN ([full termAQ]) (2002) *Globalization, Growth and Poverty: Building an Inclusive World Economy* (Washington, DC: World Bank).

Woo, Jung-en (1991) *Race to the Swift: State and Finance in Korean Industrialization* (New York: Columbia University Press).

Woo Wing Thye, Sachs, J. D. and Schwab, K. (eds) (2000) *The Asian Financial Crisis: Lessons for a Resilient Asia* (Cambridge, MA: MIT Press).

Woo-Cumings, M. (1999) *The Developmental State* (Ithaca, NY: Cornell University Press).

Wood, B. (1999) *Development Cooperation into the 21st Century*, The Inaugural K. William Taylor Memorial Lecture Brisbane, Australia, 1 November.

Woodford-Berger, P. (2007) 'Gender Mainstreaming: What is it (about) and Should We

Continue Doing It?', in A. Cornwall, E. Harrison, and A. Whitehead (eds), *Feminisms in Development: Contradictions, Contestations, and Challenges* (London: Zed Books).

Woods, N. (2008) 'Whose Aid? Whose Influence? China, Emerging Donors and the Silent Revolution in Development Assistance,' *International Affairs*, 84 (6): 1205–21.

World Bank (various years) *World Development Indicators* (Washington, DC: World Bank).

——(various years) *World Development Report* (New York: Oxford University Press).

——(1981a) *Accelerated Development in Sub-Saharan Africa: An Agenda for Action* (Washington, DC: World Bank).

——(1981b) *A Collection of Farewell Speeches on the Occasion of the Retirement of Robert S. McNamara as President of the World Bank, 1968–81,* World Bank Report 13380 (Washington, DC: World Bank).

——(1984a) *Toward Sustained Development in Sub-Saharan Africa: A Joint Programme of Action* (Washington, DC: World Bank).

——(1984b) *World Development Report: Population Change and Development* (New York: Oxford University Press).

——(1986) *Financing Adjustment with Growth in Sub-Saharan Africa* (Washington, DC: World Bank).

——(1990) *Proceedings of the World Bank Annual Conference on Development Economics* (Washington, DC: World Bank).

——(1991a) *World Development Report 1991* (Oxford: Oxford University Press).

——(1991b) *World Development Report: From Plan to Market* (New York: Oxford University Press).

——(1994) *Population and Development: Implications for the World Bank* (Washington, DC: World Bank).

——(1995) *Strengthening the Effectiveness of Aid: Lessons for Donors,* available at: www.worldbank.org (accessed on 27 September 2002).

——(1996) *Madagascar Poverty Report* (Washington, DC: World Bank).

——(1998) *Assessing Aid: What Works, What Doesn't and Why,* a World Bank Policy Research Report (Oxford: Oxford University Press).

——(2000) *First Trust Fund For East Timor Project to be Handed over to East Timorese,* press release (Washington, DC: World Bank Group).

——(2001a) 'Community Empowerment and Social Inclusion', in *Social Policy Design* (Washington, DC: World Bank).

——(2001b) *Engendering Development: Through Gender Equality in Rights, Resources and Voice* (Washington, DC: World Bank).

——(2001c) *Sustainable Development in the 21st Century* (Washington, DC: World Bank).

——(2002a) *World Development Report 2000/2001: Attacking Poverty* (Washington, DC: World Bank).

——(2002b) *Engendering Development* (Washington, DC: World Bank, available at: www.worldbank.org/gender/Prr/.

——(2002c) *The Role and Effectiveness of Development Assistance: Lessons from World Bank Experience* (Washington, DC: DEC).

——(2006a) '06 World Development Indicators', available at: www.devdata.worldbank.org/wdi2006/contents/section1_1_1.htm.

——(2006b) 'The Costs of Attaining the Millennium Development Goals', available at: www.web.worldbank.org/html/extdr/mdgassessment.pdf.

——(2006c) *Timor-Leste: Country Country Brief* (Washington, DC: World Bank).

——(2006d) *Status of Projects in Execution FY-06 – Timor-Leste* (Washington, DC: World Bank).

——(2007) *World Development Indicators 2007* (Washington, DC: World Bank).

——(2010a) *The MDGs after the Crisis: Global Monitoring Report 2010* (Washington: International Bank for Reconstruction and Development/The World Bank).

——(2010b) *Global Monitoring Report 2010: The MDGs After the Crisis* (Washington, DC: World Bank).

——(2010c) *Empowering Indonesian Communities through Developing Infrastructure and Services* (Washington, DC: World Bank) April.

——(2011) *World Development Report 2011: Conflict Security and Development* (Washington, DC: World Bank).

World Bank PovertyNet (2006) 'Pro-poor Growth', available at: www.web.worldbank. org/ WBSITE/EXTERNAL/TOPICS/EXTPOVERTY/0,menuPK:336998~pagePK: 149018~piPK:149093~theSitePK:336992,00.html.

World Commission on Environment and Development (1987) *Our Common Future* (Brundtland Report) (Oxford: Oxford University Press).

WRM (World Rainforest Movement) (2000) 'Laos: Vanishing Forests and Growing Corruption', *World Rainforest Movement Bulletin,* 35 (Montevideo: World Rainforest Movement).

WSF (World Social Forum) (2002) *World Social Forum Charter of Principles* (Sao Paulo: World Social Forum).

WTO (World Trade Organization) (2002a) *The WTO in Brief* (Geneva: World Trade Organization).

——(2002b) 'Developing Countries', in *The WTO in Brief* (Geneva: World Trade Organization).

——(2005) Ministerial Declaration, Doha Work Program 18 December 2005, available at: www.wto.org/english/thewto_e/minist_e/min05_e/final_text_e.htm#tech_coop (accessed 20 April 2007).

——(2007) *Principles of the Trading System,* available at: www.wto.org/english/ thewto_e/whatis_e/tif_e/fact2_e.htm (accessed 20 April 2007).

——(2011) 'WTO Legal Texts', World Trade Organisation, available at: www.wto. org/english/docs_e/legal_e/legal_e.htm#dispute (accessed 30 March 2011).

Wu, Y. (1946) 'International Capital Movements and the Development of Poor Countries', *Economic Journal,* March: 86–101.

WWF (World Wildlife Fund) (2002) *Living Planet Report* (Gland: World Wildlife Fund).

Yes Pakistan (2002) available at: www.yespakistan.com/people/potable_water.asp (accessed 2 December 2002).

Yusoff, M., Hasan, F. and Jalil, S. (2000) 'Globalization, Economic Policy, and Equity: The Case of Malaysia', paper presented to *Poverty and Income Inequality in Developing Countries: A Policy Dialogue on the Effects of Globalization,* (Paris: OECD), 30 November–1 December.

Zakaria, F. (1994) 'A Conversation with Lee Kwan Yew', *Foreign Affairs,* March/April 1994.

Zandstra, H. G., Price, E. C., Litsinger, J. A. and Morris, R. A. (1981) *A Methodology for on-farm Cropping Systems Research* (Los Banos: IIRI).

Zimmerman, R. (1993) *Dollars, Diplomacy and Dependency: Dilemmas of US Economic Aid* (London: Lynne Rienner).

Zysman, J. and Borrus, M. (1996) 'Lines of Fracture, Webs of Cohesion: Economic Interconnections and Security Politics in Asia', in S. L. Shirk and C. Twomey (eds), *Power and Prosperity: Economics and Security Linkages in Asia-Pacific* (New Brunswick: Transaction Publishers), pp. 77–99.

Index